NO OTHER TRIVIA LIKE THIS MASTERCLASS: VOLUME 1

SB Hilarion

RYSS

Raising Young Scholars Series by SB Hilarion

I AM Manifesto

Humongous (& Cool) Words For Kids
(British edition and U.S. edition)

Hao and Sabine Buy the World's Currencies

No Other Trivia like this Masterclass: Volume 1

Copyright © 2024 by SB Hilarion
Illustrations © SB Hilarion
Edited by Kendra Muntz
Cover design by Jerry Bennett
Printed in the USA
First Edition 2025

Cataloging-in-Publication has been obtained from the Library of Congress.
ISBN: 979-8-9910929-1-3 (Trade Paperback)
ISBN: 979-8-9910929-0-6 (eBook)

For more titles by SB Hilarion, please visit www.sbhilarion.com.

Raising Young Scholars Series®

Although the information in this book is believed to be true and accurate at the time of printing, neither SB Hilarion nor Raising Young Scholars Series LLC can accept any legal responsibility or liability for any errors or omissions that may have been made herein.

The use of both American English and British English in the Trivia Lime is deliberate.

*To my children and all
philomaths of the world*

"Creativity is intelligence having fun."—Albert Einstein

Over 2,000 questions
(including bonus questions)
for all ages!
Actually, it's more like:
for *most* ages
and for *all* philomaths!

CONTENTS

‡Lime: A Trinbagonian word for a get-together or gathering of family and/or friends.

TRIVIA LIME RULES

For each Team Trivia Lime, there can be up to 7 teams, each comprising no more than 4 players. (For Individual-player Trivia Limes, there can be up to 7 players, but teams are so much more fun!) **Teams can play IN PERSON and/or VIRTUALLY.** Teams shall play by the following designated names: **Cusco, Hamilton, Krabi, Praslin, Rotorua, Vava'u,** and **Zermatt.** One person should be designated as the impartial judge and will be referred to as **Belmont** during the game. If there is a co-scorer, that person will be referred to as **Maraval.**

Objective:
The first team or individual player to reach <u>50 points</u> (or another number of maximum points the teams agree upon) wins bragging rights. You may also up the ante and play for cryptocurrency, a pot of silver, gold, or money to donate to a charity or school. That'd make things really interesting, but no less difficult.

Fundamentals:

- *Themes:* There are 33 categories, each with 33 main questions, in Volume 1.

- Each team must have a team leader. This leader will be the player representative to provide the team's answers to the judge during the **Steals, Strategy Plays,** and **"Correct" Answer Challenges.** In all other instances, each player within a team plays first through fourth.

- Each category's main question will be worth anywhere from 1 point to 6 points. Most questions contain sub-quizzes and bonus point questions that make the points higher. Each category contains one SUPER-BONUS POINTS QUESTION worth a minimum of 7 points.

- *Order of play:* The judge will pick "out of a hat" the order in which each team shall play.

- *How to play:* A player in the team selects a category. Then the player chooses a number (1) through (33), which determines the question to be answered.

  - Play to your strength. **<u>But no single category can be selected consecutively</u>** by any team or individual player.

- <u>No player will be put on the spot.</u> For each question, a player will work with the members of his/her/their team *via* text messages, WhatsApp Messenger, online chat, in-person discussion, or however the team intends to correspond. (Please agree your method prior to the start of the Trivia Lime.) **The judge must be able to see the players at all times.** When the time allotment is up, that player **verbally** tells the judge the team's answer(s) to the question.

  - No team may use any other means to help guess the correct answers. For the avoidance of doubt, teams may not search the internet or use books, artificial intelligence (machine learning), other apps, or calculators, nor may they ask nonplayers, etc. In other words, no cheating.

  - During each team's turn, the team will have up to 3 minutes to answer after the judge reads the question(s). The judge will use a stop clock/ hourglass/ timer/ counting sheep that everyone has access to see/hear.

- ***Bonus points***: A team must answer the main question(s) correctly in order to receive the point(s) from the bonus question(s), unless otherwise indicated. If the team answers the bonus question(s) incorrectly, they still receive the points for the main question(s).

- ***Steals***: During each team's turn, the other teams will have an equal opportunity and time during the turn to steal the points in the event that the team's answers are incorrect. Those teams (*via* their team leader) must provide the correct answer(s) to the judge within a minute of the judge opening it up to them. They also can decide not to play for the Steal.

  o   In Steals, if there are bonus questions, the first team to answer BOTH the main question(s) and the bonus question(s) correctly, will receive the points and only for those that the initial team answered incorrectly.

  o   No Steals in the "True or False" category, unless indicated by an asterisk.

- ***Strategy Plays***: There are 8 strategy play cards. These cards will test each team's character and/or determination to win. The instructions of each strategy play card will be different. The judge must allow the use of at least one at any time during the Trivia Lime, and must select the team randomly (e.g., picking the team's name out of a hat). The team then chooses the card (1) to (8) without first looking at it. (The judge can change the order of the cards.) A team can only receive and use a strategy play card once during the Trivia Lime unless the judge decides otherwise, or the team happens upon the one question in the trivia that offers up a card.

- ***"Correct" Answer Challenges***: If a team disagrees with the stated correct answer, that team can challenge ONLY IF two other teams second the challenge. At that point, the team can search online for the correct answer for up to 2 minutes.

  o   If the team is correct, then the team receives the points for the question, PLUS 5 free points from the judge, along with an apology on behalf of the author. The teams that seconded the challenge each receives 3 free points.

  o   If the team is incorrect, the team gets 7 points taken away from their overall score. The teams that seconded the challenge each has 4 points taken away from their overall score. So, please don't challenge!

- ***Rules that really matter***: This Trivia Lime is about fun, laughs, strategy, intellectual challenges, meaningful conversations, nostalgia, and "smack" talk. (You'll also learn tons along the way!) If a player is sensitive and does not like to be teased, please announce that to the judge and all of the players BEFORE the Trivia Lime commences. All other players are sincerely requested to respect that wish—just poke fun at everyone else. The judge can have some discretion. If the judge is a sensitive, rigid, or partial person, then select a different judge. Lastly, feel free to modify the rules as you see fit since this is your Trivia Lime. Have fun, philomaths!

Category A:
COUNTRY LEADERS
(4-point category)

1. **(I) This individual was president/prime minister of the same country on three separate occasions. ((2) points)**
   A. José Figueres Ferrer of Costa Rica
   B. Don Benito Juárez of Mexico
   C. Florvil Hyppolite of Haiti
   D. Ingvar Carlsson of Sweden

   (II) Which Thai king was born in the USA while his father was studying at Harvard University? Hint: He is the key motif on the front side of this banknote (not shown). ((2) points)

   A. King Rama VII
   B. King Rama VIII
   C. King Rama IX
   D. King Rama X

2. **(I) Dr. Sun Yat-sen, known as the Father of the Republic of China, attended a particular school in the USA. Years later, which future U.S. president attended the same school? ((2) points)**
   A. George H. W. Bush (Senior)   C. William J. Clinton
   B. Barack H. Obama   D. George W. Bush (Junior)

   (II) Mahatma Gandhi, the Father of India, spent how many years living in South Africa? ((2) points)
   A. 1 – 10 years   C. 20+ years
   B. 11 – 15 years   D. 0 years

3. **(I) General Hannibal Barca was born in which African country? ((2) points)**
   A. Algeria   C. Tanzania
   B. Morocco   D. Tunisia

   (II) This leader was exiled to the British Overseas Territory of Saint Helena. ((2) points)
   A. Napoleon Bonaparte (France)
   B. Dinuzulu KaCetshwayo (Zulu nation)
   C. Both
   D. Neither

4. **(I) *"History has proven that all dictatorships, all authoritarian forms of government, are transient. Only democratic systems are intransient."* Which political leader made this comment? ((2) points)**
   A. Hugo Chávez   D. Ronald Reagan
   B. Vladimir Lenin   E. Joseph Stalin
   C. Vladimir Putin   F. Charles de Gaulle

   (II) This is the official residence of the president of: ((2) points)
   A. Belgium
   B. Brazil
   C. Finland
   D. Iceland

5. **(I) All or nothing: Three leaders below were instrumental in bringing about the unification of Italy on 17 March 1861. ((2) points)**
    A. Giuseppe Garibaldi   C. Count Camillo di Cavour
    B. Prince Metternich   D. Giuseppe Mazzini

    (II) Which country was fervently against the unification of Italy? ((1) point)
    A. France   C. Prussia
    B. Austria   D. Great Britain

    (III) Who was the first king of the Kingdom of united Italy? ((1) point)
    A. Victor Emmanuel I   C. Umberto I
    B. Victor Emmanuel II   D. Umberto II

6. This 14th-century ruler developed Timbuktu and Gao as great commercial centres. He had the Great Mosque and Sankoré Madrasah (Sankoré University) built during his time. He made a legendary pilgrimage to Mecca in 1324, handing out vast amounts of gold to locals along the way. At the time of his death, he had accumulated over US$400 billion in wealth (adjusted for inflation). Who was this West African leader of the Mali Empire for about 25 years who is considered one of the richest persons in history?
    A. Abu Bakr II   C. Sundiata Keita
    B. Mansa Musa   D. Sunni Ali Bar

7. **(I) "Facts": (a) Chinggis Khaan (Genghis Khan) was the founder of the largest land empire in history.**
    (b) His original name was not Chinggis.
    (c) He was known to be religiously tolerant.
    (d) The precise location of his tomb is known.
    (e) During wartime, he used a black banner.
    Which of the above statements are true? ((3) points)
    A. (a), (c), (d)   D. (a), (c), (d), (e)
    B. (a), (b), (e)   E. All
    C. (a), (b), (c), (e)

    (II) On which country's currency banknote shown is Khaan the key motif? ((1) point)

    A. Kazakhstan   C. Mongolia
    B. Kyrgyzstan   D. Tajikistan

8. **(I) This U.S. leader was stranded on an uninhabited island of Country [Y] during World War II. ((2) points) [max. 6 points]**
    A. John F. Kennedy   C. Dwight D. Eisenhower
    B. Gerald R. Ford   D. Lyndon B. Johnson

    (II) What is Country [Y]? ((2) points)
    A. Micronesia   C. Solomon Islands
    B. Japan   D. The Philippines

    For (2) bonus points: Name one of the two men (both friends) who saved him.

A. COUNTRY LEADERS
(each question at least 4 points)

9. **(I) Which leader lived in the medieval mountain cave city of Vardzia? ((3) points)**
    A. Stephen the Great (the "Greatest Romanian of all time")
    B. Tariq ibn-Ziyad
    C. Queen Tamar (called at times, the "King of Kings")
    D. Ahmad Shāh Durrānī

    (II) In which country is Vardzia located? ((1) point)
    A. Afghanistan   C. Armenia
    B. Georgia   D. Moldova

10. **This man was the first King of England who united the Anglo-Saxons.**
    A. Aethelwulf   C. Alfred the Great
    B. Edward   D. Æthelstan

11. **This ruler ascended to the throne when he was 13 years old. He was the third Mughal emperor and reigned from 1556 to 1605. He held an unbeaten military record in the Indian subcontinent. He also had a reputation for possessing a liberal attitude towards religions.**
    A. Akbar the Great   C. Humayun
    B. Bairam Khan   D. Shah Jahan III

12. **This woman was the first democratically elected female prime minister in modern times. [max. 9 points]**
    A. Prime Minister Indira Gandhi
    B. Prime Minister Sirimavo Bandaranaike
    C. Prime Minister Margaret Thatcher
    D. Prime Minister Golda Meir

    (I) For (1) bonus point: In what year did it occur?
    A. 1966   B. 1979   C. 1969   D. 1960   E. 1955

    (II) For (4) bonus points ((1) point each): Name each prime minister's country.

13. **This ruler was the Voivode (a prince or military governor) of Wallachia three times. He gained notoriety for his cruel methods of punishment against enemies. A 19th-century novel is said to be based on him. His father was known as "The Dragon."**
    A. Vlad Tepes (Vlad III)   C. Sultan Mehmed II
    B. Vlad the Monk   D. Radu I

14. **Originally from Venezuela, this military leader led many revolutions against Spanish rule in the Viceroyalty of New Granada. He became the first president of Gran Colombia and later was a dictator of Peru.**
    A. José de San Martín   C. Francisco de Miranda
    B. Antonio José de Sucre   D. Simón Bolívar

15. **Philip II ruled (or co-regented) all of the below in the 16th century except:**
    A. Portugal   C. Naples   E. England
    B. Spain   D. Venice   F. Sicily

A. COUNTRY LEADERS
(each question at least 4 points)

16. During this leader's first term as prime minister, he introduced a national minimum wage and significant constitutional reforms. However, he later became unpopular in part because of his support of the USA's invasion of Iraq. This politician led the United Kingdom for 10 years until his resignation in 2007.
    A. John Major
    B. Gordon Brown
    C. Tony Blair
    D. David Cameron

17. This person, who reigned for 40 years, was the ruler of Austria during the age of Enlightened Absolutism and was one of the most important and famous members of the House of Habsburg. He/she established lasting economic and educational reforms, such as elementary schools, introduced an income and toll tax, and removed universities from the control of the Catholic Church. [max. 6 points]
    A. Francis I
    B. Charles VI
    C. Joseph II
    D. Maria Theresa

    For (2) bonus points: What did Charles VI's Pragmatic Sanction of 1713 allow?

18. This U.S. president's administration pushed through the Enforcement Act (also known as the First Ku Klux Klan Act) that allowed state militias to restrict the KKK, stop lynchings, and disallow the suppression of the right of African Americans to vote.
    A. Andrew Johnson
    B. James A. Garfield
    C. Ulysses S. Grant
    D. Rutherford B. Hayes

19. Nawab Sultan Kaikhusrau Jahan was the Begum of this princely state of India from 1901 to 1926. She was a progressive and reforming leader who advanced the position of women and educational institutions in her state. Her other main legacy was in public health where she improved sanitation and the state's water supply; and she adopted widespread inoculation and vaccination programs in the state.
    A. Indore   B. Bhopal   C. Hyderabad   D. Gwalior

20. Who founded China's Yuan Dynasty? [max. 6 points]
    A. Kublai Khan
    B. Emperor Shunzhi
    C. Kaidu Khan
    D. Tog[h]on-Temür

    For (2) bonus points: Which dynasty did he defeat?
    A. Han Dynasty
    B. Song Dynasty
    C. Ming Dynasty
    D. Tang Dynasty

21. Who was the first democratically elected female head of state in modern times? [max. 5 points]
    A. President Corazon Aquino (The Philippines)
    B. President Ellen Johnson Sirleaf (Liberia)
    C. President Vigdís Finnbogadóttir (Iceland)
    D. President Isabel Perón (Argentina)

    For (1) bonus point: In which year was she elected?
    A. 1968   B. 1974   C. 1980   D. 1986   E. 2005

A. COUNTRY LEADERS
(each question at least 4 points)

22. [SUPER-BONUS QUESTION—at least 7 points!!!!!] Ignoring the political upheavals in the United Kingdom in 2022, match the leader below with (T) the length of time he served in office (note: each is amongst the shortest times in office) ((1) point each); and (C) the country in which he held the office ((1) point each). I can't give you 44 days to answer the question, but I can give you 5 minutes.

A.   Carlos Luz
B.   William Henry Harrison
C.   Pedro Lascuráin
D.   Louis XIX (Louis Antoine)
E.   Tommaso Tittoni
F.   Frank Forde
G.   Alec Douglas-Home

T. Time In Office	C. Country Served
(I) About 20 minutes	(I) Brazil
(II) 30 days	(II) UK
(III) 3 days	(III) France
(IV) 16 days	(IV) USA
(V) 363 days	(V) Italy
(VI) 8 days	(VI) Mexico
(VII) Around 45 minutes	(VII) Australia

23. This ruler was Queen of England and Ireland from 1553, and Queen of Spain from 1556 until her death in 1558. [max. 5 points]
A.   Lady Jane Grey
B.   Elizabeth I
C.   Catherine of Aragon
D.   Mary I

For (1) bonus point: What was the name of her husband?

24. This person was the founder and first ruler of the Kingdom of Hawaii. Standing at about seven feet tall, he is known as the greatest ruler in Hawaiian history. [max. 9 points]
A.   Kaumuali'i
B.   Kamehameha I
C.   Alapa'i
D.   Kalākaua

(I) For (2) bonus points: What is the name of the 7,000-pound mystical volcanic rock in Hilo that he overturned as a teenager?

(II) For (3) bonus points: Which ruler above was the last king of Hawaii?

25. Which U.S. president requested Congress to declare war formally on Germany and its allies after the U.S. government was presented with the secret diplomatic Zimmermann Telegram deciphered by British cryptographers? [max. 6 points]
A.   William H. Taft
B.   Woodrow Wilson
C.   Franklin D. Roosevelt
D.   Henry S. Truman

For (2) bonus points: This U.S. Founding Father said: *"Three may keep a secret, if two of them are dead."*
A.   George Washington
B.   Alexander Hamilton
C.   John Jay
D.   Benjamin Franklin

A. COUNTRY LEADERS
(each question at least 4 points)

26. This Chinese emperor, the first emperor of a unified China, was also a successful war leader. During his reign, he banned all philosophies other than Legalism and substantially curtailed freedoms of expression. He was buried with a terra cotta army in his mausoleum to protect him for eternity. [max. 8 points]

A. Xuantong Emperor   C. Emperor Gaozu of Han
B. Kangxi Emperor   D. Qin Shi Huang(di)

This woman was the first and only female emperor of China. She officially ruled the Tang Dynasty from 690 to 705. ((4) bonus points)

A. Empress Wu Zetian (Zhao)   C. Empress Dowager Cixi
B. Princess Taiping   D. Empress Xiaocheng (Zhao Feiyan)

27. This leader was the fifth emperor of the Mughal Empire. He reigned for 30 years from 1628. Major architectural achievements during his reign included the Taj Mahal and the Pearl Mosque in Agra, and the Red Fort and Jama Masjid, both in Delhi. He fought against the Safavid Empire as well as the Portuguese empire, but he maintained good relations with the Ottoman Empire. His son imprisoned him in the Agra Fort from July 1658 until his death in January 1666 at age 74.

A. Shah Jahan   C. Jahangir
B. Akbar   D. Shahryar Mirza

28. At the Battle of Bannockburn from 23 to 24 June 1314, which king led the Scottish forces to victory over England?

A. John de Balliol   C. Robert I (Robert the Bruce)
B. David II   D. Robert II

29. For (2) points each. (I) This man was the first Roman leader to be proclaimed emperor.

A. Caesar Augustus   B. Julius Caesar   C. Claudius   D. Caligula

(II) This ruler was the first Roman emperor to convert to Christianity.

A. Maximian   C. Diocletian
B. Severus II   D. Constantine the Great

30. For (2) points each. (I) Alfred the Great (849 to 899) was king of which region below? [max. 9 points]

A. Exeter   C. Wessex
B. Sussex   D. Northumbria

(II) Where was his great battle against the Danes in May 878?

A. Mercia   C. Somerset
B. Edington   D. Chippenham

(I) For (3) bonus points: Name the Danish leader that Alfred the Great fought against in that battle.

A. Sigurd Snake-in-the-Eye   C. Ragnar Lothbrok
B. Halfdan Ragnarsson   D. Guthrum

(II) For (2) bonus points: What is the name of the writings that Alfred started, which recorded the history of England during those times?

14

A. COUNTRY LEADERS
(each question at least 4 points)

31. Which leader below said the following (one leader per statement):
(I) *"Everyone wants a more simple tax system. But if this means that certain tax breaks have to be cut, people are no longer so enthusiastic."* ((2) points)

(II) *"Deeply concerning scenes from the U.S. Capitol tonight. Democratic votes must be respected. We are certain the US will ensure that the rules of democracy are protected."* ((2) points) [max. 6 points]
   A. Prime Minister Mette Frederiksen (Denmark)
   B. Prime Minister Boris Johnson (United Kingdom)
   C. President Emmanuel Macron (France)
   D. Chancellor Angela Merkel (Germany)
   E. David Sassoli (European Parliament President)
   F. Prime Minister Justin Trudeau (Canada)

   For (2) bonus points: One of the above said: *"It is easy to make promises— it is hard work to keep them."*

32. Considered the brainchild of President Xi Jinping, in 2013 China adopted the Belt and Road Initiative ("BRI"). It initially was called "One Belt One Road." BRI's infrastructure build is expected to continue until 2035. As of December 2024, at least 150 countries are part of the BRI. Which four countries below, however, are not official countries of the BRI (or are not known to have signed the Memorandum of Understanding for the BRI) with China? ((1) point each)

   A. Argentina   G. Germany
   B. Bangladesh   H. Haiti
   C. Colombia   I. Indonesia
   D. Djibouti   J. Japan
   E. Equatorial Guinea K. Kuwait
   F. Fiji   L. Luxembourg

33. This sixth pharaoh of the 18th Dynasty was the second and longest-reigning woman in ancient Egypt. She is regarded as one of its greatest pharaohs. Her mortuary temple at Deir el-Bahri is called Djeser-Djeseru ("Holy of Holiness"). Much was done after her death to erase her from history. [max. 8 points]

   A. Hatshepsut   D. Sobekneferu
   B. Nefertiti   E. Nefertari
   C. Ahmose

   (I) For (1) bonus point: Which one of the above queens was her mother?

   (II) For (3) bonus points: Which one of the above queens was the Great Royal Wife of King Ramesses II?

Answers to questions in this Category can be found starting on page 265.

A. COUNTRY LEADERS

(each question at least 4 points)

Category B:
WAIT...WHAT HAPPENED?
(2-point category)

1. On November 15, 2017, at the end of a 19-minute bidding war among four bidders on the telephone and one bidder in the room, the most expensive painting ever sold was purchased for US$450,312,500 (including auction house premium) at Christie's in New York. Who was the painter? [max. 3 points]

    A. Paul Gauguin
    C. Leonardo da Vinci
    B. Willem de Kooning
    D. Paul Cézanne

    For (1) bonus point: What was the name of the painting?

2. As part of Operation Barrel Roll, the United States dropped more than 2 million tons of bombs from 1964 to 1973 in this country's Plain of Jars region during the CIA's "Secret War" to interdict use of the Ho Chi Minh Trail.

    A. Cambodia
    C. Vietnam
    B. Laos
    D. Myanmar

3. The construction of this ancient road from Rome, stretching about 582 kilometres (362 miles), began in 312 B.C.E. during the Samnite Wars. In April 71 B.C.E., along part of this road from Capua to Rome, Roman general and politician Marcus Licinius Crassus crucified 6,000 enslaved people who had fought against their Roman masters.

    A. Via Aurelia
    C. Via Latina
    B. Via Flaminia
    D. Via Appia

4. For years, archeologists searched for Rhapta, the ancient port city and trade center on the eastern coast of Africa. In 2016, diver archeologists believed they found its ruins in an archipelago of which country or territory?

    A. Kenya
    C. Somalia
    B. Ethiopia
    D. Zanzibar

5. This lake in Central Asia mostly dried up as a result of the diversion of its main sources of in-flowing water for irrigation purposes. It was once the world's fourth-largest lake with tons of fish. Today, you'll find the "corpses" of abandoned rusting ships and fishing boats. [max. 4 points]

    A. Aral Sea
    C. Lake Alakol
    B. Lake Kaindy
    D. Lake Song-Kul

    For (1) bonus point each: It straddles the boundary between which two countries?

    A. Kazakhstan
    C. Kyrgyzstan
    E. Tajikistan
    B. Turkmenistan
    D. Uzbekistan
    F. Mongolia

6. On 31 October 2019, this region became a union territory of India, and prior to that it was part of another state (also now a separate union). Once a Buddhist kingdom, this region has picture-perfect gompas situated on rocky outcrops. It is the highest plateau in India, and there are two main districts: Leh and Kargil. What is its name?

    A. Jammu and Kashmir
    C. Ladakh
    B. Dadra and Nagar Haveli and Daman and Diu
    D. Himachal Pradesh

B. WAIT…WHAT HAPPENED?
(each question at least 2 points)

7. On April 30, 1975, at the launch of "Operation Frequent Wind," the coded message *"The temperature in Saigon is 105 degrees and rising"* went out over the radio. Which Christmas song followed the message to signal the emergency final evacuation of American personnel and "at-risk" Vietnamese out of Saigon (now Ho Chi Minh)?
    A. "Let It Snow"   C. "I'll Be Home for Christmas"
    B. "Silent Night"   D. "White Christmas"

8. On 25 September 1396, the armies of the European Crusaders (that included the Knights Hospitaller) and the armies of the Ottoman Empire (that included the Janissary Guards, an elite corps of infantry archers), fought a great catastrophic military battle along the Danube River. Both sides suffered heavy losses, but the Ottomans were victorious in the end, and several European nobles were taken prisoner, only to be released following the payment of a huge ransom. What was the name of the battle?
    A. Battle of Nicopolis   C. Varna Crusade
    B. Siege of Belgrade   D. Battle of Vienna

9. On July 9, 1958, an earthquake of 7.8 magnitude resulted in a landslide that sent about 90 million tons of rock plunging into a narrow bay. Both events then generated a mega-tsunami with waves of about 700 feet (213 metres) high around the bay. As the waves travelled inland, they rose to an elevation of 1,720 feet (524 metres), shearing forest and destroying all vegetation in their path. To put into context, that elevation is taller than the Empire State Building in New York City! Sadly, yet miraculously, five people died. Where was this mega-tsunami?
    A. Valdivia, Chile   C. Sumatra, Indonesia
    B. Alaska, USA   D. Lisbon, Portugal

10. This long-lost ancient city from the Maya civilization was uncovered in the deep jungles of Mexico, in the Calakmul Biosphere Reserve, by an American archeologist in 1970. But the scientist neither published his work nor recorded the site's location. In August 2014, Slovenian archeologist Dr. Ivan Šprajc, along with his team, local guides, aerial surveys, and geodesy, rediscovered this ancient city with its pyramids, temples, stelae, chultuns, and plazas, and another ancient site nearby it.
    A. Ocomtún   C. Xiol
    B. Lagunita   D. Chactún (Chaktún)

11. On January 11, 2013, four volcanoes on this peninsula—Shiveluch, Bezymianny, Tolbachik, and Kizimen—erupted at the same time.
    A. Kola Peninsula   C. Kamchatka Peninsula
    B. Labrador Peninsula   D. Alaska Peninsula

12. Ivar the Boneless led the Viking attack of the city of York in England on [DATE 1], but they did not capture the Northumbrian kings Ælle and Osberht. The Vikings attacked York again on [DATE 2] in a very violent battle that resulted in their recapture of the city as well as the deaths of both kings. Identify the two dates below. ((1) point each date)
    A. 21 March 866   C. 1 March 867   E. 1 November 867
    B. 1 November 866   D. 21 March 867

B. WAIT…WHAT HAPPENED?
(each question at least 2 points)

13. In this year: A series of earthquakes hit Japan, triggering a major tsunami. U.S. Navy Seals killed Osama bin Laden. Adele's "Someone Like You" topped music charts globally. Kim Clijsters won her fourth and final Grand Slam. Muammar al-Gaddafi was overthrown and later killed in Libya. India won the Cricket World Cup. *The Oprah Winfrey Show* ended. Calvin Harris released his major EDM hit "Feel So Close."
    A. 2010   B. 2011   C. 2012   D. 2013

14. On January 30, 2014, El Salvadorian fisherman José Salvador Alvarenga was rescued on Ebon Atoll, a remote coral atoll that is part of this country below. Alvarenga spent 438 days drifting west from Mexico where he lived, across 6,700 miles (10,800 kilometres) of open Pacific Ocean. He survived on rainwater, fish, turtles, birds, and his urine. Sadly, his young companion Ezequiel Córdoba did not survive. In which country was Alvarenga, a castaway, rescued?
    A. Marshall Islands   C. North Mariana Islands
    B. Micronesia   D. Nauru

15. 2022 was the third year of the <u>modern era</u> (since the advent of satellites in 1960) without a single named tropical hurricane or cyclone over the Atlantic Ocean during the month of August. (So, we are not considering 1941 and 1929.) What was the only other year after 1961?
    A. 1988   B. 1989   C. 1997   D. 2002

16. Before 21 July 2024, 6 July 2023 was the hottest day ever recorded globally (breaking the record first reached on 3 July). What temperature did the <u>global</u> average temperature reach on the 6th? [max. 6 points]
    A. 17.18°C (62.92°F)   C. 17.23°C (63.01°F)
    B. 16.92°C (62.46°F)   D. 17.01°C (62.62°F)

    (I) For (1) bonus point: During the week of 18 July 2022, a "red extreme" heat warning was issued for England. This warning meant that there was a risk to life. What temperature did it hit on 19 July 2022, the highest temperature ever recorded there?
    A. 40.3 °C (104.5°F)   C. 39.1°C (102.4°F)
    B. 38.7°C (101.7°F)   D. 40.5°C (104.9°F)

    (II) For (1) bonus point: On 27 April 2023, Spain recorded its hottest temperature ever during the month of April. (Spring!)
    A. 40.1°C (104.2°F)   C. 42.1°C (107.8°F)
    B. 44.2°C (111.6°F)   D. 38.8°C (101.8°F)

    (III) For (2) equally alarming bonus points: On 15 April 2023, northwest Thailand experienced this temperature. (Again…Spring!)
    A. 45.4°C (113.7°F)   C. 42.7°C (108.9°F)
    B. 38.8°C (101.8°F)   D. 46.2°C (115.2°F)

17. On this date, the largest percentage single-day decline in history occurred in the Dow Jones Industrial Average.
    A. Tuesday 29th October 1929   C. Monday 15th September 2008
    B. Monday 19th October 1987   D. Monday 16th March 2020

B. WAIT…WHAT HAPPENED?
(each question at least 2 points)

18. During this century: Edward the Confessor rebuilt Westminster Abbey. Norsemen landed in North America. The construction of the Tower of London commenced. William the Conqueror won the Battle of Hastings and later became the first Norman king of England. The University of Bologna, the oldest university in Europe, was founded. The "Great Schism" occurred between the Eastern Orthodox Church and the Roman Catholic Church.
   A. 10th century
   B. 11th century
   C. 12th century
   D. 13th century

19. In this year: Mount Etna erupted. Archaeologist Howard Carter opened the burial chamber of King Tutankhamen (King Tut) in Egypt. The first home game at the original Yankee Stadium was played between the New York Yankees and the Boston Red Sox. Canadian scientists introduced insulin as a treatment for diabetes. The Irish Civil War ended. The Great Kanto earthquake devastated Tokyo and Yokohama. The Republic of Turkey was established. The great jazz musician Louis Armstrong's fame was on the rise.
   A. 1923   B. 1928   C. 1922   D. 1925

20. On 14 August 2021, rainfall was recorded for the first time in history in this location, which already is considered melting passed the point of no return. Interestingly, the subsequent effect of heat on the snow surface was worse. [max. 4 points]
   A. Antarctic Ice Sheet
   B. Greenland Ice Sheet
   C. Barnes Ice Cap (Canada)
   D. Quelccaya Ice Cap (Peru)

   For (2) disturbing bonus points: Between October 2021 and October 2022, the world's 40-odd reference glaciers (i.e., those glaciers that have been observed scientifically over a long-term period) saw an average thickness loss that was larger than their average loss over the last decade. How much was this thickness loss within that one-year period?
   A. More than 0.75 metre / 2.5 feet
   B. More than 1 metre / 3.3 feet
   C. More than 1.3 metres / 4.3 feet
   D. More than 1.5 metres / 4.9 feet

21. In 1661, on the 12th anniversary of the execution of Charles I on 30 January 1649, this man's body was exhumed and subjected to a posthumous execution. His head was displayed atop a pole outside Westminster Hall for almost 30 years before it went missing.
   A. George Monck
   B. Richard Cromwell
   C. John Lambert
   D. Oliver Cromwell

22. In this year: The USA invaded Grenada. There were attacks at the French Army and the United States Marine Corps barracks in Beirut Lebanon. A Soviet Union Air Force fighter shot down Korean Air Lines Flight 007. Motorola received government-approval for DynaTAC, the world's first commercial mobile phone. The song "Every Breath You Take" by The Police was the longest-running number one single of the year. Spanish painter Joan Miró passed away on Christmas Day.
   A. 1982   B. 1983   C. 1984   D. 1985

B. WAIT…WHAT HAPPENED?
(each question at least 2 points)

23. At the 2021 Laver Cup held in Boston USA, which tennis player said: *"That's the last point they're going to win"* after the match in which his team was defeated? [max. 4 points]

A. Matteo Berrettini
B. Denis Shapovalov
C. Alexander Zverev
D. Reilly Opelka

For (2) bonus points: In which tournament in 2022 did the Swiss maestro Roger Federer play his last professional tennis match before retirement? (*Sob.*)

A. Wimbledon
B. Laver Cup
C. Swiss Indoors Basel
D. Nitto ATP Finals

24. In this year, the Atlantic hurricane season was extremely active with a record 30 named storms. After all 21 names on the World Meteorological Organization's list for that season were used, meteorologists turned to the Greek alphabet to name the rest of the storms. [max. 4 points]

A. 2018
B. 2019
C. 2020
D. 2021

For (2) bonus points: This was the second time in history that the Greek alphabet was utilized. When was the first time?

A. 1993
B. 2005
C. 1987
D. 2012

25. In March 1968, Soviet ballistic missile submarine K-129 sank to the floor of the Pacific Ocean, about 1,600 miles (2,600 kilometres) northwest of Hawaii. The U.S. Navy subsequently located it. In 1974, working with billionaire Howard Hughes, the CIA tried to recover the wreck under the elaborate cover story of a Hughes deep-sea mining exploration using a new ship called the Glomar Explorer. The recovery was partially successful as the submarine broke apart during its extraction by "Clementine," the giant steel claw. What was the name of this CIA operation? [max. 4 points]

A. Project Azorian
B. Operation Odessa
C. Project Artichoke
D. Operation Gold

For (2) bonus points: When the story broke and the media requested information, the official comment was: *"We can neither confirm nor deny."* What has that line since been called in U.S. law?

26. In July 2021, this country launched what military strategists consider to be the world's first nuclear-capable titanium hypersonic weapon that flies at around 10 times the speed of sound, cannot be seen by early warning radars, can change direction in flight, and can evade other missile defenses.

A. USA
B. Russian Federation
C. North Korea
D. China

B. WAIT…WHAT HAPPENED?
(each question at least 2 points)

27. On Monday 26 September 2022, NASA's Dart mission saw it deliberately crash a 19-metre-wide, 570-kilogram space probe into 163-metre-wide Dimorphos at over 20,000 km/h. What is Dimorphos? [max. 3 points]

    A. Asteroid   C. Dwarf planet
    B. Comet   D. Meteor

    For (1) bonus point: Dart reduced the orbital period of Dimorphos by about:

    A. 15 minutes   C. 1 hour
    B. 33 minutes   D. 1 hour 15 minutes

28. In late 2022 in the Bellingshausen Sea in Antarctica, around 10,000 young chicks of Emperor penguin colonies were killed when Antarctic sea-ice under them broke apart before the chicks could fledge the waterproof feathers needed for swimming. Which island had the least loss of life?

    A. Verdi Inlet   D. Bryan Peninsula
    B. Smyley Island   E. Pfrogner Point
    C. Rothschild Island

29. In this year: Dolly the Sheep became the first mammal to be cloned successfully in July. Internet Explorer 3 web browser was released for Microsoft Windows. Kofi Annan was elected as the seventh Secretary-General of the United Nations (U.N.). The U.N. adopted the Comprehensive Nuclear Test Ban Treaty. Tickle Me Elmo was the most sought-after toy for the Christmas season. The Billboard Hot #1 song was Los Del Rio's "Macarena (Bayside Boys Mix)."

    A. 1995   C. 1997
    B. 1996   D. 1998

30. [SUPER-BONUS QUESTION—at least 7 points!!!!!] On this date, the historical figure named in the table was born. No female figures deliberately are included, and no offense is intended. ((1) point each) Appreciating the difficulty of the question, answer five correctly for (7) points. Each incremental correct answer is (2) points.

    A. 18 July 1918
    B. On or about 31 October 1760
    C. 4 January 1643
    D. 1 October 1541
    E. 2 October 1869
    F. December 1770 (baptized 17th)
    G. On or about 23 April 1564
    H. 11 February 1847
    I. 10 July 1856
    J. 17 January 1706

Historical Figure
I. Thomas Edison
II. El Greco
III. William Shakespeare
IV. Ludwig van Beethoven
V. Nelson Mandela
VI. Mahatma Gandhi
VII. Sir Isaac Newton
VIII. Benjamin Franklin
IX. Katsushika Hokusai
X. Nikola Tesla

B. WAIT...WHAT HAPPENED?
(each question at least 2 points)

31. **In this year: NASA unveiled the first group of female astronauts. Dominica became an independent nation. The Camp David Accords between Egypt and Israel were signed. Japanese explorer Naomi Uemura became the first person to reach the North Pole in a solo expedition. The world's population was estimated at 4.29 billion. Sweden became the first nation to ban aerosol sprays, which were thought to be damaging Earth's protective ozone layer. (*Tack, Sverige!*) [max. 4 points]**

    A. 1978   C. 1979
    B. 1980   D. 1981

    For (2) bonus points:
    In this year: Expedition 1 arrived on the International Space Station for the first long-duration stay of 136 days. The Tate Modern opened in London, England. Sony's gaming console, PlayStation 2, was released. Bill Gates stepped down as the CEO of Microsoft. Tiger Woods became the youngest player to complete a career Grand Slam in golf.

    A. 1999   C. 2002
    B. 2003   D. 2000

32. **In 2019, the U.N.-backed Net-Zero Insurance Alliance (NZIA) was formed to encourage insurers to commit to reducing greenhouse gas emissions in their underwriting portfolios to a net-zero level by 2050. Which of the below member-insurers dropped out of NZIA in May 2023, soon after receiving a letter from some U.S. states that threatened, in part, legal action over anti-competitive behavior pushing up prices?**

    A. Allianz   E. Sompo
    B. AXA   F. Tokio Marine
    C. MAPFRE   G. All
    D. SCOR   H. None

33. **On December 21, 2020, there was a "Christmas Star," the alignment between Jupiter and Saturn making them appear to be very close to each other (the great conjunction). On this date, Jupiter and Saturn were 0.1 degree apart (less than the diameter of a full moon). When was the last observable time there was such a <u>similar</u> great conjunction of these two planets?**

    A. August, 3 B.C.E.   D. July 16, 1623
    B. September 6, 1487   E. November 2, 1812
    C. March 4-5, 1226

Answers to questions in this Category can be found starting on page 265.

B. WAIT...WHAT HAPPENED?
(each question at least 2 points)

Category C:
"INDEPENDENCE"
(1-point category)

1. How many individuals signed the U.S. Declaration of Independence?
    [max. 3 points]
    A. 47   B. 56   C. 42   D. 53

    (I) For (1) bonus point: One woman signed the Declaration of
    Independence. Unscramble her full name:
    KDANRDAIAHYGTROADERM

    (II) (1) bonus point: How many individuals
    are on the back of the US$2-banknote?
    Hint: It's one of the answers above.

2. The world's oldest republic, which uses the Euro as its functional
    currency, is:
    A. Monaco   C. Vatican City
    B. Andorra   D. San Marino

3. King and Chief Hendrik Witbooi, affectionately known as "the snake in
    the grass," wrote in an official letter:
    *"We did not give our land away, and what has not been
    given by the owner, cannot be taken by another person."*
    In what present-day country did he live at the time
    of writing? [max. 2 points]
    A. Namibia   C. The Gambia
    B. São Tomé and Principe   D. Mozambique

    For (1) bonus point: From 1884 to 1915, his country was under colonial
    occupation by which European country, who in 2021 officially
    acknowledged that it committed genocide during its occupation?
    A. Great Britain   D. The Netherlands
    B. France   E. Belgium
    C. Germany   F. Denmark

4. Who said this quote: *"To find yourself, think for yourself."*
    A. Karl Marx   C. Socrates
    B. René Descartes   D. Epicurus

5. In return for France's recognition of its independence in 1804, in 1825
    Haiti initially agreed to make a payment of what amount over a five-
    year period to France?
    A. 20 million French francs   C. 150 million French francs
    B. 60 million French francs   D. 200 million French francs

6. Of the countries below, only one became independent in the 21st
    century. Which one?
    A. Azerbaijan   C. Palau
    B. Moldova   D. Timor-Leste

7. Who sang "Chimes of Freedom"?
    A. Johnny Cash   C. Neil Diamond
    B. Bob Dylan   D. Bruce Springsteen

C. "INDEPENDENCE"   25
(each question at least 1 point)

8. **When did Ukraine declare its independence from the USSR?**
   A. 21 August 1991
   C. 26 August 1991
   B. 24 August 1991
   D. 27 August 1991

9. **When did Nabopolassar seize Babylonia's throne from the control of the Assyrian Empire?**
   A. 726 B.C.E.
   C. 626 B.C.E.
   B. 605 B.C.E.
   D. 631 B.C.E.

10. **In 1825, Juan Antonio Lavalleja and Manuel Oribe led the *Treinta y Tres Orientales* ("Thirty-Three Orientals") in their efforts for this country's independence. [max. 2 points]**
    A. Uruguay
    C. Argentina
    B. Brazil
    D. Portugal

    For (1) bonus point: Against which above country's rule were they fighting for independence?

11. **This country gained dominion status from the British Empire on 1 July 1867.**
    A. Australia
    C. Canada
    B. South Africa
    D. New Zealand

12. **Which two governments signed the Evian Accords on 18 March 1962 that agreed to end a war between them and paved the way for independence of a colony?**
    A. France and Tunisia
    C. France and Morocco
    B. France and Algeria
    D. France and Mali

13. **In what year did South Sudan gain its independence from Sudan?**
    A. 2012
    C. 2009
    B. 2010
    D. 2011

14. **In 1918, Iceland was granted its independence, valid for 25 years from which country? That country continued to manage Iceland's defense and foreign affairs until 1944.**
    A. Denmark
    C. Norway
    B. Sweden
    D. Finland

15. **This island is the only full member of CARICOM that is not an independent nation.**
    A. Antigua and Barbuda
    C. Montserrat
    B. St. Kitts and Nevis
    D. St. Lucia

16. **Who said this quote: "*It is very nearly impossible…to become an educated person in a country so distrustful of the independent mind.*"**
    A. Marcus Garvey Jr.
    C. Langston Hughes
    B. Booker T. Washington
    D. James Baldwin

C. "INDEPENDENCE"
(each question at least 1 point)

17. **[SUPER-BONUS QUESTION—at least 7 points!!!!!] (1)** Match the country in the table with the country from which it gained independence. But only one country in the table was always an independent nation. ((1) point each)

Independent Country
I. USA
II. Brazil
III. Equatorial Guinea
IV. Ivory Coast
V. Palau
VI. Indonesia
VII. Nepal
VIII. Singapore
IX. Cyprus

A. France
B. The Netherlands
C. Great Britain
D. USA
E. Portugal
F. Spain
G. Malaysia

(2) Which country in the table was always an independent nation? ((2) points)

18. From which country did Norway gain its independence? [max. 2 points]
    A. Denmark
    B. Finland
    C. Germany
    D. Sweden

    For (1) bonus point: Which country above ruled Norway prior to that country?

19. When did India gain its independence from Britain?
    A. 14 August 1947
    B. 14 August 1948
    C. 15 August 1947
    D. 15 August 1948

20. This country gained its independence from Britain, but it is not a republic.
    A. Fiji
    B. Jamaica
    C. Mauritius
    D. Malta

21. This company announced in June 2022 that it was spinning off into three independent public companies.
    A. General Electric Co.
    B. 3M Co.
    C. Johnson & Johnson
    D. Kellogg Co.

22. Iraq became a republic in 1958. However, it attained its independence as a kingdom from Britain in which year?
    A. 1932
    B. 1933
    C. 1946
    D. 1948

23. This island officially became part of Greece in December 1913. But prior to this, it gained independence from the Ottoman Empire in 1898.
    A. Naxos
    B. Lesbos
    C. Rhodes
    D. Crete

24. This country achieved independence in 1984 after being a British protectorate since 1888.
    A. Bermuda
    B. Burkina Faso
    C. Brunei
    D. Bahrain

C. "INDEPENDENCE"
(each question at least 1 point)

25. Who said this quote: "*I wanted to be an independent woman, a woman who could pay for her bills, a woman who could run her own life—and I became that woman.*"

    A. Britney Spears   C. Janet Jackson
    B. Diane von Fürstenberg   D. Charlotte Brontë

26. French troops completely withdrew from Lebanon in 1946; but on which date was Lebanon proclaimed an independent nation from France?

    A. 22 November 1941   C. 22 November 1943
    B. 22 November 1942   D. 22 November 1944

27. This country does not have an independence day, though it celebrates Constitution Day.

    A. Armenia   C. Cyprus
    B. Bulgaria   D. Denmark

28. This country was never invaded or colonized by another foreign country or power. As such, there is no independence day celebration.

    A. The Netherlands   C. Mongolia
    B. Thailand   D. Seychelles

29. When did Pakistan gain its independence from (British) India?

    A. 14 August 1947   C. 16 August 1947
    B. 14 August 1948   D. 15 August 1948

30. How many of the world's sovereign states have "Republic" as part of their official names?

    A. 148   C. 159
    B. 200   D. 177

31. In what year did South Korea gain its independence from Japanese rule? On August 15th every year, the South Korean president also grants special prison pardons in honor of the day of liberation.

    A. 1915   C. 1945
    B. 1930   D. 1948

32. Who released the then-controversial song "Independence Day" in 1994?

    A. Gloria Gaynor   C. Aretha Franklin
    B. Martina McBride   D. Ani DiFranco

33. Who said this quote: "*The only real prison is fear, and the only real freedom is freedom from fear.*"

    A. Aung San Suu Kyi   C. Winnie Mandela
    B. Rosa Parks   D. Malala Yousafzai

Answers to questions in this Category can be found starting on page 265.

C. "INDEPENDENCE"
(each question at least 1 point)

Category D:
SPORTS CHAMPION
(3-point category)

1. **(I) This grandmaster was the ninth World Chess Champion. ((1 ½) points) [max. 4 points]**

   A. Bobby Fischer   C. Max Euwe
   B. Tigran Petrosian   D. Boris Spassky

   For (1) bonus point to (I): In which country was he born?
   A. USA   C. The Netherlands
   B. Armenia   D. Soviet Union (Russia)

   (II) Name the World Chess Champion who defeated Boris Spassky in 1972. He also held Icelandic citizenship. ((1 ½) points)
   A. Bent Larsen   C. Anatoly Karpov
   B. Wilhelm Steinitz   D. Bobby Fischer

2. **In what years did Venus Williams win her first and second Wimbledon? [max. 7 points]**
   A. 1999, 2000   C. 2001, 2002
   B. 2000, 2001   D. 2002, 2005

   For (2) bonus points each:
   (I) How many Singles Grand Slam titles has Venus Williams won?
   A. 5   B. 6   C. 7   D. 9
   (II) How many Olympic Gold Medals has she won?
   A. 2   B. 3   C. 4   D. 5

3. **Sport climbing has become quite popular. (I) Both or nothing. In the 2024 Paris Summer Olympics, who won the Olympic Gold in each of the Men's and Women's Bouldering and Lead Combined? ((1) point)**
   A. Brooke Raboutou (USA) C. Janja Garnbret (SLO)
   B. Toby Roberts (GBR)   D. Sorato Anraku (JPN)

   (II) Who won Olympic Gold in Women's Speed Climbing? ((1) point)
   A. Deng Lijuan (CHN)   C. Aleksandra Kalucka (POL)
   B. Rajiah Sallsabillah (INA) D. Aleksandra Miroslaw (POL)

   (III) Who won Olympic Gold in Men's Speed Climbing? ((1) point)
   A. Veddriq Leonardo (INA) C. Wu Peng (CHN)
   B. Reza Alipour (IRI)   D. Sam Watson (USA)

4. **This team won the Rugby Olympic Gold medal in 2016. [max. 5 points]**
   A. Great Britain   B. Fiji   C. France   D. New Zealand

   (2) bonus points: Which team above did they beat to win gold?

5. **Who is the winningest golfer in LPGA Tour history? [max. 7 points]**
   A. Patty Berg   C. Kathy Whitworth
   B. Mickey Wright   D. Annika Sorenstam

   (I) For (3) bonus points: Only one female golfer has shot a score of 59 in competition. Who is she above?
   (II) For (1) bonus point: How many majors has that golfer won?
   A. 13   B. 10   C. 15   D. 6

D. SPORTS CHAMPION
   (each question at least 3 points)

6. **As of July 2024, which franchise has won the most NBA Finals championships? [max. 8 points]**
   - A. Boston Celtics
   - B. Chicago Bulls
   - C. Golden State Warriors
   - D. Los Angeles Lakers

   (I) For (1) bonus point each: Name two famous starting players for that franchise in the 1980s.
   (II) For (1) bonus point each: 1. Another franchise has won just one fewer NBA Finals championships. What is it? 2. Name two famous starting players who played anytime from 1983 to 1989 for this franchise.

7. **Each of these athletes is among the best cricketers ever in the world. Match them with the World Cup team for whom they played: (1) point for two correctly identified; (3) points for four correct; and (6) points for all seven correctly identified. [max. 9 points]**

Cricketer
(I) Wasim Akram
(II) Ian Botham
(III) Sunil Gavaskar
(IV) Richard Hadlee
(V) Brian Lara
(VI) Don Bradman
(VII) Hashim Amla

   - A. Australia
   - B. England
   - C. India
   - D. New Zealand
   - E. Pakistan
   - F. South Africa
   - G. Sri Lanka
   - H. West Indies

   (I) For (1) bonus point: As of 2024, which of the above has won the most World Cup titles?
   (II) For (2) bonus points: As of 2024, which batsman held the record of highest individual score ever in a Test?
   - A. Matthew Hayden
   - B. Mahela Jayawardene
   - C. Brian Lara
   - D. Gary Sobers

8. **This ice hockey league was the first to allow the goalie to leave his feet and fall to the ice to cover a puck. [max. 7 points]**
   - A. World Hockey Association (est. 1972)
   - B. National Hockey League (est. 1917)
   - C. Liiga (est. 1975)
   - D. The Coloured Hockey League of the Maritimes (est. 1895)

   For (2) bonus points each: (I) Who was the first player to use the slapshot technique in ice hockey? (II) Who was the first Black player to play in the National Hockey League?
   - A. Willie O'Ree
   - B. Eddie Martin
   - C. Henry "Braces" Franklyn
   - D. Grant Fuhr

9. **(I) Which female runner has won the most Major Marathons? ((1 ½) points.) For (1) bonus point: What is her nationality? [max. 8 points]**
   - A. Mary Jepkosgei Keitany
   - B. Catherine Ndereba
   - C. Sifan Hassan
   - D. Edna Kiplagat
   - E. Paula Radcliffe
   - F. Brigid Kosgei

   (II) Which male runner has won the most? ((1 ½) points.) For (3) bonus points: As of 2024, which male runner had run the fastest distance on a record-eligible course? What was the exact time for an additional point?
   - A. Wilson Kipsang
   - B. Samuel Wanjiru
   - C. Eliud Kipchoge
   - D. Meb Keflezighi
   - E. Geoffrey Mutai
   - F. Kelvin Kiptum

D. SPORTS CHAMPION
(each question at least 3 points)

10. **(I) This nation has won the most Men's FIS World Cups across the disciplines. ((½) point) [max. 7 points]**

A.	Austria	D.	Italy
B.	Switzerland	E.	Norway
C.	France	F.	USA

(II) This nation has won the most Women's FIS World Cups across the disciplines. ((½) point)

A.	Austria	D.	Italy
B.	Switzerland	E.	Germany
C.	France	F.	USA

(III) Who is the only racer in history to have won all disciplines—downhill, slalom, giant slalom, super-G, combined, and parallel slalom? ((2) points)

A.	Ingemar Stenmark	C.	Marcel Hirscher
B.	Mikaela Shiffrin	D.	Lindsey Vonn

If you answer (III) correctly:
(1) For (3) bonus points: As of the end of 2024, how many World Cup wins did that skier have?

A. 67   B. 82   C. 86   D. 88   E. 99

(2) For (1) bonus point: From which country is the skier?

11. **How many Formula One Drivers' World Championships did Michael Schumacher win? [max. 5 points]**

A. 5   B. 6   C. 7   D. 8

For (2) bonus points: For which racing team did he not compete?

A.	Benetton	C.	Red Bull
B.	Ferrari	D.	Mercedes

12. **Who won the men's singles title and the women's singles title of the below Tennis Grand Slams? (Answer three below fully correct for (3) points. No partially correct answers accepted. Answer all seven fully correct for (7) points.) [max. 9 points]**
(A) Wimbledon 2003. (B) Australian Open 2017. (C) Wimbledon 2009. (D) Wimbledon 2012. (E) Australian Open 2007. (F) Australian Open 2010. (G) U.S. Open 2008.

Male Tennis Player	Female Tennis Player
I. Juan Martín del Potro	I. Victoria Azarenka
II. Novak Djokovic	II. Kim Clijsters
III. Roger Federer	III. Justine Henin
IV. Juan Carlos Ferrero	IV. Ana Ivanovic
V. Andy Murray	V. Svetlana Kuznetsova
VI. Rafael Nadal	VI. Maria Sharapova
VII. Andy Roddick	VII. Serena Williams
VIII. Stan Wawrinka	VIII. Venus Williams

Bonus: What is the pattern? (If you have (3) points, the bonus question is worth (1) point; if (7) points, the bonus question is worth (2) points.)

D. SPORTS CHAMPION
(each question at least 3 points)

13. **(I) On October 30, 1974, "The Rumble in the Jungle" between Muhammad Ali and George Foreman took place at the then-named 20th of May Stadium in Kinshasa. Who won this boxing match? ((2) points)**
    A.   Muhammad Ali   B.   George Foreman

    (II) In what country, <u>its name at the time</u>, did "The Rumble in the Jungle" take place? ((1) point) [max. 6 points]

    For (1) bonus point each: (I) The heavyweight belt in that fight sold at auction in 2022 for about how much? A. $4.5M B. $6.18M C. $9.45M

    On October 1, 1975, Muhammad Ali squared off with Joe Frasier in "Thrilla in Manila"—their third and final boxing match for the heavyweight champion of the world. (II) Who won by technical knockout? (III) In which round? (Back then there were 15 rounds.)

14. **This gymnast has the most world medals, the most world gold medals, and the most all-round titles. She has won 11 Olympic medals, seven of which are gold.**
    A.   Simone Biles   C.   Lilia Podkopayeva
    B.   Vitaly Scherbo   D.   Věra Čáslavská

15. **In September 2022, Michael Jordan's red Chicago Bulls jersey sold for a record US$10.1 million at auction. He wore this jersey at the opening game of the NBA Finals in 1998. [max. 7 points]**
    (I) Which team did the Chicago Bulls play in this Finals? ((2) points)
    A.   Portland Trail Blazers   C.   L.A. Lakers
    B.   Utah Jazz   D.   Seattle Sonics

    (II) In the 1998 Finals, in which game did the Chicago Bulls secure the title? ((1) point)
    A.   Fourth   B.   Fifth   C.   Sixth   D.   Seventh

    (1) Bonus: How many NBA titles did Michael Jordan win? ((2) points)
    A.   3   B.   4   C.   5   D.   6

    (2) Bonus: In which year's NBA Finals did Jordan play his famous "Flu Game"? ((2) points)
    A.   1997   B.   1991   C.   1993   D.   1998

16. **For (1) point each. (I) Which team won the FIFA Women's World Cup in 1995? [max. 7 points]**
    A.   Norway   B.   USA   C.   Japan   D.   Germany

    (II) Which team won the FIFA Women's World Cup in 2007?
    A.   Brazil   B.   Germany   C.   Sweden   D.   USA

    (III) Which team won the FIFA Women's World Cup in 2011?
    A.   The Netherlands   B.   USA   C.   Japan   D.   Germany

    For (4) bonus points, (2) points each: (1) What was the first year of the FIFA Women's World Cup? (2) Which team won the coveted trophy?

D. SPORTS CHAMPION
(each question at least 3 points)

17. **On April 30, 2022, for the first time in the history of Madison Square Garden, two women headlined for a major boxing event: Ireland's Katie Taylor versus Puerto Rico's Amanda Serrano. Who was declared world lightweight champion in a split decision, after going the full 10 rounds against her opponent?**

A.   Amanda Serrano   B.   Katie Taylor

18. **This ice hockey player scored 894 career goals. He won four Stanley Cups with his team. Hint: He was born in Canada. [max. 7 points]**

A.   Bobby Orr   C.   Mario Lemieux
B.   Gordie Howe   D.   Wayne Gretzky

For (2) bonus points each:
(I) Name the team with which he won all four Stanley Cups.

A.   Pittsburg Penguins   C.   Boston Bruins
B.   Edmonton Oilers   D.   Detroit Red Wings

(II) How many times was he named the NHL's MVP?

A.   1   B.   3   C.   9   D.   6

19. **This Formula One driver has won seven World Drivers' Championship titles. He holds the record for the most wins, the most pole positions, and the most podium finishes. [max. 7 points]**

A.   Juan Manuel Fangio   C.   Sebastien Vettel
B.   Lewis Hamilton   D.   Max Verstappen

(I) Bonus: With which race car has he won the most races? ((2) points)

A.   Red Bull   B.   Mercedes   C.   McLaren   D.   Ferrari

(II) Bonus: Which race car did he drive when he commenced his professional Formula One career? It's one of the cars above. ((2) points)

20. **(I) This team won the FIFA Men's World Cup in 2018. ((1) point) [max. 11 points]**

A.   Germany   C.   France
B.   Croatia   D.   Belgium

(II) This team won the FIFA Men's World Cup in 2006. ((1) point)

A.   France   C.   Portugal
B.   Germany   D.   Italy

(III) This team won the FIFA Men's World Cup in 1994. ((1) point)

A.   Sweden   C.   Argentina
B.   Brazil   D.   Italy

(1) For (2) bonus points: In the FIFA Men's World Cup 2006 finals, for which one of these countries was it not its first appearance?

A.   Ghana   C.   Côte d'Ivoire   E.   Saudi Arabia
B.   Trinidad & Tobago   D.   Angola   F.   Togo

(2) Both or nothing. For (6) bonus points: Name the only two countries to have won the FIFA Men's and Women's World Cups as of 2024.

D. SPORTS CHAMPION
(each question at least 3 points)

21. **Which baseball player was the first to break Babe Ruth's career home run record of 714?**

    A. Mickey Mantle
    B. Willie Mays
    C. Hank Aaron
    D. Barry Bonds
    E. Roger Maris

22. **This rugby player is considered the first true international superstar of the sport, and he is one of the greatest rugby players of all time. [max. 4 points]**

    A. Jonah Lomu
    B. Dan Carter
    C. Richie McCaw
    D. Gareth Edwards

    From which country is he? ((1) bonus point)

    A. England
    B. Wales
    C. New Zealand
    D. Australia

23. **(I) Which tennis player has won two Calendar Grand Slams? ((1) point) [max. 5 points]**

    A. Martina Navratilova
    B. Björn Borg
    C. Ivan Lendl
    D. Rod Laver

    (II) As of 2024, which tennis player was the last player to win a Calendar Grand Slam? ((1) point)

    A. Steffi Graf
    B. Andre Agassi
    C. Serena Williams
    D. Novak Djokovic

    (III) Who is the most decorated tennis player in men's wheelchair tennis, with a record 50 major titles, including 28 Slams? ((1) point)

    A. Joachim Gérard
    B. Shingo Kunieda
    C. Stéphane Houdet
    D. Nicolas Peifer

    If you get (III) correct, for (2) bonus points: Who above is the first tennis player in men's wheelchair doubles to have won a Calendar Grand Slam?

24. **(I) Which golfer(s) has/have won the most events on the PGA Tour? ((2) points)**

    A. Jack Nicklaus
    B. Tiger Woods
    C. Sam Snead
    D. Ben Hogan

    (II) Which golfer(s) above has/have won the most majors? ((1) point)

25. **Which country/countries has/have won the most FIFA Men's World Cups in the tournament's history? [max. 6 points]**

    A. Germany
    B. Italy
    C. Brazil
    D. Argentina
    E. France

    (I) For (2) "sudden death" bonus points that if answered incorrectly, you lose (1) of the (3) points above: Which country won the first FIFA Men's World Cup held in 1930?
    (II) For (1) easy bonus point without "extra time": Which country was the third-place winner in the FIFA Men's World Cup 2022?

D. SPORTS CHAMPION
(each question at least 3 points)

26. **[SUPER-BONUS QUESTION—at least 7 points!!!!!]**
(I) In which year did Serena Williams win the Australian Open while pregnant? (*Wow!*) ((3) points)

A. 2015   B. 2016   C. 2017   D. 2018

(II) In what year was the first "Serena Slam" completed at the Australian Open? ((2) points)

A. 2003   B. 2005   C. 2007   D. 2009

(III) Since the age of 30, how many Singles Grand Slam titles has Serena won? ((3) points)

A. 5   B. 8   C. 10   D. 15

(IV) At the Hopman Cup in 2015, which drink did Serena Williams request after losing the first set 0-6 against Flavia Pennetta? ((2) points)

A. Diet Coke   C. Fanta
B. Espresso   D. Seltzer Water

(V) For how many weeks did the Women's Tennis Association (WTA) rank Serena Williams at World No. 1 in Singles? ((3) points)

A. 165   B. 223   C. 296   D. 319

(VI) Which WTA 500 or WTA 1000 event did Serena Williams boycott for 14 years after being subjected to overwhelming boos and racism at the tournament? Yet, she still won the tournament! ((1) point)

A. Miami Open   C. Winston-Salem Open
B. Indian Wells Open   D. Cincinnati Open

(VII) How many Doubles Grand Slam titles has Serena won with her sister Venus Williams? ((3) points)

A. 6   B. 10   C. 14   D. 17

27. **(I)** As of 2024, which men's team holds the most World Cup Rugby championship titles? ((1 ½) points) [max. 6 points]

A. South Africa (The Springboks)   C. England (The Lions)
B. New Zealand (The All Blacks)   D. Australia (The Wallabies)

For **(3)** bonus points to **(I)**: All or nothing. In which years did they win?

(II) As of 2024, which women's team holds the most World Cup Rugby Cup championship titles? ((1 ½) points)

A. New Zealand (The Black Ferns)   C. England (The Red Roses)
B. Australia (The Wallaroos)   D. USA (The Eagles)

28. How many Olympic medals does Michael Phelps have? [max. 7 points]

A. 30   B. 16   C. 22   D. 28

For **(2)** bonus points each:
(I) In which Summer Olympics did he win a record eight gold medals?
(II) In which Summer Olympics did he win a total of eight medals?

A. Athens 2004   C. London 2012
B. Beijing 2008   D. Rio 2016

D. SPORTS CHAMPION
(each question at least 3 points)

29. **(I)** The year 2022 might be known for the "biggest chess scandal in history." However, there was another infamous drama during the 1978 World Chess Championship played between Anatoly Karpov and Viktor Korchnoi in The Philippines. There were accusations of X-raying of chairs, hypnotists, and psychic yogis all influencing the match; mirror glasses were worn; and demands that the players' restroom be searched for hidden devices. Which food below also prompted a cheating protest at this event, with the claim that it was a code sent to a player by his team? **((1) point)**

   A. Green apple
   B. Blueberry yoghurt
   C. Five carrots
   D. Donut

   (II) Who ultimately won this championship? **((1) point)**

   A. Karpov
   B. Korchnoi

   (III) What was the final score? **((1) point)**

   A. 6 – 2
   B. 6 – 5

30. Who was the youngest women's tennis player in the Open Era to attain the WTA World Number 1? **[max. 12 points]**

   A. Steffi Graf
   B. Monica Seles
   C. Iga Świątek
   D. Martina Hingis

   (I) For **(2)** bonus points: Which top player above used or uses LEGOs as part of her mental training regimen?

   (II) For **(3)** bonus points: Which female tennis player has won the most Roland Garros (French Open) singles titles in the Open Era? She may or may not be on the list above.

   (III) For **(3)** bonus points: This athlete was the youngest men's tennis player to become World Number 1 in ATP history.

   A. Pete Sampras
   B. Boris Becker
   C. Carlos Alcaraz
   D. Rafael Nadal
   E. John McEnroe
   F. Lleyton Hewitt

   (IV) For **(1)** bonus point: In which year?

31. **(I)** There's no point asking who is considered the fastest athlete ever in the world. Rather, the question is: What's the fastest time in which Jamaica's Usain Bolt ran the 100-metre sprint? **((2) points)**

   A. 9.72 seconds
   B. 9.58 seconds
   C. 9.63 seconds
   D. 9.69 seconds

   (II) What's the fastest time in which Bolt ran the 200-metre dash? **((1) point) [max. 7 points]**

   A. 19.26 seconds
   B. 19.30 seconds
   C. 19.19 seconds
   D. 19.67 seconds

   Bonuses: How many **(I)** World Championship gold medals, and **(II)** Olympic gold medals does Bolt have? **((2) points each)**

   A. 14
   B. 8
   C. 11
   D. 13

D. SPORTS CHAMPION
(each question at least 3 points)

32. **This athlete is the first male tennis player to win 21 Singles Grand Slam titles in the Open Era. [max. 9 points]**
    A. Pete Sampras   C. Rafael Nadal
    B. Roger Federer   D. Novak Djokovic

    (I) For (3) bonus points: In what Grand Slam did he win his 21st title?
    A. Australian   C. Wimbledon
    B. U.S.   D. Roland Garros (French)

    (II) For (1) bonus point: In what calendar year?

    (III) For (2) bonus points: Rafael Nadal played his last match in 2024 at which tournament before his retirement?
    A. Roland Garros (French)   C. Nitto ATP Finals
    B. Davis Cup   D. Laver Cup

33. **This horse won the 2018 Triple Crown, i.e., it won the Kentucky Derby, then the Preakness Stakes, and finally the Belmont Stakes. [max. 12 points]**
    A. American Pharoah
    B. Justify
    C. Audible
    D. Authentic

    (I) For (3) bonus points: Who was the horse's jockey in all three races?
    A. Javier Castellano
    B. Victor Espinoza
    C. Mike E. Smith
    D. John Velazquez

    This is not the horse!

    (II) Get (1) bonus point if you know his trainer's name.

    (III) For (3) bonus points: Which filly won the Longines Kentucky Oats race in 2018?
    A. Wonder Gadot   C. Chocolate Martini
    B. Midnight Bisou   D. Monomoy Girl

    (IV) For (2) "fascinator" bonus points: Which three-year-old horse won the 150th Kentucky Derby in 2024, by a nose?
    A. Mystik Dan   C. Forever Young
    B. Sierra Leone   D. Catching Freedom

Answers to questions in this Category can be found starting on page 266.

Are you and your team ready for a strategy play card?

D. SPORTS CHAMPION
(each question at least 3 points)

Category E:
"JAMS"
(3-point category)

1. All of these charting R&B singles were released in 1990 except: [max. 7 points]
   A. "Feels Good" by Tony! Toni! Toné!
   B. "Hold On" by En Vogue
   C. "All Around the World" by Lisa Stansfield
   D. "Emotions" by Mariah Carey
   E. "Poison" by Bell Biv DeVoe

   (I) For (2) bonus points: Which LL Cool J's "Jam" was released in 1990 and reached No. 1 on the U.S. Hot Rap Singles Chart? It complimented one of the above singles well. Hint: "C-O-O-L-I-N-F-R-O-N-T-I-N."

   (II) For (2) bonus points: Magiun de Prune, one of the most expensive jams in the world, is produced in:
   A. Slovenia   C. Moldova
   B. Romania   D. North Macedonia

2. (I) Both of these are hit songs by Chicago-born Jody Watley. "Real Love" was released before "Looking For A New Love." ((1) point)
   A. True   B. False

   (II) What was the name of her debut solo album? ((1) point)
   A. *Affairs of the Heart*   C. *Larger Than Life*
   B. *Jody Watley*

   (III) With which rap artist(s) did Jody Watley collaborate for another hit song (and video), "Friends"? ((1) point) [max. 5 points]
   A. LL Cool J   C. Big Daddy Kane
   B. Eric B. and Rakim D. Kid 'N Play

   For (2) bonus points: Where / with whom did she get her first big break? ((2) points)
   A. TV dance show Soul Train   C. As a solo musical artist
   B. R&B group Shalamar   D. U.K. Reggae group Musical Youth

3. Match the Eurovision Song Contest winning "Jam" with its artist(s) and the country the artist(s) represented. Three fully correct for (3) points; all correct for (11) points. [max. 14 points]
   A. "Arcade" (2019)
   B. "Love Shine a Light" (1997)
   C. "Stefania" (2022)
   D. "Zitti E Buoni" (2021)
   E. "Hold Me Now" (1987)
   F. "Diva" (1998)
   G. "Euphoria" (2012)

Eurovision Artist(s)	Country
I. Dana International	I. Ukraine
II. Johnny Logan	II. Italy
III. Loreen	III. UK
IV. Kalush Orchestra	IV. Israel
V. Katrina and the Waves	V. The Netherlands
VI. Duncan Laurence	VI. Sweden
VII. Måneskin	VII. Ireland

   For (3) bonus points: As of 2024, which two countries had the most wins?
   A. France   D. Ireland
   B. United Kingdom   E. Sweden
   C. The Netherlands   F. Luxembourg

E. "JAMS"
(each question at least 3 points)

4. **Match four British artists with their "Jam" for (3) points. Match all for (13) points. [max. 19 points]**

		British Artist(s)
A.	"Addicted to Love"	I. Duran Duran
B.	"Another Brick in the Wall (Part 2)"	II. Eurythmics
C.	"Everybody Wants to Rule the World"	III. Pink Floyd
D.	"Back to Life"	IV. Soul II Soul
E.	"Owner of a Lonely Heart"	V. Tears for Fears
F.	"Sweet Dreams (Are Made Of This)"	VI. Yes
G.	"The Reflex"	VII. Lisa Stansfield
H.	"Yellow"	VIII. David Bowie
I.	"Start Me Up"	IX. Robert Palmer
J.	"You Can't Deny It"	X. Rolling Stones
K.	"Let's Dance"	XI. Coldplay

(I) For (1) bonus point: How many of the "Jams" were released in 1983?

(II) For (3) bonus points: Which two "Jams" were first released in 1989?

(III) For (2) bonus points: Which "Jam" was released in April 1984?

5. **The group Guy's "Groove Me" was a hit *New Jack Swing* style "Jam" of producer Teddy Riley in the late 1980s. Which song with its artist(s) below did Riley not produce? [max. 5 points]**
   - A. "Is It Good to You" by Heavy D and the Boyz
   - B. "Never Let You Go" by New Kids on the Block
   - C. "My Prerogative" by Bobby Brown
   - D. "I Want Her" by Keith Sweat
   - E. "Remember the Time" by Michael Jackson
   - F. "Sorry Belmont, but they all were. We know our Jams!"

   For (2) bonus points: According to a world of statistics report, which city had the worst daily traffic jam in the world in 2024?

A.	Jakarta, Indonesia		D.	London, England
B.	Istanbul, Turkey		E.	New York City, USA
C.	Mexico City, Mexico		F.	Delhi, India

6. **Match the EDM song of DJ and music producer David Guetta with the artist(s) he collaborated for the "Jam." Any four correct for (3) points. All eight correct for (10) points. [max. 11 points]**

		Featuring Artist(s)
A.	"Titanium"	I. Kelly Rowland
B.	"Memories"	II. Emeli Sandé
C.	"Without You"	III. Nicki Minaj
D.	"Shine Your Light"	IV. Usher
E.	"When Love Takes Over"	V. Kid Cudi
F.	"Dákiti Remix"	VI. Sia
G.	"Turn Me On"	VII. Bad Bunny & Jhayco
H.	"What I Did for Love"	VIII. Master KG & Akon

(1) bonus point: Which country below in the European Union consumes the most jams and jellies?

A.	Belgium	B.	France	C.	Italy	D.	Spain

E. "JAMS"
(each question at least 3 points)

41

7. **(I) Both or nothing. TLC is the best-selling American girl group. In which album were their hit singles "Ain't 2 Proud 2 Beg" and "What About Your Friends"? In what year was the album released? ((2) points) [max. 12 points]**

A. *CrazySexyCool*   C. *3D*
B. *Ooooooohhh…On the TLC Tip*   D. *FanMail*
Year: 1. 1992   2. 1994   3. 1999   4. 2002

(II) Kid 'N Play was one of the top hip hop duos in the late 1980s and early 1990s, known also for their dances. Their famous dance "Kid 'N Play Kick Step" first appeared in which music video? ((1) point)

A. "Do This My Way"   C. "Ain't Gonna Hurt Nobody"
B. "Gittin' Funky"   D. "Rollin with Kid 'N Play"

(I) For (5) bonus points: All or nothing. In which album(s) were TLC's number one singles (1) "No Scrubs," (2) "Creep," and (3) "Baby-Baby-Baby"? Select from sub-question (I) above.

(II) For (2) bonus points: What was the name of Kid 'N Play's DJ?

A. DJ Jazzy Jeff   C. Biz Markie
B. DJ Wiz   D. Hurby Love Bug

(III) For (1) bonus point each: There were five *House Party* films.
(1) In which film did Kid 'N Play actually not appear?
(2) In which *House Party* film did TLC appear?

A. *House Party 1*   C. *House Party 3*   E. *House Party 5*
B. *House Party 2*   D. *House Party 4*

8. **[SUPER-BONUS QUESTION—at least 7 points!!!!!] (I) Chicago DJ Marshall Jefferson's house music national anthem "Move Your Body" (vocals by Curtis McClain) was released in which year? ((6) points)**

A. 1985   B. 1986   C. 1987   D. 1988

(II) *Bring out the acid wash jeans, roller skates, and the Sony Walkman.* If you do, receive (2) free points, regardless. Freestyle singer Shannon had two ground-breaking hit singles in the early 1980s: "Let the Music Play," and "Give Me Tonight." For (4) points, when was each song released?

A. 1982, 1983   C. 1983, 1984
B. 1983, 1983   D. 1984, 1984

(III) All correctly or nothing. Place the songs in order of first to fourth release from freestyle legend Stevie B. ((4) points)

A. "I Wanna Be the One"   C. "In My Eyes"
B. "Because I Love You"   D. "Party Your Body"

(IV) In what year did Noel release his hit debut freestyle single "Silent Morning"? (The "Extended Version" was on fire!) ((3) points)

A. 1986   B. 1987   C. 1988   D. 1989

(V) Which "Godfather of House Music" recorded "Tears"? ((5) points)

A. Frankie Knuckles   C. Marshall Jefferson
B. Larry Heard   D. David Morales

E. "JAMS"
(each question at least 3 points)

9. Match the artist(s) with their hit song. Get any three correct for (1) point; six correct for (3) points; all 13 correctly for (14) points. No other in-betweens. No Steals, so please don't squander this question.

A. "Wishing Well"	
B. "Caribbean Queen"	
C. "Don't You (Forget About Me)"	
D. "I Will Survive"	
E. "Don't You Want Me"	
F. "Never Gonna Give You Up"	
G. "Take On Me"	
H. "You Spin Me Round (Like a Record)"	
I. "Get Down on It"	
J. "Ain't Nobody"	
K. "Let Me Be the One"	
L. "Funky Sensation"	
M. "Our House"	

Artist(s)
I. A-ha
II. Billy Ocean
III. Dead or Alive
IV. The Human League
V. Madness
VI. Terence Trent D'Arby
VII. Rufus & Chaka Khan
VIII. Simple Minds
IX. Exposé
X. Rick Astley
XI. Gwen McRae
XII. Kool & The Gang
XIII. Gloria Gaynor

10. (I) The Wop was a popular 1980s dance that was a "must do" with this rap song by Eric B. and Rakim, an excerpt of which is below: ((2) points) [max. 5 points]
    Don't get excited, you've been invited to a quiet storm
    But now it's out of hand 'cause you told me you hate me
    And then you ask what have I done lately
    A. "I Ain't No Joke"   C. "Don't Sweat the Technique"
    B. "Eric B. Is President"   D. "Move the Crowd"

    (II) In what year were Gen Xers wopping to this song while belting out its lyrics? ((1) point)
    A. 1985   B. 1986   C. 1987   D. 1988

    For (2) bonus points: Confirm which verse of the song is the above excerpt, but if you are wrong, you'll lose (1) of your original points.
    A. First   B. Second   C. Third   D. Fourth

11. One of these alternative rock bands is originally from Washington state; sued Ticketmaster for anti-competitiveness and monopolistic tactics in the concert ticket market; is a pro-choice activist; has been called "the most popular American rock 'n' roll band of the 1990s"; and was named one year "Planet Defenders" by Rock the Earth for their environmental activism. Who is it? [max. 11 points]
    A. Nirvana   C. Soundgarden
    B. Pearl Jam   D. Green Day

    (I) For (2) bonus points: Which 1980s mega-hit song had the names "Tommy" and "Gina" in the lyrics?
    A. "Jack and Diane"   C. "Livin' On a Prayer"
    B. "Sweet Child O' Mine"   D. "Need You Tonight"
    (II) For (3) bonus points: Name the artist(s) of the song.

    (III) Which band above released the mega-hit "Smells Like Teen Spirit" in the 1990s? ((3) bonus points)

E. "JAMS"

(each question at least 3 points)

12. Match four of these iconic 1980s songs with the artist(s) for (3) points. Match seven for (6) points. Match all of the songs with their artist(s) for (15) points.

	Artist(s)
A. "(You Are My) All and All"	I. Fonda Rae
B. "Set It Off"	II. Cameo
C. "Candy"	III. Joyce Sims
D. "Point of No Return"	IV. Strafe
E. "Show Me"	V. Inner City
F. "People are People"	VI. Nocera
G. "Lifetime Love"	VII. The Jets
H. "Crush On You"	VIII. Cover Girls
I. "Summertime, Summertime"	IX. Slick Rick with Doug E. Fresh
J. "Tuch me"	X. Depeche Mode
K. "I Want to Thank You"	XI. Nu Shooz
L. "Sign O' The Times"	XII. Alicia Myers
M. "La-Di-Da-Di"	XIII. Prince
N. "Big Fun"	

13. **(I)** Before there was JLo, there was another Boricua sensation Lisa Lisa & Cult Jam. Their mega hit "I Wonder If I Take You Home" was released in which year? ((1) point)

A. 1984   B. 1985   C. 1986   D. 1987

(II) They released another mega hit "Can You Feel the Beat" in which year? ((1) point)

A. 1985   B. 1986   C. 1987   D. 1988

(III) Their producer Full Force hailed out of which New York City borough? ((1) point)

A. The "boogie down" Bronx   C. (Harlem) Manhattan
B. (East Flatbush) Brooklyn   D. (Hollis) Queens

14. All of the below were major Jamaican dancehall artists during the 1980s and 1990s except: [max. 15 points]

A. Koffee   C. Shabba Ranks   E. Bounty Killer
B. Shaggy   D. Capleton   F. Super Cat

(1) For (7) bonus points (all or nothing): Which artist(s) above sang "Tour," "Toast," "Mud Up," and "Ting-a-Ling"?

(2) For (2) bonus points: The reggaeton song "Mi Gente" is one of the biggest songs ever viewed / heard on YouTube, with over 3 billion views. Who is/are the artist(s)?

A. J. Balvin   D. J. Balvin and Black Eyed Peas
B. J. Balvin and Ozuna   E. J. Balvin and Maluma
C. J. Balvin and Willy William

(3) For (1) bonus point: In what year did the above "Jam" drop?

A. 2016   B. 2017   C. 2018   D. 2019

(4) For (2) bonus points: In what year did Maluma release "Agua de Jamaica"?

A. 2020   B. 2021   C. 2022   D. 2023

E. "JAMS"
(each question at least 3 points)

15. This question is dedicated to the Gen Xers who "jammed" to these songs during the 1980s and 1990s. "Can I Kick It?" Match any five songs with the rap group for (3) points. Earn (9) extra points if you correctly match the six remaining songs with the rappers. No other derivatives. "Yes, You Can." [max. 15 points]

	Rap Group
A. "Me, Myself and I"	I. Salt N Pepa
B. "Hip Hop Hooray"	II. Doug E. Fresh and The Get Fresh Crew
C. "Rebel Without a Pause"	III. A Tribe Called Quest
D. "Scenario"	IV. Black Sheep
E. "The Show"	V. Run D.M.C.
F. "Sucker MC's"	VI. Rob Base and DJ EZ Rock
G. "It Takes Two"	VII. Public Enemy
H. "Get Up Everybody (Get Up)"	VIII. Naughty by Nature
I. "Ready or Not"	IX. De La Soul
J. "The Choice Is Yours"	X. Digable Planets
K. "Rebirth of Slick (Cool Like Dat)"	XI. Fugees

For (3) bonus points: Which Fatman Scoop song below, though not from the 1980s or 1990s, sampled a couple of the songs on the list above? The song was a major club hit in Europe before it became popular in the USA.

A.   "Clap Your Hands"   B.   "Be Faithful"

16. Which group sang "If It Isn't Love," "Can You Stand the Rain," and "You're Not My Kind Of Girl"? Their choreography was top of the class! [max. 8 points]

A.   New Edition   D.   New Kids On the Block
B.   NSYNC   E.   Backstreet Boys
C.   Menudo   F.   Tony! Toni! Toné!

(I) For (2) bonus points: What was the name of the classic album in which these songs were, with "If It Isn't Love" being the first single and music video released?

(II) For (3) bonus points: Which group above sang "Larger Than Life"?

17. *If you or someone on your team happens to be wearing a thick hair bow, fingerless lace gloves, stacks of bracelets, and/or strands of necklaces, take (1) free bonus point, regardless of this outcome. Both or nothing.* Which two Madonna "Jams" were not released in the 1980s? [max. 10 points]

A.   "Into the Groove"   D.   "Ray of Light"
B.   "Holiday"   E.   "Like a Prayer"
C.   "Justify My Love"   F.   "Lucky Star"

(I) For (3) bonus points: What was the name of Madonna's first album before it was retitled for the 1985 reissue?

(II) For (3) bonus points, (1) point each: 1. Which of the above songs was a theme song in a film? 2. Name that film in which Madonna played the title role. 3. State the year that the film was released.

E. "JAMS"
(each question at least 3 points)

18. Time to "Fog Up De Place." We can't have a proper "Jams" category without matching some Caribbean artists and their songs. "Who Am I?" Answer any four correctly for (3) points; seven for (6) points; "Play Harder": all correctly for (13) points. [max. 18 points]

Caribbean Artist(s)
I. Rihanna
II. Bad Bunny
III. Kes
IV. Beenie Man
V. Bunji Garlin
VI. Bob Marley
VII. Nailah Blackman and Skinny Fabulous
VIII. Ozuna
IX. Buju Banton
X. Destra featuring Machel Montano
XI. El Alfa El Jefe
XII. Kevin Lyttle

A.   "The Savannah Grass (Road Mix)"
B.   "Romie"
C.   "It's Carnival (Remix)"
D.   "No Woman No Cry"
E.   "Síguelo Bailando"
F.   "Suave"
G.   "Come Home"
H.   "Champion"
I.   "Yo Perreo Sola"
J.   "Umbrella"
K.   "Hard Fete"
L.   "Turn Me On"

For (5) bonus points, all or nothing: Which six Caribbean islands are represented by the artists? (Note: By birth.) And if you (or someone on your team) were born in the Caribbean, take (1) extra point. *Just kidding!*

19. What was the first international hit of Boy George and the Culture Club from their first album? [max. 6 points]
A.   "I'll Tumble 4 Ya"   C.   "Do You Really Want to Hurt Me?"
B.   "Karma Chameleon"   D.   "Church of the Poisoned Mind"

For (3) bonus points: What is the group's second album?
A.   *Colour by Numbers*   B.   *Kissing to Be Clever*

20. (I) In tribute to Mozart, this singer / group released "Rock Me Amadeus" in 1985. ((1 ½)) points)
A.   Scorpions   B.   A-ha   C.   Falco   D.   Nena

(II) This singer popularized the idea of wearing one's "Sunglasses at Night" in 1983. ((1 ½)) points)
A.   Huey Lewis   C.   Corey Hart
B.   Bryan Adams   D.   George Michael

21. For (1) point each. (I) Janet Jackson showed us how to "jam" with a chair. In what year was her song "The Pleasure Principle" released?
A.   1985   B.   1986   C.   1987   D.   1988
For (3) bonus points to (I): In what music video did she bring back "the chair"?

(II) In what year did she release the album *Rhythm Nation 1814*?
A.   1989   B.   1990   C.   2001   D.   1993

(III) Who produced *Control* and *Rhythm Nation 1814* with Janet Jackson? [max. 6 points]
A.   Teddy Riley   C.   L.A. Reid and Babyface
B.   Jimmy Jam and Terry Lewis   D.   Quincy Jones

E. "JAMS"
(each question at least 3 points)

22. A dedication to aficionados of 1980s and 1990s house music. A shout-out also to Greek-letter fraternity and sorority step teams. "Party People," match the three songs directly below with the artist(s) in the table. ((1) point each) [max. 16 points]

A. "Follow Me"   B. "Can You Party"   C. "Can You Feel It"

House Music Artist(s)
I. Steve "Silk" Hurley
II. Royal House
III. The Jungle Brothers
IV. Aly-Us
V. Mr. Fingers
VI. Ten City
VII. Black Box
VIII. Raze
IX. LNR
X. Ralphi Rosario featuring Xavier Gold
XI. Nightcrawlers
XII. Two Without Hats

If at least two of the above songs are answered correctly, for (1) bonus point each plus (4) extra "house" points if all nine are correct: Which artist(s) recorded the house music hits below?

D. "I'll House You"
E. "Devotion (Club Mix)"
F. "Push the Feeling On"
G. "Jack Your Body"
H. "You Used to Hold Me"
I. "Break 4 Love"
J. "Work It to The Bone"
K. "Everybody Everybody"
L. "Try Yazz"

23. U.S. East Coast meets U.S. West Coast meets U.S. Southern hip hop. Get (1) point for each different question correctly answered.
Q1: (I) 1 Notorious B.I.G. (Biggie Small) song.
Q2: (II) 1 Tupac Shakur (2Pac) song; or (III) 1 Snoop Dogg song.
Q3: (IV) 1 Ludacris song; (V) 1 Lil Jon song; or (VI) 1 OutKast song.
[max. 10 points]

A. "Dear Mama"   F. "Hypnotize"
B. "What's My Name"   G. "Keep Ya Head Up"
C. "One More Chance" H. "Act a Fool"
D. "Turn Down For What" I. "Hey Ya!"
E. "Ms. Jackson"   J. "Gin and Juice"

If you received the (3) points, get (7) bonus points (all or nothing), if you can identify correctly the artists of the remaining songs above.

24. Slow "Jams" for when you're in love, when you have tabanca, when you've just experienced a break-up, when you need a good cry, when you're getting married, or when you're just being you. Match four artists with his/her song to receive (3) points. Answer all 10 songs correctly, receive (12) points. No other derivatives.

Artist
I. Lisa Fischer
II. Toni Braxton
III. Babyface
IV. Sade
V. Luther Vandross
VI. Anita Baker
VII. George Michael
VIII. Whitney Houston
IX. Phil Collins
X. Billy Joel

A. "Here and Now"
B. "How Can I Ease the Pain"
C. "One More Try"
D. "Honesty"
E. "I Have Nothing"
F. "Un-Break My Heart"
G. "Whip Appeal"
H. "Sweet Love"
I. "Against All Odds"
J. "No Ordinary Love"

E. "JAMS"
(each question at least 3 points)

25. **Decades of dance, EDM, and house music classics. Match any four hit songs with the artist(s) for (3) points. Match seven songs for (6) points, and all 12 songs for (14) points.**

	Song		Artist(s)
A.	"Call on Me"	I.	Stardust
B.	"Wake Me Up"	II.	Faithless
C.	"Lady (Hear Me Tonight)"	III.	Daft Punk
D.	"Music Sounds Better with You"	IV.	Eric Prydz
E.	"Summer"	V.	Modjo
F.	"Don't You Worry Child"	VI.	Haddaway
G.	"Insomnia"	VII.	Deee-Lite
H.	"Groove Is in the Heart"	VIII.	Avicii
I.	"Rhythm Is a Dancer"	IX.	Swedish House Mafia
J.	"What is Love"	X.	Snap!
K.	"One More Time"	XI.	Calvin Harris
L.	"Levels"		

26. **Musician Rick James wrote the songs below. Match the song with its artist(s). All or nothing. [max. 7 points]**

A. "Ebony Eyes"   C. "All Night Long"
B. "Square Biz"

Artist(s)
I. Teena Marie
II. Mary Jane Girls
III. Smokey Robinson

(I) For (3) bonus points: Which rapper sampled "All Night Long" in his hit 1989 song "Smooth Operator"?

A. Kool Moe Dee   C. Big Daddy Kane
B. LL Cool J   D. Slick Rick

(II) For (1) bonus point: In what year was Rick James's "Super Freak" released?

A. 1980   B. 1981   C. 1982   D. 1983

27. **Match each sociopolitical 1980s rap song with its artist(s). ((1) point each) [max. 11 points]**

A. "The Message"
B. "Don't Believe the Hype"
C. "Philosophy"

Artists
I. Grandmaster Flash and the Furious Five
II. Boogie Down Productions
III. N.W.A
IV. Public Enemy
V. The Roots

(I) For (3) bonus points (both or nothing): In which film by director Spike Lee was the theme song "Fight the Power"? Who was the musical group?

(II) For (2) bonus points: The proceeds of the following socially conscious song went to the National Urban League in the USA. In what year was "Self Destruction" by The Stop the Violence Movement released?

A. 1987   B. 1988   C. 1989   D. 1990

(III) For (3) bonus points: Where is Bar-le-Duc, one of the most expensive jams in the world, produced?

A. Pau, France   C. Liège, Belgium
B. Alsace, France   D. Lorraine, France

E. "JAMS"
(each question at least 3 points)

28. **(I) In what year did U2 release their mega "Jam," "With or Without You?" ((1) point) [max. 7 points]**
   A.   1980   B.   1984   C.   1987   D.   1988

   (II) In which album was the song featured? ((2) points)
   A.   *Boy*   C.   *The Unforgettable Fire*
   B.   *The Joshua Tree*   D.   *Rattle and Hum*

   (1) For (2) bonus points: Which songs below sampled the "Jam"?
   A.   "On and On" by Girl Talk   E.   All
   B.   "Come Over" by Kenny Chesney   F.   B and C
   C.   "With or Without You" by Machel   G.   A and C
        Montano feat. Walker Hornung   H.   None
   D.   "Take Me to the Clouds Above" by LMC

   (2) For (2) bonus points: From where on the island of Ireland are the members of U2?
   A.   Galway   B.   Belfast   C.   Cork   D.   Dublin

29. **Which two songs were a Wu-Tang Clan group song and not a song released by a member of the group as a solo artist? [max. 6 points]**
   A.   "Brooklyn Zoo"
   B.   "C.R.E.A.M. (Cash Rules Everything Around Me)"
   C.   "I'll Be There for You/You're All I Need to Get By"
   D.   "Criminology"
   E.   "Triumph"

   For (3) bonus points: Name Wu-Tang Clan's secret album.

30. **Hype Williams directed all of the following hit music video "Jams" except for two. Both or nothing for the (3) points. [max. 6 points]**
   A.   Mary J. Blige's "Enough Cryin"
   B.   TLC's "No Scrubs"
   C.   Kendrick Lamar's "Not Like Us"
   D.   Beyoncé's "Drunk in Love" featuring Jay-Z
   E.   Missy Elliott's "The Rain (Supa Dupa Fly)"
   F.   2Pac's "California Love" featuring Dr. Dre
   G.   Eminem's "Without Me"
   H.   Busta Rhymes's "Put Your Hands Where My Eyes Can See"

   For (3) bonus points: Which of the above Williams-directed videos was based on Eddie Murphy's 1988 film *Coming to America*?

31. **Rapper and record producer Dr. Dre has produced songs for each of the following artists except: [max. 4 points]**
   A.   Tupac   D.   Gwen Stefani
   B.   Eminem   E.   Snoop Dogg
   C.   Heavy D   F.   Mary J. Blige

   For (1) bonus point: In what year was Dr. Dre's "Nuthin' But A 'G' Thang" with Snoop Dogg released?
   A.   1991   B.   1992   C.   1993   D.   1994

E. "JAMS"

(each question at least 3 points)

32. Some songs have "jump" or "jumping" themes. Match the songs with the artists. ((½) point each) [max. 5 points]
    A. "Jump (For My Love)" (1983)
    B. "Jump" (1983)
    C. "Jump Around" (1992)
    D. "Jump" (1992)
    E. "Jump and Wave" (1994)
    F. "Jump" (2004)

Artist(s)
I. Kris Kross
II. Preacher
III. Van Halen
IV. Rupee
V. House of Pain
VI. Pointer Sisters

(I) For (1) bonus point: In what year was French Montana's "Jump" featuring Travis Scott released?
    A. 2016   C. 2018
    B. 2017   D. 2019

(II) For (1) bonus point: In what year was Rihanna's "Jump" released?
    A. 2008   C. 2011
    B. 2009   D. 2012

33. Slow "Jams" are eternal; slow "Jams" give you hope; slow "Jams" are medicinal; and slow "Jams" uplift you. Match four artist(s) with his/her/their song to receive (3) points. Match eight for (7) points. Answer all 13 artists correctly, receive (15) points for being a good sport. No other derivatives.
    A. "My, My, My"
    B. "Come & Talk to Me"
    C. "Time After Time"
    D. "Shake You Down"
    E. "Total Eclipse of the Heart (Turn Around)"
    F. "End of the Road"
    G. "Halo"
    H. "Home"
    I. "Holding Back the Years"
    J. "Have You Ever Loved Somebody"
    K. "Broken Wings"
    L. "I Want to Know What Love Is"
    M. "Sarvesham Svastir Bhavatu"

Oy, tears are welling up here, mates.

Artist(s)
I. Simply Red
II. Beyoncé
III. Johnny Gill
IV. Gregory Abbott
V. Jodeci
VI. Foreigner
VII. Boyz II Men
VIII. Cyndie Lauper
IX. Mr. Mister
X. Freddie Jackson
XI. Stephanie Mills
XII. Tina Turner
XIII. Bonnie Tyler

Answers to questions in this Category can be found starting on page 266.

Now, I need a mix tape of these "Hilarion Jams: Volume 1"!

Rest in Peace, all the "Jams" Artists who no longer are with us. Thank you for your timeless and transformational songs and music.

E. "JAMS"
(each question at least 3 points)

Category F:
GEOGRAPHY 235
(3-point category)

1. [SUPER-BONUS QUESTION—at least 7 points!!!!!] Name 16 countries / territories that begin with the letter C and are geographically (not politically) located in the continents below.
    (I) Name 6 in the Americas
    (II) Name 1 in Europe
    (III) Name 5 in Africa
    (IV) Name 4 in Asia

    > No points if you answer fewer than 8 correctly
    > (7) points if you answer 8 - 10 correctly
    > (15) points if you answer 11 – 14 correctly
    > (23) points if you answer 15 – 16 correctly

    If you earn at least (7) points above, for (3) points: Name 1 in Oceania.

2. Below is the English translation of the full name of a city in which country? [max. 6 points]
    "*The city of angels, the great city, the residence of the Emerald Buddha, the impregnable city (of Ayutthaya) of God Indra, the grand capital of the world endowed with nine precious gems, the happy city, abounding in an enormous Royal Palace that resembles the heavenly abode where reigns the reincarnated god, a city given by Indra and built by Vishnukarn.*"

    A. Laos   C. Nepal
    B. Indonesia   D. Thailand

    (1) For (1) bonus point: How many English letters are in the name?
    A. 96   B. 125   C. 168   D. 202

    (2) For (2) bonus points: What is a shortened name of this city either used locally or by non-locals?

3. On March 1, 1954, the USA tested the 15-megaton Bravo Hydrogen Bomb in Bikini Atoll. This was one of several nuclear tests done at the atoll between July 1946 and July 1958. However, the 1954 test was 1,000 times the magnitude of the Hiroshima and Nagasaki nuclear weapons dropped on Japan during WWII. The blast also vaporized three islands. Where is this coral reef, Bikini Atoll?

    A. Guam   D. American Samoa
    B. Wake Island   E. Northern Mariana Islands
    C. Marshall Islands

4. All of these countries no longer exist as a separate country except one, which exists still as a single country but with a different name. Which one? [max. 5 points]

    A. Ceylon   C. Czechoslovakia
    B. Yugoslavia   D. Sikkim

    For (2) bonus points: What is it known as today?

5. Vikings from this country played a notable role in European history. A bridge links this country's capital to another European country. This country administers and controls the foreign policy and defense of Faroe Islands and Greenland. It operates under a constitutional monarchy. Its municipality Roskilde annually hosts one of the largest music festivals in Europe.

A. Norway   C. Sweden

B. The Netherlands   D. Denmark

6. Name eight countries / territories that begin with the letter E. Get (1) point if you answer 2 – 4 correctly; (2) points if you answer 5 – 6 correctly; or (3) points, only if you answer 7 – 8 correctly.

7. Name countries / territories that begin with the letter P and are located in the continents below. Get (1) point if 2 – 3 correct; (2) points if 4 – 6 correct; or (3) points, but only if 7 – 8 are correct. [max. 6 points]

(I) Name **4** in **the Americas**

(II) Name **2** in **Asia**

(III) Name **2** in **Oceania**

If you have the (3) points, for (3) bonus points: Name 2 in Europe.

8. Indicate which number on the map corresponds to Nicaragua.
[max. 7 points]

A. 1   D. 5

B. 2   E. 6

C. 3   F. 7

(I) For (1) bonus point: Name its official currency.

(II) For (3) bonus points: Indicate which country corresponds to 4.

9. Which country has made territorial claims to land areas 1 on the map of Antarctica? [max. 5 points]

A. Argentina

B. Australia

C. Chile

D. France

E. Norway

F. United Kingdom

G. United States of America

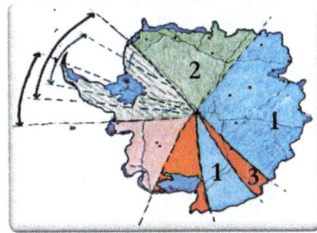

Get (1) bonus point each if you name:

(I) Which country has claimed territory 2;

and (II) Which country has claimed territory 3?

(It could be same as (I), or it could be different.)

10. **(I) Greenland is the largest island in the world. What is the second largest island? ((2) points)**
   A.   Madagascar   C.   Honshū
   B.   Borneo   D.   New Guinea

   (II) Each of these European countries is landlocked except: ((1) point)
   A.   Switzerland   C.   Liechtenstein
   B.   The Netherlands   D.   Austria

11. **This province's capital is the oldest city in Canada. Its largest city is Montreal. Ungava Peninsula is in its north, while Gaspe Peninsula is in the south.**
   A.   Alberta   B.   Ontario   C.   Nova Scotia   D.   Québec

12. **This is the most populous island on Earth that is not also a continent.**
   A.   Java   C.   Great Britain
   B.   Honshū   D.   Luzon

13. **Name countries / territories / departments in the continents below that begin with the letter M. Get (1) point if 3 – 5 are correct; (2) points if 6 – 9 are correct; or (3) points if 10 – 13 are correct. [max. 9 points]**
   (I) Name **3** in **the Americas**
   (II) Name **3** in **Europe**
   (III) Name **5** in **Asia**
   (IV) Name **2** in **Oceania**

   If you earn the (3) points, for (6) bonus points: Name 5 in Africa.

14. **Tomorrow, you head to Versilia. But today, you're drinking a local three-year-old Chianti Classico DOCG Reserva with your *pappardelle al cinghiale*, while your friend is eating *seppie in zimino*. You spent already a few hours visiting Filippo Brunelleschi's Il Duomo, stood in front of Sandro Botticelli's *Birth of Venus*, and squeezed amongst other people staring at Michelangelo's *David*, wondering why there was such a big fuss in the USA over it. Which Italian region are you visiting?**
   A.   Lazio   B.   Liguria   C.   Tuscany   D.   Umbria

15. **At a point in history, Hong Kong and Macau were part of this province in China. [max. 5 points]**
   A.   Sichuan   C.   Hebei
   B.   Jiangsu   D.   Guangdong

   (I) For (1) bonus point: Hong Kong was a colony of which country from 1841 until 1 July 1997?

   (II) For (1) bonus point: Macau was a colony of which country from 1557 until 20 December 1999?

16. **This Australian state's capital is Adelaide. The state is home to Kangaroo Island. Barossa Valley is its renowned wine country.**
   A.   Queensland   C.   South Australia
   B.   Victoria   D.   New South Wales

F. GEOGRAPHY 235
(each question at least 3 points)

17. The official languages of this country are Dari and Pashto. Two iconic 6th and 7th-century Buddha statues (Salsal and Shahmama) in its Bamiyan Valley were destroyed in 2001. One of its borders is at the Durand Land. What is this central Asian country?

    A.   Pakistan   C.   Afghanistan
    B.   Turkmenistan   D.   Tajikistan

18. (I) What is the largest country in Africa, <u>by area</u>? ((1 ½) points)

    A.   Algeria   C.   Democratic Republic of the Congo
    B.   Nigeria   D.   Sudan

    (II) What is the smallest country in the African <u>mainland</u>? ((1 ½) points)

    A.   Cabo Verde   B.   Namibia   C.   The Gambia   D.   Lesotho

19. Name nine countries / territories that begin with the letter I. Get (1) point if 2 – 4 correct; (2) points if 5 – 6 correct; or (3) points if 7 – 9 are correct. [max. 5 points]
    (2) bonus points: Name a country capital that begins with the letter I.

20. This country's capital is Port Louis. The dodo bird, now extinct, once lived primarily in Rodrigues, one of its islands.

    A.   Mauritius   C.   St. Vincent & the Grenadines
    B.   Rwanda   D.   Jamaica

21. Kyoto, once the capital of Japan where the emperors resided up to the mid-nineteenth century, is in which region? Hint: Osaka, Nara, and Kobe also are in this region.

    A.   Chubu   C.   Kanto
    B.   Kinki / Kansai   D.   Chugoku

22. The capital of this unincorporated U.S. territory is Hagåtña. [max. 6 points]

    A.   Northern Mariana Islands   C.   Guam
    B.   Marshall Islands   D.   American Samoa

    For (3) bonus points: Which of the above places no longer is an unincorporated territory and is now an independent nation?

23. (I) This African nation's capital is Bangui. In 1977, the president was coronated as emperor in a ceremony similar to Napoleon's in 1804. It legally recognized Bitcoin in 2022 and launched its first crypto hub called "Sango," named after one of its official languages. ((2) points)

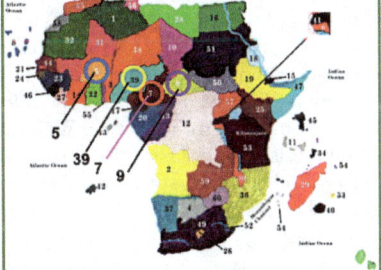

    A.   Cameroon
    B.   Burkina Faso
    C.   Republic of the Congo
    D.   Central African Republic

    (II) Where is it located on this map? ((1) point)
    A. 39   B. 9   C. 5   D. 7

24. Which South American country is (11); which is (14); and which is (15) on the map? ((1) point each) [max. 4 points]
    A. Ecuador
    B. Venezuela
    C. Uruguay
    D. Peru

    For (1) bonus point if all the above are answered correctly:
    One of the countries uses the USD as its official currency. Which one?

25. This Mexican state contains the ruins of Teotihuacán. Its capital is Toluca de Lerdo. Popocatépetl and Iztaccíhuatl stratovolcanoes are also in this state.
    A. Baja California   C. State of Mexico
    B. Mexico City   D. Michoacán

26. Goldeneye, the estate of novelist Ian Fleming, is located in the town of Oracabessa in this country.
    A. Barbados   C. Samoa
    B. Jamaica   D. Bermuda

27. Where in India has the 14th Dalai Lama of Tibetan Buddhism been living for at least six decades since fleeing Tibet?
    A. Narkanda   C. Manali
    B. Dharamshala   D. Fagu

28. In 1867, the USA purchased this territory, which was in dispute between Russia and Great Britain, from Russia for US$7.2 million. Its original inhabitants include the Aleut, Athabascan, Haida, Inupiat, Tlingit, and Yuit. Mount Denali is located here. Its capital is Juneau, and it became the 49th state to join the USA. [max. 4 points]
    A. Hawaii   C. Alaska
    B. Arizona   D. Oregon

    For (1) bonus point: What U.S. state above was the 48th to be admitted to the Union?

29. Vikings settled in this region in the early 9th century. Henry III relinquished this region to Louis IX in the 1259 Treaty of Paris. In a war against Philip II, John of England lost this region and almost all of his other possessions in France. William the Conqueror grew up here and ruled this region. From this region, he led his conquest to England. Its coastline is amongst the world's most famous coasts.
    A. Île-de-France   C. Normandy
    B. Brittany   D. Burgundy

30. Name nine countries / territories that begin with the letter N. Receive (1) point if 2 – 4 correct; (2) points if 5 – 6 correct; or (3) points only if 7 – 9 are correct. [max. 9 points]

    For (6) bonus points: Name four other countries / territories that begin with the letter N. All or nothing.

31. (I) These two countries squabbled for 50 years in their "Whisky War" row over the ownership of a small, uninhabited Arctic island. They reached a deal in June 2022 to divide the island into two almost equally large parts, so no more war with schnapps and whiskey. ((1) point)

    A.   Canada and USA   C.   Denmark and USA
    B.   Canada and Denmark   D.   Denmark and Iceland

    (II) What is the name of the island? ((2) points)

    A.   Ellesmere Island   C.   Axel Heiberg Island
    B.   Hans Island   D.   Somerset Island

32. India comprises 28 states and 8 union territories.
    (I) What is the largest state in India by population? ((1) point)

    A.   Madhya Pradesh   C.   Rajasthan
    B.   Uttar Pradesh   D.   Maharashtra

    (II) What is the largest state by area? ((1) point)

    A.   Madhya Pradesh   C.   Rajasthan
    B.   Uttar Pradesh   D.   Maharashtra

    (III) What is the smallest state in India by area? ((1) point)

    A.   Sikkim   C.   Chandigarh
    B.   Tripura   D.   Goa

33. (I) How many countries border France? ((1) point)

    A.   4   C.   7
    B.   5   D.   8

    (II) How many countries border Botswana? ((1) point)

    A.   2   C.   4
    B.   3   D.   5

    (III) How many countries border Bhutan? ((1) point)

    A.   1   C.   3
    B.   2   D.   0

Answers to questions in this Category can be found starting on page 267.

F. GEOGRAPHY 235

(each question at least 3 points)

Category G:
BIG SCREEN, SMALL SCREEN
(2-point category)

1. **Which film won the Oscar's Best Picture at the 65th Academy Awards in 1993?**
    A. *A Few Good Men*
    B. *The Crying Game*
    C. *Howards End*
    D. *Scent of a Woman*
    E. *Unforgiven*

2. **For (1) point each. (I) The 1950s movie *The King and I* is banned in Thailand because its depiction of which King is considered disrespectful and false?**
    A. King Rama III
    B. King Rama IV
    C. King Rama V
    D. King Rama VI

    (II) How many children did this king have?
    A. 23   B. 43   C. 75   D. 82   E. 95

3. **In what year did Ang Lee's film *Crouching Tiger Hidden Dragon* win an Oscar award? (Note: It's not the year of its release.) [max. 4 points]**
    A. 2000   B. 2001   C. 2002   D. It didn't

    For (2) bonus points: Who played the lead actress in the film?
    A. Zhang Ziyi   B. Michelle Yeoh   C. Cheng Pei-pei

4. **One of these films won the Oscar's Best Picture award in 2010.**
    A. *An Education*
    B. *The Hurt Locker*
    C. *District 9*
    D. *Up in the Air*
    E. *Inglourious Basterds*
    F. *The Blind Side*
    G. *Avatar*
    H. *Precious*
    I. *Up*

5. **In what year was *Weird Science* released? [max. 6 points]**
    A. 1984   B. 1985   C. 1986   D. 1987

    For (4) bonus points: Name two of the director's other films from the 1980s or 1990s (sorry, I won't tell you the director's name as a hint).

6. **Who won Best Director at the 85th Academy Awards in 2013?**
    A. Michael Haneke (*Amour*)
    B. David O. Russell (*Silver Linings Playbook*)
    C. Steven Spielberg (*Lincoln*)
    D. Benh Zeitlin (*Beasts of the Southern Wild*)
    E. Ang Lee (*Life of Pi*)

7. **All of the following binge-worthy shows are/were aired on Netflix.**
    1. *Money Heist*   3. *Extrapolations*   5. *Stranger Things*   7. *Bear*
    2. *Supacell*   4. *Squid Game*   6. *Bridgerton*   8. *Lioness*
    A. True   B. False

8. **Both or nothing. Which two blockbusters below are not Disney-released animated films?**
    A. *Incredibles*
    B. *Toy Story*
    C. *Chicken Run*
    D. *How to Train Your Dragon*
    E. *Lilo & Stitch*
    F. *Tangled*
    G. *Zootopia*

G. BIG SCREEN, SMALL SCREEN
(each question at least 2 points)

9. Regina King has acted in and/or directed which of the following? [max. 4 points]

    A. *Watchmen*
    B. *Boyz n the Hood*
    C. *Shirley*
    D. *One Night in Miami…*
    E. A and D only
    F. All

    For (2) bonus points: In which TV sitcom did she make her acting debut?

10. (I) In what year was director Tony Scott's film *Top Gun* originally released? ((1) point) [max. 7 points]

    A. 1985   B. 1986   C. 1987   D. 1988

    (II) All of the below actors starred in that film except: ((1) point)

    A. Val Kilmer
    B. Tom Cruise
    C. Anthony Edwards
    D. Ed Harris
    E. Kellie McGillis
    F. Tom Skerritt

    (I) For (3) bonus points (all or nothing): Identify three hit songs from the film.

    A. "Let's Hear It for the Boy"
    B. "Take My Breath Away"
    C. "Danger Zone"
    D. "Playing With the Boys"

    (II) For (2) bonus points: Who directed the 2022 blockbuster sequel *Top Gun: Maverick*?

    A. James Cameron
    B. John Woo
    C. Joseph Kosinski
    D. Antoine Fuqua

11. In what years were Jason Blum's (I) *The Purge*, and (II) *The Purge: Anarchy* originally released? ((1) point each) [max. 4 points]

    A. 2012
    B. 2013
    C. 2014
    D. 2015

    (I) For (1) bonus point: On which date of the year is the purge held?

    (II) For (1) bonus point: Which of *The Purge* franchise films did Gerard McMurray direct?

    A. *The Purge: Anarchy*
    B. *The First Purge*
    C. *The Purge: Election Year*
    D. *The Forever Purge*

12. These documentary films won Best Documentary Feature at the Academy Awards held within a year after their release. Choose two films and select the year each was originally released. ((1) point each) [max. 3 points]

Film
I. *Man on Wire*
II. *Inside Job*
III. *Born Into Brothels*
IV. *An Inconvenient Truth*
V. *March of the Penguins*

    A. 2003
    B. 2005
    C. 2006
    D. 2007
    E. 2008
    F. 2009
    G. 2010

    For (1) bonus point: Which documentary above was released in 2004?

G. BIG SCREEN, SMALL SCREEN
(each question at least 2 points)

13. In no particular order, these are the *Austin Powers* spy action movies:
    (I) *Austin Powers in Goldmember*
    (II) *Austin Powers: International Man of Mystery*
    (III) *Austin Powers: The Spy Who Shagged Me*
    Give the order in which each film was released. "Yeah baby, yeah!"
    "Oh, behave!" "Smashing!" ((½) point each)

A.	1995	D.	2002
B.	1997	E.	2004
C.	1999		

    (IV) What was the name of his spy car? ((½) point)

14. Bolivia's Cochabamba Water War from November 1999 to April 2000 in
    the city of Cochabamba was the inspiration for which *James Bond* film?

A.	*Casino Royale*	C.	*Quantum of Solace*
B.	*Skyfall*	D.	*Spectre*

15. Which British comedy show won Best Comedy Programme or Series at
    the BAFTA TV Awards for two consecutive years, 2004 and 2005?

A.	*The Office*	C.	*Little Britain*
B.	*Coupling*	D.	*Harry Hill's TV Burp*

16. Motown celebrated its 25th anniversary with *Motown 25: Yesterday, Today,
    Forever,* during which Michael Jackson dazzled the world with The
    Moonwalk while performing "Billie Jean." The final episode of *M.A.S.H.*
    aired with record viewers. *Star Wars: Episode VI – Return of the Jedi, Terms of
    Endearment,* and *Trading Places* were blockbuster movies worldwide.
    What year was this?

A.	1982	B.	1983	C.	1981	D.	1984

17. This is the highest grossing horror film of all time, adjusted for
    inflation. [max. 4 points]

A.	*The Exorcist*	D.	*It*
B.	*The Sixth Sense*	E.	*Jaws*
C.	*I Am Legend*	F.	*Scream*

    (2) bonus points: Which above is the highest grossing, before inflation?

18. Acclaimed Nigerian novelist, playwright, and filmmaker Biyi Bandele's
    final film premiered at the Toronto International Film Festival in
    September 2022. Sadly, he passed away a month before the premiere.
    Which film was it?

A.	*Elesin Oba, The King's Horseman*	C.	*Half of a Yellow Sun*
B.	*Blood Sisters*	D.	*Fifty*

19. Which TV show(s) below did not use cold opens? [max. 6 points]

A.	*The Wire*	D.	*Hawaii Five-O* (not the 21st century edition)
B.	*The Office*	E.	*Breaking Bad*
C.	*Bewitched* (the '60-'70s edition)	F.	They all did

    For (4) bonus points (each answer (2) points), especially for staunchly
    loyal fans of *The Wire* within the teams: In what year did *The Wire* begin
    airing, and when did the acclaimed series end?

G. BIG SCREEN, SMALL SCREEN
(each question at least 2 points)

NO OTHER TRIVIA LIKE THIS MASTERCLASS: VOLUME 1

20. **Two of these individuals have won an Oscar as well as a Nobel Prize. ((1) point each)**
    A. George Bernard Shaw
    B. Angelina Jolie
    C. Meryl Streep
    D. Bob Dylan

21. **Who directed *Bad Boys*, *The Rock*, *Transformers*, and *Pearl Harbor*?**
    A. Michael Mann
    B. George Miller
    C. Michael Bay
    D. Tony Scott

22. **Christopher Nolan's *Oppenheimer* was nominated for several movie awards. Which Nolan film was not nominated for an Academy Award?**
    A. *Interstellar*
    B. *Tenet*
    C. *Dunkirk*
    D. *Inception*
    E. *Following*
    F. *The Dark Knight*

23. **[SUPER-BONUS QUESTION—at least 7 points!!!!!] (1) Match the films in the table with the year each one originally was released. ((1) point each)**

				Film
A.	1977	G.	2002	I. *Stomp the Yard*
B.	1978	H.	2003	II. *Flashdance*
C.	1983	I.	2007	III. *Streets of Fire*
D.	1984	J.	2023	IV. *The Five Heartbeats*
E.	1987	K.	2024	V. *Purple Rain*
F.	1991			VI. *8 Mile*
				VII. *La Bamba*
				VIII. *School of Rock*
				IX. *Saturday Night Fever*
				X. *Footloose*
				XI. *Chicago*
				XII. *Taylor Swift: The Eras Tour*
				XIII. *Dirty Dancing*

(2) From which film is each song ((1) point each): A. "Lose Yourself" B. "I Can Dream About You" C. "Baby I'm A Star" and D. "A Heart is a House for Love"?

(3) Who won an Oscar for the 2006 film *Dreamgirls*? ((2) points)
    A. Beyoncé
    B. Jennifer Hudson
    C. Eddie Murphy
    D. Jamie Foxx

24. **Match each film with its lead actor in the table. ((½) point each)**

	Lead Actor
A. *Moneyball*	I. Leonardo DiCaprio
B. *Wall Street*	II. Christian Bale
C. *The Wolf of Wall Street*	III. Brad Pitt
D. *The Big Short*	IV. Michael Douglas

25. **Match two films with its actor or actress for (2) points. Match all the films correctly with their actor and actress for the total of (10) points, as there are up to 10 answers. Be strategic.**

	Actor and Actress
A. *Invictus*	I. Angela Bassett
B. *Erin Brockovich*	II. George Clooney
C. *Black Panther: Wakanda Forever*	III. Sandra Bullock
D. *Gravity*	IV. Morgan Freeman
E. *Sicario*	V. Julia Roberts
F. *Syriana*	VI. Robert De Niro
G. *The Deer Hunter*	VII. Benicio del Toro
H. *Olympus Has Fallen*	

G. BIG SCREEN, SMALL SCREEN
(each question at least 2 points)

26. **Who wrote the screenplay for *Get Out*?**
    - A. Mati Diop
    - B. Ryan Coogler
    - C. Jordan Peele
    - D. Emmanuel Osei-Kuffour

27. **(I) Guillermo del Toro directed all of the following films except: ((1) point) [max. 4 points]**
    - A. *Pinocchio*
    - B. *The Shape of Water*
    - C. *Pan's Labyrinth*
    - D. *Amores Perros*

    For (2) bonus points to (I): Who directed that film?

    (II) For which film above did del Toro win both the Academy's Best Director and Best Picture awards? ((1) point)

28. **Match any four films with the lead actor or actress in the table for (2) points. If you answer all ten films correctly, you'll receive (12) points.**

	Lead Actor & Actress
A. *The Shadow Strays*	I. Jet Li
B. *Speed*	II. Halle Berry
C. *Hero*	III. Chadwick Boseman
D. *Aliens*	IV. Anne Parillaud
E. *La Femme Nikita*	V. Denzel Washington
F. *Black Panther*	VI. Keanu Reeves
G. *Hard Boiled*	VII. Sigourney Weaver
H. *Kill Bill*	VIII. Chow Yun Fat
I. *Moonfall*	IX. Aurora Ribero
J. *The Equalizer*	X. Uma Thurman

29. **(I) *Friday the 13th* was originally released on May 9th of which year?**
    (II) In which year was *The Terminator* originally released? ((1) point each) [max. 6 points]
    - A. 1981   B. 1984   C. 1985   D. 1980

    1. For (1) bonus point each:
    (I) Who directed that version of *Friday the 13th*?
    (II) Who directed *The Terminator*?
    - A. John Carpenter
    - B. James Cameron
    - C. John McTiernan
    - D. Sean S. Cunningham

    2. For (2) bonus points (both or nothing): In what month and year was Michael Jackson's blockbuster *Thriller* music video first broadcasted?

30. **Which animation studio produced Christian Linke's and Alex Yee's *Arcane*, based on *League of Legends* by Riot Games? [max. 10 points]**
    - A. Mappa
    - B. Illumination
    - C. Fortiche
    - D. Studio Ghibli

    (I) For (4) bonus points (both or nothing): Name the two main cities.
    - A. Exandria   B. Night City   C. Piltover   D. Zaun

    (II) For (2) bonus points each: As of 2024, how many (1) Primetime Emmy Awards, and (2) Annie Awards has *Arcane* won?
    - A. 4   B. 6   C. 7   D. 8   E. 9   F. 10

G. BIG SCREEN, SMALL SCREEN
(each question at least 2 points)

31. How well do you know director Spike Lee's films? Answer three films with their respective release date correctly for (2) points. Answer six correctly for (5). Answer all eight correctly for (8) points. No other derivatives. [max. 10 points]

A. 1986
B. 1988
C. 1989
D. 1992
E. 1997
F. 2002
G. 2006
H. 2018

Film
I. *Malcolm X*
II. *Inside Man*
III. *School Daze*
IV. *BlacKkKlansman*
V. *4 Little Girls*
VI. *She's Gotta Have It*
VII. *25th Hour*
VIII. *Do The Right Thing*

For (2) bonus points: What is the name of his Vietnam War drama film that was released in 2020?

32. These documentary films won Best Documentary Feature at the Academy Awards held within a year after their release. Select the year in which each was originally released. ((½) point each) [max. 4 points]

A. 2015
B. 2021
C. 2018
D. 2016

Film
I. *Summer of Soul*
II. *Free Solo*
III. *O.J.: Made In America*
IV. *Amy*

For (2) bonus points: Which of the following won the Primetime Emmy Award for Outstanding Documentary or Nonfiction Series at the 71st Primetime Creative Arts Emmy Awards?

A. *American Masters*
B. *Hostile Planet*
C. *30 for 30*
D. *Our Planet*
E. *Chef's Table*

33. All of these films won Best Animated Feature at the Academy Awards. In which year was each film originally released? Answer three correctly for (2) points. Answer six correctly for (5) points. Answer all ten correctly for (14) points. No other derivatives.

A. 2003
B. 2006
C. 2008
D. 2010
E. 2012
F. 2013
G. 2015
H. 2017
I. 2018
J. 2020

Animated Feature
I. *Coco*
II. *Happy Feet*
III. *Inside Out*
IV. *Finding Nemo*
V. *Soul*
VI. *Brave*
VII. *Toy Story 3*
VIII. *Spider-Man: Into the Spider-Verse*
IX. *WALL-E*
X. *Frozen*

Answers to questions in this Category can be found starting on page 268.

G. BIG SCREEN, SMALL SCREEN
(each question at least 2 points)

Category H:
COUNTRY FLAGS
(2-point category)

1. **Flag 1 and Flag 2 are of which countries?**
   A. Moldova, Samoa
   B. Romania, Chad
   C. Romania, Moldova
   D. Samoa, Chad

(1)   (2)

2. **Which Aztec god is represented on the Mexico flag?**
   A. Huītzilōpōchtli
   B. Ometecuhtli
   C. Quetzalcoatl
   D. Tezcatlipoca

3. **[SUPER-BONUS QUESTION—at least 7 points!!!!!]**
   (I) Islamic symbols are found on the national flags of six countries in Africa. Match the flag with its country.
   ((2) points each)
   A. Libya
   B. Tunisia
   C. Algeria
   D. Mauritania
   E. Comoros
   F. Morocco

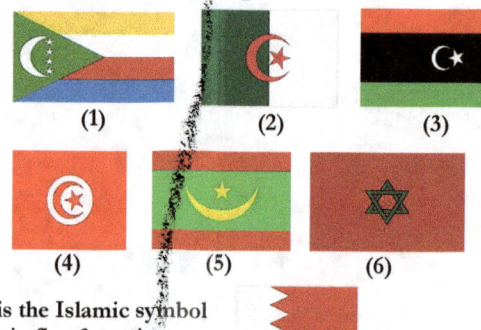

(1)   (2)   (3)

(4)   (5)   (6)

(II) For (1) point: What is the Islamic symbol represented on the Bahrain flag featuring five white triangles?

4. **Flag 1 and Flag 2 are of which countries? [max. 5 points]**
   A. Denmark, Estonia
   B. Norway, Iceland
   C. Iceland, Norway
   D. Estonia, Denmark

(1)   (2)

For (3) bonus points: One of these countries is at the forefront of dissolving CO2 in water then injecting it into sedimentary basalt rock where it is eventually mineralized, rather than releasing carbon emissions into the atmosphere. ("*Much respect!*")

5. **Which country's government has stated the following about its national flag: "*The crescent moon represents a young nation on the ascendant, and the five stars depict [the country's] ideals for democracy, peace, progress, justice and equality.*" [max. 3 points]**
   A. Brunei
   B. Jordan
   C. Maldives
   D. Singapore

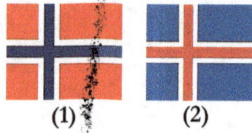

For (1) bonus point: What is one of this country's national symbols?

66   **H. COUNTRY FLAGS**
          (each question at least 2 points)

6. **All or nothing. Which flag corresponds to each island below? [max. 5 points]**
   A. Norfolk Island
   B. Christmas Island
   C. Cocos (Keeling) Islands
   For fun, what is the animal in the circle on Flag 1?

   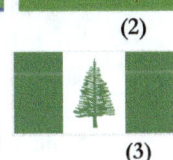

   (1)   (2)

   (I) For (2) bonus points: Every year, millions of bright red crabs migrate across one of the above islands. Which one?

   (3)

   (II) For (1) bonus point: What is the official currency of the islands?
   A. Australian Dollar   C. New Zealand Dollar
   B. Indonesian Rupiah   D. British Pound

7. **Buddhism and/or Hinduism symbols appear on five national flags.**

      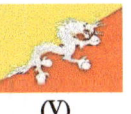

   (I)   (II)   (III)   (IV)   (V)

   Identify the flag with its country below: (1) point for any two correctly identified; (2) points for any three correctly identified; and (3) bonus points if all five are correct. [max. 5 points]
   A. Bhutan   C. India   E. Sri Lanka
   B. Cambodia   D. Nepal   F. Thailand

8. **Flag 1 and Flag 2 are of which countries?**
   A. Italy, Ireland
   B. Ireland, Ivory Coast
   C. Ivory Coast, Ireland
   D. Ireland, Italy

   (1)   (2)

9. **Flag 1 and Flag 2 are of which territories?**
   A. Cayman Islands, Bermuda
   B. Bermuda, Cayman Islands
   C. Pitcairn Islands, Saint Helena
   D. Saint Helena, Pitcairn Islands

   (1)   (2)

10. **Flag 1 and Flag 2 are of which countries? [max. 4 points]**
    A. Paraguay, Uruguay
    B. Uruguay, Paraguay
    C. Bolivia, Ecuador
    D. Ecuador, Bolivia

    (1)   (2)

    For (2) bonus points: One of these four countries has a two-sided national flag. Name that country.

11. **Flag 2 is of which country?**
    A. Indonesia
    B. Monaco
    C. Poland
    D. Latvia

    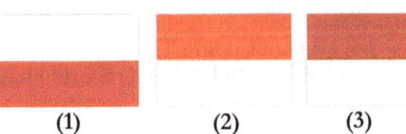

    (1)   (2)   (3)

H. COUNTRY FLAGS   67
(each question at least 2 points)

12. **(1) Flag 1 is of a country that had the first Anglican (Episcopalian) church constructed in its region. (2) Flag 2's country was a party to the Royal Ordinance of Charles X. ((1) point each)**
    A. Haiti
    B. Belize
    C. Dominican Republic
    D. Costa Rica

    (1)   (2)

13. **Name the only country / territory in the world whose flag is non-quadrilateral shaped. [max. 3 points]**
    A. Vanuatu   C. Nepal
    B. Easter Island   D. French Polynesia

    For (1) bonus point: Name the only country in the world whose national flag depicts an AK-47 rifle.
    A. Guatemala   C. Bolivia
    B. Burkina Faso   D. Mozambique

14. **For (1) point each. (I) This is the flag of which Italian city / region? [max. 4 points]**
    A. Tuscany   C. Sicily
    B. Milan   D. Venice

    (II) In which year was the current flag officially approved and adopted?
    A. 1848   B. 1282   C. 2000   D. 1945

    For (1) bonus point each: (I) What do the three feet symbolize; and (II) Who in Greek mythology does the head of the figure represent?

15. **Flag 1 and Flag 2 are of which countries?**
    A. Moldova, Andorra
    B. San Marino, Spain
    C. Andorra, Moldova
    D. Spain, San Marino

    (1)   (2)

16. **These flags are of countries in Europe. Name the countries for both flags (1) and (2). Hints: One country's currency is the Lev. One country reveres a statesman who has been called the "Sage of the Nation." ((1) point each) [max. 3 points]**
    A. Liechtenstein
    B. Bulgaria
    C. Italy
    D. Hungary
    E. Lithuania

    (1)   (2)

    (3)

    For (1) bonus point: This flag above is of a country located in Europe that has over 50 UNESCO World Heritage Sites.

H. COUNTRY FLAGS
(each question at least 2 points)

17. **(I) This flag is of a country / territory located in Oceania. It is home to one of the best diving sites in the world, Blue Corner. ((1) point)**

A. Samoa   C. Niue
B. Pitcairn Islands   D. Palau

(II) This second flag is of a country / territory located about halfway between Australia and Hawaii. Legend has it that *te Pusi mot e Ali* (the Eel and the Flounder) created its islands. ((1) point)

A. Tuvalu   C. Nauru
B. Fiji   D. Kiribati

18. **Each flag shown is of a country located in Europe. They are all member states of the European Union. They are also members of NATO. Select any two for (2) points. Select all for (5) points. No other derivatives.**

(I) **(II)**

A. Belgium   E Sweden
B. Montenegro   F. Germany
C. Romania   G. Malta
D. Finland   H. Albania

(III) **(IV)**

19. **Flag 2 is from which country? [max. 3 points]**

A. Colombia   C. Armenia
B. Cyprus   D. Venezuela

(1)   **(2)**

For (1) bonus point: Flag 1 is of which country?

20. **(I) This flag is of a country located in Africa. Hint: The country is a major producer of cashew nuts. ((1) point)**

A. Guinea   C. Cameroon
B. Benin   D. Guinea-Bissau

(II) This flag is of a country located in Africa. Hint: Lots of bronze objects and sculptures were looted from this country and never returned. ((1) point)

A. Benin   C. Cameroon
B. Republic of the Congo   D. Guinea-Bissau

21. **Selecting from the list below: Flag 1 is of which country? Flag 2 is of which country? ((1) point each) [max. 3 points]**

A. Costa Rica
B. Nicaragua
C. Honduras
D. El Salvador

(1)   **(2)**

For (1) bonus point: Flag 3 is of which country? Hint: The flag previously was a darker blue color.

(3)

H. COUNTRY FLAGS   69
(each question at least 2 points)

22. **(I) This flag is of a country in geographic Asia. The country has one of the highest valued currencies in the world. ((1) point) [max. 4 points]**

A. Oman   C. Kuwait
B. Qatar   D. Jordan

For (1) bonus point: Name the country's capital.

(II) This flag is of a country in mainland Africa. Hint: Chad borders this country to its west, while Libya and Egypt each borders on the north. ((1) point)

A. Ethiopia   C. Eritrea
B. Sudan   D. Eswatini

For (1) bonus point: Name the country's capital.

23. **Flag 1 and Flag 2 are of which countries?**

A. Chile, Malaysia
B. Malaysia, Chile
C. Malaysia, Liberia
D. Liberia, Malaysia

(1)   (2)

24.

(1)   (2)   (3)   (4)

Which country / territory is: (I) Flag 1; (II) Flag 2; (III) Flag 3; and (IV) Flag 4? Choose from the list below. ((½) point each) Hint: Each country / territory is in a different continent. [max. 7 points]

A. Trinidad & Tobago   E. Iraq
B. United Arab Emirates   F. Papua New Guinea
C. Uganda   G. Angola
D. St. Vincent & the Grenadines   H. New Caledonia

(I) For (2) bonus points, (1) point each: For any two flags answered correctly, name its country's / territory's capital. OR
(II) If you answer all four capitals correctly, you receive (5) bonus points.

25.

(1) Flag of   (2) Flag of   (3) Flag of Pomeranian
Tibet   Wales   Voivodeship, Poland

First thing's first: These flags are fearlessly cool!!! But only one of them depicts Y Ddraig Goch. Which one? [max. 4 points]

For (2) bonus points: Name one other European country that depicts a dragon on its national flag. Hint: It's a member state of the European Union as well as a member of the Commonwealth of Nations.

H. COUNTRY FLAGS
(each question at least 2 points)

26. Flag 1 is of the only landlocked country in its region. Flag 2 is of a country that is one of two doubly landlocked countries in the world. ((1) point each) [max. 6 points]

(1)   (2)

A. Uzbekistan	D. Myanmar
B. Laos	E. North Macedonia
C. Liechtenstein	F. Slovenia

(I) For (1) bonus point: Flag 3's country has a representation of Archangel Gabriel on one of its banknotes.

(II) For (3) bonus points, (1) point each: Name the capital of each country.

(3)

27. Flag 1 and Flag 2, respectively, are of two countries that are landlocked within one other country. Name both. ((1) point each)

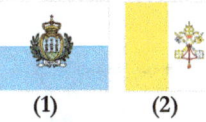

(1)   (2)

A. Andorra	C. Moldova
B. Vatican City	D. San Marino

28. Which country uses Flag 1, and which uses Flag 2? [max. 5 points]

(1)   (2)

A. Lesotho	C. Antigua & Barbuda
B. Tanzania	D. Saint Kitts & Nevis

Bonus: There are three countries in the world with the colour purple in their national flag, albeit it is applied sparingly. Name them. Hint: One is in the Caribbean; the other two are in Central America. ((1) point each)

29.

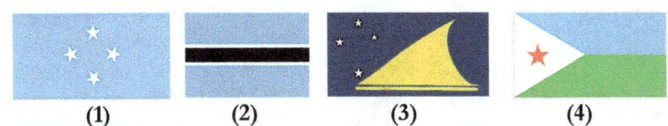

(1)   (2)   (3)   (4)

Which country / territory is: (I) Flag 1; (II) Flag 2; (III) Flag 3; and (IV) Flag 4? Choose from the list below. ((½) point each) [max. 7 points]

A. Tokelau	C. Djibouti
B. Botswana	D. Federated States of Micronesia

(I) For (2) bonus points, (1) point each: For any two flags answered correctly, name its country's / territory's capital. OR
(II) If you answer all four capitals correctly, you receive (5) bonus points.

30. Which country uses Flag 1, and which uses Flag 2? ((1) point each)

(1)   (2)

A. Senegal
B. South Sudan
C. Zambia
D. South Africa

31.

(1)   (2)   (3)   (4)

Which country is: (I) Flag 1; (II) Flag 2; (III) Flag 3; and (IV) Flag 4?
Choose from the list below. ((½) point each) No Steals. [max. 7 points]

A.   Denmark   C.   Switzerland
B.   Tonga   D.   Georgia

(I) For (2) bonus points, (1) point each: For any two flags answered
correctly, name its country's capital. OR
(II) If you answer all four capitals correctly, you receive (5) bonus
points.

32.   Let's focus on North Korea and South Korea.
      Which flags are A and B, respectively,
      below? ((1) point each) [max. 6 points]

      A.   The royal flag of the Goryeo Dynasty
      B.   The royal flag of the Joseon Dynasty
      C.   The flag used during the Joseon Dynasty
           and the Empire of Korea
      D.   The flag of the People's Republic of Korea

(1)   (2)

(3)   (4)

(I) Both or nothing. For (2) bonus points:
Which flags above are C and D, respectively?

(II) For (2) bonus points:
Flag 5 and Flag 6, respectively,
are of which countries?

 (5)    (6)

33.

(1)   (2)   (3)   (4)

What is the country represented by the following: (I) Flag 1; (II) Flag 2;
(III) Flag 3; and (IV) Flag 4? ((½) point each) [max. 4 points]

A.   France   C.   The Netherlands
B.   Luxembourg   D.   Russian Federation

For (1) bonus point each:
(I) Which is the oldest country of the four?
(II) What is its capital?

Answers to questions in this Category can be found starting on page 268.

H. COUNTRY FLAGS
              (each question at least 2 points)

Category I:
EARTH'S "SPHERES"
(5-point category)

1. Let's have fun with Earth's <u>lithosphere</u>. [max. 9 points]
(I) Sedimentary rock covers most of Earth's land surface. About what percentage of the land surface does igneous rock cover? ((2) points)
A.   1%   B.   5%   C.   10%   D.   15%

(II) What percentage of Earth's crust is made up of igneous and metamorphic rocks? ((2) points)
A.   5%   B.   50%   C.   75%   D.   95%

(III) Which is an example of sedimentary rock? ((1) point)
A.   Shale   B.   Gypsum   C.   Conglomerate   D.   All

For (2) bonus points each: Which below is an example of: (1) igneous rock, and (2) metamorphic rock?
A.   Marble   B.   Breccia   C.   Obsidian   D.   Limestone

2. Which of these is not one of the so-called "Seven Summits" on Earth? [max. 9 points]
A.   Aconcagua   C.   Mount Damāvand
B.   Denali   D.   Mount Elbrus

Get (1) bonus point for each correct answer naming the country where each summit above is located. [max. (4) bonus points] But for each country answered incorrectly, you lose (1) of your original (5) points.

3. There are officially 17 rare earth elements (REEs). Which of the below are not REEs? [max. 7 points]
A.   Ytterbium (Yb), Cerium (Ce)   C.   Niobium (Nb), Rhodium (Rh)
B.   Scandium (Sc), Erbium (Er)   D.   Lutetium (Lu), Holmium (Ho)

For (1) bonus point each:
(I) Much of the world's REEs are produced in Baotou, China. In which province or region is this large industrial city located?
A.   Gansù   C.   Inner Mongolia Autonomous Region
B.   Jiangsù   D.   Hunan

(II) Which country below is not considered a large producer of REEs?
A.   Australia   C.   Russia   E.   Vietnam
B.   Myanmar   D.   Libya   F.   Thailand

4. (I) Despite the global shutdowns as a result of the COVID-19 pandemic, the amount of CO_2 in the atmosphere reached record levels. In May 2020, it had hit 417 parts per million (ppm). When was the time before then that CO_2 levels first exceeded 400 ppm? ((2 ½) points)
A.   2 million years ago   C.   4 million years ago
B.   2016   D.   2013

(II) In the summer of 2020, air temperatures reached 38°C (100.4°F) in Siberia, while land surface temperatures in several parts of the Arctic Circle hit 45°C (113°F), accelerating the thawing of permafrost in that region. ((2 ½) points)
A.   True   B.   False   C.   Partially True

I. EARTH'S "SPHERES"
(each question at least 5 points)

5. Each correct answer relating to Earth's <u>atmosphere</u> is (1) point.
    (I) The northern and southern lights occur in this layer that also absorbs harmful radiation from the Sun.
    (II) Almost all weather occurs within this dense layer.
    (III) This layer contains helium and hydrogen that rarely collide.
    (IV) The ozone is in this layer; and wildfires can spread smoke up into this layer triggering chemical reactions that erode its ozone.
    (V) This very cold layer burns up meteors. *Merci!* [max. 9 points]

A. Ionosphere	C. Stratosphere	E. Mesosphere
B. Thermosphere	D. Troposphere	F. Exosphere

    For (4) bonus points (and only if you answer all five questions above correctly): What region influences radio communication?

6. (I) Earth's <u>hydrosphere</u> covers approximately what percentage of Earth? ((1) point)

    A. 65%   B. 71%   C. 78%   D. 82%

    (II) A massive iceberg below that carved off from the Larsen C ice shelf in western Antarctica in July 2017 was on a collision course with the remote South Georgia Island in 2020. There was great concern over the destruction of the marine life in the area. Fortunately for the seals, penguins, and us, mini "child bergs" broke off the iceberg and followed their own path. Crisis averted. ((2) points)

    A. A23a   B. A68a   C. A38   D. B-15

    (III) Twirling in an ocean vortex, this iceberg is in the Southern Ocean. Its total average thickness is over 280 metres (920 feet); its mass covers an area of almost 4,000 square kilometres (1,500 square miles); and it weighs nearly a trillion tonnes. Which of the above is it? ((2) points)

7. This two-part question is both or nothing.
    (I) About what percentage of Earth's water is non-saline (non-salty)?

    A. 3%   B. 4.5%   C. 97%   D. 95.5%

    (II) What is the lowest freshwater lake on Earth?
    A. Lake Kinneret / Sea of Galilee / Lake Tiberias
    B. Yam ha-Melakh / The Dead Sea
    C. Khor Al Udaid / The Inland Sea
    D. Lake Superior

8. (I) All of these glaciers are melting at alarming rates (almost to the point of no return), but one of them is not located in Antarctica. (i) Which one? ((2) points) (ii) In which country is it located? ((½) point)

A. Ronne Glacier	C. Furtwängler Glacier
B. Pine Island Glacier (PIG)	D. Thwaites Glacier

    (II) One of these volcanoes in Iceland officially has been declared "dead" due to global climate change. Which one? ((2 ½) points)

A. Eyjafjallajökull	D. All of these are "alive"
B. Okjökull	E. All of these are "dead"
C. Skjaldbreiður	

I. EARTH'S "SPHERES"
(each question at least 5 points)

9. **(I) The Equator does not pass through: ((3) points)**
    A. São Tomé and Principe   C. Maldives
    B. Uganda   D. American Samoa

    (II) The Sun's path follows the celestial equator plane twice per year at which equinoxes? ((2) points)
    A. January and July equinoxes   C. May and November equinoxes
    B. March and September equinoxes   D. June and December equinoxes

10. **(I) If you ignore (for this trivia) Earth's natural gift of the "Sergio black diamond" unearthed in Brazil, the largest rough gemstone diamond to date was found in: ((3) points)**
    A. Botswana   C. Sierra Leone
    B. Democratic Republic of Congo   D. South Africa

    (II) How many carats was its weight? ((2) points)
    A. 3,167   B. 3,106   C. 2,998   D. 1,758

11. **[SUPER-BONUS QUESTION—at least 7 points!!!!!] (1) Earth's biosphere covers plants and trees. Plants can clean the air and remove pollutants/toxins, such as formaldehyde, trichloroethylene, and benzene from the air in your home. Identify the plants below with their names: (I) Mother-in-law's Tongue plant, (II) Baby Rubber Tree, (III) Fiddle Leaf plant, (IV) Prayer plant, (V) Jade plant, (VI) ZZ plant, (VII) Red Leaf Philodendron, (VIII) Dracaena Marginata, (IX) Rattlesnake plant, (X) Golden Pothos, (XI) Monstera Deliciosa. ((2) points each)**

    A. ..
    B. ..
    C. ..
    D. ..
    E. ..
    F. ..
    G. ..
    H. ..
    I. ..
    J. ..
    K. ..

    (2) Plants scream when stressed, thirsty, or injured. ((5) points)
    A. Uhh…no. Their leaves just turn yellow or brown.
    B. Of course, they do. Listen to their xylem, dude.

I. EARTH'S "SPHERES"
(each question at least 5 points)

12. **What kind of bird's foot is this?**
    A. Tridactyl foot
    C. Anisodactyl foot
    B. Zygodactyl foot
    D. Pamprodactyl foot

13. **(I) This metal can be found in the rare mineral galena. Its more important ore mineral is argentite. The metal is a very resistant mineral and does not dissolve most solvents. What is this metal, feared by werewolves? ((3) points)**
    A. Copper
    C. Silver
    B. Gold
    D. Platinum

    (II) Which country produces the most of this metal in the world? ((2) points)
    A. Chile   B. China   C. Mexico   D. South Africa

14. **(I) One of these minerals, typically hexagonal in shape, is among the rarest and most expensive on Earth. It often is confused with ruby or garnet. ((4) points)**
    A. Red Beryl (or Bixbite)
    C. Painite
    B. Rhodium
    D. Kyawthuite

    (II) In which country is this metal predominantly (or only) found? ((1) point) [max. 10 points]
    A. USA
    C. South Africa
    B. Mongolia
    D. Myanmar

    For (5) bonus points: Only one crystal of one of the rare minerals in (I) above is known to exist. It has a chemical formula of $Bi^3 + Sb^5 + O_4$, with traces of tantalum. What is this mineral?

15. **(I) Perigee is where the Moon is…. ((2 ½) points)**
    (II) Apogee is where the Moon is…. ((2 ½) points)
    A. farthest from Earth.   B. nearest to Earth.

16. **(I) In the biosphere, the human vertebral column consists of how many small bones (the vertebrae)? ((2) points) [max. 7 points]**
    A. 33   B. 24   C. 39   D. 44

    (II) How many cervical vertebrae are there in the neck? ((1) point)
    A. 4   B. 5   C. 7   D. 12

    (III) How many lumbar vertebrae are there in the lower back? ((1) point)
    A. 12   B. 4   C. 5   D. 7

    (IV) How many thoracic vertebrae are there in the torso? ((1) point)
    A. 5   B. 12   C. 4   D. 8

    For (1) bonus point each: To complete, how many (1) sacral, and (2) coccygeal vertebrae (typically) are there?
    A. 7   B. 5   C. 8   D. 4

I. EARTH'S "SPHERES"
(each question at least 5 points)

17. This chemical element is very volatile and rare. Its atomic number is 70. It is named after a village in Sweden, where it was first found in a quarry. It is radioactive. What is it?
   A. Uranium
   C. Yttrium
   B. Zinc
   D. Ytterbium

18. (I) Earth's atmosphere is roughly: ((4) points)
   A. 78% nitrogen, 21% oxygen, 1% other gases
   B. 21% nitrogen, 78% oxygen, 1% other gases
   C. 50% nitrogen, 49% oxygen, 1% other gases
   D. 39% nitrogen, 60% oxygen, 1% other gases

   (II) Of the 1% other gases, what percentage is argon? ((1) point)
   A. 0.1%   B. 0.4%   C. 0.5%   D. 0.9%

19. For (2) points each. What is the imaginary latitude line: (I) 23.5° north of the Equator called? and (II) 23.5° south of the Equator called?
   A. Tropic of Cancer   B. Tropic of Capricorn

   (III) How many degrees north and south of the Equator are the Arctic Circle and Antarctic Circle, respectively? ((1) point)
   A. 55.5°   B. 66.5°   C. 80.5°   D. 76.5°

20. (I) Which of the following elements is not a type of halogen? ((4) points)
   A. Argon (Ar)
   C. Chlorine (Cl)
   B. Bromine (Br)
   D. Iodine (I)

   (II) Name one other element that is part of the halogen Group 17. ((1) point)
   A. Zirconium (Zr)   B. Astatine (At)

21. One of these trees can survive in harsh desert environments.
   A. Weeping willow
   C. Red maple tree
   B. Pine tree
   D. Jojoba

22. This marine mammal is born blind, deaf, and toothless. Its skin is jet black. Its liver accumulates lots (and lots) of vitamin A and is poisonous to humans—even lethal.
   A. Bearded seal
   C. Polar bear
   B. Manatee
   D. Walrus

23. (I) Which clouds below are created by intense heat, such as wildfires or volcanic eruptions, and can lead to thunder and lightning? ((1) point)
   (II) Formed when water vapor freezes into ice crystals that cling to dust and particles from falling meteors, these clouds below are the highest, driest, coldest, and among the rarest clouds on Earth. ((2) points)
   (III) Looking like flying saucers, these clouds listed below are a sign of mountain waves in the air. ((1) point)
   (IV) Which rare clouds take the form of rippling waves? ((1) point)
   A. Noctilucent clouds
   C. Pyrocumulonimbus clouds
   B. Asperitas clouds
   D. Lenticular clouds

I. EARTH'S "SPHERES"
(each question at least 5 points)

24. **(I) Name this noble, malleable metal with chemical symbol Au and atomic number 79. ((3) points)**
    A. Aluminum   C. Platinum
    B. Gold   D. Copper

    (II) What type of metal is it? ((?) points)
    A. Transition   C. Metalloid
    B. Post-Transition   D. Alkali

25. **Earth's lithosphere. Which fine-grained, extrusive igneous rock is formed from the rapid cooling of lava? More than half of Earth's ocean floor is of this rock. It is the primary component of Earth's crust and the Lunar Maria on the Moon. It is found also on Mars, Jupiter, and Venus.**
    A. Andesite   B. Scoria   C. Pumice   D. Basalt

26. **This large, beautiful flower emits an odor of rotting flesh or animal dung.**
    A. Wisteria   C. Rafflesia
    B. Virginia creeper   D. Hydrangea

27. **Match Earth's crust layers to the diagram. 1. All or nothing. (I) Inner Core; (II) Lower Mantle; (III) Continental Crust; (IV) Upper Mantle; and (V) Outer Core. ((3) points) [max. 8 points]**
    A.   B.   C.   D.   E.

    2. Earth's inner core is [ ]. ((1) point)
    3. Earth's outer core is [ ]. ((1) point)
    A. Liquid   B. Solid   C. Gas

    (I) For (1) bonus point: What is the name of the layer at the bottom of the lower mantle?

    (II) For (1) bonus point each:
    What two layers constitute the lithosphere?

28. **For (1 ½) points each. (I) One species of penguins is found only on the Antarctic continent; (II) Another species is found there too and in certain neighboring islands.**
    (III) Name one of the other types of penguins that lives primarily on subantarctic islands and southern South America. ((1) point)
    (IV) Which of these penguins lives only in New Zealand? ((1) point)
    A. Adélie penguin   D. Yellow-eyed/Hoiho penguin
    B. Emperor penguin   E. Magellanic penguin
    C. King penguin

29. **André-Marie Ampère discovered this chemical element in 1810. However, it was Henri Moissan who first isolated the element successfully through electrolysis in 1886. It is the most reactive and most electronegative element on the Periodic Table. It also is the thirteenth most abundant element in Earth's crust. *Quest-ce que c'est?***
    A. Hydrogen   C. Fluorine
    B. Chlorine   D. Potassium

I. EARTH'S "SPHERES"
(each question at least 5 points)

30. Receive (1) point for each question:
     (I) What divides the continental crust and the oceanic crust?
     (II) What separates the Earth's crust and mantle?
     (III) What separates the upper mantle from the lower mantle?
     (IV) What separates the lower mantle and the outer core?
     (V) What separates the outer core and the inner core?

     A. Mohorovičić discontinuity   D. Lehmann discontinuity
     B. Gutenberg discontinuity   E. Repetti discontinuity
     C. Conrad discontinuity

31. The most abundant vertebrate on Earth is:

     A. Human   B. Bristlemouth   C. Herring   D. Chicken

32. 1) This climate phenomenon keeps temperatures down since water
     cools more than usual in parts of the Pacific Ocean between South
     America and Australia. ((1 ½) points) [max. 11 points]

     A. La Niña   B. El Niño

     2) This climate phenomenon generally suppresses Atlantic hurricane
     activity. ((1 ½) points)

     A. La Niña   B. El Niño

     If 1) and 2) above are correct, for (3) bonus points each:
     (I) Countries in Asia, Oceania, and Central and Southern Africa
     generally experience more drought during this phenomenon.

     A. La Niña   B. El Niño

     (II) La Niña events occur less frequently than El Niño events.

     A. True   B. False

     3) I) In the Northern hemisphere, the right side of a hurricane is the
     stronger, more dangerous side; and II) in the Southern hemisphere, the
     right side of a hurricane also is the stronger side. ((1) point each)

     A. True   B. False

33. (I) Oceans produce at least 50% of the oxygen supply in the
     atmosphere. One particular phytoplankton is a cyanobacterium that is
     estimated to be solely responsible for one in every five breaths a human
     takes. *Wow! And Thank You!* Scientists believe it also fueled the
     explosion of early life in our oceans. What is it? ((3) points)

     A. Diatom   C. Synechococcus
     B. Dinoflagellate   D. Prochlorococcus

     (II) About how much carbon does the ocean store, by gigaton (note: 1
     gigaton (Gt) = 1 billion tons)? ((2) points)

     A. 2,375 Gt   C. 38,000 Gt
     B. 633 Gt   D. 65,500 Gt

Answers to questions in this Category can be found starting on page 269.

Win "spherically," ask the judge to offer a strategy play card.

I. EARTH'S "SPHERES"
(each question at least 5 points)

Category J:
LAND AND SEA FORMS
(5-point category)

1. A study released in 2019 revealed that on the beaches of this place,
    marine scientists found about 414 million pieces of plastic (primarily
    bottles, cutlery, bags, and straws) weighing about 238 metric tonnes,
    977,000 shoes, and 373,000 toothbrushes. What was this place, which
    has a population of about 500 people?
    A. Galapagos Islands   C. Cocos (Keeling) Islands
    B. Henderson Island   D. Bora Bora

2. Where is this natural beauty? [max. 7 points]
    A. Mainland China   C. Hong Kong
    B. Macau   D. Taiwan

    For (2) bonus points: What is its name?

3. This mountain is considered the most sacred
    mountain in China. Hint: It also appears on
    one of the country's banknotes.
    A. Bei-Heng-Shan   C. Song-Shan
    B. Hua-Shan   D. Tai-Shan

4. This reef is also called the "Amazon of the Sea" and it has the richest
    marine biodiversity in the world. [max. 7 points]
    A. Coral Triangle   C. Mesoamerican Reef
    B. Great Barrier Reef   D. New Caledonian Barrier Reef

    For (2) bonus points: This adorable marine mammal, sadly endangered,
    can be seen in the Amazon of the Sea if you're lucky.
    According to one myth, it is the inspiration behind
    mermaids. And in some cultures, it is considered to
    be the reincarnations of women. What is it?

5. Statement: "In 2019, Greenland overall lost 532 gigatons of ice mass."
    (I) That's 532 billion tons of ice mass.
    (II) That's 66 tons of ice per person on Earth.
    (III) That's the equivalent of filling six Olympic-sized swimming pools
    full of ice every second of the calendar year.
    (IV) That statement and (I), (II), and (III) above are entirely fake news.
    (V) That's less than what it lost in 2014, so it's not *that* bad. Don't be
    such an alarmist, Greta-Thunberg-wannabe.
    Which is/are true?
    A. (I), (II), (III)   D. (II), (V)
    B. (IV)   E. (I), (V)
    C. (V)

6. This is the world's most perfectly formed volcano.
    A. Nevado Sajama (Bolivia)
    B. Mount Fiji (Japan)
    C. Momotombo Volcano (Nicaragua)
    D. Mount Mayon (Philippines)

J. LAND AND SEA FORMS
(each question at least 5 points)

7. Legend states that Hercules rested within the Caves of Hercules before
    heading on to his next labour. Where are the Caves of Hercules located?
    [max. 7 points]
    A. Algeria   B. Morocco   C. Portugal   D. Spain

    For (2) bonus points: To which labour was he headed?
    A. His 9th   B. His 10th   C. His 11th   D. His 12th

8. The deepest point on continental Earth is a canyon under Denman
    Glacier in Antarctica. But the deepest point on Earth is the Challenger
    Deep in Mariana Trench, which is nearest to Northern Mariana Islands
    and which of these other Pacific islands? [max. 7 points]
    A. Marshall Islands   C. Guam
    B. Micronesia   D. American Samoa

    For (2) bonus points, (1) point each: Who were the first two explorers to
    descend into the Challenger Deep? Hint: It was on January 23, 1960.
    They spent 20 minutes there after a five-hour descent.

9. Match each of these five man-made (artificial) islands with their
    location: (I) Amwaj Islands; (II) Île aux Cygnes; (III) Flevopolder;
    (IV) The Pearl; and (V) The Venetian Islands. ((1) point each)
    A. USA   C. The Netherlands   E. France
    B. Qatar   D. Bahrain   F. Italy

10. These falls are among the widest in the world. They are made up of
    about 275 separate vertical waterfalls (the most in the world).
    A. Iguazú Falls   D. Niagara Falls
    B. Victoria Falls   E. Pará Falls
    C. Kongou Falls

11. 1) Name the longest mountain range (on land) in the world. ((3) points)
    A. Rocky Mountains   D. Transantarctic Mountains
    B. Andes Mountains   E. Great Dividing Range
    C. Caucasus Mountains

    2) In what country is the Great Dividing Range? ((2) points)
    A. Russia   B. Argentina   C. USA   D. Australia

12. (I) Where is the Mid-Atlantic Ridge, a divergent plate boundary, mostly
    located? ((2) points)
    A. Above land   B. Underwater

    (II) Which one of the volcanic islands below is not part of the Mid-
    Atlantic Ridge? ((1) point)
    A. Azores   D. Tristan da Cunha
    B. Jan Mayen   E. Iceland
    C. South Sandwich Islands   F. St. Paul's Rock

    (III) With the exception of Iceland, the other islands above are
    territories or possessions of countries. Select two and name the country
    that owns each. ((1) point each)

J. LAND AND SEA FORMS
(each question at least 5 points)

83

13. **(I) Like McMurdo Dry Valleys of Antarctica, this desert is a cold desert. It also is the driest nonpolar desert in the world. It is exposed to some of the highest levels of ultraviolet radiation. Some areas of it hadn't recorded any rain in more than 500 years! NASA uses it as a testing site for its Mars program. There are several astronomy facilities in this desert, including the European Southern Observatory's Paranal Observatory. Which desert is this that receives as much sunlight as the planet Venus in certain spots? ((4) points)**

   A. Al-Kufrah   C. Atacama Desert
   B. Wadi Halfa   D. Desert of Ica

   (II) In what country is it? ((1) point)
   A. Chile   B. Peru   C. Libya   D. Sudan

14. **This is not a trick question. One of these mountains is the tallest mountain on Earth from its base, i.e., beneath sea level, to its peak.**
   A. Mount Everest   C. Olympus Mons
   B. Mount Chimborazo   D. Mauna Kea

15. **(I) One of these volcanoes in Iceland erupted from March to May 2010, causing major air traffic disruptions across Europe (and unintentionally put Iceland on the map as a major tourist destination). ((3) points)**
   A. Grímsvötn   C. Eyjafjallajökull
   B. Mount Hekla   D. Fagradalsfjall

   (II) Not to be outdone, which other volcano above erupted on 19 March 2021 and remained active for about six months? ((2) points)

16. **This place is the most remote spot in the world. It is a location in the Pacific Ocean that is farthest from land at 48°52.6′S 123°23.6′W. It is so far away from land that the nearest humans are actually the astronauts on the International Space Station. Hint: It is officially known as "the oceanic pole of inaccessibility." [max. 17 points]**
   A. Tristan da Cunha   D. Point Nemo
   B. Moto Nui (of Easter Islands)   E. Diego Garcia
   C. Ducie Island (of Pitcairn Islands) F. Maher Island

   (1) For (4) bonus points: Which one of the places above is the most isolated inhabited place in the world?

   (2) For (5) bonus points: Which one of the above places is horse-shoe shaped with numerous areas of exposed rock, and is part of Antarctica?

   (3) For (3) bonus points: Which one of the above places is in the Indian Ocean, not the Pacific Ocean, and serves as a highly-secretive military installation?

17. **Two of these large seamounts are in the Atlantic Ocean; the others are in the Pacific Ocean. Which two? ((2 ½) points each)**
   A. Meiji Seamount   D. Vema Seamount
   B. Great Meteor Seamount   E. Bowie Seamount
   C. Rodriguez Seamount   F. Davidson Seamount

J. LAND AND SEA FORMS
(each question at least 5 points)

18. This large, inland, basin-like desert, whose name translates as "the great thirst" is found in Botswana, Namibia, and South Africa. The Okavango River Delta flows through it. It has been home to the native San people for tens of thousands of years.
    A. Karoo Desert   C. Sahara Desert
    B. Namib Desert   D. Kalahari Desert

19. Under U.S. President Theodore Roosevelt, the USA controlled the construction and operation of this artificial waterway, which opened in 1914. [max. 14 points]
    A. Suez Canal   C. Panama Canal
    B. Corinth Canal   D. Grand Canal

    For (3) bonus points each:
    (I) Which of the above is the oldest and longest canal in the world?
    (II) Which is the narrowest canal?
    (III) For which canal was the Statue of Liberty in the USA originally designed?

20. One of these organisms has not been found in the Challenger Deep.
    A. Small sea cucumbers (Holothurians)
    B. Persistent organic pollutants such as industrial products or chemicals (Polychlorinated biphenyls)
    C. Portuguese dogfish (Centroscymnus coelolepis)
    D. PBDEs flame retardants (Polybrominated diphenyl ethers)
    E. Shrimp-like crustaceans (Amphipods)

21. All or nothing. Match the coral reef with its country. [max. 10 points]

    A. Fiji   D. The Bahamas
    B. Mexico   E. Philippines
    C. Indonesia   F. Puerto Rico

    For (5) bonus points: Which reef drops about 8 feet (2.4 metres) on its island side and approximately 6,000 feet (1,829 metres) in the deep region Tongue of the Ocean?

Coral Reef
I. Raja Ampat
II. Grand Central Station and Chimneys
III. Palancar Reef
IV. Tubbataha Reef
V. Andros Coral Reef

22. [SUPER-BONUS QUESTION—at least 7 points!!!!!] Match the strait (a narrow natural passage of water that connects two large bodies of water) with the seas or oceans or land area it connects. ((1) point each) If you get all correct, you earn (8) "straight" extra points. No other derivatives.

    A. Gulf of Mexico and Caribbean Sea
    B. Tasmania from mainland Australia
    C. Tyrrhenian Sea and Ionian Sea
    D. Atlantic Ocean and Pacific Ocean
    E. Baffin Bay and Labrador Sea
    F. Gulf of Oman and Persian Gulf
    G. Arctic Ocean and East Pacific Ocean
    H. Atlantic Ocean to Mediterranean Sea
    I. Sea of Okhotsk and Sea of Japan
    J. Adriatic Sea and Ionian Sea

Strait
I. Strait of Tartary
II. Hormuz Strait
III. Strait of Magellan
IV. Otranto Strait
V. Yucatán Strait
VI. Davis Strait
VII. Bering Strait
VIII. Bass Strait
IX. Messina Strait
X. Gibraltar Strait

J. LAND AND SEA FORMS
(each question at least 5 points)

23. For (2 ½) points each.
(I) Which lost ancient port city below did archeologists discover underwater in 2000?
(II) One other ancient city that had been submerged by a tsunami around 373 B.C.E. was discovered in 2001. Which of the below was it?

A. Helike (Greece)
B. Thônis-Heracleion (Egypt)
C. Dwarka (India)
D. Pavlopetri (Greece)

24. (I) This village and research station is home to fewer than 200 people. It is so remote that the people who live here as long-term residents (adults and their children alike) must have their appendix removed before arriving. This is because the nearest major hospital is more than 1,000 kilometres (625 miles) away. ((4) points)

A. Ittoqqortoormiit
B. Oymyakon
C. Villas Las Estrellas
D. Yakutsk

(II) Which pet is not allowed in the village? ((1) point)
A. Cat   B. Hamster   C. Dog   D. Bird

25. Longyearbyen is one of the world's northernmost civilian settlements. A couple of its rules are: (1) No dying, and no being buried here. (2) If venturing outside the settlement limits, one must carry a weapon and know how to use it against the resident polar bears (it is not to be used against humans). Located on the island of Spitsbergen, on which archipelago is it?

A. Oodaaq   B. Svalbard   C. Nunavut   D. Josef Land

26. What is the world's largest marine area?
A. Ross Sea Region Protected Area (Antarctica)
B. Coral Sea Commonwealth Marine Reserve (Australia)
C. Papahānaumokuākea Marine National Monument (USA)
D. South Georgia Marine Protected Area (South Georgia Island)

27. (I) What is the world's largest salt flat? ((2) points) [max. 7 points]

A. Atacama Desert
B. Makgadikgadi Pan
C. Etosha Salt Pan
D. Uyuni Salt Flat

(II) Where is it located? ((1) point)
A. Namibia   B. Bolivia   C. Chile   D. Botswana

(III) What vegetation grows on this salt flat, to the point where there are islands full of it? ((1) point)

A. Cactus
B. Bromeliad
C. Blue-green algae
D. Mopane tree

(IV) This salt flat contains 50% to 70% of the world's reserves of this metal or compound. ((1) point)
A. Sodium   B. Copper   C. Lithium   D. Beryllium

Bonus: Which salt flat above is so extraordinarily flat that it is the world's largest natural mirror? It can be seen from space and after a rain, it can reflect stars, galaxies, and at least one planet. ((2) points)

J. LAND AND SEA FORMS
(each question at least 5 points)

28. During the Paleozoic-Mesozoic transition, all the continents formed a single continent mass and a single mega ocean that surrounded the mass. Name (I) the supercontinent and (II) its ancient global ocean. ((2 ½) points each)

    A. Panthalassa Ocean
    B. Gondwana
    C. Pangaea
    D. Tethys Ocean
    E. Pannotia
    F. Poseidon Ocean

29. Which is the world's largest lake on an island?

    A. Lake Toba
    B. Nettilling Lake
    C. Lake Manitou
    D. Lake Taal

30. What is the world's largest recursive island (i.e., an island in a lake within an island in a lake within another island)? [max. 9 points]

    A. Pomona Island (New Zealand)
    B. An unnamed island in Victoria Island (Canada)
    C. Samosir (Indonesia)
    D. Okishima (Japan)
    E. Treasure Island (Canada)

    For (4) bonus points: In which first lake specifically is Treasure Island located?

    A. Lake Mindemoya   B. Lake Huron   C. Lake Ontario

31. What is the world's largest freshwater island?

    A. René-Levasseur Island (Canada)
    B. Manitoulin Island (Canada)
    C. Isle Royale (USA)
    D. Olkhon Island (Russia)

32. What is the world's largest hot spring? Its acidic water maintains a temperature of about 35°C - 80°C (95°F - 176°F). [max. 9 points]

    A. Blue Lagoon (Iceland)
    B. Boiling Lake (Dominica)
    C. Grand Prismatic Spring (USA)
    D. Inferno Crater Lake or the adjacent Frying Pan Lake (New Zealand)

    For (4) bonus points: Which of the above is the second largest hot spring in the world?

33. These are some of the hottest places on Earth: (I) Oodnadatta; (II) Lut Desert; (III) Kebili; (IV) Turbat; and (V) Death Valley. *Persistently*. Match each place with its country below. ((1) point each) [max. 10 points]

    A. Tunisia
    B. Australia
    C. Pakistan
    D. USA
    E. Iran

    For (5) bonus points: A meteorological study in 2021 reported that one of the above places had been recording a blistering surface temperature of 80.8°C (177.4°F), surpassing its prior record of 70.7°C (159.3°F). (*Yikes!*) Which one?

Answers to questions in this Category can be found starting on page 269.

J. LAND AND SEA FORMS
(each question at least 5 points)

Category K:
WORLD SLANGS / SAYINGS / COOL WORDS
(2-point category)

HUMONGOUS (& COOL) WORDS FOR KIDS

Written and Illustrated by SB Hilarion

1. This Croatian word means "a state of mind where you want to do nothing and you do nothing."

   A. Možda   B. Kuna   C. Fjaka   D. Bok

2. When was the first "Yo Mama" joke known to be told "for the masses' ears"?

   A. On a 1500 B.C.E. Babylonian tablet
   B. In Shakespeare's *Titus Andronicus* (written between 1588 and 1593)
   C. In Shakespeare's *Twelfth Night* (written around 1601 – 1602)
   D. In the 1975 *Monty Python and the Holy Grail* film
   E. In the 1980s within Black and Latino communities in the USA
   F. In a 1993 episode of *In Living Color* during a game called "The Dirty Dozens"

3. If you want to "get cozy, cuddly, comfortable, or safe" in Denmark, you want to:

   A. Flygskam   C. Pyt
   B. Hygge   D. Friluftsliv

4. What does the Iraqi-origin slang "*Shaku maku*" mean?

   A. That's cool!   C. What's up?
   B. You're awesome.   D. Get out of here!

5. Both or nothing. (I) The word "*Eh-heh*" means something different than (II) the word "*Eh-eh*" in Trinbagonian slang. What do they each mean?

   A. No, no way, oh no.   C. Oh really? / I understand. Yes.
   B. What did you say?   D. Is that not so? / Isn't that true?

6. This is a two-part question, (1) point each.
   (I) Where did the slang "*packing a sad*," which means "someone is throwing a tantrum," originate and is used most commonly?

   A. England   C. Australia
   B. Ireland (Republic of) D. New Zealand

   (II) Where did the slang "*You're a hard case*," which means "You're witty / funny," originate and is used most commonly?

   A. Australia   C. New Zealand
   B. England   D. Scotland

7. This is a two-part question, (1) point each. [max. 3 points]
   (I) What does the Jamaican slang "*Weh yuh deh pun*" mean?

   A. See you tomorrow.   C. I'll be right there.
   B. What are you up to?

   (II) Under what circumstances is the Jamaican slang "*Small up yuhself*" usually applied?

   A. To encourage someone to lose weight
   B. To tell someone to show respect and stop being rude
   C. To create space for someone, such as on a bus or maxi-taxi

   For (1) bonus point: What does "*Gwaan*" mean in Jamaica?

K. WORLD SLANGS / SAYINGS / COOL WORDS   89
(each question at least 2 points)

8. If you're in *Straya*, and someone gives you a "pineapple," what are they really giving you?

   A. A black eye / beat-down   C. An AU$50 bill
   B. A smooch   D. A ride home

9. Where did the slang "*no wucking furries*" originate and is used most commonly?

   A. England   C. Australia
   B. Northern Ireland   D. New Zealand

10. Not slangs or sayings, but these words mean the same in English—*Tatik, Elisi, Grosi, Maimeó, Lǎo Lao.*

    A. Grandma   C. Hello
    B. Goodbye   D. Grandpa

11. Which of these German words is slang for money?

    A. Dicht   C. Geil
    B. Kohle   D. Alter

12. All or nothing question. A proverb is a short, well-known saying stating a general truth or piece of advice. Match the proverb with its origin: (I) Cuban; (II) Bulgarian; and (III) Ethiopian.

    A. "Coffee and love taste best when hot."
    B. "Cheese, wine, and friends must be old to be good."
    C. "Tell me who your friends are, so I can tell you who you are."

13. The word "arseling" is…

    A. …a real word dating from Old English to mean "on the back" or "backwards"
    B. …a made-up word used by Leofric to describe Uhtred in Netflix's *The Last Kingdom*

14. Each of the words below means "respect" in its country's language. Match each word with the following language: (I) Korean; (II) Swahili; (III) Japanese; and (IV) Yoruba. ((½) point each)

    A. Ọwọ   C. Sonkei
    B. Jongyeong   D. Heshima

15. The following are examples of which figure of speech?
    "Put on your shoes and socks."
    "I conquered. I saw. I came."
    "Putting the cart before the horse."

    A. Adage   C. Metonym
    B. Hysteron proteron   D. Idiom

16. From which country are the following words: (I) Bichulsan, (II) Bihon, (III) Bisekseu, and (IV) Biyeonae? [max. 5 points]

    A. Japan   C. Malaysia
    B. South Korea   D. Laos

    For (3) bonus points: What is the English meaning of any two of the words?

K. WORLD SLANGS / SAYINGS / COOL WORDS
(each question at least 2 points)

17. **[SUPER-BONUS QUESTION—at least 7 points!!!!!]**
    AA-CHOO! AA-CHOO! AA-CHOO! "(God) Bless you." "Gesundheit."
    1. What are the typical responses to sneezes in the following countries / cultures: (I) Serbia; (II) The Netherlands; (III) Zulu; (IV) Romania; (V) Bosnia; (VI) Spain; (VII) certain Latin American countries; (VIII) Turkey; and (IX) India? ((2) points each)
    A. "Thuthuka" ("grow")
    B. "Shatam Jeevah" ("live to 100 years")
    C. "Norac" ("good fortune")
    D. "Morgen mooi weer" ("good weather tomorrow" said after third sneeze)
    E. "Salud" ("health" after first sneeze). "Dinero" ("money" after second sneeze). "Amor" ("love" after third sneeze)
    F. "Nazdravlje" ("to your good health")
    G. "Çok yaşa" ("live long" after first sneeze). "Sağlikli yaşa" ("live healthily" after second sneeze)
    H. "Jesús, María, José" ("Jesus, Mary, Joseph")
    I. "Pis maco" ("go away kitten" and mostly said to children)

    2. During which plague is it often said that the pope first encouraged people to say "God bless you" after someone sneezed? ((1) point)
    A. Justinian   B. Roman Plague of 590   C. Black Death

18. **This is an ancient, fearless, and feared Norse elite warrior who wore bearskin coverings and fought naked (neither of which was traditional battle wear!). Before battle, through certain ritual processes, this warrior worked himself/herself into a self-induced, trance-like fury that culminated in his/her reckless, frenzy behavior during battle. It is believed that the warriors would even bite into their shields, and they were immune to fire and iron! [max. 4 points]**
    A. Berserker   B. Defiler   C. Valkyrie   D. Seer

    For (2) bonus points: Who were the *úlfheðnar*?

19. **These Samurai swords each served a different purpose. (I) Which one was the warrior's primary weapon? (II) Which one was reserved for court and ceremonial occasions? ((1) point each) [max. 3 points]**
    A. Wakizashi   C. Katana
    B. Nodachi   D. Tachi

    For (1) bonus point: Which one above was called "little sword"? It was used to take off the head of an honored opponent after his death.

20. **This island's indigenous names were created by its first inhabitants, the Amerindians, and are pretty cool: *"Oualichi"* (oo-ah-lee-kee), which means "Land of Brave Women," and *"Soualiga"* (swa-ler-guh), "Land of Salt." Which Caribbean island is this?**
    A. St. Kitts and Nevis   C. Cayman Islands
    B. Antigua   D. St. Martin and Sint Maarten

21. **With around 30 languages, which ethnic group's languages include K'iche', Mam, Chol, Tsotzil, and Yucatec?**
    A. Toltec   B. Olmec   C. Mayan   D. Aztec

K. WORLD SLANGS / SAYINGS / COOL WORDS
(each question at least 2 points)

22. *La floraj estas belaj.* (The flower is beautiful.)
    Vi ŝatas min. (You like me.)
    Mi ŝatas min. (I like you.)
    Kato kuris. (A cat ran.)
    In what language are these statements?
    A. Spanish
    B. Esperanto
    C. Portuguese
    D. Italian
    E. "Belmont, you made these up."

23. *"They are so extra."* **What does this slang phrase mean? [max. 4 points]**
    A. They are so rich.
    B. They are in such a bad mood.
    C. They are so kind.
    D. They are over the top, unnecessarily dramatic.

    For (2) bonus points: What is a cold way of dismissing someone in American slang?
    A. Bye, Karen!
    B. Bye, Stan!
    C. Bye, Felicia!
    D. Bye, Ricardo!

24. **The term "quiet quitting" was used quite a lot in 2022. Match these other 2022 buzz words with their meaning. Answer two for (2) points; answer all for (7) points. No other "great" derivatives. [max. 8 points]**
    A. Workers who quit their jobs to move to other jobs or into other positions express regret.
    B. Workers feel increasingly disconnected from their employers.
    C. Where workers are motivated to request changes or move positions after re-examining their relationships with their jobs.
    D. Women and millennials are leaving their jobs at record-rates in search of better opportunities for advancement.
    E. Workers who resigned from their jobs are with regret as they struggle to find new positions.
    F. Employers silently nudge out workers instead of outright firing them or laying them off.

    "The Great" Terms of 2022
    I. "The Great Rethink"
    II. "Quiet Firing"
    III. "The Great Regret"
    IV. "The Great Remorse"
    V. "The Great Breakup"
    VI. "The Great Disengagement"

    For (1) bonus point: What is the term for the strategy where leadership looks at talent across their organization to acquire new skills and capabilities for their group, without acquiring new full-time employees?

25. **This Spanish slang/expression means to be a kind and good person.**
    A. Ser un trozo de pan
    B. Dejar plantado
    C. Estar chupado
    D. Dar la lata

26. **All of these can mean "dude" except:**
    A. Mate
    B. Tío
    C. Frate
    D. Bro
    E. They all mean it
    F. B and C

K. WORLD SLANGS / SAYINGS / COOL WORDS
(each question at least 2 points)

27. **When was the verb "diss" or "dis" (a term first used within African American communities) first known to appear cited?**
A. 1979   B. 1984   C. 1986   D. 1989

For conversation and not bonus points: Who won the diss battle between rap artists Drake and Kendrick Lamar in 2024?
A. Kendrick Lamar   C. Neither
B. Drake   D. Both

28. **What is the Chinese slang for what many have done or have considered doing: "Quitting one's job without another one lined up"?**
A. Dēngpào   C. Luǒ hūn
B. Fán'ěrsài   D. Luǒ cí

29. **What is the slang phrase for catching someone red-handed and with the evidence to prove it?**
A. Caught in UHD   C. Caught in Sus
B. Caught in 4K   D. Caught in Reel

30. **If you hear a French person saying any of these slang words _fric_, _pognon_, _oseille_, or _thune_, what is the meaning in English?**
A. Soda   C. Money
B. A nice car   D. A group of friends

31. **By the time you're playing this Trivia Lime, this word might be cheugy, but "tea" is not merely tea, it is also... [max. 4 points]**
A. An insult   C. A nice haircut
B. Hot gossip   D. A cool outfit

For (2) bonus points: If you're called a "sigma," you're considered as:
A. Cool   C. An idiot
B. Weird   D. A brat

32. **_"Flat out like a lizard drinking"_ is Australian slang for:**
A. Someone is extremely busy
B. Someone has no money
C. Someone is a royal pain in the butt
D. Someone is extremely thirsty

33. **If someone / something is the "blueprint," they are…. [max. 10 points]**
A. An exact replica   C. A wannabee
B. Very good-looking   D. The original

For (2) bonus points each: What was Oxford English Dictionary's word of the year for: (I) 2022; and (II) 2023? What was Merriam-Webster Dictionary's word of the year for: (III) 2022; and (IV) 2023?
A. Dystopian   E. Deepfake
B. De-influencing   F. Rizz
C. Goblin-mode   G. Vax
D. Gaslighting   H. Authentic

Answers to questions in this Category can be found starting on page 270.

K. WORLD SLANGS / SAYINGS / COOL WORDS   93
(each question at least 2 points)

Category L:
"SHOW ME THE $¥€£"
(3-point category)

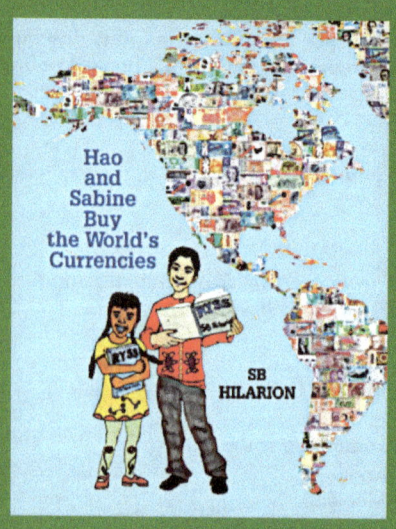

1. **On the front of this country's 10-denominated banknote is a Black businesswoman who was the first known woman to bring a legal challenge against racism in that country. [max. 4 points]**

   A.   The Bahamas   C.   Dominican Republic
   B.   Canada   D.   Aruba

   (1) bonus point: What is the fourth most traded currency in the world?

   A.   British Pound   C.   Australian Dollar
   B.   Japanese Yen   D.   Canadian Dollar

2. **Match the Euro currency with the European architectural style on its banknote: (I) Romanesque; (II) Gothic; (III) Baroque and Rococo; (IV) Modern 20th Century; and (V) Renaissance? Answer two correctly, (1) point; three correctly, (2) points; all correctly, (3) points. [max 6 points]**

   A.   €10   D.   €100
   B.   €20   E.   €500
   C.   €50

   If you have (3) points, for (3) bonus points: €5 and €200, respectively, are of which style: (VI) 19th Century Iron & Glass; (VII) Classical?

3. **Which one of these Japanese women attended college in the USA? She received her degree in three years with a double major in Biology and Education. [max. 4 points]**

   A.   Ichiyō Higuchi
   B.   Tsuda Umeko

   Ichiyō Higuchi

   For (1) bonus point: What was the name of her all-female college, located in the Northeast of the USA?

   Tsuda Umeko

4. **According to the World Gold Council, which was the best-selling gold coin in the world in 1992, 1995, 1996, and 2000?**

   A.   American Eagle   C.   South African Krugerrand
   B.   Australian Kangaroo   D.   Vienna Philharmonic

5. **(I) Who was on the obverse of the US$100,000 bill? ((1 ½) points)**

   A.   "You can't be a U.S. citizen! There's no such bill!"
   B.   Salmon P. Chase
   C.   Woodrow Wilson   D.   James Madison

   (II) Alexander Hamilton first appeared on the US$500 bill in 1918. ((1 ½) points)

   A.   True   B.   False

L. "SHOW ME THE $¥€£"
(each question at least 3 points)

6. **[SUPER-BONUS QUESTION—at least 7 money-making points!!!!!]**
    (1) Match the statement with the European coin image. ((1) point each)
    Get all 10 below correct, (16) points.
    A. This person won a Nobel Prize for Peace.
    B. This person competed in bobsleigh.
    C. This coin has a representation of the Idol of Pomos.
    D. This coin depicts a *cláirseach*.
    E. This person was a proofreader.
    F. This is a coin within a coin.
    G. This person said: "Will cannot be quenched against its own will."
    H. This person flew as a commercial pilot.
    I. This coin depicts *hellas*.
    J. This coin depicts a royal seal from the 12th century.

(I)　　(II)　　(III)　　(IV)　　(V)　　(VI)

(VII)　　(VIII)　　(IX)　　(X)　　(XI)　　(XII)

    (2) For (3) points each. (I) What country has Vytis, its national emblem, on a Euro coin? (II) Which country has the 19th-century poet France Prešeren on its Euro coin? (None of these coins is shown above.)

7. We know about Monaco and its tax-free status attraction to the ultra-high-net-worth elite (UHNWE). Which of the following has the highest personal/individual income tax rate of the group? [max. 4 points]
    A. Andorra
    B. The Bahamas
    C. Cayman Islands
    D. United Arab Emirates
    E. Bermuda
    F. They all have 0% income tax rate

    For (½) tax-free bonus point each:
    (I) What is a native of Monaco called?
    A. Monégasque
    B. A Monacoian
    (II) What is the official language of the principality?
    A. French
    B. Gallo-Italian
    C. Monégasque

8. In April 2023, a signed pair of Michael Jordan's Nike Air Ships sold at a Sotheby's auction for:
    A. US$3.8 million
    B. US$1.18 million
    C. US$2.2 million
    D. US$1.47 million

9. What is the commonly known attribute of the following individuals who are the key motifs on Israel's current banknotes? Rachel Bluwstein, Shaul Tchernichovsky, Leah Goldberg, and Natan Alterman were all....
    A. Medical doctors
    B. University professors
    C. Playwrights
    D. Poets

L. "SHOW ME THE $¥€£"

(each question at least 3 points)

10. **Which one of these individuals also wrote letters, essays, etc., under a female pseudonym?**
    A. Thomas Jefferson
    B. Andrew Jackson
    C. Ulysses S. Grant
    D. Benjamin Franklin
    E. "None of them would have even considered doing that, you liberal."

11. **(I) Let's be honest, art and tax evasion can go hand-in-hand, especially when you're an UHNWE art collector who can take the opportunity to store your art collection at a freeport in a tax-free zone. In which scenario will sales or use tax be imposed <u>and</u> capital gains tax be recognized? ((1) point)**
    A. UHNWE Collector A has been storing a piece of artwork with good provenance at a freeport and sells it at a substantial gain to UHNWE Collector B who decides to store it at the same freeport.
    B. UHNWE Collector A sells a much-appreciated artwork stored at a freeport through an auction house to UHNWE Collector B.

    (II) There are the world-renowned Geneva Freeport and the Zurich Freeport. Which of the following places below does not have a freeport? ((2) points)
    A. Chiasso
    B. Singapore
    C. Delaware
    D. Mauritius
    E. Luxembourg
    F. Liechtenstein

12. **(I) The Cayman Islands Dollar is one of the highest valued currencies in the world. However, this other Caribbean country's currency was the only legal tender of Cayman Islands until the end of August 1972. ((1 ½) points)**
    A. Barbados
    B. Bermuda
    C. Jamaica
    D. Trinidad & Tobago

    (II) For how much did Denmark sell its territory of Virgin Islands to the United States in 1917? ((1 ½) points)
    A. US$10 million in gold
    B. US$15 million in gold
    C. US$20 million in gold
    D. US$25 million in gold

13. **(I) In 2022, Amazon announced a stock split of 20:1. What was the last year prior to this that Amazon split its stock? ((1 ½) points) [max. 6 points]**
    A. 2009   B. 2002   C. 1999   D. 1998

    (II) In 2022, Alphabet announced a stock split of its GOOG and GOOGL stocks. What was the last year prior to this that Alphabet split its stock? ((1 ½) points)
    A. 2016   B. 2015   C. 2014   D. 2009

    For (3) bonus points: What two research units did Alphabet merge in 2023?

L. "SHOW ME THE $¥€£"
(each question at least 3 points)

14. Match each country with its official currency below: (I) Malawi; (II) Oman; (III) Malaysia; (IV) Niue; (V) Haiti; and (VI) Guatemala. ((½) point each)
    A. Gourde
    B. Kwacha
    C. Quetzal
    D. New Zealand Dollar
    E. Rial
    F. Ringgit

15. (I) In March 2022, what was the highest valued company (by market capitalization) in the world? ((2) points) [max. 5 points]
    A. Alphabet Inc. (GOOG)
    B. Amazon.com Inc. (AMZN)
    C. Apple Inc. (AAPL)
    D. Microsoft Corp. (MSFT)
    E. Saudi Aramco (2222.SR)
    F. Tesla (TSLA)

    (II) On which stock exchange does it primarily trade? ((1) point)
    A. NYSE
    B. NASDAQ
    C. Saudi Stock Exchange

    For (2) bonus points: Which company (also shown above) overtook it as the highest valued company (by market cap) in early May 2022? In 2023, it regained its position as the highest valued, but in 2024....

16. In which country does the Beckham Law apply? It's a law applicable to foreign workers where their income earned in that country up to €600,000 is taxed at a fixed rate of 24%, and amounts in excess are taxable at the rate of 45%.
    A. France
    B. Spain
    C. Portugal
    D. Italy

17. If you're based at each of the following research stations in Antarctica, what is the main currency there: (I) Bharati; (II) McMurdo; (III) Troll; (IV) Concordia; (V) Rothera; and (VI) Marambio? ((½) point each) [max. 6 points]
    A. Euro
    B. Krone
    C. Argentine Peso
    D. Indian Rupee
    E. US Dollar
    F. Great Britain Pound

    For (3) bonus points: If you're a research scientist at Mawson located in the claimed territory land of Holme Bay in Antarctica, what is the main currency there? Hint: It's not listed above.

18. In May 2022, a type of Stablecoin (a cryptocurrency meant to offer a safe harbor against wild volatility and fluctuations of the greater crypto market) collapsed. (*Go figure!*) What is its name? [max. 5 points]
    A. Tether (USDT)
    B. Binance USD (BUSD)
    C. USD Coin (TUSD)
    D. TerraUSD (UST)
    E. Dai (DAI)

    For (2) bonus points: There's Bitcoin and there's Altcoin (another type of cryptocurrency). Which one of these is an exchange-traded product (ETP) that enables investing in Bitcoin?
    A. MONERO
    B. RIPPLE
    C. IBIT
    D. DASH

L. "SHOW ME THE $¥€£"
(each question at least 3 points)

19. Which hedge fund made a profit of USD 16 billion in 2022, the biggest annual windfall on record?
    A. Renaissance Technologies   C. Bridgewater Associates
    B. Man Group   D. Citadel

20. Match the country with its official currency below: (I) Switzerland; (II) Anguilla; and (III) Liechtenstein. ((1) point each)
    A. US Dollar   C. Franc
    B. East Caribbean Dollar   D. Euro

21. Match the country with its official currency below: (I) Bahrain; (II) Israel; and (III) United Arab Emirates. ((1) point each)
    A. Shekel   C. Rial
    B. Pound   D. Dirham

22. All of these African countries use the West African CFA Franc (XOF) as their official currency except:
    A. Comoros   C. Côte d'Ivoire
    B. Senegal   D. Mali

23. On the newest Egyptian 10-pound banknote issued in 2022, who is the main motif represented on the reverse side below? [max. 5 points]

    A. Pharaoh Sneferu
    B. Pharaoh Hatshepsut
    C. Pharaoh Khufu
    D. Pharaoh Khafre
    E. Pharaoh Menkaure

    For (2) bonus points: Who is depicted on the back side of the older, but still in circulation, Egyptian 10-pound note?

24. What is the name of each company whose stock ticker symbol is listed below? ((1) point each) [max. 15 points]
    A. MS   B. NTDOY   C. TCEHY

    For (2) bonus points each, and provided all are correct above: What company has the stock ticker symbol: (I) BRK-B; (II) NVDA; (III) TSM; (IV) JOBY; and (V) RGTI? (VI) Which exchange-traded fund (ETF) has the ticker symbol of QTUM?

25. Match the official currency below with its country: (I) Honduras; (II) Romania; (III) Aruba; (IV) Denmark; (V) Serbia; and (VI) Estonia. ((½) point each) [max. 6 points]
    A. Florin   D. Leu
    B. Lempira   E. Dinar
    C. Euro   F. Krone

    For (3) bonus points, (1) point each: For which language of an EU member is the linguistic variant (I) ESB; (II) BĊE; and (III) ЕЦБ, respectively, on Euro banknotes?

L. "SHOW ME THE $¥€£"
(each question at least 3 points)

26. **All or nothing. Which stock ticker symbol is: (I) Technology Select Sector SPDR Fund; (II) Consumer Staples Select Sector SPDR Fund; (III) Materials Select Sector SPDR Fund; and (IV) Consumer Discretionary Select Sector SPDR Fund? [max. 6 points]**

    A.   XLP   B.   XLY   C.   XLK   D.   XLB

    For (1) bonus point each: What do the terminologies (I) TAPAS; (II) TARA; and (III) TIARA, coined by certain financial institutions, mean?

27. **Match the musical artist(s) with the popular song about money. Five correct answers for (3) points; answer all 12 correctly for (10) "guap-making" points!**

	Artist(s)
A. "Money for Nothing" (1985)	I. The Pet Shop Boys
B. "I Don't Want Your Money" (2019)	II. Donna Summer
C. "Bills Bills Bills" (1999)	III. Dire Straits
D. "For the Love of Money" (1973)	IV. Divine Sounds
E. "Opportunities (Let's Make Lots of Money)" (1986)	V. The O'Jays
F. "Money Changes Everything" (1983)	VI. Notorious B.I.G.
G. "Mo Money Mo Problems" (1997)	VII. Pink Floyd
H. "She Works Hard For the Money" (1983)	VIII. Johnny Kemp
I. "Just Got Paid" (1986)	IX. The Beatles
J. "Money" (1973)	X. Cyndi Lauper
K. "Can't Buy Me Love" (1964)	XI. Destiny's Child
L. "What People Do for Money" (1984)	XII. Ed Sheeran

28. **What is the name of each company whose stock ticker symbol is listed below? ((1) point each correct answer) [max. 8 points]**

    A.   COST   B.   BABA   C.   GS

    Provided all the above are answered correctly, for (5) bonus points, all or nothing: What is the name of each company whose stock ticker symbol is listed below?

    A.   MC.PA (on Euronext Paris)   C.   KER (on Euronext Paris)
    B.   HESAY (on the OTC markets)   D.   MA (on the NYSE)

29. **On 19 March 2023, as part of their response to the turmoil in the banking industry, which six central banks agreed upon a coordinated action to boost liquidity (daily) in their U.S. dollar swap line arrangements? All or nothing.**

    A.   Swiss National Bank   F.   European Central Bank
    B.   Norges Bank   G.   Bank of Japan
    C.   U.S. Federal Reserve System   H.   People's Bank of China
    D.   Reserve Bank of New Zealand   I.   Bank of England
    E.   Bank of Canada   J.   Reserve Bank of Australia

30. **Match the official currency below with its country: (I) Sweden; (II) Lesotho; (III) Costa Rica; (IV) Tuvalu; (V) Macau; (VI) Colombia; and (VII) Tokelau. ((½) point each)**

    A.   Colón   D.   Maloti
    B.   Kronor   E.   Australian Dollar
    C.   Peso   F.   Pataca

L.   "SHOW ME THE $¥€£"
                    (each question at least 3 points)

31. **Show the $¥€£, someone will sell you the car (and you can store it at a freeport). Which car, as of 2024, set the record for most expensive car ever sold at auction? [max. 6 points]**
    A. 1956 Aston Martin DBR1 Roadster
    B. 1955 Mercedes-Benz 300 SLR Uhlenhaut Coupé
    C. 1957 Ferrari 335 Sport Scaglietti
    D. 1962 Ferrari 250 GTO
    E. 1962 Ferrari 330 LM / 250 GTO

    For (3) bonus points: What was the approximate price in USD?

    A. $35,700,000   D. $156,000,000
    B. $70,000,000   E. $51,700,000
    C. $48,400,000   F. $142,800,000

32. **Which three below are Biotechnology Sector stocks? ((1) point each)**
    A. CRSP   D. MELI
    B. ONON   E. ABBV
    C. NVO   F. PLTR

33. **The World Bank was created in 1944 to provide grants and economic assistance to countries. Which country in 1947 was the first beneficiary of a loan from it? [max. 4 points]**
    A. USA   D. Ecuador
    B. Great Britain   E. The Netherlands
    C. France   F. Chile

    For (1) bonus point: In February 2022, the World Bank approved a loan of US$700 million for which country above "to create opportunities, generate employment, guarantee transparency and fiscal sustainability with equity, and promote climate action"?

Answers to questions in this Category can be found starting on page 270.

$¥€£ for a strategy play card?
Only if your judge is corrupt.

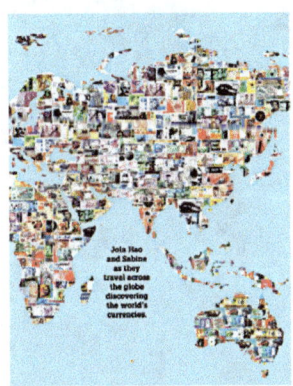

Jola Hao and Sabine as they travel across the globe discovering the world's currencies.

Category M:
SCIENTISTS
AND GENIUSES
(3-point category)

1. **Match the following hacker(s) with what he/she/they did: (I) Marc Maiffret; (II) Loyd Blankenship; (III) Joanna Rutkowska; (IV) Kevin Mitnick; (V) Phineas Fisher; (VI) Richard Matthew Stallman; and (VII) Robert Tappan Morris. Get (3) points if you have three correct; and (3) bonus points if you answer all seven correctly. [max. 6 points]**
   A. He/she/they are credited as being the creator of the world's first known computer worm
   B. Known as The Mentor, he/she/they wrote an essay called "Hacker Manifesto"
   C. He/she/they breached spyware companies Gamma Group and Hacking Team, and then posted the details of the breaches online
   D. He/she/they founded the GNU Project, an open-source operating system and mass collaborative project
   E. He/she/they exposed vulnerabilities in Microsoft products, such as the Code Red worm
   F. Also known as The Condor, he/she/they wrote the books *The Art of Deception* and *The Art of Intrusion*
   G. He/she/they are known for the Blue Pill rootkit technique and Qubes OS, and wrote the seminal essay "State Considered Harmful – A Proposal for a Stateless Laptop"

2. **(I) As of 2024, how many individuals born in the Caribbean have been awarded the distinguished Nobel Prize? ((1 ½) points)**
   A. 0   B. 1   C. 2   D. 3   E. 4

   (II) This scientist / genius said, *"Wisdom was not created from books, but books were created from wisdom."* ((1 ½) points) [max. 4 points]
   A. Albert Einstein   D. (Hryhorii) Grigory Skovoroda
   B. Admiral Grace Hopper   E. Nikola Tesla
   C. Beatrix Potter

   For (1) bonus point: One of the above individuals purportedly was petrified of earrings, especially those with pearls.

3. **We're familiar with the Black-Scholes theorem for which Robert Merton and Myron Scholes won the 1997 Nobel Prize in economics. Match the Nobel Prize winners below with their economic theory. Get (3) points for any two answered correctly; (7) points for all identified correctly.**

Nobel Prize Winner(s) in Economic Sciences
(I) James M. Buchanan Jr. (1986)
(II) John C. Harsanyi, John F. Nash Jr., Reinhard Selten (1994)
(III) George Akerlof, A. Michael Spence, Joseph Stiglitz (2001)
(IV) Daniel Kahneman (2002)
(V) Elinor Ostrom (2009)

   A. Analyses of markets with asymmetric information
   B. Equilibria in the theory of non-cooperative games
   C. Contributions to political decision-making and public economics theory
   D. Analysis of economic governance, especially the commons
   E. Behavioral economics especially concerning human judgment and decision-making under uncertainty

M. SCIENTISTS AND GENIUSES
(each question at least 3 points)

4. Match the physicist and/or chemist with his/her discoveries/invention: (I) Galileo Galilei; (II) Marie Curie; (III) Niels Bohr; (IV) Paul Dirac; (V) Adolf von Baeyer; and (VI) Alessandro Volta. Get any three correct for (3) points; and (4) bonus points if all six correct. [max. 7 points]
   A. Determined that electrons travel in set orbits around the nucleus
   B. Developed the field of quantum electrodynamics and predicted the existence of antimatter
   C. Invented the first electric battery
   D. Showed that all freely falling bodies have the same constant acceleration
   E. Discovered the elements radium and polonium, and coined the term radioactivity
   F. Synthesized the plant pigment indigo and formulated its structure

5. (I) Ancient Indian mathematician and astronomer, Aryabhata the Elder (476 to 550), applied trigonometry tables to measure Earth's distance from the Sun. Also importantly, he introduced the versine into trigonometry. How old was he when he did the latter? ((1 ½) points)
   A. 13   B. 23   C. 52   D. 65

   (II) This individual discovered the boundary layer between Earth's crust and its mantle. ((1 ½) points)
   A. Beno Gutenberg   C. Milutin Milanković
   B. Andrija Mohorovičić   D. Mihajlo Pupin

6. Called a "human computer," Katherine Johnson (née Coleman) was a scientist and mathematician at NASA for about 35 years. Her calculations of orbital mechanics were critical in NASA's first successful and subsequent U.S.-crewed spaceflights. Specifically, she calculated the flight path for the USA's first crewed space mission and moon landing. Which U.S. Historically Black College / University did she attend and graduated from at age 18? [max. 5 points]
   A. Hampton University
   B. Howard University
   C. North Carolina A&T State University
   D. West Virginia State College (now West Virginia State University)

   For (2) bonus points: What was the name of the book and later 2016 film in which she was profiled (along with two other prolific African American women NASA alumni)?

7. [SUPER-BONUS QUESTION—at least 7 points!!!!!] 1. Match the scientist with his/her discoveries/invention: (I) Lise Meitner; (II) C.V. Raman; (III) Mario J. Molina; (IV) George Carruthers. ((4) points each)
   A. Created the ultraviolet camera/spectrograph for NASA to use when it launched Apollo 16 in 1972
   B. Discovered the element protactinium and the process of nuclear fission
   C. Discovered that chlorofluorocarbons (CFCs) could destroy the ozone in the atmosphere
   D. Discovered that when light traverses a transparent material, some of the light that is deflected changes in wavelength

   2. In which country was each scientist born? ((1) point each))

M. SCIENTISTS AND GENIUSES
(each question at least 3 points)

8. Name this subject that Gottfried Leibniz and Sir Isaac Newton invented independently. (Lots of dispute over the independence.)
    A. Statistics
    B. Geometry
    C. Calculus
    D. Applied Mathematics

9. This chemist and physicist is internationally recognized as the Father of Nuclear Physics, and he is a Nobel Prize winner. He is featured also on his native country's banknote. Who is he?
    A. Werner Heisenberg
    B. Max Planck
    C. Ernest Rutherford
    D. J. Robert Oppenheimer
    E. James Chadwick
    F. Niels Bohr

10. This 9th-century mathematician and astronomer invented algebra and algorithm while at the House of Wisdom in Iraq.
    A. Ulūgh Beg
    B. Al-Khwārizmī
    C. Abū'Alī al-Husayn ibnī'Abdallāh ibn Sīnā
    D. Abū'Abd Allah Ja'far ibn Muhammad al-Rūdhakī

11. This scientist studied the use of peanuts—creating about 300 different uses of this crop. He developed the concept of restoring nitrogen in soil via crop rotation. He made dye from sweet potatoes and paint from soybeans. He was dubbed a "Black Leonardo."
    A. Ernest Everett Just
    B. Frederick McKinley Jones
    C. George Washington Carver
    D. Benjamin Banneker

12. This physicist worked on the Manhattan Project at Columbia University. She helped develop the process for separating uranium into uranium-235 and uranium-238 isotopes by gaseous diffusion. She is called the First Lady of Physics.
    A. Maria Goeppert Mayer
    B. Barbara McClintock
    C. Rosalind Franklin
    D. Chien-Shiung Wu

13. This scientist is considered to be the earliest female physician in the history of science. *Two answers will be accepted as correct. No Steals.
    A. Agamede
    B. Merit-Ptah
    C. Agnodice
    D. Theano
    E. Peseshet

14. This astronomer and astrophysicist discovered that the Sun was composed largely of hydrogen and helium. Her discovery was disparaged at the time because it contradicted scientific belief that the Sun's composition was similar to Earth's. One of her most important works is *The Stars of High Luminosity and Variable Stars*.
    A. Antonia Maury
    B. Annie Jump Cannon
    C. Adelaide Ames
    D. Cecilia Payne-Gaposchkin

15. This scientist theorized that radiation emitted by a black hole over a very, very long (*very long!*) timescale could cause the black hole to lose its mass and possibly evaporate. He wrote *The Theory of Everything, On the Shoulders of Giants*, and *A Brief History of Time*.
    A. Isaac Newton
    B. Stephen Hawking
    C. Edwin Hubble
    D. Kip Thorne

M. SCIENTISTS AND GENIUSES
(each question at least 3 points)

16. **This scientist wrote the books *Dialogues Concerning Two New Sciences* and *Starry Messenger*.**
    A.   Nicolaus Copernicus   C.   Johannes Kepler
    B.   Robert Hooke   D.   Galileo Galilei

17. **Who solved the 30-year-old Sensitivity Conjecture in computer science in 2019?**
    A.   "Uhh…an insensitive git?"   C.   Prof. Noam Nisan
    B.   Prof. Hao Huang   D.   Prof. Mario Szegedy

18. **This mathematician tried to refute the idea of 19th-century mathematician Ada Lovelace (who's been referred to as "the Prophet of the Computer Age") that the Analytical Engine "can follow analysis, but it has no power of anticipating any analytical relations or truth."**
    A.   John Searle   C.   Alan Turing
    B.   Selmer Bringsjord   D.   Admiral Grace Hopper

19. **The geographic work** 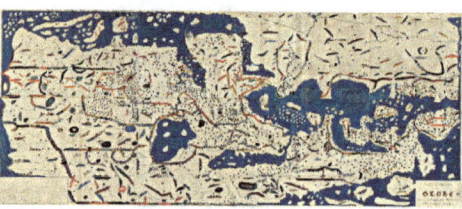 ***Kitab Rudjdjar* was commissioned by the Norman King Roger II of Sicily in Palermo. The map, drawn in 1154, showed the Eurasian continent in** its entirety, but only the northern part of Africa. It was oriented with the North at the bottom. For three centuries, it was considered the most accurate world map. It was the most significant source of information on the cultural, political, social, and physical conditions of the territories that were studied. Who was its esteemed and renowned mapmaker and geographer?
    A.   Muhammad al-Idrisi   C.   Claudius Ptolemy
    B.   Abraham Ortelius   D.   Anaximander

20. **This Scottish physicist and mathematician's four equations are the foundations of electromagnetism. [max. 9 points]**
    A.   James Clerk Maxwell   C.   Michael Faraday
    B.   Henry Moseley   D.   Heinrich Hertz

    For (3) bonus points each:
    (1) Which one of the above scientists conclusively proved the existence of electromagnetic waves?
    (2) Who of the above discovered a way to convert mechanical energy into electricity?

21. **Who designed a prototype leather diving suit in the 1500s, complete with glass goggles, a bag-like mask that went over the head with two flexible cane-tubes attached, and an inflatable buoying aid?**
    A.   Galileo Galilei   C.   Tycho Brahe
    B.   Leonardo da Vinci   D.   Leonhard Fuchs

M. SCIENTISTS AND GENIUSES
        (each question at least 3 points)

22. All of the below won the prestigious Turing Award and are considered the "godfathers" of AI (or machine learning) except: [max. 5 points]
    A. Yoshua Bengio
    B. Geoffrey Hinton
    C. Sam Altman
    D. Yann LeCun

    For (2) bonus points: Renowned futurist and former computer scientist Ray Kurzweil has predicted that: AI will surpass human intelligence and will master the Turing Test by 2029; and that humans will merge with the AI they created by 2054 (the "Singularity" phenomenon).
    A. True   B. False   C. Partially True

23. This physicist used mathematical equations to theorize that the behavior of electrons in an atom could be explained by treating them as matter waves. His model is known as the quantum mechanical model of the atom. He also introduced a theoretical experiment that a cat could be alive and dead at the same time. [max. 6 points]
    A. Niels Bohr
    B. Erwin Schrödinger
    C. Max Born
    D. Werner Heisenberg

    For (3) bonus points: Who above reportedly told Einstein "*Stop telling God what to do*" during their great debate about quantum theory?

24. Along with his discovery of infrared radiation, William Herschel discovered this planet in 1781 that he originally called the "Georgium Sidus" (the "Georgian Planet").
    A. Neptune   B. Pluto   C. Mercury   D. Uranus

25. Who is believed to have discovered the concept of the perfect number? [max. 7 points]
    A. Leonhard Euler
    B. Pythagoras
    C. Pierre de Fermat
    D. Euclid
    E. Apollonius of Perga
    F. Aryabhata the Elder

    For (4) bonus points, (1) point each: What did he consider as the first four perfect numbers?
    A. 36   D. 496   G. 28
    B. 268   E. 2,246   H. 9,236
    C. 6   F. 8,128   I. 108

26. Who is considered the Mother of Botany? [max. 5 points]
    A. Janaki Ammal
    B. Katherine Esau
    C. Gertrude Jekyll
    D. Emma Lucy Braun

    For (2) bonus points: Who is considered the Father of Modern Taxonomy?
    A. Jean-Baptiste Lamarck
    B. Carl Linnaeus
    C. Charles Darwin
    D. Georges Cuvier

27. Who discovered the Law of Conservation of Mass, which states that mass can neither be created nor destroyed in chemical reactions?
    A. John Dalton
    B. Julius Robert Mayer
    C. Wolfgang Pauli
    D. Antoine Lavoisier

M. SCIENTISTS AND GENIUSES
(each question at least 3 points)

28. This scientist, who has done extensive work on stem cell research, carried out the first-ever induced pluripotent stem cell clinical study for the treatment of age-related macular degeneration (a disease that affects a person's central vision). [max. 6 points]
    A. Shinya Yamanaka
    B. Masayo Takahashi
    C. Martin Evans
    D. Howard Green

    For (3) bonus points: One of the above scientists was a joint winner of the 2007 Nobel Prize for Physiology or Medicine. In 1981, this person was the first scientist to isolate embryonic stem cells from early mice embryos and cultivate them successfully in a laboratory. This scientist genetically modified the stem cells and implanted them into adult female mice to create genetically modified pups.

29. This scientist currently is one of the leading theoretical physicists in the world. When she was 14 years old, she became the youngest person to build an airworthy-certified airplane, and then she conducted the first flight in the aircraft. In 2016, Stephen Hawking cited her solo research paper on electromagnetic memory in one of his published works. She has been dubbed "the next Albert Einstein." [max. 6 points]
    A. Lene V. Hau
    B. Fabiola Gianotti
    C. Sabrina Gonzalez Pasterski
    D. Lucie Green

    For (3) bonus points: Which scientist above is the first person to slow down and freeze light?

30. This chemist developed a medical treatment and cure for leprosy (Hansen's disease) at the age of 23 years old. [max. 6 points]
    A. Alice Augusta Ball
    B. Marie Maynard Daly
    C. Harry T. Hollman
    D. Arthur Dean

    For (3) bonus points: One of the above scientists was the first African American woman (also of Caribbean ancestry) to earn a Ph.D. in chemistry in the USA. Her pioneering research examined the relationship between clogged arteries in heart health and high cholesterol.

31. This person was the first female scientist to earn a salary in the United Kingdom for her work in astronomy. She was the first woman to be officially recognized in a scientific position. She discovered several comets and nebulae. She also was one of two women first elected as an Honorary Member of the Royal Astronomical Society in 1835.
    A. Maria Margaretha Kirch
    B. Caroline Lucretia Herschel
    C. Henrietta Swan Leavitt
    D. Mary Sommerville

M. SCIENTISTS AND GENIUSES
(each question at least 3 points)

32. This Chinese chemist below discovered artemisinin, a drug therapy for malaria, for which she was awarded a Nobel Prize in Physiology or Medicine in 2015. [max. 12 points]

A.	Yi Xing	D.	Ma Jun (Deheng)
B.	Cai Lun	E.	Tu Youyou
C.	Zhang Heng	F.	Tsai-Fan Yu

For (3) bonus points each:
(I) One of the above persons was an astronomer and mathematician, born in the first century, who created the first seismoscope. This person also recognized that the Moon was not a source of light, but rather reflected the Sun. He was an acclaimed poet too!

(II) One of the above persons was an 8th-century Buddhist mathematician and monk who developed an astronomical instrument that later was renamed the astronomical clock.

(III) What Chinese inventor above devised the idea of paper and the papermaking process in the early second century?

33. This mathematical genius made substantial contributions to number theory, elliptic functions, infinite series, and game theory, despite having no university education. The number 1,729, which is the smallest integer expressible as the sum of two cubes in two different ways, is named after him. National Mathematics Day is observed annually on 22 December, the date of his birthday. Who is he? [max. 8 points]

A.	Srinivasa Ramanujan	C.	Subrahmanyan Chandrasekhar
B.	C. R. Rao	D.	D. R. Kaprekar

For (2) bonus points each, (I) and (II): What are the two different ways to represent 1,729?

(III) For (1) bonus point:
"…[J]ust guessing at numbers and figures
Pulling puzzles apart…."
In what year did Coldplay release their mega hit "The Scientist" with these lyrics?

A.	2005	C.	2002
B.	2011	D.	2008

Answers to questions in this Category can be found starting on page 271.

M. SCIENTISTS AND GENIUSES
(each question at least 3 points)

Category N:
LANDMARKS
AND MONUMENTS
(1-point category)

1. **Mäñgilik Yel Triumphal Arch was unveiled in December 2011 to celebrate the 20-year anniversary of this country's independence. The monument is shown in the foreground of this banknote. [max. 4 points]**

    A. Afghanistan
    B. Kazakhstan
    C. Kyrgyzstan
    D. Turkmenistan

    All or nothing question for (3) bonus points: Name three more countries that end with 'stan.'

2. **In what Middle Eastern country is this museum that French architect Jean Nouvel designed?**

    A. Bahrain   C. Oman
    B. Kuwait   D. Qatar

3. **Which famous stalactite and stalagmite is this landmark (the top images), which contains its country's longest wooden path? [max. 2 points]**

    A. Mammoth Cave (USA)
    B. Škocjan Caves (Slovenia)
    C. Reed Flute Cave (China)
    D. Động Thiên Đường (Vietnam)

    For (1) bonus point: This second landmark is believed to preserve the world's longest cave system. Choose from the above answers.

4. **[SUPER-BONUS QUESTION—at least 7 points!!!!!]**
    (I) Match the type of order with the architectural image: (1) Doric; (2) Ionic; (3) Corinthian; (4) Tuscan; and (5) Composite. ((2) points each)

    (A) Arch of Titus   (B) New York Stock Exchange   (C) St. Paul's Church Covent Garden

    (D) Erechtheum   (E) Temple of Hephaestus

    (II) Which is the earliest and simplest of the five orders? ((2) points)
    (III) Is the Composite order: (1) Greek or (2) Roman architecture? ((1) point)

N. LANDMARKS AND MONUMENTS

(each question at least 1 point)

5. There are major opera houses around the world that also serve as landmarks. With its horseshoe-shaped auditorium and its room considered as having the best acoustics for opera, which opera house is shown? [max. 3 points]

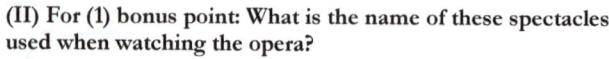

    A. El Teatro Colón (Argentina)
    B. Palais Garnier (France)
    C. Vienna State Opera House (Austria)
    D. Bolshoi Theatre (Russia)

    (I) For (1) bonus point: Which is the oldest working opera house in the world?
    A. Teatro di San Carlo (Naples Italy)
    B. Teatro alla Scala (Milan Italy)

    (II) For (1) bonus point: What is the name of these spectacles used when watching the opera?

6. In late 1841, the justices within this landmark, the U.S. Supreme Court, decided on the "Amistad Rebellion" international legal case. The justices ruled in favor that Sengbe Pieh and the other incarcerated Africans were not Spanish citizens and of "slave" status, but instead were illegally kidnapped Africans, and thus not enslaved persons under U.S. or Spanish law. How exactly was the case decided amongst the justices? [max. 2 points]

    A. 5 - 3
    B. 6 – 2
    C. 7 – 1
    D. 8 – 0

    For (1) bonus point: From what modern-day country was Sengbe Pieh?
    A. Ghana   C. Nigeria
    B. Liberia   D. Sierra Leone

7. The Banteay Srei Temple and some of its buildings were dedicated to which Hindu gods / goddesses? [max. 2 points]
    A. Lakshmi and Indra
    B. Shiva and Vishnu
    C. Saraswati and Parvati
    D. Ganesha and Krishna

    For (1) bonus point: In which country is it located?
    A. Cambodia   C. Nepal
    B. India   D. Sri Lanka

8. Where is this iconic landmark, Taktsang Palphug Monastery, located?
    A. Bhutan
    B. Cambodia
    C. Laos
    D. Tibet

N. LANDMARKS AND MONUMENTS
(each question at least 1 point)

9. Where is this archeological complex, the ruins of this most ancient city of the Americas? [max. 2 points]

   A. Monte Albán
   B. Ciudad Perdida
   C. Xunantunich
   D. Sacred City of Caral-Supe

   For (1) bonus point: In which country is it located?

10. This is the world's highest palace at an altitude of about 3,700 metres (12,139 feet) above sea level. Where is it located? [max. 2 points]

   A. Mongolia   C. Nepal
   B. Japan   D. Tibet

   For (1) bonus point: What is its name?

11. Ludwig II had this castle built in the "authentic style of the old German knights' castles" in the German state of Bavaria. [max. 2 points]
   A. Neuschwanstein Castle   C. Nuremberg Castle
   B. Würzburg Residence   D. Plassenburg Castle

   For (1) bonus point: In what century was it built?
   A. 12th century   C. 18th century
   B. 17th century   D. 19th century

12. The major buildings of this ancient city in Mexico deliberately were destroyed by fire in the 6th century.
   A. Teotihuacán   C. Tulum
   B. Tenochtitlan   D. Chichén Itzá

13. This Initiation Well was not used for collecting water. It was part of a mysterious ritual within the Knights Templar tradition. An initiate would descend nine flights of 139 steps of a spiral staircase blindfolded. The nine flights represented Dante's Inferno and/or the nine founders of the Knights Templar. Where is this particular Initiation Well?
   A. Castle of Montalbán, Toledo (Spain)
   B. Commandery of Richerenches, Vaucluse (France)
   C. Quinta da Regaleira, Sintra (Portugal)
   D. Castelo de Tomar, Tomar (Portugal)

14. Name this famous pillar that contains a 90-letter, 5-line inscription that states, in part, that the Mauryan emperor King Piyadasi made a royal visit during the 20th year of his reign to the birthplace of Buddha Shakyamuni. The pillar was erected to commemorate the historic location.

   A. Ashoka Pillar of Lumbini (Nepal)
   B. Iron Pillar of Delhi (India)

N. LANDMARKS AND MONUMENTS

(each question at least 1 point)

15. **Inaugurated in March 1979, where are these iconic towers located?**

    A. Bahrain
    B. United Arab Emirates
    C. Qatar
    D. Kuwait

16. **This monument is a statue of the Roman god Neptune in front of the Palace of Versailles. But he goes by another name in Greek mythology. What is it? [max. 2 points]**

    A. Palaemon   C. Poseidon
    B. Plutus   D. Prometheus

For (1) bonus point: Which leader of France originally built on the site of the Palace of Versailles?
    A. Henry IV   C. Louis XIV
    B. Louis XIII   D. Napoleon III

17. **This is the tallest minaret in the world. In which predominantly Muslim country is it located? [max. 2 points]**

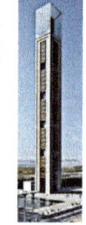

    A. Algeria
    B. Morocco
    C. Saudi Arabia
    D. United Arab Emirates

For (1) bonus point: Name the minaret.

18. **This monument is the Steilneset Memorial to Victims of Witch Trials. In the 17th century, 91 so-called "witches" (77 women, 14 men) were burned at the stake after witch trials in Vardø, an extreme northeastern part of this country. The monument consists of two structures: a long, wooded-framed enclosure with 91 windows and a burning chair. In what country is it located?**

    A. Sweden
    B. Denmark
    C. Norway
    D. Finland

19. **Rapa Nui is its indigenous name. Most of the world knows this place as Easter Island, with its amazing giant stone figures, the *Moai*, strewn across the 63-square-mile island. It is not an independent country but rather a territory of which country?** (*In October 2022, a ferocious fire damaged hundreds of the iconic Moai statues!*)

    A. Australia
    B. Chile
    C. Indonesia
    D. New Zealand

N. LANDMARKS AND MONUMENTS
(each question at least 1 point)

20. These bronze, cast iron, lion statues are symbols of the bank HSBC. Which one is Stephen, and which is Stitt?

(I)   (II)

 A. (I) is Stephen; (II) is Stitt
 B. (I) is Stitt; (II) is Stephen
 C. Actually, HSBC does not have lions as symbols
 D. "You uploaded the incorrect pics, dimwit"

21. In which city is the iconic Broken Chair installed? The monumental sculpture was designed to raise awareness about the impact of landmines on civilians in conflict zones.

 A. Hanoi
 B. Brussels
 C. Geneva
 D. Cairo

Ping, ping, ping! Pick any strategy play card not yet selected.

22. What is the name of this Zen Buddhist temple in Japan? [max. 3 points]

 A. Kinkaku-ji
 B. Sensō-ji
 C. Tōdai-ji
 D. Kiyomizu-dera

1. For (1) bonus point: Where in Japan is the temple located?

 A. Nara
 B. Kamakura
 C. Kyōtō
 D. Tōkyō

2. For (1) bonus point: What is the name of this famous shrine, also in Japan?

 A. Itsukushima Shinto Shrine
 B. Fushimi Inari Taisha
 C. Kashima Shrine
 D. Hie Shrine

23. (I) TRAJAN'S COLUMN: Roman Emperor Trajan had this marble monument erected from 106 to 113 to celebrate his two military campaigns in Dacia.

(II) INFINITY COLUMN: This marble monument was created by Constantin Brâncuşi to commemorate the Romanian fallen soldiers who defended the town of Târgu-Jiu against German forces during World War I.

Match each fact above with its image. [max. 2 points]

Image A: [**I**] or [**II**]
Image B: [**II**] or [**I**]

For (1) bonus point: In which modern-day country was Dacia located?

(A)   (B)

N. LANDMARKS AND MONUMENTS

(each question at least 1 point)

24. The Intihuatana ritual stone was used by the ancient Incas in South America. It was pointed directly at the Sun to measure the winter solstice. At what archeological site is it located? [max. 2 points]
    A. Ciudad Perdida   C. Chan Chan
    B. Coral-Supe   D. Machu Pichu

    For (1) bonus point: During the summer solstice, the Sun rises over this prehistoric monument's Heel Stone. Its outer edge contains 56 chalk pits called Aubrey Holes. What is the monument?
    A. Carnac Stones   C. Stonehenge
    B. Cairns   D. Zorats Karer

25. Where was the Dragon Throne of the Emperor of China located?
    A. Huizhou Ancient City   C. Pingyao Ancient City
    B. Langzhong Ancient City   D. Forbidden City

26. British architect Richard Rogers, along with Italian architect Renzo Piano, designed this art gallery in Paris, intentionally placing all of its pipes on the outside of the building. [max. 2 points]
    A. Musée de l'Orangerie   C. Louvre
    B. Centre Georges Pompidou   D. Musée D'Orsay

    Rogers designed two European airport terminals. For (1) bonus point: Name one of them.

27. Göbekli Tepe is the oldest known temple in the world, dating to 10000 B.C.E., and thus predating the pottery Neolithic period. In what modern-day country was it discovered?
    A. Greece   C. Turkey
    B. North Macedonia   D. Armenia

28. This famous department store is a landmark for luxury goods. It dates to the 1800s. In fact, it burned to the ground in December 1883 but was rebuilt in an even grander style soon afterward. Its motto is "*Omnia Omnibus Ubique*" ("All things for all people, everywhere"). It is Europe's largest department store.
    A. Galeries Lafayette   C. Selfridges
    B. Harrods   D. Kaufhaus des Westens

29. This Baroque palace located in Vienna was the main summer residence of the Habsburgs. Today, nonroyals can rent out apartments in the palace. [max. 3 points]
    A. Belvedere Palace   C. Hofburg Palace
    B. Schönbrunn Palace   D. Schloss Hetzendorf

    (I) For (1) bonus point: Which one of the above palaces holds the world's largest collection of Gustav Klimt's paintings?

    (II) For (1) bonus point: One of these palaces was the home of the last Austrian emperor Archduke Franz Josef. During World War II, it was heavily bombed, but it has since been restored to its former glory.

N. LANDMARKS AND MONUMENTS
(each question at least 1 point)

30. This palatial complex is one of the most famous landmarks in Islamic architecture with its enchanting gardens, courtyards, and fountains. Its walls are full of calligraphy, including the Kūfic text *"Only God is Victor"* and epigraphic poems by court poets Ibn al-Yayyab, Ibn al-Khatib, and Ibn Zamrak.

A. Citadel of Aleppo
B. Mshatta
C. Al Jawsaq al-Khāqanī
D. Alhambra

31. What temple holds the Nara Daibutsu, one of the largest bronze Buddha statues in the world? [max. 4 points]

A. Kōtoku-in Temple
B. Bongeunsa Temple
C. Tōdai-ji
D. Vĩnh Tràng Temple

For (1) bonus point each:
1. In what country is it located?

A. Vietnam
B. Japan
C. South Korea
D. Taiwan

2. What is the world's largest religious monument?

A. Angkor Wat Temple (Cambodia)
B. Hassan II Mosque (Morocco)
C. Temple of Zeus (Libya)
D. Al-Masjid al-Harām (Saudi Arabia)

3. Badaling is the most famous stretch of this landmark structure below, sections of which were built originally by Qin Shi Huang.

A. Amarbayasgalant Monastery (Mongolia)
B. Golden Bridge in Bà Nà Hills (Vietnam)
C. Great Wall of China (China)
D. Kiyomizu-dera Temple (Japan)

32. The Door of No Return is located in the House of Slaves, a memorial to the Atlantic African slave trade on Gorée Island. In which country is it?

A. The Gambia
B. Senegal
C. Ghana
D. Guinea

33. This stunning Benedictine nunnery with its walled Victorian garden is located in the Republic of Ireland. Benedictine nuns purchased the property in 1920 after they were forced to leave Belgium during World War I. What is the name of the nunnery?

A. Tintern Abbey
B. Blarney Castle
C. Muckross Abbey
D. Kylemore Abbey

Answers to questions in this Category can be found starting on page 271.

N. LANDMARKS AND MONUMENTS

(each question at least 1 point)

Category O:
"ENLIGHTENMENT"
(3-point category)

1. Certain of Lord Buddha's remains are believed to rest in Sanchi Stupa (illustration right), a UNESCO World Heritage Site. Where is it located?

   A. Tibet   C. India
   B. Nepal   D. Thailand

2. (I) What is considered the world's oldest religion? ((1) point)

   (II) What below was the state religion of various Persian empires between the 10th and 5th century B.C.E.? ((1) point)

   (III) With which religion or philosophy below are Parshvanatha and Mahavira associated? ((1) point) [max. 4 points]

   A. Buddhism   E. Islam
   B. Zoroastrianism   F. Jainism
   C. Judaism   G. Christianity
   D. Hinduism   H. Confucianism

   For (1) bonus point: With which religion or philosophy is the philosopher Laozi associated? It may or may not be listed above.

3. The pinnacle in the diagram was first found in which grimoire (or "book of spells") manuscript below?

   A. *Three Books of Occult Philosophy (De occulta philosophia)*
   B. *Key of Solomon (Clavicula Salomonis)*
   C. *The Book of St. Ciprian (El Libro de San Cipriano)*
   D. *The Lesser Key of Solomon (Clavicula Salomonis Regis)*

4. Which of the following is not a prayer bead? [max. 4 points]

   A. Japa Mala   C. Rosary
   B. Misbaha   D. They all are prayer beads

   For (1) bonus point: Britain's oldest known prayer beads that were found in Lindisfarne are made out of which material?

   A. Salmon vertebrae   C. Cod bone
   B. Whale bone   D. Human vertebrae

5. Who is not considered an "official" archangel? [max. 4 points]

   A. Uriel   C. Lamassu
   B. Jophiel   D. Metatron

   For (1) bonus point: Which commandment in the Bible is *"Thou shalt not have any other Gods before me"*?

   A. First   B. Second   C. Third   D. Fourth

6. Both or nothing. (I) Which cleansing mantra below is associated with the Heart Chakra / Anahata (the 4th chakra)?
   (II) Which is associated with the Throat Chakra / Vishuddha (the 5th chakra)?

   A. Aum   C. Lam   E. Vam
   B. Ham   D. Ram   F. Yam

O. "ENLIGHTENMENT"
(each question at least 3 points)

7. **Match the "enlightening" saying with its origin: (I) Yiddish; (II) Russian; (III) Italian; (IV) Turkish; and (V) Māori. Three correct for the (3) points. All correct for (5) points. [max. 6 points]**
   A. "There is no shame in not knowing, the shame lies in not finding out."
   B. "Even though you know a thousand things, ask the man who knows one."
   C. "A mother understands what a child does not say."
   D. "Turn your face toward the sun and the shadows fall behind you."
   E. "If you can't live longer, live deeper."

   Get (1) bonus point if at least three other teams (or individual players, as the case may be) agree that you should receive it.

8. **In Western Christianity, the Three Wise Men are named (I) Balthasar; (II) Melchior; and (III) Gaspar (Caspar). Identify the country from which each is believed to have represented. [max. 4 points]**
   A. Ethiopia   B. India   C. Persia

   For (1) bonus point (all or nothing): What were their three main luxurious gifts? (By no means am I suggesting there weren't more.)

9.

   These symbols of different religions are in the correct order only once below:
   A. Buddhism, Hinduism, Ásatrú, Taoism, Christianity, Islam, Akom, Judaism
   B. Akom, Taoism, Ásatrú, Buddhism, Christianity, Islam, Hinduism, Judaism
   C. Hinduism, Buddhism, Ásatrú, Akom, Christianity, Islam, Taoism, Judaism
   D. Ásatrú, Buddhism, Akom, Hinduism, Christianity, Islam, Taoism, Judaism

10. **The ancient Chinese divination text *I Ching* (or *Book of Changes*), an image below, consists of how many hexagrams? [max. 11 points]**

    A. 16   C. 32
    B. 64   D. 28

    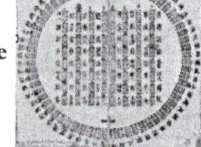

    (1) For (3) bonus points: Who is believed to have authored *I Ching*?
    A. Confucius   C. Mozi
    B. Lao Zhu   D. Fu Xi

    (2) For (1) bonus point each: Identify each hexagram below. (I) Qián (The Creative); (II) Gòu (The Royal Bride/Encounter); (III) Dà Zhuàng (Great Strength); (IV) Duì (Joy); and (V) Xián (Reciprocity).

    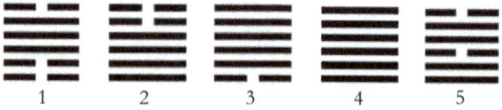

    1   2   3   4   5

O. "ENLIGHTENMENT"
(each question at least 3 points)

11. **[SUPER-BONUS QUESTION—at least 7 points!!!!!]**
(I) Match the auspicious symbol of Buddhism with its representation:
(1) Dharma Wheel; (2) Parasol; (3) Two Golden Fish; (4) Conch Shell;
(5) Lotus Flower; (6) Banner of Victory; (7) Treasure Vase; and (8)
Eternal Knot. ((3) points each)

A. Purification of mind, spirit, speech, and body
B. The teachings of Buddha
C. Long life, prosperity, balance, and abundance
D. Far reaching sound of Buddha's teachings
E. Protection from suffering
F. Interconnectedness of everything in life; the eternal wisdom of Buddha and his endless compassion
G. Happiness, impulsiveness, good fortune
H. Triumph of wisdom over ignorance, negativity, hindrances

(II-1) According to Buddhist tradition, where did Lord Buddha die? ((1) point)

A Kusinara (now Kushinagar)   C. Sarnath
B. Lumbini   D. Lhasa

(II-2) What is believed to have caused his death? ((1) point)

A. Natural causes   C. Injuries sustained from a fall off an animal
B. Killed   D. Food poisoning (tainted pork or wild mushrooms)

12. **(I) Ibadi Islam was started about how many years after the death of the Prophet Muhammad (Peace be upon Him) in 632 C.E.? ((2) points)**

A. Within 10 years after his death   C. 20 – 60 years after his death
B. 10 – 15 years after his death   D. More than 100 years after his death

(II) This country is the only one in the world where Ibadi Islam is the majority religion. ((1) point)

A. Indonesia   B. Kuwait   C. Oman   D. Yemen

13. **(I) In what country are the sacred rocks, known as the Wedded Rocks, situated? A thick, straw sacred Shinto rope connects the couple who represent the deities Izanagi and Izanami, in marriage. The rocks also are regarded as a shrine for the worship of a sun goddess. ((1 ½) points)**

A. China   B. South Korea   C. Thailand   D. Japan

(II) This temple has 1001 statues of the Buddhist deity Kannon, the Goddess of Compassion, made of Japanese cypress covered in gold leaf during the 12th and 13th centuries of the Kamakura period. ((1 ½) points)

A. Hase-dera Temple   C. Ōfuna Kannon Temple
B. Sanjūsangen-dō Temple   D. Ryōzen Kannon Temple

14. **St. Ignatius of Loyola founded this Catholic religious order.**

A. Benedictines (Order of St. Benedict)
B. Dominican (Order of Preachers)
C. Jesuits (Society of Jesus)
D. Franciscans (Order of Friars Minor)

O. "ENLIGHTENMENT"
(each question at least 3 points)

15. **All or nothing. Match the religious writings/texts/scriptures in the religion with which each is associated: (I) Shintoism; (II) Jainism; (III) Buddhism; and (IV) Hinduism.**
    A. Agam Sutras   C. Vedas
    B. Tripitaka   D. Kojiki

16. **"Simulation theory" is the hypothesis that our human existence and experiences are a simulated reality. Our existence is an ultra-high-tech computer simulation of how we live, eat, work, and love—in a *Matrix*-like world. This theory has gained much attention and proponents of it in recent years. However, a version of this hypothesis was first theorized by a philosopher/physicist below, who said: "*It is possible that I am dreaming right now and that all of my perceptions are false.*"**
    A. Neil deGrasse Tyson   C. Nick Bostrom
    B. René Descartes   D. Hans Moravec

17. **This Hindu deity is known also as the "Preserver." He is one of the supreme deities in the Hindu Trimurti. [max. 6 points]**
    A. Brahma   C. Shiva
    B. Krishna   D. Vishnu

    For (1) bonus point each: Who are his three wives/consorts?

18. **(I) The image on the right is an example of which type of tattoo? ((1) point)**
    A. Tatau   D. Mehndi
    B. Sak Yant   E. Horimono
    C. Tā Moko

    (II) Match the other above-named tattoos with the country or ethnic group below with which each is associated. ((½) point each)
    (1) Japan   (3) Samoa   (5) Thailand
    (2) Māori   (4) India

19. **The dreamcatcher, a talisman to keep away nightmares, especially from children, was and remains sacred to Native Americans. In which tribe did it originate?**
    A. The Ojibwe Nation   C. The Cherokee Nation
    B. The Lakota Nation   D. The Navajo Nation

20. **All or nothing. What do the master numbers 11, 22, and 33, respectively, symbolize in numerology? [max. 5 points]**
    A. Master Teacher—pure love, wisdom, understanding, altruistic
    B. Master Intuitive—intuition, spiritual awakening, insight
    C. Master Builder—creates something out of nothing, disciplined

    For (2) bonus points: Who is credited with starting the field of numerology?
    A. Plato   C. Archimedes
    B. Pythagoras   D. Aryabhata I

O. "ENLIGHTENMENT"
                    (each question at least 3 points)

21. **(I) Methuselah, a biblical patriarchal figure, pivotal in Judaism, Christianity, and Islam, lived to which age? ((2) points) [max. 6 points]**

   A. 365   B. 528   C. 867   D. 969

   (II) Of whom was he a grandfather? ((1) point)

   A. David   C. Lamech
   B. Noah   D. Enoch

   (I) For (1) bonus point: Who was Methuselah's father? He is listed above.

   (II) For (2) bonus points: Who was Methuselah's mother?

   A. Eve   C. Edna
   B. Betenos   D. Lilith

22. **Match the following statement with the person who made it:**
   "I have held and hold souls to be immortal….[Catholics teach] they do not pass from body to body, but go to Paradise, Purgatory or Hell. But I have reasoned deeply, and, speaking as a philosopher, since the soul is not found without body and yet is not body, it may be in one body or in another, and pass from body to body. This, if it be not [proved] true, seems at least likely, according to the opinion of Pythagoras…."

   A. Giordano Bruno (1548 - 1600)
   B. Leonardo da Vinci (1452 - 1519)
   C. Paracelsus (1493 - 1541)
   D. Edmund Spenser (1552? - 1599)

23. **This Jewish festival commemorates the Maccabean Revolt. The religious holiday celebrates the revolt against Antiochus IV, the Seleucid leader who invaded Judea and built an altar to Zeus in the Second Temple. Celebrations of this holiday include gift giving, playing a game using a dreidel, and eating latkes.**

   A. Purim   C. Sukkot
   B. Hanukkah   D. Rosh Hashanah

24. **This Chinese philosopher and political adviser advocated for the adherence to Zhou cultural forms and beliefs. He compiled *The Book of Rites*. *The Analects* is a written record of his life, sayings, and principles by his disciples.**

   A. Confucius   C. Mencius
   B. Lao Tzu   D. Xunzi

25. **The Cathars strongly held all of the following beliefs except: [max. 6 points]**

   A. Abstinence   D. Cosmic dualism
   B. Marriages were encouraged E. Equality of men and women
   C. Reincarnation   F. Vegetarianism

   (I) For (1) bonus point: In what country did they mainly live?

   (II) For (2) bonus points: What was another name by which they were known?

O. "ENLIGHTENMENT"
(each question at least 3 points)

26. **What is believed to be the first Christmas hymn? [max. 7 points]**
    A. "Resonet in laudibus" ("Let the voice of praise resound" / "Christ was born on Christmas Day")
    B. "O Holy Night" originally "Minuit, Chrétiens" ("Midnight, Christians")
    C. "Adeste Fideles" ("O Come, All Ye Faithful")
    D. "Jesus Refulsit Omnium" ("Jesus, Light of All Nations")

    For (2) bonus points: What was one controversy about the Christmas carol "O Holy Night" whose lyrics focused on humanity and championed humility? If you identify three controversies, you earn instead (4) bonus points.

27. **Match the following statement with the person who made it:**
    "[T]he doctrine of metempsychosis is, above all, neither absurd nor useless....It is not more surprising to be born twice than once; everything in nature is resurrection."
    A. Henry Fielding (1707 - 1754)
    B. Voltaire (1694 - 1778)
    C. David Hume (1711 - 1776)
    D. Benjamin Franklin (1706 - 1790)

28. **This Moabite woman refused to leave her also widowed mother-in-law Naomi over returning to her family. She declared:** *"Where you go, I will go, where you lodge, I will lodge; your people shall be my people, and your God my God. Where you die, I will die—there will I be buried."*
    She is one of two women to have a book in the Bible named for her. She is considered a symbol of abiding loyalty and devotion. Who is she?
    A. Sarah   C. Ruth
    B. Deborah (the Prophetess) D. Esther

29. **In which canonical gospel of the Bible is the text:** *"Beware of false prophets who come to you in the guise of sheep, but inwardly they are ferocious wolves. By their fruit you will recognize them."* **[max. 7 points]**
    A. Matthew   B. Mark   C. Luke   D. John

    For (2) bonus points each:
    (I) Who above is considered to have written the first gospel?

    (II) Until the 19th century, who was regarded as having written the first gospel?

30. **Who was the first Sikh Guru? [max. 7 points]**
    A. Guru Ram Das   C. Guru Nanak
    B. Guru Amar Das Ji   D. Guru Angad

    For (2) bonus points each:
    (I) Which Sikh Guru above composed the *Laavan*—the Sikh wedding ceremony song, as well as the four "Engagement Shabads"?

    (II) Which Sikh Guru above composed the *Anand Sahib* (the Song of Bliss), which is one of the five daily prayers for someone who has taken *Amrit*?

O. "ENLIGHTENMENT"
(each question at least 3 points)

31. **Which date has not been put forth as the actual date of birth of the Lord Jesus?**

    A. March 20
    B. March 27
    C. April 6
    D. April 17
    E. July 30
    F. September 17

32. **The supreme deity of this early religion is Ahura Mazda ("Lord of Wisdom"). One of the most important prayers is the "Ashem Vohu":** *"Righteousness is the best. It is happiness. Happiness comes to the person who is righteous for the sake of righteousness alone."*

    A. Taoism
    B. Judaism
    C. Islam
    D. Zoroastrianism

33. **Answer any of the two questions for (3) points, both correctly for (8) points. [max. 11 points]**

    (I) Match the following statement with the person who wrote it:
    "We have all some experience of a feeling, that comes over us occasionally, of what we are saying and doing having been said and done before, in a remote time—of our having been surrounded, dim ages ago, by the same faces, objects, and circumstances—of our knowing perfectly what will be said next, as if we suddenly remembered it!"

    A. Richard Wagner (1813 - 1883)
    B. Honoré de Balzac (1799 - 1850)
    C. Johann Wolfgang von Goethe (1749 - 1832)
    D. Charles Dickens (1812 - 1870)

    (II) One of the above persons wrote the following:
    "Who can tell how many times the human being lives in the sphere of Instinct before he is prepared to enter the sphere of Abstractions, where thought expends itself on erring science, where mind wearies at last of human language? For, when Matter is exhausted, Spirit enters."

    For (3) bonus points: Finish this quote. "On the other side of fear is …"

    A. Success.
    B. Freedom.
    C. Joy.
    D. Love.
    E. Bravery.
    F. Life.

Answers to questions in this Category can be found starting on page 272.

O. "ENLIGHTENMENT"
(each question at least 3 points)

Category P:
"DOCTOR"
(2-point category)

1. **For many COVID-19 patients in 2020, this cerebral cortex lobe did not process or pick up information relating to taste and smell. [max. 4 points]**
    A. Frontal lobe (A in image)
    B. Motor cortex (B in image)
    C. Parietal lobe (D in image)
    D. Cerebellum (G in image)
    E. Occipital lobe (E in image)

    For (2) bonus points: Which lobe is responsible for visual processing?

2. **In reflexology, reflexology point 11 corresponds to which part of our body? [max. 5 points]**
    A. Thyroid   C. Pituitary gland
    B. Shoulder   D. Lung

    Both or nothing. Get (3) bonus points if you can say to which parts of our body reflexology points 14 and 23 each corresponds.
    A. Stomach   C. Neck
    B. Adrenal gland   D. Small intestine

3. **The cardiac pacemaker was invented in 1950 by an engineer from which country? Hint: Two heart surgeons from the same country recruited this electrical engineer to co-develop the device. [max. 3 points]**
    A. USA   C. UK   E. Australia
    B. Canada   D. Germany

    For (1) fun bonus point: Joe Cocker, the singer of the 1987 hit "Unchain My Heart," was from which of the above countries?

4. **Both or nothing. (I) The emotion of fear is associated with this organ. (II) The emotion of anger is associated with this organ. [max. 5 points]**
    A. Liver   C. Mesentery
    B. Kidney   D. Brain

    1. For (1) bonus point each: Match the organ in (I) and (II) with its respective element.
    A. Water   D. Earth
    B. Metal   E. Wood
    C. Fire

    2. For (1) bonus point: What is a rhytid?
    A. Lipstick line   C. Another name for colon
    B. A skin wrinkle   D. A gland that can cause rheumatoid arthritis

5. **Which country below was the first to fully legalize cannabis?**
    A. Canada   C. Austria
    B. Thailand   D. Uruguay

P. "DOCTOR"   127
(each question at least 2 points)

6. Avicenna's greatest work is *The Canon of Medicine*, a five-volume medical encyclopedia that was used for about five centuries in European universities. Name the present-day country in which the area where he was born is located. [max. 5 points]

    A. North Macedonia   C. Italy
    B. Turkey   D. Uzbekistan

    How cautious or adventurous are you? For (3) bonus points: Do you wish to open this vintage doctor's bag and guess the hidden question, which appears after **Q.33**? If your answer is wrong, you lose your (2) points above.

7. This is a two-part question of (1) point each.
    (I) Of the following DNA genome editing nucleases, which one is based on the bacterial immune system and is composed of two RNAs?

    A. MNs   C. ZFNs
    B. CRISPR/Cas9   D. TALENs

    (II) Which of the above comprises a DNA-binding bacterial protein and a Fok1 endonuclease?

8. All of these plants below play important roles in traditional Māori healing, which focuses on treating the whole person and not just the symptom(s). But which one of them is considered as extremely important to the Māori?

    A. Kawakawa   D. Kūmarahou
    B. Mamaku   E. Harakeke
    C. Mānuka

9. The Solfeggio frequencies have been around for thousands of years. They are associated with ancient meditational chants and sacred music to promote health and healing. Two of the frequencies (I) Mi – 528 Hz and (II) Sol – 741 Hz, respectively, are used for which health issues below? ((1) point each)

    A. Turns grief to joy and liberates one from guilt and fear
    B. DNA repair and restores equilibrium
    C. Awakens intuition
    D. Cleanses the body of toxins, and helps with problem solving and self-expression

    Fun fact: The syllables of the frequencies relate to the first stanza from a Gregorian hymn. Does it sound familiar?
    Ut quéant laxis Resonáre fibris
    Mira gestórum Famuli tuórum
    Solve pollúti Lábii reátum
    Sancte Joánnes.

10. This vitamin's precursor is beta-carotene. Chemical sources of it are retinol and retinyl ester. It is found in spinach, kale, sweet potatoes, and carrots. The vitamin supports vision health, and it regulates cell growth and division.

    A. Vitamin A   B. Vitamin B   C. Vitamin C   D. Vitamin D

P. "DOCTOR"
(each question at least 2 points)

11. It has been proven scientifically that certain indoor plants like peace lilies, spider plants, English ivy, areca palms, parlor palms, aloe vera, dracaenas, rubber plants, lady palms, gerbera daisies, and snake plants effectively clean the air by filtering and removing pollutants/toxins, such as: (I) Ammonia; (II) Benzene; (III) Formaldehyde; (IV) Styrene; (V) Trichloroethylene; (VI) Toluene; and (VII) Xylene. These are Mother Nature's "doctor" plants. (*Appreciated!*)
   For (2) points, identify any three of the above dangerous toxins with the objects where each is commonly found. For (1) bonus point each, identify the others. [max. 6 points]
   A. Toxin ( ) is commonly found in varnishes, rubber, paints, plastics, inks, oils, detergents, detergents, and floor finishes.
   B. Toxin ( ) is commonly found in printing inks, adhesives, and lacquers.
   C. Toxin ( ) is commonly found in paper towels, facial tissues, tobacco smoke, adhesive binders in floor coverings, carpet backing, grocery bags, and gas stoves.
   D. Toxin ( ) is commonly found in cleaning products.
   E. Toxin ( ) is commonly found in fiberglass, home insulation, packaging, wiring insulation, carpet backing, and drinking cups.
   F. Toxin ( ) is commonly found in stain removers, oils, paints, paint thinner, paintbrush cleaner, nail polish, and inks.
   G. Toxin ( ) is commonly used as a solvent for rubber and leather processing.

12. Name this first commercial antibiotic that Alexander Fleming accidentally discovered. Its V variant can be taken orally, while the G variant must be administered intravenously or intramuscularly.
   A. Amoxicillin
   B. Penicillin
   C. Carbapenem
   D. Cephalosporin

13. Sunlight promotes Vitamin D production, which then helps our body to absorb which element naturally?
   A. Calcium
   B. Potassium
   C. Magnesium
   D. Sodium

14. A sphygmomanometer instrument first developed by Samuel Siegfried Karl Ritter von Basch in 1881 is used to measure or examine:
   A. Blood glucose levels
   B. Ear drum and ear canal
   C. Blood pressure
   D. Anal canal and part of rectum

15. For (1) point each. (I) Which of these animals could shoot out its guts to distract and repel a predator?
   A. Sea slug
   B. Sea cucumber
   C. Seahorse
   D. Sea sponge

   (II) Which of the above could self-decapitate (you heard me!) using the "breakage plane" on its neck in order to completely regrow its body?

16. The Incas used this medical technique to relieve pressure in the head as well as to release demons.
   A. Acupuncture
   B. Cranioplasty
   C. Trepanning
   D. Lobotomy

17. This South American entheogenic brewed tea is made from the *Banisteriopsis caapi* vine along with leaves of other plants. Traditionally, making the tea follows a certain ritual process. There are varied uses for the tea, including religious, medicinal, and ceremonial purposes.
   A. Mescaline   C. Peyote
   B. Ayahuasca   D. Salvia

18. This organ stores blood and filters blood by removing old and damaged red blood cells. It also makes white blood cells and antibodies that help fight infection. Sickle cell anemia can cause the organ to scar and be sequestered, and thereby not function effectively. Also, the Bajau people of Southeast Asia have enlarged forms of this organ (about 50% larger than normal), which makes more oxygen available in their blood for diving.
   A. Heart   C. Kidneys
   B. Liver   D. Spleen

19. In the 1880s, Cuban physician Carlos Finlay theorized that this viral disease was transmitted through *Aedes aegypti* mosquitoes. He was ridiculed. His theory was confirmed to be correct by U.S. army physician Walter Reed almost 20 years later. Also known as "Bronze John," this virus can cause jaundice. A vaccine for it now exists.
   A. Yellow fever   C. Malaria
   B. Dengue fever   D. Zika virus

20. This organ detoxifies the blood in our body and breaks down poisonous substances. It regulates most chemical levels in the blood; and it excretes bile that helps digest fats and carries away waste products from it. The organ stores vitamins, glycogen, and minerals, and it synthesizes plasma proteins. Humans cannot live without it.
   A. Heart   C. Liver
   B. Kidney   D. Gallbladder

21. This chemist and microbiologist discovered that microorganisms cause fermentation and disease. He then developed a namesake process of heating certain foods and beverages to destroy pathogenic microorganisms. [max. 4 points]
   A. Gregory Mendel   C. Joseph Lister
   B. Robert Koch   D. Louis Pasteur

   For (2) bonus points: He developed vaccines for all of the following except:
   A. Rabies   C. Chicken/fowl cholera
   B. Anthrax   D. Chickenpox

22. Tens of thousands of years ago, homo sapiens interbred with each of these groups. The genetic inheritance of one of the hominins below aids survival at high altitudes, and it helps the body to cope with low levels of oxygen.
   A. Denisovan
   B. Neanderthal

P. "DOCTOR"
(each question at least 2 points)

23. Two of these scientists were awarded the Nobel Prize in Physiology or Medicine for "their discoveries concerning a novel therapy against infections caused by roundworm parasites." ((1) point each correct name) [max. 4 points]

A. Satoshi Ōmura
B. César Milstein
C. William C. Campbell
D. Yoshinori Ohsumi

For (2) bonus points: One of the above scientists was awarded the Nobel Prize in Physiology or Medicine for "his discoveries of mechanisms for autophagy," essentially how cells degrade and recycle proteins and other cellular components, and renew their content. His pioneering research has enabled a better understanding of the correlation between autophagy and health conditions and diseases such as cancer, diabetes, and Parkinson's disease.

24. The "immortal" cells of a 31-year-old African American woman with cervical cancer have been one of the most important cell lines exploited globally in modern medical and scientific research. Notably and unfortunately, in 1951, two samples (healthy tissue and cancerous tissue) were taken from her cervix without her consent or her knowledge at Johns Hopkins Hospital in Maryland, USA. The HeLa cells (as they are known) were the first human cells to survive and grow outside the body in a test tube. The HeLa cells have been used for all of the following except: [max. 6 points]

A. Development of the polio vaccine
B. Research linking human papillomavirus 18 with cervical cancer
C. Genome mapping
D. Treatments for Parkinson's disease
E. Development of COVID-19 vaccines
F. Treatments for HIV and AIDS
G. Sent into space to determine the impact of zero gravity on human cells
H. Testing potential side effects of new cosmetic products
I. C, E, and G
J. E, G, H
K. They've been used for all of the above

For (4) bonus points: What is the full name of this African American woman who lived from 1920 until 1951, and has been described also as the "Mother of Modern Medicine"?

25. All of these "nuts" have high nutritional value for humans. Which one actually is not a nut? [max. 3 points]

A. Acorn
B. Peanut
C. Chestnut
D. Hazelnut

For (1) bonus point: What then is it?

26. Argentina-born Dr. Julio C. Palma invented which of the following?
A. Cardiac defibrillator
B. Stethoscope
C. Balloon expandable coronary stent
D. Transcatheter heart valve

P. "DOCTOR"
(each question at least 2 points)

27. Which engineer co-developed the first commercial CT scanner, and later won a Nobel Prize in Physiology or Medicine for his work?
    A. Wilhelm Conrad Röntgen   C. Claude Beck
    B. Raymond V. Damadian   D. Godfrey Hounsfield

28. This physician is known for performing the first human dissection in India using Western medicine. [max. 6 points]
    A. Pandit Madhusudan Gupta   C. Charaka
    B. Sushruta   D. Acacio Gabriel Viegas

    For (2) bonus points each: (1) Which person above is known as the Father of Surgery and the Father of Plastic Surgery in India?
    (2) Who above is known as the Father of Ayurveda?

29. One of these is not a very rich source of Vitamin K.
    A. Dried basil   C. Sweet potatoes
    B. Green (spring) onions   D. Kale

30. Rufaida Al-Aslamia is recognized as the first female Muslim nurse and the first female surgeon in Islamic history. During which century did she live and practise medicine? [max. 14 points]
    A. 7th century   C. 15th century
    B. 10th century   D. 18th century

    If the above is correct, you get (2) bonus points for each correct answer below. If the above is incorrect, you get (1) bonus point for each below. For the teams that participate in the Steal, the main question must be answered correctly to receive the (2) points each bonus question.
    (I) Who was the first Native American female to earn a medical degree in the USA?

    (II) Who was the first African American female to earn a medical degree in the USA?

    (III) Who was the first East Asian American female to earn a medical degree in the USA?

    (IV) Who was the first South Asian female to earn a medical degree in the USA?

    (V) Who was the first woman worldwide to earn a medical degree?

    (VI) Who was the first woman to have her name entered in the British General Medical Council's medical register? She was also the first woman (irrespective of race) to become a medical doctor in the USA in modern times.
    A. Elizabeth Blackwell   F. Anandibai Joshee
    B. Susan La Flesche Picotte   G. Kaku Sudo
    C. Gurubai Karmarkar   H. Patricia Bath
    D. Rebecca Lee Crumpler   I. Dorothea Erxleben (née Leporin)
    E. Margaret Chung   J. Madeleine Brès

P. "DOCTOR"
                         (each question at least 2 points)

31. **SUPER-BONUS QUESTION—at least 7 points!!!!!] 2 EXTRA MINUTES. (1) Match the ancient forms of healing technique below with its origin in the table. ((1) point each technique) If you answer (1) and (2) fully correct, then you receive (3) extra points.**

    A. Lomilomi massage
    B. Vedic
    C. Qigong
    D. Shamanism
    E. Reiki
    F. Hilot
    G. Acupuncture
    H. Smudging
    I. Shiatsu
    J. Tri Hita Karana
    K. Drinking chocolate
    L. Rongoā
    M. Sowa-Rigpa
    N. Ayurveda
    O. Walking backwards

Origin
I. China
II. Japan
III. India
IV. Tibet
V. Hawaii
VI. Native American
VII. Māori
VIII. Indonesia
IX. Mayan
X. The Philippines
XI. Siberia

    (2) The first flu vaccine was made available to the public in: ((1) point)
    A. 1933   B. 1945   C. 1957   D. 1968

32. **If you "think in words," and are more "logical" and "analytical," and your partner is "visual," more "intuitive" and more "creative," you are: [I], and your partner is: [II]**
    A. [I] Right brain; [II] Left brain
    B. [I] Left brain; [II] Right brain
    C. It has nothing to do with the cerebral hemisphere of the brain
    D. "Who gives an O****?! We balance each other out."

33. **One of these India-educated physicians was the first practising female doctor of Western medicine in India. [max. 6 points]**
    A. Anandibai Joshee   C. Kadambini Ganguly
    B. Mary Poonen Lukose   D. Rukhmabai Raut

    For (2) bonus points each:
    (I) One of the above physicians was a staunch activist for female's rights of consent. Her own landmark case against her husband led to the enactment of India's Age of Consent Act in 1891.

    (II) One of the above physicians was India's first female surgeon general in 1938.

Bonus question to Q.6. Inside the doctor's medical bag, for (3) bonus points:
What is Avicenna's real name?
A. Duhh..., Avicenna   D. Oghuz Khan
B. Ulūgh Beg   E. Ibn Sīnā
C. al-Rūdhakī

Answers to questions in this Category can be found starting on page 272.

P. "DOCTOR"
(each question at least 2 points)

Category Q:
MASTERPIECES
(3-point category)

1. **This is a representation of a masterpiece by which Baroque painter? [max. 5 points]**

   A. Gian Lorenzo Bernini
   B. Peter Paul Rubens
   C. Nicolas Poussin
   D. Rembrandt Harmenszoon van Rijn

   For (1) bonus point each: (I) In which city was he born? (II) In which city did he make his living?
   A. Naples   E. Madrid
   B. Siegen   F. Leiden
   C. Amsterdam   G. Antwerp
   D. Florence   H. Rome

2. **Who created the famous painting *Black Irises III*? [max. 7 points]**
   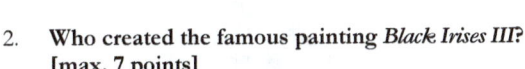
   A. Louise Bourgeois   C. Tracey Emin
   B. Tamara de Lempicka   D. Georgia O'Keeffe

   For (1) bonus point each: Specify in which country each artist was born. Options: USA, FR, ENG, POL, BEL, IRE.

3. **The masterpiece *Eagle Standing on Pine Tree* sold for RMB 425.5 million (US$65.5 million) at a Beijing auction in 2011. Who created it? Hint: A crater on Mercury is named after him.**
   A. Huang Gongwang   C. Qi Baishi
   B. Li Cheng   D. Tang Yin

4. **Who created these masterful *Irises* folding screen panels?**

   A. Ogata Kōrin
   B. Ogata Kenzan
   C. Vincent Van Gogh
   D. Edouard Manet

5. **The masterpiece below, *Miguel Hidalgo y Costilla, leader of the Mexican War of Independence*, is by a Mexican muralist who is one of "los tres grandes." [max. 5 points]**

   A. José Clemente Orozco
   B. Diego Rivera
   C. David Alfaro Siqueiros
   D. Rufino Tamayo

   For (2) bonus points: Which one of the above artists painted *El hombre de fuego* (right)? Hint: His artworks focused on social injustice.

6. **Who created the manga classics series *One Piece*? [max 6 points]**
   A. Osamu Tezuka
   B. Eiichiro Oda
   C. Akira Toriyama
   D. Golgo 13

   For (3) bonus points: Which manga artist above of the *Dragon Ball* mega series gave up drawing in 2023 after he lost the pen holder that he used to ink for 51 years?

7. **The masterpiece, *Defender of His Country*, is by an Ethiopian artist whose medium of choice was stained glass. His self-portrait was the first work by an African artist to enter the permanent collection of the Uffizi Galleries in Florence, Italy.**

   A. Alexander "Skunder" Boghossian
   B. Afewerk Tekle
   C. Wosene Worke Kosrof
   D. Agegnehu Engida

8.

   (I) In which museum is Claude Monet's *Impression, Sunrise* permanently exhibited? ((1) point)
   (II) In which museum is Monet's *Bridge Over a Pond of Water Lilies* permanently exhibited? ((1) point)
   (III) In which museum is Monet's *The Poppy Field* permanently exhibited? ((1) point) [max. 5 points]
   A. Metropolitan Museum of Art (USA)
   B. Musée de l'Orangerie (France)
   C. Musée Marmottan Monet (France)
   D. Musée d'Orsay (France)

   For (2) bonus points: In which museum above is Claude Monet's *Water Lilies–The Clouds* below permanently exhibited?

9. **This 18th-century Buddhist masterpiece painting is of which style? It depicts six bodhisattvas surrounding Buddha giving a sermon in paradise. Hint: This style tended to depict the figures in more human form.**

   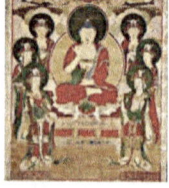

   A. Chinese
   B. Japanese
   C. Korean
   D. Tibetan

Q. MASTERPIECES
(each question at least 3 points)

10. **Which is not a National Treasure (NT) of South Korea?**

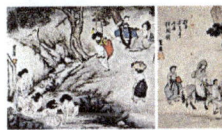   

Hyewon Pungsokdo

A. Hyewon Pungsokdo
B. Cheomseongdae
C. Wongaksa Pagoda
D. Bell of King Seongdeok
E. They all are not NTs
F. They all are NTs

Cheomseongdae

Bell of King Seongdeok

Wongaksa Pagoda

11. **From which region of the world are these masterpieces?**
    A. South America
    B. Africa and neighbouring territories
    C. Geographic Asia
    D. Oceania
    E. Central America

12. **An Andy Warhol 1964 silk-screen portrait of Marilyn Monroe was sold in May 2022 for an astronomical price at a Christie's auction. What was the price (before surcharges, etc.)?**
    A. US$145 million
    B. US$165 million
    C. US$195 million
    D. US$230 million

13. **Which of these "most valuable treasures" are still missing?**
    A. The sarcophagus from Menkaure's pyramid in Giza
    B. The Honjo Masamune samurai sword
    C. The Peking Man fossils
    D. All
    E. None

14. **(I) This famous fresco painting includes representations of the philosophers Socrates, Diogenes, Plato, and Aristotle, mathematician Euclid, and painter Protogenes. ((2) points)**
    A. *The Allegory of Good and Bad Government*
    B. *The School of Athens*
    C. *Sistine Chapel ceiling*
    D. *The Expulsion of Heliodorus from the Temple*

    (II) Who is the painter? ((1) point)
    A. Giotto
    B. Ambrogio Lorenzetti
    C. Raphael
    D. Michelangelo

Q. MASTERPIECES 137
(each question at least 3 points)

15. **Which of these missing "most valuable treasures" have been found?**
    A. The Jules Rimet Trophy (World Cup)
    B. Michelangelo's *Leda and the Swan*
    C. Raphael's *Portrait of a Young Man*
    D. Poland's Princess Izabela Czartoryska's Royal Casket
    E. None   F. All

16. **The Catholic Church banned these masterpieces except: [max. 4 points]**
    A. *Madame Bovary* by Gustave Flaubert
    B. *On the Revolutions of the Celestial Spheres* by Nicolaus Copernicus
    C. *On the Origin of Species* by Charles Darwin
    D. *The Hunchback of Notre Dame* by Victor Hugo
    E. *Critique of Pure Reason* by Immanuel Kant
    F. *The Count of Monte Cristo* by Alexandre Dumas
    G. It banned all of these   H. A, B, C, and E

    What was the name of the Church's list? ((1) bonus point)

17. **Who wrote the poems "The Waste Land" and "Ash Wednesday"?**
    A. Alexander Pushkin   C. William Butler Yeats
    B. Edgar Allan Poe   D. T. S. Eliot

18. **This mural-sized painting by Pablo Picasso was an overtly political painting in which Picasso conveyed his abhorrence of the civil war in his homeland Spain, and the bombing by the Nazis of a Spanish village and its civilian population in 1937. Completing the 132" x 300" painting in less than one month, Picasso displayed it at the 1937 Paris World Fair for the Spanish Pavilion. What is the name of this powerful and timeless anti-war artwork? [max. 5 points]**
    A. *Still Life With Guitar*   C. *Guernica*
    B. *The Weeping Woman*   D. *The Charnel House*

    For (2) bonus points: In which museum is it permanently exhibited?
    A. Reina Sofia (Spain)   D. The Louvre (France)
    B. Picasso Museum (Spain)   E. Tate Modern (UK)
    C. The Prado (Spain)   F. Museum of Modern Art (USA)

19. **Which playwright wrote the plays *The Pittsburgh Cycle, Fences,* and *Ma Rainey's Black Bottom*?**
    A. Louis S. Peterson   C. Amiri Baraka
    B. August Wilson   D. Douglas Turner Ward

20. **The author of the masterpieces *War and Peace* and *Anna Karenina* is one of the greatest authors of all time. His works influenced personalities such as Mahatma Gandhi and Martin Luther King Jr. [max. 9 points]**
    A. Victor Hugo   C. James Joyce   E. Oscar Wilde
    B. Franz Kafka   D. Leo Tolstoy   F. Samuel Beckett

    For (6) bonus points: Both or nothing. In what year below was the all-time masterpiece *Ulysses* published in its entirety? Who is the author?
    A. 1918   B. 1920   C. 1922   D. 1924

Q. MASTERPIECES
    (each question at least 3 points)

21. The epic *Shāhnāmeh* (*Book of Kings*) is considered one of the greatest masterpieces of world literature. It recounts the history, legends, and lore of ancient Persia. Completed in 1010, who wrote it?

    A. Daqīqī
    B. Daqīqī then Ferdowsī
    C. Ferdowsī
    D. Sanai

22. From which tribe or culture are the African masks and figures that inspired artist Amedeo Modigliani? [max. 5 points]

    A. Baule (Côte d'Ivoire)
    B. Dogon (Niger)
    C. Chokwe (Angola and Zambia)
    D. Vili (DRC)

    For (2) bonus points: From which country were the Kuba cloths that so inspired and influenced Henri Matisse, as seen in his artworks *Red Interior Still Life on a Blue Table* (1942) and *Snow Flowers* (1951)?

    A. Nigeria
    B. Mali
    C. Democratic Republic of the Congo
    D. Burkina Faso

23. World-renowned Nigerian Modern artist Ben Enwonwu's *Tutu* (1974) painting of Adetutu Ademiluyi, a princess and the daughter of the former Oni of Ife, was rediscovered in a London apartment. For nearly 50 years, *Tutu* (1974) had been presumed lost. It sold at auction in March 2008 for USD equivalent:

    A. $100,500   B. $275,600   C. $1.67 million   D. $2.3 million

24. New York Neo-expressionist-graffiti-street art artist Jean-Michel Basquiat (1960 - 1988) of Haitian and Puerto Rican descent was the youngest artist to take part in *documenta* (an exhibition of contemporary art that takes place every five years in Kassel, Germany) at age 21. At age 22, he was one of the youngest artists to exhibit at the Whitney Biennial in New York. One of his masterpieces below was sold for a record-breaking US$110.5 million in May 2017 at Sotheby's.

    A. *In this Case* (1983)
    B. *Dustheads* (1982)
    C. *Versus Medici* (1982)
    D. *Untitled* (1982)

25. On May 2, 2006, this Pablo Picasso painting was sold at Sotheby's for US$95.2 million to an unknown gentleman sitting near the back, waving paddle No. 1340. [max. 6 points]

    A. *Dora Maar With Cat*
    B. *Seated Woman in an Armchair*
    C. *Boy With a Pipe (The Young Apprentice)*
    D. *Harlequin With Baton*

    For (3) bonus points: What other Picasso painting named above sold for US$104.2 million just two years earlier, also at a Sotheby's auction?

26. The French author Jules Verne (1828 - 1905) is known as the Father of Science Fiction. He authored all of the books below except:

    A. *Journey to the Center of the Earth*
    B. *War with the Newts*
    C. *Around the World in Eighty Days*
    D. *Twenty Thousand Leagues Under the Sea*
    E. *The Mysterious Island*

Q. MASTERPIECES
(each question at least 3 points)

27. **[SUPER-BONUS QUESTION—at least 7 points!!!!!]**
(1) Lin-Manuel Miranda is best known for his smash-hit, Tony-award winning Broadway musicals *In the Heights* and *Hamilton*, the latter being one of a kind not seen before on Broadway. He's since created musical scores for films. Match each song below written by Miranda with its play or film. ((2) points each)

		Musical Play / Film
A.	"We Don't Talk About Bruno"	I. *In the Heights*
B.	"How Far I'll Go"	II. *Hamilton*
C.	"Keep the Beat"	III. *Vivo*
D.	"My Shot"	IV. *Moana*
E.	"96,000"	V. *Encanto*
F.	"Satisfied"	

(2) For (3) points: How many Tony Awards did *Hamilton* win?
A. 9   B. 16   C. 11   D. 13

(3) For (3) points: How many Tony Awards has Miranda won to date?

(4) For (2) points: Which character did Miranda play in the television adaptation of *Percy Jackson and the Olympians*?
A. Apollo   B. Hermes   C. Dionysus   D. Grover Underwood

(5) For (4) points: Who authored the *Percy Jackson* fantasy series?

28. **Who wrote *Crime and Punishment* and *The Brothers Karamazov*?**
A. Nikolai Gogol   C. Franz Kafka
B. Leo Tolstoy   D. Fyodor Dostoevsky

29. **Known for his photography, films, and printed fabrics, one of this Moroccan artist's most iconic photography series is *Kesh Angels*.**
A. Zakaria Ramhani   C. Hassan Hajjaj
B. Ismail Zaidy   D. André Elbaz

30. **William Shakespeare's *Comedies, Histories, & Tragedies* (commonly referred to as *The First Folio*) was published in 1623, seven years after the playwright's death. It consists of 36 of his masterpieces. Which three plays of Shakespeare are not in *The First Folio*? ((1) point each) [max. 6 points]**
A. *King Lear*   E. *The Two Noble Kinsmen*
B. *Macbeth*   F. *The Two Gentlemen of Verona*
C. *Pericles*   G. *Edward III*
D. *Henry VIII*   H. *Measure for Measure*

(I) For (1) bonus point: On July 21, 2022, a copy of *The First Folio*, originally owned by a Scottish family who acquired it in the 17th century, sold at a Sotheby's auction in New York City for:
A. US$1.6 million   D. US$6.1 million
B. US$2.4 million   E. US$9.98 million
C. US$3.2 million   F. US$11.6 million

(II) For (2) bonus points: What is the highest price paid for a copy of *The First Folio* at an auction? Hint: It is one of the amounts above.

Q. MASTERPIECES
(each question at least 3 points)

31. This Ethiopian composer (1923 - 2023), known as the "Piano Queen," was a piano virtuoso nun. For a decade, she walked barefoot on the isolated mountains of northern Ethiopia. She composed more than 150 works, including the masterpieces "The Homeless Wanderer," "Homesickness," and "Mother's Love."
    A. Bizunesh Bekele
    B. Emahoy Tsegué-Maryam Guèbrou
    C. Asnakech Worku

32. This epic poem is based on the Kurukshetra War. It describes the legendary 18-day conflict between the Kauravas and the Pandavas for the throne of Hāstinapura. [max. 6 points]
    A. *The Mahābhārata*   C. *Rigveda*
    B. *Rāmāyana*   D. *The Upanishads*

    For (3) bonus points: Name the other Sanskrit epic poem of ancient India. It is listed above.

33. All or nothing: Match three of these famous masterpieces with their Latin American and South American artists for the (3) points. If you answer all six correctly, then (9) points awarded. No in-betweens. [max. 15 points]

	Artist(s)
A. *Los Derechos de la Mujer*	I. Débora Arango
B. *La marcha de la Humanidad en la Tierra y hacia el Cosmos*	II. Fernando Botero
C. *Dos Fridas*	III. Leo Chiachio y Daniel Giannone
D. *Las Etnias*	IV. Frida Kahlo
E. *Bailarina en la barra*	V. Eduardo Kobra
F. *Nacimiento*	VI. David Alfaro Siqueiros

    1. For (3) bonus points ((1) point each): Identify the nationality of three of the artists. The artists listed in (III) are of the same nationality, so that counts as (1) point.

    2. For (3) bonus points: Which artist above said: "*En realidad no sé si mis cuadros son surrealistas o no, pero sí sé que representan la expresión más franca de mi misma.*"
    Translation: "In reality, I don't know if my paintings are surrealist or not, but I do know that they represent the most honest expression of myself."

    Answers to questions in this Category can be found starting on page 273.

Category R:
TRUE OR FALSE
(2-point category)

1. *(I) Permafrost contains a huge amount of greenhouse gases, including CO_2 and methane. ((1) point)
    A. True B. False

    *(II) Methane has over 80 times the warming power of CO_2 over a 20-year period after it reaches the atmosphere. ((1) point)
    A. True B. False

2. All of these are currently UNESCO World Heritage Sites:
    Wadi Al-Hitan, Dresden Elbe Valley, Western Ghats, Works of Antoni Gaudí, Arabian Oryx Sanctuary, and Wood Buffalo National Park. [max. 5 points]
    A. True B. False

    For (3) bonus points ((1) point each): In what three countries are Wadi Al-Hitan, Western Ghats, and the Works of Antoni Gaudí located?

3. A sloth poops once every week. It can even be once every three weeks.
    A. True B. False

4. Each question (1) point.
    *(I) The Olmecs are the oldest of the following four peoples: Aztecs, Incas, Mayans, and Olmecs.
    A. True B. False

    *(II) The Incas and Aztecs lived in South America.
    A. True B. False C. Partially True

5. The letter E is the most common letter of the English alphabet.
    A. True B. False

6. According to China and Nepal in 2020, Sagarmāthā (Mount Everest) grew by almost two metres (six feet).
    A. True B. False

7. The Amazon River is the third longest river in the world. [max. 4 points]
    A. True B. False

    For (2) bonus points: The Amazon River does not flow through Bolivia and Uruguay.
    A. True B. False C. Partially True

8. *(I) There are three species of zebras. ((1) point)
    A. True B. False

    *(II) A group of zebras can be called a dazzle. ((1) point)
    A. True B. False

9. A newborn baby scoring 8 or more on an APGAR test is a bad thing for parents to hear.
    A. True B. False

10. **The earliest Christians celebrated Jesus's birthday on December 25th because that was the date specifically referenced in the Bible.**
A. True   B.   False

11. **Whale sharks are known to be friendly and non-aggressive.**
A. True   B.   False

12. **Chi Phi is the oldest fraternity in the world.**
A. True   B.   False

13. **The publicly traded BRKa.N stock reached US$500,000 for the first time in 2022.**
A. True ("Yep, yep! Such a great investment!")
B. False ("Duhh, were you not following the market?!")

14. **The letters K and W are not native of the French language.**
A. True   B.   False

15. ***(I) The universe is a subset of ether. ((1) point)**
A. True   B.   False

    *(II) A galaxy is a subset of the universe. ((1) point)
A. True   B.   False

16. ***(I) Nijo Castle in Kyoto was built in the 17th century by Tokugawa Ieyasu, the founder and first Shogun of the Tokugawa Shogunate. ((1) point) [max. 4 points]**
A. True   B.   False

    *(II) Edo Castle, the site of the Imperial Palace in Tokyo, was built in the 17th century by Tokugawa Ieyasu, the founder and first Shogun. ((1) point)
A. True   B.   False

    For (2) bonus points: These two images are of structures from the Imperial Palace in Tokyo.
A. True   B.   False

17. **The FUNKO CHASE Edition of Demogorgon from *Stranger Things* looks like this image. [max. 3 points]**
A. True   B.   False

    For (1) bonus point: What is the name of the baby/adolescent Demogorgon?

18. **Human remains do not decompose quickly without humidity.**
A. True   B.   False

19. **Marie Antoinette was the youngest daughter of the Holy Roman Emperor Francis I and Empress Maria Theresa.**
A. True   B.   False   C.   Partially True

R. TRUE OR FALSE
(each question at least 2 points)

20. Novelist Mo Yan is the first Chinese citizen to win the Nobel Prize in Literature.
    A.   True   B.   False

21. For (1) point each. *(I) Bebbanburg (from Netflix's *The Last Kingdom*) was a real historical place. [max. 3 points]
    A.   True   B.   False

    *(II) Uhtred the Bold from Northumbria was a real historical figure.
    A.   True   B.   False

    For (1) bonus point: FUNKO released its limited edition Uhtred vinyl figure for the 2022 San Diego Comic Con: True or False?

22. Lewis Carroll, author of *Alice in Wonderland*, was obsessed with the number 44.
    A.   True   B.   False

23. When there are two or more unknowns in a math problem, only the integers are studied.
    A.   True   B.   False

24. *(I) Viking Ragnar Lothbrok was a legendary king of Denmark and Sweden. He raided England in the 8th century. ((1) point)
    A.   True   B.   False   C.   Partially True

    *(II) Viking Rollo was the great-great-great grandfather of William the Conqueror. ((1) point)
    A.   True   B.   False

25. Socrates wrote / authored two books during his lifetime.
    A.   True   B.   False

26. All of these are Romance languages: French, Romanian, English, Italian, and Catalan.
    A.   True   B.   False

27. The snailfish has loose gelatinous skin and no scales.
    A.   True   B.   False

28. Images of living creatures on Islamic architecture are strictly forbidden in Islamic art.
    A.   True   B.   False

29. Beer is a type of lager.
    A.   True   B.   False

30. *(I) There are no national parks in Northern Ireland. ((1) point)
    A.   True   B.   False

    *(II) There are ten national parks in England. ((1) point)
    A.   True   B.   False

R. TRUE OR FALSE
(each question at least 2 points)

31. *(I) Ice that forms in polar seas affects sea levels significantly when it melts. ((1) point)

A. True   B. False

*(II) Land-based ice that melts and ends up in the sea does not cause the sea levels to rise. ((1) point)

A. True   B. False

32. *[SUPER-BONUS QUESTION—at least 7 points!!!!!] (I) through (IV) is (2) points each; (V) through (XI) is (3) points each.
(I) A pumpkin is a fruit.

A. True   B. False

(II) Spain beat The Netherlands in the 2014 FIFA World Cup Final.

A. True   B. False

(III) Alexander McQueen was a fashion designer from Scotland.

A. True   B. False

(IV) Venus has no moon.

A. True   B. False

(V) Novak Djokovic won Roland Garros in 2015, 2016, and 2023.

A. True   B. False   C. Partially True

(VI) Australia is the only continent with no glaciers.

A. True   B. False

(VII) The longest word in the world is made up of 189,819 letters.

A. True   B. False

(VIII) Warmer waters have greater ability to absorb carbon dioxide.

A. True   B. False

(IX) England beat Argentina for the third-place finish in the 2023 Men's Rugby World Cup.

A. True   B. False

(X) The gale-force, westerly winds of the Roaring Forties, the Furious Fifties, and the Screaming Sixties batter the Southern Hemisphere.

A. True   B. False   C. Partially True

(XI) About 100 Greubel Forsey timepieces are handmade annually in Switzerland, and each can cost about CHF 1 million (USD 1.1 million).

A. True   B. False

33. This highly classified United States Air Force facility in southern Nevada is associated with UAP (or UFO) conspiracy theories. It officially is called Homey Airport and is located at Groom Lake. However, it commonly is known as Area 71 or Baikonur Site 31.

A. True   B. False

Answers to questions in this Category can be found starting on page 273.

R. TRUE OR FALSE
(each question at least 2 points)

Category S:
"FIRST" OR "ONLY"
(3-point category)

1. What is the only (known) bird in the world that can fly forward, backward, sideways, and upside down? [max. 8 points]
   A. Northern crested caracara falcon
   B. Hummingbird
   C. Troupial songbird
   D. Cenzontle ("Mexican northern mockingbird")

   (I) For (2) bonus points: Which country is known as the "land of the hummingbirds"?

   (II) For (3) bonus points: Name the only mammal that naturally can fly.

2. (1 ½) points each. (I) The book widely considered as the world's first novel was written by an author from what country? [max. 9 points]
   A. England   B. France   C. China   D. Japan

   (II) In which century was the novel written?
   A. 10th   B. 11th   C. 12th   D. 13th

   Earn (3) bonus points if you can name the title; and
   (3) additional bonus points if you can name the author.

3. Who is the only male tennis player to have won each Major at least three times to date? [max. 6 points]
   A. Björn Borg   C. Ivan Lendl
   B. Novak Djokovic   D. Rafael Nadal

   For (3) bonus points: As of 2024, who is the only singles tennis player (male or female) to win a Golden Slam (four Grand Slams and one Olympic Gold medal) in the same calendar year?

4. This country was the first in the world to ban the use of thin/lightweight plastic bags.
   A. Bangladesh   B. Israel   C. New Zealand   D. Rwanda

5. In which city is the world's first singularly focused artificial intelligence (AI) research university located? The AI research institute intends to develop natural language processing tools in Arabic; AI applications that address climate change and health care challenges; and other AI products. [max. 5 points]
   A. Riyadh   B. Abu Dhabi   C. Dubai   D. Doha

   For (2) bonus points: The development of the Middle East's first quantum computer is in which one of the above cities?

6. This country was the first in the world to grant women the right to vote. The white camellia flower is a hint (or maybe not). [max. 5 points]
   A. Ecuador   C. Iceland
   B. Finland   D. New Zealand

   Bonuses: (I) Which European country was the last to grant women's suffrage; and (II) In what year? ((1) point each)

S. "FIRST" OR "ONLY"
   (each question at least 3 points)

7. **In 1978, LEGO introduced this first ever LEGO minifigure to the world.**
   A. The Fireman
   B. The Birthday Party Girl
   C. The Cowboy
   D. The Clown
   E. The Police Officer

8. **(I) This company is widely considered the world's first multinational company. [max. 8 points]**
   A. Dutch East India Company
   B. Swedish Africa Company
   C. Hudson's Bay Company
   D. British East India Company

   > Rule: Answer either (I) or (II) for (3) points; or answer both for (8) points. But if you answer both and one of them is incorrect, your final points will be (1) point. *"What's your risk appetite?"*

   (II) This company is considered the world's first insurance company.
   A. The Sun (predecessor to Royal & Sun Alliance Group)
   B. Hamburger Feuerkasse (Hamburg Fire Office)
   C. The Philadelphia Contributionship for the Insurance of Houses from Loss by Fire
   D. Lloyds of London

9. **Which country's national flag is thought by many academics to be the oldest, continuously used flag in the world?**
   A. Mongolia
   B. Denmark
   C. England
   D. France
   E. Spain

10. **As of 2024, this is the only English Premier League (EPL) team to have reached 100 points in an EPL season. [max. 9 points]**
    A. Manchester United
    B. Tottenham Hotspur
    C. Chelsea
    D. Manchester City
    E. Arsenal
    F. Liverpool
    For (6) bonus points: To date, only two EPL teams have won the Treble (EPL, FA Cup and Champions League) in a single season. Name them.

11. **At the onset of the COVID-19 pandemic in 2020, toilet paper seemed almost as valuable as gold. [*LOL*] Paper was invented in China. But who created the first commercially available packaged toilet paper in 1857? [max. 5 points]**
    A. James Gamble
    B. Clarence Wood Scott
    C. Joseph Gayetty
    D. John Harvey Kellogg

    For (2) bonus points: Pre-1857, all of the following were used to wipe people's bottoms except:
    A. Seashell
    B. Marble
    C. Communal sponge
    D. (Hygiene) sticks
    E. Corncob
    F. Animal fur

12. **Waterproof wristwatches emerged after World War I. (*Does anyone on your team own a Rolex Oyster or an Omega Marine?*) Fast-forward to 1953 when the first and second modern dive watches were introduced. Which dive watch came out first commercially? [max. 8 points]**
    A. Orca Edge
    B. Rolex Submariner
    C. Blancpain Fifty Fathoms
    D. Panerai Radiomir

    (I) For (2) bonus points: Which dive watch was second?
    (II) For (3) bonus points: Which of the above was the first commercially viable dive computer?

S. "FIRST" OR "ONLY"
(each question at least 3 points)

13. **Chinese astronomers first observed this phenomenon on c. 4 July 1054.**
    A. Supernova
    C. Comet
    B. Asteroid
    D. Black hole

14. **What is the world's oldest computer?**
    A. Z1
    C. Universal Automatic Computer 1
    B. Atanasoff-Berry
    D. Antikythera Mechanism

15. **This is the first unmanned vehicle to complete a circumnavigation of Antarctica.**
    A. Salidrone (SD 1020)
    C. Anduril (Dive-LD)
    B. Planys (ROV Beluga)
    D. Kraken Robotics (Katfish)

16. **This is the only remaining completely walled city in South Korea.**
    A. Busan
    C. Seoul
    B. Suwon
    D. Incheon

17. **This Sūrah is the only chapter in the Quran that does not open with the Bismillah (i.e., the invocation "*In the name of Allah, the most Merciful, and the most Compassionate*").**
    A. 16th (Sūrah An-Nahl)
    C. 9th (Sūrah At-Tawbah)
    B. 107th (Sūrah Al-Ma'un)
    D. 55th (Sūrah Ar-Rahman)

18. **What event first occurred in 776 B.C.E.?**
    A. The first Olympics Games took place
    B. The first historic solar eclipse is recorded in China
    C. The establishment by Greece of colonies in Italy and Sicily
    D. The adoption by Rome of the Etruscan alphabet

19. **(I) Which explorer below was the first person to solo descent the Challenger Deep in the Mariana Trench? ((1 ½) points)**
    (II) Which explorer below was the first person to reach the deepest part in all five of the world's oceans, the Five Deeps? ((1 ½) points)
    A. Victor Vescovo
    C. James Cameron
    B. Dawn Wright
    D. John Rost

20. **Which artist had his/her first and only solo art show in 1917 that caused quite the scandal due to its shocking content? Police closed the show within a few hours of the opening on the grounds that seven nude paintings were obscene.**
    A. Chaïm Soutine
    C. Amedeo Modigliani
    B. Dora Maar
    D. Paul Cézanne

21. **What was the first document to put into writing the principle that the king and his government were not above the law? [max. 6 points]**
    A. The Code of Hammurabi
    B. The Salic Law of Succession
    C. The Code of Justinian
    D. The Magna Carta

    For (3) bonus points: With its 12th issue released on 29 February 2024, what is the world's only quadrennial (or four-yearly) newspaper?

S. "FIRST" OR "ONLY"
    (each question at least 3 points)

22. **All of these names except one have been associated (whether correctly or not) with being the inventor of homework or being the Father of Homework. Which one?**
    A. Horace Mann
    B. Pliny the Younger
    C. Roberto Nevilis
    D. Pliny the Elder

23. **(I) All of the animals below are among the first domesticated animals except: ((2) points)**
    A. Goat
    B. Pig
    C. Sheep
    D. Dog
    E. Horse
    F. Cow

    (II) Which bird is believed to be the first domesticated bird? ((1) point)
    A. Duck
    B. Pigeon
    C. Goose
    D. Raven
    E. Chicken
    F. Crow

24. **For (1 ½) points each.**
    (I) What was the first commercial home video game console released?
    A. Gran Trak 10
    B. Pong
    C. Space Race
    D. Magnavox Odyssey Games

    (II) When was Pac-Man introduced to the world? [max. 6 points]
    A. 1979   B. 1980   C. 1981   D. 1982

    For (3) bonus points: Go is considered the oldest strategy board game. Where is it believed to have originated 2,500 – 4,000 years ago?
    A. China   B. India   C. Japan   D. Korea   E. Mongolia

25.

(I) What is the first published modern world atlas? ((1 ½) points)
    A. Catalan Atlas
    B. Theatrum Orbis Terrarum
        (Epitome of the Theatre of the World)
    C. Genoese Map
    D. Cantino World Map

(II) What is considered the world's oldest map? It was found at Sippar, an ancient Sumerian, then later a Babylonian, city southwest of modern-day Baghdad, Iraq. In the form of a clay tablet with cuneiform texts, the world (as known at the time) is depicted as a disc surrounded by water. The map is kept at the British Museum.
((1 ½) points)

    A. Imago Mundi
    B. Kitab Rudjdjar
        (Tabula Rogeriana)
    C. Hereford Mappa Mundi
    D. The map of Eratosthenes

26. What was the first compact galaxy group ever discovered? [max. 6 points]
    A. Copeland Septet (in the constellation Leo)
    B. Seyfert's Sextet (in the constellation Serpens)
    C. Stephan's Quintet (in the constellation Pegasus)
    D. Hickson Compact Group 10: NGC 536, NGC 529, NGC 531, NGC 542 (in the constellation Andromeda)

    For (3) bonus points: What was the first humanoid robot sent to space?
    A. Sophia   B. Robonaut 2   C. Valkyrie   D. Robonaut

27. For (1 ½) points each. (I) The first beer in the world was brewed in what country or city-state below?
    (II) The process that most experts in the West recognize as beer brewing began in which country or city-state below?
    A. Mesopotamia   C. China   E. Denmark   G. Rome
    B. Germany   D. England   F. Norway   H. Egypt

28. Who is the first non-European to be awarded the Nobel Prize in Literature? [max. 9 points]
    A. Naguib Mahfouz   D. Derek Walcott
    B. Rabindranath Tagore   E. Gabriel García Márquez
    C. Gabriela Mistral   F. Yasunari Kawabata

    For (3) bonus points each: (I) One of the below is the only Nobel recipient to have won the Prize three times. Which one?
    (II) Only one of the below has won the Nobel Peace Prize for advocacy work on nuclear weapons abolition.
    A. Linus Pauling
    B. International Committee of the Red Cross (ICRC)
    C. Marie Curie
    D. Nihon Hidankyo
    E. United Nations High Commissioner for Refugees (UNHCR)

29. [SUPER-BONUS QUESTION—at least 7 points!!!!!]
    1. For (5) points: What was the first animal on Earth?

    2. For (2) points each:
    (I) What was the first whale called?
    (II) What was the first horse?
    (III) What is the oldest domesticated breed of cat?
    (IV) What was the first proboscidean that reasonably looked like a modern-day elephant called?
    (V) What is believed to be the earliest dinosaur to have lived on Earth?
    (VI) What is the name of the oldest penguin fossil uncovered to date?
    (VII) What was the first fish on Earth?
    A. Nyasasaurus Parringtoni   E. Pakicetus
    B. Egyptian Mau   F. Eohippus
    C. Haikouichthys   G. Palaeomastodon
    D. Waimanu manneringi   H. Ctenophore (Comb Jelly) or Sponge

    Until someone reveals evidence to the contrary.

S. "FIRST" OR "ONLY"
(each question at least 3 points)

30. **(I)** Nomadic warriors in Central Asia played a version of polo that was part sport and part war training. But in what place below did polo first become a national sport played by nobility and military men between 600 B.C.E. and 100 C.E.? ((1) point)

    (II) In which place below did modern polo originate? ((1) point)

    (III) The word "polo" is believed to be derived from "pholo" meaning "ball" or "ballgame" from a spoken language in which of the below places? ((1) point)
    A. Turkey   C. Persia (modern day Iran)
    B. India   D. Tibet

31. **(I)** One of the below music videos was the first rap video to air on MTV. ((1 ½) points)

    (II) One of the below was the first new wave single that featured rap vocals to reach number one in the USA. It also was the first music video with rap broadcasted on MTV. Graffiti artists Jean-Michel Basquiat and Lee Quiñones made cameo appearances in the video. ((1 ½) points)
    A. "Rapture"   C. "8TH Wonder"
    B. "Rapper's Delight"   D. "Rock Box"

32. This may be the first country in the world where parents who are stressed out (or close to being burned out) could spend up to three weeks, every four years, at a health retreat clinic for "Kur." Prescribed by a doctor...Kur. Mostly funded by health insurance...Kur. Childcare, meals, and therapies—all included...Kur. It's not to be confused with "Kinder-Reha," where the child is the focus.
    A. Finland   B. Germany   C. Denmark   D. Sweden

33. For (1) point each. **(I)** In which year did the marathon first become an event at the modern Olympics? [max. 6 points]
    A. 1968   B. 1892   C. 1900   D. 1896

    (II) In which year did polo first become an event at the modern Olympics?
    A. 1968   B. 1892   C. 1900   D. 1896

    (III) In which year did cricket first become an event? Hint: It is also the only year it was played...but look out 2028 Summer Olympics.
    A. 1968   B. 1892   C. 1900   D. 1896

    For (3) bonus points: In which year did sport climbing become an event at the modern Olympics?
    A. 2012   B. 2016   C. 2020 (held in 2021)   D. 2024

Answers to questions in this Category can be found starting on page 273.

Have you used yet your first strategy play card? It might be your only chance.

S. "FIRST" OR "ONLY"
(each question at least 3 points)

Category T:
POTPOURRI
(2-point category)

1. **To date, all of the following sports legends featured in Louis Vuitton's Core Values Campaign photographed by Annie Leibovitz, except:**
   A. Diego Maradona, Pelé et Zinedine Zidane
   B. André Agassi et Steffi Graff
   C. Michael Jordan, Kobe Bryant et LeBron James
   D. Lionel Messi et Cristiano Ronaldo
   E. Muhammad Ali
   F. Roger Federer et Rafael Nadal

2. **What is the name of the headpiece worn by the young woman? [max. 4 points]**
   A. Fascinator   C. Karimojong
   B. Vinok   D. Dupatta

   For (2) bonus points: In what country is it a traditional headwear?

3. **How well do you know luxury sports cars? Match the car manufacturer and model with the model years. ((½) point each)**
   A. AC Cars' AC Shelby Cobra, Shelby Cobra, AC Roadster
   B. Lamborghini Aventador S Coupé
   C. Ferrari 458 Italia Coupé
   D. Ford Mustang Shelby GT350R Coupe

Circa Model Year
I. 2016 - 2020
II. 2009 - 2015
III. 2017 - 2021
IV. 1962 - 1969

4. **Which is the most expensive LEGO set ever released (as of 2024)?**
   A. Titanic (10294)   C. Star Wars Millennium Falcon (75192)
   B. Eiffel Tower (10307)   D. Star Wars AT-AT (75313)

5. **Place the following in the correct order by year of acquisition, from earliest to most recent:**
   (I) Redditt acquired Dubsmash
   (II) Google (Alphabet) acquired YouTube
   (III) Facebook (Meta) acquired Instagram
   (IV) Microsoft acquired LinkedIn
   (V) Apple acquired BEATS Electronics
   A. I, II, III, IV, V   C. III, IV, II, V, I
   B. II, III, V, IV, I   D. II, IV, I, III, V

6. **[SUPER-BONUS QUESTION—at least 7 points!!!!!] Match the famous attendee / alum with her college or university. ((1) point each)**
   A. University of Exeter
   B. Cambridge University
   C. Paris Nanterre University
   D. Oxford University
   E. Tennessee State University
   F. Leipzig University
   G. University of Iceland
   H. University of Chicago
   I. ETH Zürich
   J. Dartmouth College

Famous Alumna
I. Christine Lagarde
II. Oprah Winfrey
III. J. K. Rowling
IV. Emma Thompson
V. Malala Yousafzai
VI. Angela Merkel
VII. Shonda Rhimes
VIII. Yrsa Sigurðardóttir

T. POTPOURRI
(each question at least 2 points)

7. **What is Stuxnet?**
   A. An AI start-up company with some "heavy" VC-funding behind it
   B. Supposedly a U.S. and Israeli government-sponsored cyberwarfare mission to dismantle / kneecap Iran's nuclear programme
   C. The NSA code name for the malicious hacking attacks in the USA in 2020 supposedly carried out by Sandworm
   D. A privately owned carbon capture company headquartered in Switzerland
   E. A quantum computer with 569 functional qubits being used by NASA

8. **This sport is the second most popular and played sport in the world (after Football/Soccer).**
   A. Hockey
   B. Basketball
   C. Cricket
   D. Rugby
   E. Tennis
   F. Volleyball

9. **For (1) point each. (I) The Code of Hammurabi from the ancient Mesopotamian civilization is one of the earliest and most complete written legal codes. How many laws does it have?**
   A. 111
   B. 235
   C. 282
   D. 358

   (II) What is this alphabet?
   A. Egyptian *mdju netjer* (hieroglyphics)
   B. Elder Futhark alphabet
   C. Old Türkic Script
   D. Phoenician alphabet

10. **In 2021 and 2022, Trinidad & Tobago did not host its annual Carnival celebrations because of the COVID-19 pandemic. What other year did it not hold its "greatest show on Earth"?**
    A. 1972
    B. "What a dotish question! 2021 was the first time."
    C. 1923
    D. 1961

11. **The 1980s was one of the greatest decades for dances and music. Many know of The Moonwalk because of Michael Jackson (who didn't create the dance but made it mainstream). But certain other dances were more popular. For instance, The Wop was created by B-Fats in his 1986 song "Woppit." Now match the dance below with the artist(s) who either created it or popularized it. ((½) point each) No Steals. [max. 7 points]**
    A. The Alf
    B. The Butt
    C. Cabbage Patch
    D. The Roger Rabbit

Artist(s)
I. Bobby Brown
II. Boss Patrol
III. Experience Unlimited
IV. Gucci Crew II

    (I) Even if you don't get full points above, for (2) bonus points: Perform two of these dances <u>flawlessly</u> once, while Belmont and the other competing teams judge you.

    (II) For (1) bonus point each: In which country did: (1) The Bogle originate; (2) The Butterfly originate; and (3) Chipping originate?

T. POTPOURRI
(each question at least 2 points)

12. If you were born the Year of the Rooster, your zodiac sign corresponds to which number in the 12-year Chinese astrology cycle? [max. 5 points]
    A. 2   B. 3   C. 10   D. 12

    For (1) bonus point each: To which animal does each of the other years correspond?

13. This material was used to make bracelets for Queen Nefertiti as well as robes for King Solomon, and vestments for pharaohs and popes. It is referenced in the Bible about 40 times and the Greek script of the Rosetta Stone slab.
    A. Cotton   B. Byssus   C. Wool   D. Linen

14. (I) If you (or your parents) clubbed/partied at places like the Garage, Studio 54, the Palladium, the Limelight, and the Tunnel, in which U.S. city were you/they? ((1) point) [max. 4 points]
    A. Manhattan   C. Chicago
    B. Miami   D. Los Angeles

    For (2) bonus points to (I): Who sang "Love to Love You Baby," a hit song played at these clubs?

    (II) If you (or your parents—smile) clubbed and still are clubbing in Ibiza, in which country are you/they? ((1) point)
    A. Greece   C. Spain
    B. Portugal   D. Denmark

15. (I) The ampersand was once part of the English alphabet. ((1) point)
    A. True   B. False

    (II) What type of expression is the following SB Hilarion's coined sentence: *"Quiet & jazzy philomaths believe knowledge expands cultures & life."*? ((1) point)
    A. A neologism   B. A palindrome   C. A pangram

16. Which Nirvana song is about a young man finding religion after the death of his girlfriend?
    A. "Verse Chorus Verse"   C. "Drain You"
    B. "Come As You Are"   D. "Lithium"

17. All or nothing. Match the country with its official currency below:
    (I) Samoa; (II) Vietnam; and (III) Saudi Arabia.
    A. US Dollar   B. Dồng   C. Riyal   D. Tālā

18. This educational institution's first major benefactor bequeathed £800 and his personal library of over 400 books to it. It was not, however, founded by him. [max. 4 points]
    A. Oxford University   C. Yale University
    B. Harvard University   D. Cambridge University

    For (2) bonus points: Which university above developed rapidly after English students were banned from attending the University of Paris?

T. POTPOURRI
(each question at least 2 points)

19. **Which of these Bo-Katan Kryze FUNKO Pops is the CHASE variant (that rare Funko pop variant that is always coveted)?**
    A. (I)
    B. (II)

    (I)   (II)

20. **Using the first row as a clue, what word does the second hieroglyphic spell out?**

    A. Philosophies
    B. Philomaths
    C. Philologists
    D. Philatelists

21. **What is this Native American tent called?**
    A. Teepee (tipi)
    B. Yurt
    C. Wigwam
    D. Bivy

22. **Which nation below has the fewest public holidays in any given year?**
    A. Cambodia
    B. France
    C. Colombia
    D. United Kingdom
    E. India

23. **First, a shout-out to Coney Island's Wonder Wheel in NYC and to the London Eye. What is the current tallest observation wheel in the world? [max. 3 points]**
    A. High Roller
    B. Star of Nanchang
    C. Singapore Flyer
    D. Ain Dubai (Dubai Eye)

    For (1) bonus point: Where is the world's tallest indoor Ferris wheel?
    A. Turkmenistan
    B. China
    C. Tajikistan
    D. USA

24. **All of these birds, in addition to the Dodo, are extinct except:**
    A. Elephant bird
    B. Carolina parakeet
    C. African grey parrot
    D. Great auk

25. **Who defeated the Mongols of Chinggis Khaan in the Battle of Ain Jalut in 1260?**
    A. Mamluk empire
    B. Ottoman empire
    C. Khwarazmian empire
    D. Kievan Rus'

26. **Who first argued that nothing comes into being because everything must derive from something that already exists? [max. 4 points]**
    A. Plato
    B. Socrates
    C. Heraclitus
    D. Parmenides
    E. Aristotle

    For (2) bonus points: Which Greek philosopher above introduced the three laws of logic: the law of identity, the law of non-contradiction, and the law of the excluded middle?

T. POTPOURRI
(each question at least 2 points)

27. The modern carnivals of New York City, Toronto, Notting Hill, Miami, Rotterdam, Berlin, and most Caribbean islands have their influence, "DNA," and patterns from this country's annual carnival festival. Hint: "No place like home!" "Carnival Contract!" 🎵 [max. 3 points]

    A. Trinidad & Tobago   C. Brazil
    B. Barbados   D. France

    For (1) bonus point: When you hear "Get in your section" during any of the above modern carnivals, what does it mean, other than "time to misbehave"?

28. How many full-length operas did Beethoven complete? [max. 4 points]

    A. 1   B. 2   C. 3   D. 4

    For (2) bonus points: Name it/them.

29. Which leader promulgated the Yassa law code that remained a secret, and not ever made public? No manuscript of it has been discovered.

    A. Genghis Khan   C. Ismail Samani
    B. Hammurabi   D. Alexander the Great

30. Pope Julius II hired this artist to paint a series of frescos, including *The Creation of Adam.*

    A. Bramante   C. Michelangelo
    B. Raphael   D. Botticelli

31. Which of these is/are considered language isolates: (I) Burushaski; (II) German; (III) Basque; (IV) Haida; and (V) Luxembourgish?

    A. All   D. (I), (III), (IV)   G. (III)
    B. (I), (IV)   E. (I), (II), (III)   H. (IV)
    C. (II), (III), (V)   F. None   I. (I)

32. Which country has the longest national anthem in the world?

    A. Japan   C. Greece
    B. Uruguay   D. Italy

33. This trivia question really belongs in "Jams" but brings some lyrical fun to Potpourri. In what year did DJ Kool release "Let Me Clear My Throat (Old School Reunion Remix)" with Biz Markie and Doug E. Fresh? [max. 5 points]

    A. 1995   B. 1996   C. 1997   D. 1999

    For (3) bonus points (all or nothing): Which of (I) DJ Kool / (II) Biz Markie / (III) Doug E. Fresh rapped the following lyrics in this ultimate party song?

    A. "Jamming and cramming the party people on the dance floor."…. "Let me see those hands in the air, y'all."
    B. "Yeah, rock to the rhythm of the funky rhyme."…. "Shaking and breaking, no mistaking the identity."
    C. "Can I kick it?"…. "No matter what I say, it always comes out fly."

Answers to questions in this Category can be found starting on page 274.

T. POTPOURRI

(each question at least 2 points)

Category U:
"WHO SAID THIS?"
(5-point category)

1. **This is a three-part question. Who said the following:**
   (I) "To know is to know that you know nothing. That is the meaning of true knowledge." ((2) points)
   (II) "Those that know, do. Those that understand, teach." ((1) point)
   (III) "Patience is the companion of wisdom." ((2) points)
   A. Socrates   B. Plato   C. Aristotle   D. St. Augustine

2. **"If you find it in your heart to care for somebody else, you will have succeeded."**
   A. Maya Angelou   C. Toni Morrison
   B. Zora Neale Hurston   D. Oprah Winfrey

3. **"In a time of crisis, the peoples of the world must rush to get to know each other."**
   A. Winston Churchill   C. Jose Martí
   B. Joe Biden   D. Angela Merkel

4. **"We are all one. Only egos, beliefs, and fears separate us."**
   A. Mahatma Gandhi   C. Nikola Tesla
   B. Nelson Mandela   D. Martin Luther King Jr.

5. **(I) Diogenes Laërtius *quoting* Zeno of Citium**
   (II) Dante Alighieri
   (III) Giovanni Boccaccio
   (IV) Yamamoto Tsunetomo
   Who said which of the below? Get one correct for (2 ½) points; get two correct for (5) points; get all four correct, earn "Kudos" and (9) points.
   A. "We have two ears and only one tongue in order that we may hear more and speak less."
   B. "Human it is to have compassion on the unhappy."
   C. "Eternal love made me."
   D. "It is difficult for a fool's habits to change to selflessness."

6. **"Life appears to me too short to be spent in nursing animosity, or registering wrongs."**
   A. Jane Austen   C. Zadie Smith
   B. Coco Chanel   D. Charlotte Brontë

7. **Match the quote below with the philosopher or poet who said it.**
   ((1) point for each correct answer)

Who Said It?
I. Hāfez Shirāzi
II. Saadi
III. Rumi
IV. Yunus Emre
V. Dante Alighieri

   A. "He who sees a need and waits to be asked for help is as unkind as if he refused it."
   B. "Yesterday I was clever, so I wanted to change the world. Today I am wise, so I am changing myself."
   C. "Even after all this time, the Sun never says to the Earth: 'You owe me.' Look what happens with a love like that. It lights the whole sky."
   D. "Whatever separates you from the truth, throw it away, it will vanish anyhow."
   E. "Whoever acquires knowledge but does not practise it is as one who ploughs but does not sow."

U. "WHO SAID THIS?"
(each question at least 5 points)

8. **Match the quote below with the person who said it. ((1) point each)**

   A. "No society can surely be flourishing and happy, of which the far greater part of its members are poor and miserable."

   B. "You're not to be so blind with patriotism that you can't face reality. Wrong is wrong, no matter who does it or says it."

   C. "Be realistic, demand the impossible."

   D. "The philosophers have only interpreted the world, in various ways. The point, however, is to change it."

   E. "Insults are the arguments employed by those who are in the wrong."

Who Said It?
I. Malcolm X
II. Karl Marx
III. Jean-Jacques Rousseau
IV. Adam Smith
V. Che Guevara

9. **Match the quote below with the philosopher / poet / author / political leader / motivational speaker who said it. ((1) point each)**

   A. "As we cultivate peace and happiness in ourselves, we also nourish peace and happiness in those we love."

   B. "Be courteous to all, but intimate with a few, and let those few be well tried before you give them your confidence."

   C. "Chaperons, even in their days of glory, were almost never able to enforce morality; what they did was to force immorality to be discreet. This is no small contribution."

   D. "Self-worth comes from one thing—thinking that you are worthy."

   E. "Unless it grows out of yourself no knowledge is really yours, it is only borrowed plumage."

Who Said It?
I. D. T. Suzuki
II. George Washington
III. Wayne Dyer
IV. Thich Nhat Hanh
V. Judith Martin

10. **(I) "If you want something said, ask a man; if you want something done, ask a woman." ((1) point)**
    (II) "Never feel like you have to tick all of the boxes on everything to be able to feel like you can do a job." ((2) points)
    (III) "Gender equality struggles cannot be fought selectively; they have to involve all social groups." ((2) points)
    A. Prime Minister Margaret Thatcher
    B. Prime Minister Jacinda Ardern
    C. Prime Minister Sanna Marin
    D. Prime Minister Katrín Jakobsdóttir

11. **"Who wishes to fight must first count the cost."**
    "The wise warrior avoids the battle."
    The person who made these statements was a military general, strategist, writer, and philosopher. Who is he? [max. 8 points]
    For (3) bonus points: What is the name of his famous book?

12. **All or nothing. Match the quotes with the person(s) who said them:**
    (I) Confucius; (II) King Sejong the Great; and (III) Frederick Douglass.
    A. "The life of the nation is secure only while the nation is honest, truthful, and virtuous."
    B. "Our greatest glory is not never falling, but in rising every time we fall."
    C. "The people are the roots of a nation; and the roots should be strong so as to create a peaceful nation."

U. "WHO SAID THIS?"
(each question at least 5 points)

13. **All or nothing.** Match the quotes below with the Ukrainian poet / activist / philosopher who said them: (I) Ivan Franko; (II) Hryhorii Skovoroda; and (III) Mykhailo Drahomanov.
    A. "Everything will be difficult, if there's no dream."
    B. "The preponderance of national differences between Ukraine and Muscovy can be explained by the fact that until the 18ᵗʰ century, Ukraine was more closely bound to Western Europe."
    C. "I care not if my name perishes, as long as Ukraine lives and flourishes."

14. **"If the first woman God ever made was strong enough to turn the world upside down all alone, these women together ought to be able to turn it back, and get it right side up again! And now they is asking to do it, the men better let them."**
    A. Sojourner Truth
    B. Maria W. Stewart
    C. Harriet Tubman
    D. Mary Prince

15. **For (2 ½) points each. Which physicist(s) said:**
    (I) "God is subtle, but not malicious." And years later, "I have second thoughts. Maybe God *is* malicious."
    (II) "I do not mind if you think slowly, but I do object when you publish more quickly than you think."
    A. Erwin Schrödinger
    B. Albert Einstein
    C. Niels Bohr
    D. Wolfgang Pauli

16. **(I) "There is no short cut to achievement. Life requires thorough preparation—veneer isn't worth anything." ((2 ½) points)**
    (II) "When you can do the common things of life in an uncommon way, you will command the attention of the world." ((2 ½) points)
    A. George Washington Carver
    B. Garrett A. Morgan
    C. Benjamin Banneker
    D. Sarah E. Goode

17. **"Man does not live by bread alone.... It is the mind that makes the body rich. There is no class so pitiably wretched as that which possesses money and nothing else."**
    A. J. P. Morgan
    B. Cornelius Vanderbilt
    C. John D. Rockefeller
    D. Andrew Carnegie

18. **"If I must lose because I am a woman, I want to lose like a man."**
    A. Æthelflæd, Lady of the Mercians
    B. Khawlah Bint al-Kindiyyah
    C. Lagertha
    D. Caterina Sforza

19. **Who below had the following rules included in his pirate ship's articles?**
    "To desert the ship or their quarters in battle is punished with death or marooning [abandonment on a desert island or small boat without provisions]."
    "Every man has a vote in affairs of moment, has equal title to the fresh provisions of strong liquors, at any time seized, and may use them at pleasure, unless a scarcity make it necessary, for the good of all, to vote a retrenchment."
    "The musicians to have rest on the sabbath day."
    A. Captain Hook
    B. Blackbeard
    C. Black Bart
    D. William Kidd

U. "WHO SAID THIS?"
(each question at least 5 points)

20. "How the little piglets would grunt if they knew how the old boar suffers." No Steals.
    A. Sigurd Snake-in-the-Eye   C. Björn Ironside
    B. Ragnar Lothbrok   D. Ivar the Boneless

21. "Kill them all—God will recognize his own."
    A. King Louis VIII
    B. Cistercian abbot Arnaud Amaury (Amalric)
    C. Pope Innocent III
    D. Simon de Montfort, 5th Earl of Leicester

22. "One good thing about music, when it hits you, you feel no pain."
    A. Marvin Gaye   C. Sting
    B. Prince   D. Bob Marley

23. Who ran through the streets of Syracuse naked, shouting "Eureka! Eureka!" after he discovered the law of buoyancy? He is known also for the quote, "Give me a place to stand, and I will move the Earth."
    A. Archimedes   C. Apollonius
    B. Thales   D. Eratosthenes

24. "I know I have the body but of a weak and feeble woman, but I have the heart and stomach of a king, and of a king of England too...."
    A. Queen Victoria   C. Queen Elizabeth I
    B. Emma of Normandy   D. Queen Anne

25. "I do not copy traditional art. I like what I see in the works of people like Giacometti, but I do not copy them....I would not be influenced by Giacometti, because he was influenced by my ancestors."
    A. Julie Mehretu   C. Gerard Sekoto
    B. Uzo Egonu   D. Ben Enwonwu

26. "The planet is just too small for these developing countries to repeat the economic growth in the same way that the rich countries have done it in the past. We don't have enough natural resources; we don't have enough atmosphere. Clearly, something has to change."
    A. David Suzuki   C. Vandana Shiva
    B. Mario J. Molina   D. David Attenborough

27. "I am utterly convinced that science and peace will triumph over ignorance and war, that nations will eventually unite not to destroy but to edify, and that the future will belong to those who have done the most for the sake of suffering humanity."
    A. Anatole France   C. Louis Pasteur
    B. Fritz Haber   D. Noam Chomsky

28. (I) "It is from the hands of death that people get immortality."
    (II) "All has gone to rest, and I don't know whether I'm alive or will live or whether I'm rushing like this through the world for I'm not longer weeping or laughing." ((2 ½) points each)
    A. Taras Shevchenko   C. Lesya Ukrainka
    B. Ivan Franko   D. Mykhailo Drahomanov

U. "WHO SAID THIS?"
(each question at least 5 points)

29. **"Realize that everything connects to everything."**
   A. Leonardo da Vinci   C. John Lennon
   B. Mikhail Prishvin   D. Paulo Coelho

30. **"Man is the master of his destiny and his destiny is the Earth, and he himself is destroying it until he is left with no destiny."**
   A. Joan Mitchell   C. Jaune Quick-to-See Smith
   B. Yayoi Kusama   D. Frida Kahlo

31. **"It is not events that disturb people, it is their judgments concerning them."**
   A. Diogenes   C. Epictetus
   B. Epicurus   D. Zeno of Citium

32. **"How dare you! You have stolen my dreams and my childhood."**
   A. Ineza Umuhoza Grace   C. Txai Suruí
   B. Greta Thunberg   D. Xiuhtezcatl Martinez

33. **[SUPER-BONUS QUESTION—at least 7 points!!!!!] Who said the following?**
   (I) "Kind words can be short and easy to speak, but their echoes are truly endless." ((5) points)
   A. Mahatma Gandhi   C. Mary Seacole
   B. Mother Teresa   D. Pope Francis

   (II) "The most terrible poverty is loneliness, and the feeling of being unloved." ((5) points)
   A. 14th Dalai Lama   C. Mother Teresa
   B. Florence Nightingale   D. Pope John Paul II

   (III) "I think we all have empathy. We may not have enough courage to display it." ((5) points)
   A. Maya Angelou   C. Toni Morrison
   B. Zora Neale Hurston   D. Angela Davis

   (IV) "A human being does not cease to exist at death. It is change, not destruction, which takes place." ((4) points)
   A. Pope Vigilius   C. Walt Whitman
   B. Florence Nightingale   D. Carl Jung

   (V) "Unnecessary noise is the most cruel absence of care that can be inflicted on the sick or the well." ((3) points)
   A. Mary Seacole   C. Mother Teresa
   B. Harriet Tubman   D. Florence Nightingale

   (VI) "Unless I am allowed to tell the story of my life in my own way, I cannot tell it at all." ((5) points)
   A. Fannie Lou Hamer   C. Florence Nightingale
   B. Mary Seacole   D. Walt Whitman

Answers to questions in this Category can be found starting on page 274.

U. "WHO SAID THIS?"
(each question at least 5 points)

Category V:
WHAT'S OUT THERE
IN THE UNIVERSE?
(4-point category)

1. **One of these is not a star of constellation Orion. [max. 5 points]**
   A. Bellatrix   B. Saiph   C. Antares   D. Alnilam

   For (1) bonus point: What happened during 2020 or so to Betelgeuse, Orion's second-brightest star?
   A. She dimmed dramatically
   B. She went supernova, i.e., exploded in a violent death
   C. She got much larger

2. **(I) In one of these exoplanets (i.e., a planet outside our solar system that orbits a star), it rains possibly molten glass sideways. Its winds blow up to 5,400 mph at seven times the speed of sound! ((2) points)**
   A. HR 8799b   C. Kepler 22b
   B. Kepler-186f   D. HD 189733b

   (II) In this exoplanet, its surface temperature on its hottest side is about 2427° Celsius (about 4400° Fahrenheit), while the coolest temperature is 1127° Celsius (about 3000° Fahrenheit). [A SCORCHER!!!!!] ((2) points)
   A. Kepler 10b   C. 55 Cancri e
   B. HD 209458b   D. 51 Pegasi b

3. **Each question is (2) points. (I) The universe is made up of about 5% baryonic (ordinary) matter, about 26% dark energy, and 69% dark matter.**
   A. True   B. False

   (II) How many recognized constellations are there?
   A. 74   B. 88   C. 96   D. 108

4. **This is the first plant in 2019 to have sprouted on the Moon as part of China's Chang'e program. [max. 8 points]**
   A. Cotton   B. Rice   C. Maize   D. Wheat

   For (4) bonus points: Which mineral on the Moon did Chinese scientists find while analyzing particles of lunar basalt taken from it?
   A. Scandium   C. Helium-3
   B. Changesite-(Y)   D. Yttrium

5. **(I) Neptune has how many known moons? ((2) points) [max. 6 points]**
   A. 3   B. 7   C. 11   D. 14

   (II) A day in Neptune lasts about how many Earth hours? ((1) point)
   A. 10 hours   D. 25 hours
   B. 1,408 hours   E. "Joke's on you—there's no day."
   C. 16 hours   F. "We haven't been yet, so no idea."

   (III) What is the name of its largest moon? ((1) point)
   A. Triton   B. Titan   C. Larissa   D. Nereid

   For (2) bonus points: Neptune's color is:
   A. A greenish blue, similar to Uranus
   B. A rich cobalt blue, darker than Uranus

V. WHAT'S OUT THERE IN THE UNIVERSE?   167
(each question at least 4 points)

6. Each question is (2) points. **(I) This crater on Earth's Moon is on the far side that permanently faces away from Earth. What is its name?**

    A. Copernicus   C. Russell
    B. Janssen   D. Von Kármán

    (II) Which probe did China launch in 2024 to retrieve about 2 kilograms (4.4 pounds) of samples from the far side of the Moon? [max. 6 points]

    A. Queqiao   C. Chang'e 6
    B. Tiandu   D. Queqiao-2

    For (2) bonus points to (II): Which relay signal satellite above did China launch into space in 2024 to facilitate communications with spacecraft to and from the far side of the Moon?

7. Each question is (2) points. **(I) When was the celebrity-status comet NEOWISE discovered?**

    A. December 2019   C. March 2020
    B. July 1995   D. 239 B.C.E.

    (II) Halley's Comet will be visible again in Earth's skies in what year?
    A. 2050   B. 2061   C. 2040   D. 2064

8. Each question is (2) points. **(I) The Sombrero Galaxy (M104) can be seen in which of these constellations?**

    A. Andromeda   C. Scorpius
    B. Virgo   D. Ursula Major

    (II) The Whirlpool Galaxy (M51) can be seen in which of these constellations?

    A. Andromeda   B. Canes Venatici   C. Orion   D. Libra

9. **India's Mangalyaan was the first satellite orbiting Mars to capture images of Mars's two moons. What are their names?**

    A. Athena, Apollo   C. Phobos, Deimos
    B. Poseidon, Prometheus   D. Europa, Artemis

10. **Which rocky exoplanet was the first to be confirmed by the James Webb Space Telescope in early 2023? [max. 11 points]**
    A. EPIC 201170410.02 (K2-327)   C. LHS 475 b
    B. Kepler-1649c   D. TOI 700 d

    (I) For (2) bonus points each: Which two exoplanets above are good matches to Earth in terms of size, temperature, and habitability? Each orbits in its star's habitable zone, so it possibly could support water.

    (II) For (3) bonus points: Detected in 2017, what can "Oumuamua" be?
    A. A cigar-shaped interstellar alien spaceship
    B. Interstellar "dandelion seeds" probes used for exploration of our planet
    C. A comet-like space rock releasing hydrogen trapped in ice below its surface
    D. An asteroid   E. An exoplanet

V. WHAT'S OUT THERE IN THE UNIVERSE?
(each question at least 4 points)

11. **Each question is (2) points. (I) Asteroids revolve around the Sun between which of the following two planets?**
    A. Earth and Venus
    B. Earth and Mars
    C. Mars and Jupiter
    D. Jupiter and Saturn

    (II) If energy cannot be created or destroyed (the First Law of Thermodynamics), why do stars shine?
    A. Because of God, and God alone
    B. Because nuclear fusion transforms mass to energy
    C. We don't know but the James Webb Space Telescope will inform us now that it's launched into space
    D. Because of a fusion of solar radiation, solar wind, hydrogen, and nitrogen

12. **This astronomical object can be found between a planet and a star. A typical object has a mass of about 60 to 80 times that of Jupiter. What is this failed star that does not have enough mass to perform a normal hydrogen fusion?**
    A. Asteroid
    B. Brown dwarf planet
    C. Comet
    D. Red dwarf planet

13. **(I) Astronomers Reinhard Genzel and Andrea Ghez, and mathematician Roger Penrose were awarded the 2020 Nobel Prize in Physics. The first two received it for their discovery of which super-massive black hole at the center of the Milky Way Galaxy? ((2) points)**
    A. TON 618
    B. Sagittarius B2
    C. Sagittarius A*
    D. Monoceros (The Unicorn)

    (II) Penrose won the other half of the Nobel Prize for proving that black hole formation is a robust prediction of which of Albert Einstein's theories of relativity: [A] General, or [B] Special? ((2) points)

14. **Each question is (2) points. (I) This is the largest and most massive moon in the solar system.**
    A. Ganymede
    B. Titan
    C. Earth's Moon
    D. Europa

    (II) The above moon orbits which planet?
    A. Earth
    B. Saturn
    C. Jupiter
    D. Neptune

15. **This major spiral galaxy is closest to the Milky Way.**
    A. Andromeda Galaxy
    B. Draco II Galaxy
    C. Triangulum Galaxy
    D. Cigar Galaxy

16. **This astronomical body in the Kuiper Belt has moons called Charon, Hydra, Kerberos, Nix, and Styx.**
    A. Eris
    B. Ceres
    C. Makemake
    D. Pluto

17. **Astronomers and physicists hypothesize that which two planets rain diamonds?**
    A. Neptune and Uranus
    B. Jupiter and Venus
    C. Mercury and Neptune
    D. Venus and Uranus

V. WHAT'S OUT THERE IN THE UNIVERSE?

(each question at least 4 points)

18. This planet is: (a) the smallest in the solar system; (b) shrinking; (c) the most cratered in the solar system; and (d) the second densest planet. It also has the shortest year.
    A. Earth   B. Mercury   C. Venus   D. Uranus

19. Each question is (2) points. (I) With the exception of Ariel, Belinda, and Umbriel, all of Uranus's other known moons are named after characters from William Shakespeare's plays.
    A. True   B. False

    (II) From what are the names Ariel, Belinda, and Umbriel taken?
    A. Norse gods and goddesses
    B. Celtic mythology
    C. William Shakespeare's plays in *The First Folio*
    D. Alexander Pope's poem "The Rape of the Lock"

20. One of the below is not one of the known stages of the Universe.
    A. Primordial Era   D. Infinity Era
    B. Stelliferous Era   E. Degenerate Era
    C. Dark Era   F. Black Hole Era

21. (I) What is Mars's south pole called? ((2) points) [max. 6 points]
    A. Planum Australe   B. Planum Boreum

    (II) What is known to lie beneath the permanent carbon dioxide ice cap of Mars's south pole? ((2) points)
    A. Helium   C. Argon
    B. Water   D. Nickel

    For (2) bonus points: How many south poles does Jupiter have?
    A. Duhh…1   B. 2   C. 3   D. 4

22. This region is named after a Dutch astronomer who discovered it. It is considered the outermost region of the solar system. It is believed that comets originate from the region.
    A. Interstellar Medium (ISM)   C. Large Magellanic Cloud (LMC)
    B. Kuiper Belt   D. Oort Cloud (or Öpik-Oort Cloud)

23. What is the tallest and largest known mountain in the solar system? No Steals.
    A. Mauna Kea   C. Tharsis Montes
    B. Olympus Mons   D. Rheasilvia

24. Match any four galaxies with their constellation below. (I) Porpoise Galaxy; (II) Messier 81 Galaxy; (III) Backward Galaxy; (IV) Sunflower Galaxy; and (V) Tadpole Galaxy. ((1) point each) [max. 6 points]
    A. Canes Venatici   D. Ursa Major
    B. Hydra   E. Orion
    C. Centaurus   F. Draco

    If you answer all four correctly, for (2) bonus points: Which constellation above is associated with the fifth remaining galaxy?

170   V. WHAT'S OUT THERE IN THE UNIVERSE?
         (each question at least 4 points)

25. This planet has a lot of helium. Humans cannot stand on it. Its thin yet huge rings are made up of ice, dust, and rock. It is very windy, e.g., winds can travel as fast as 1,800 km/hr (1,118 miles/hr) around its equator. One year is more than 29 Earth years.
   A. Venus   B. Uranus   C. Jupiter   D. Saturn

26. Enormous fragments of this object collided with Jupiter in July 1994.
   A. Comet P/Shoemaker-Levy 9   C. Halley's Comet
   B. Comet Hale-Bopp   D. Comet Hyakutake

27. (I) A third exoplanet, Proxima d, has been detected orbiting Proxima Centauri, Earth's closest stellar neighbor. In which solar system that is only 4.3 light-years from Earth is Proxima Centauri? ((3) points)
   A. Kruger 60   C. 61 Cygni
   B. Alpha Canis Majoris D. Alpha Centauri

   (II) Of the three exoplanets thus far detected, which one orbits in the habitable zone around its host star? ((1) point)
   A. Proxima b   C. Proxima d
   B. Proxima c

28. Each question is (2) points. (I) Which nation was the first to launch a satellite into space?
   A. USA   C. USSR   E. China
   B. UK   D. Germany

   (II) Which nation was the first to have a successful spacecraft reach Mars on its maiden attempt and the first nation to land a space mission near to the south pole of the Moon?
   A. Russia   C. Japan   E. China
   B. India   D. USA

29. Which moon in the solar system has a substantial nitrogen atmosphere, though we cannot breathe on it plus the moon is brutally cold?
   A. Earth's Moon   C. Titan
   B. Phobos   D. Triton

30. Which large M-type asteroid is believed to contain minerals such as metallic iron, nickel, and gold, estimated to be worth about US$10 quintillion? We'll know for sure once NASA's spacecraft launched on 13 October 2023 reaches this asteroid around August 2029. [max. 5 points]
   A. 1986 DA   C. 22 Kalliope
   B. 21 Lutetia D. 16 Psyche

   For (1) bonus point: Which fashion house is designing the spacesuits for NASA's mission to the Moon?

31. Which large C-type asteroid is estimated to contain about US$27 quintillion (i.e., $27,000,000,000,000,000,000!) worth of precious minerals, such as gold, nickel, iron, cobalt, and water?
   A. 162173 Ryugu   C. 52 Europa
   B. 511 Davida   D. 10 Hygiea

V. WHAT'S OUT THERE IN THE UNIVERSE?

(each question at least 4 points)

32. What is the brightest star in Earth's night sky? It is about 8.6 light-years away from Earth. It has a mass that is two times that of the Sun. The three stars of Orion's Belt always point south directly to it. [max. 6 points]

A. Sirius A (in constellation Canis Major)
B. Sirius B (in constellation Canis Major)
C. Arcturus (in constellation Boötes)
D. Canopus (in constellation Carina)

For (2) bonus points: Which is the second brightest star in Earth's night sky?

33. [SUPER-BONUS QUESTION—at least 7 points!!!!!] 2 EXTRA HUMAN MINUTES to answer. A light-year is the distance that light can travel in one year. Light travels about 5.88 trillion miles / 9.46 trillion kilometres per year. Earth is approximately 8.3 light-minutes (about 93 million miles / 150 million kilometres) away from the Sun. Thus, we always see the Sun as it was about 8.3 minutes ago. *Cool!*

1. The Moon is approximately how far from Earth? ((4) points)

A. 1 light-minute away
B. 1.3 light-seconds away
C. 1.8 light-seconds away
D. 3 light-minutes away

2. Light travels at a speed of approximately (to the nearest round number) per second: ((3) points)

A. 186,000 miles / 300,000 kilometres
B. 250,000 miles / 402,000 kilometres
C. 137,000 miles / 220,500 kilometres
D. 346,000 miles / 557,000 kilometres

3. How many approximate light-years away is Earth from: (I) Polaris (or North Star); (II) the centre of the Milky Way; (III) Andromeda; (IV) TRAPPIST-1 system; and (V) HD1 galaxy candidate? ((2) points each)

A. 26,000 light-years
B. 2.5 million light-years
C. 40 light-years
D. Between 320 and 434 light-years
E. 13.5 billion light-years

4. The time it takes for a human to travel one light-year is approximately how many human years? ((4) points)

A. 576 human years
B. 13,823 human years
C. 37,200 human years
D. 96,700 human years

5. On 24 December 2024, NASA's Parker Solar Probe made history. It zoomed within a mind-boggling 6.16 million kilometres (3.83 million miles) from the Sun's photosphere ("surface"), at an incredible speed of about 195 km/s (700,000 km/h or 435,000 mph). This speed is the equivalent of flying from London to New York in about: ((4) points)

A. 30 seconds   B. 20 minutes   C. 45 minutes   D. 75 seconds

6. In what year did Machel Montano with Beenie Man release the hit soca song "Outta Space"? ((1) point)

A. 1997   B. 1999   C. 2000   D. 2005

Answers to questions in this Category can be found starting on page 275.

V. WHAT'S OUT THERE IN THE UNIVERSE?
(each question at least 4 points)

Category W: "MORE THAN INGREDIENTS" (3-point category)

1. **One of these is not a dumpling:**
   A. Ethiopian Tihlo
   B. Georgian Khinkali
   C. Japanese Dango
   D. Indonesian Gado-gado

2. **During which battle can the origin of the delicious Peruvian papas rellenas dumpling dish be traced?**
   A. Ecuadorian-Peruvian War of 1941
   B. Cenepa War (1995)
   C. War of the Pacific (1879 – 1884)
   D. Chincha Islands War (1864 – 1866)

3. **(I) One of these Japanese breed of cattle gives us the exquisite A-5 graded Wagyu. ((1) point) [max. 6 points]**
   A. Nihon Tankaku Washu   C. Mukaku Washu
   B. Kuroge Washu   D. Akage Washu

   (II) The four most famous Wagyu beef are: (i) Kobe, (ii) Matsusaka, (iii) Ōmi, and (iv) Miyazakigyu. Select any two and name the Japanese prefectures from which they originate. ((1) point each)
   A. Mie   D. Miyazaki
   B. Shiga   E. Kagoshima
   C. Hyōgo   F. Gunma

   Both or nothing. (3) bonus points: The Wagyu Olympics is held every five years in Japan. Which two prefectures were the winners at the October 2022 event, the theme of which was *Shining a spotlight on the power of regional Wagyu beef*? The winners are from the list of prefectures above.

4. **Fårikål is the national dish of which Nordic country? Hint: It's so special, it has its own national day!**
   A. Denmark   C. Iceland   E. Sweden
   B. Finland   D. Norway

5. **This pizza is considered "like no pizza anywhere else in the world." What is it? [max. 6 points]**
   A. Kelantan pizza (from Malaysia)
   B. Delhi pizza (from India)
   C. Malé pizza (from Maldives)
   D. Zanzibar pizza (from Zanzibar)

   For (3) bonus points: One ingredient/condiment below is added to further make this hodgepodge-of-flavors pizza so unique (other ingredients aren't specified as they'd give the above answer away).
   A. Cinnamon   C. Mayonnaise
   B. Curry powder   D. Saffron

W. "MORE THAN INGREDIENTS"
(each question at least 3 points)

6. (I) The world's largest collection of seed crop diversity is stored here. ((1) point) [max. 4 points]
    A. Andøya   C. Svalbard
    B. Sommarøy   D. Tromsø

    For (1) bonus point to (I): When did this Global Seed Vault facility officially open for collection?
    A. 1984   B. 1995   C. 2004   D. 2008

    (II) This is one of the fastest growing plants on Earth. It is the main source of food for pandas. It is a crucial element in the balance of carbon dioxide and oxygen in the atmosphere. It also withstands compression better than concrete, and it is more durable than most hardwoods. ((2) points)
    A. Wolffia (duckweed)   C. Bamboo
    B. Asian jasmine   D. Neem tree

7. What is the main ingredient in a traditional Armenian side dish called *eetch*?
    A. Amaranth   C. Millet
    B. Bulgur   D. Quinoa

8. The dish *älplermagronen* is this country's version of macaroni and cheese.
    A. Austria   C. Liechtenstein
    B. Germany   D. Switzerland

9. If you're eating authentic and locally made *kkotgetang*, *maeuntang*, *ganjang-gejang*, and *haemul pajeon* in this country, where are you?
    A. Brunei   C. Laos
    B. South Korea   D. Vietnam

10. As of October 2023, one of these four hot peppers is the hottest of them all, with an average rating of 2,693,000 Scoville Heat Units. Which one?
    A. Pepper X   C. Carolina Reaper
    B. Trinidad Moruga Scorpion   D. 7 Pot Douglah

11. Prior to amendments, all of these were the sole and required ingredients of Bavarian beer in adherence to the 1516 law *Reinheitsgebot*, except:
    A. Water   B. Barley   C. Hops   D. Yeast

12. [SUPER-BONUS QUESTION—at least 7 cheesy points!!!!!]
    1. Match the cheeses below with their origin: (I) India; (II) Mexico; (III) Nepal; (IV) Denmark; (V) China; (VI) England; (VII) Serbia; (VIII) France; (IX) Poland; and (X) Belgium. ((2) points each)
    A. Chhurpi   E. Paneer   I. Oscypek
    B. Cotija   F. Danablu
    C. Pule   G. Rushan
    D. Beaufort d'été   H. White Stilton Gold

    2. Which one is the most expensive cheese in the world? ((3) points)

W. "MORE THAN INGREDIENTS"

175

(each question at least 3 points)

13. **(I) Gunpowder tea is a dried green or oolong tea in which each tea leaf is rolled tightly into a small round pellet. This type of tea product dates back to which Chinese dynasty? ((1 ½) points)**
   A. Han Dynasty C. Tang Dynasty
   B. Sui Dynasty D. Zhou Dynasty

   (II) Who is considered the Father of Teas in Japan? ((1 ½) points)
   A. Soen Nagatani C. Saisho
   B. Eisai D. Yin Yuan

14. **(I) Noodles originated in China. ((1 ½) points)**
   A. True B. False
   (II) Linguine is made of flour and eggs. ((1 ½) points)
   A. True B. False

15. **All or nothing. Match the Norden cheeses with their origin: (I) Norway; (II) Finland; (III) Sweden; and (IV) Iceland.**
   A. Herrgårdsost B. Jarlsberg C. Juustoleipä

16. **One of these is a savory Danish open-faced sandwich.**
   A. Smørrebrød C. Stegt flæsk med persillesovs
   B. Rugbrød D. Karbonader

17. **The Okinawa diet from Okinawa Japan is one of the healthiest traditional diets in the world, with Okinawans known to live healthily to at least 100 years old. The diet focuses on high fiber vegetables, low-calorie foods, lean protein, and the *Hara hachi bu* ("stop eating when you're 80% full") concept. Which below is not a main part of the typical Okinawan diet? (It is eaten, but in low consumption.)**
   A. Purple sweet potato D. Kelp
   B. Seaweed E. Daikon radish
   C. Rice F. Turmeric

18. **If you've been feasting on the culinary delights of *Amok* (curry coconut fish steamed in banana leaves), *Char kroeung sach ko* (stir fried lemongrass beef), *Bai sach chrouk* (grilled pork and broken rice), *Samlor machu* (sweet and sour soup), and *Kuy teav* (noodle soup), in what country in Southern Asia are you?**
   A. Laos B. Indonesia C. Vietnam D. Cambodia

19. **If you're indulging in some "disco fries" with your "ripper" hot dog, in what U.S. state are you?**
   A. Pennsylvania C. New York
   B. New Jersey D. Massachusetts

20. **Keeping your pinkie down, what three items below will not be offered or served during a proper afternoon tea in the UK? ((1) point each)**
   A. Finger sandwiches E. Champagne
   B. Fish and chips F. Pastries
   C. Coffee G. Ale or lager
   D. Warm scones with jam H. Warm scones with jelly and
      and clotted cream cream cheese

W. "MORE THAN INGREDIENTS"
(each question at least 3 points)

21. Select from the two answers below to complete the statements.
    (I) Most stouts are made primarily from…. ((1) point)
    (II) Porters are made traditionally from…. ((1) point)
    A. Malted barley   B. Unmalted, roasted barley

    (III) Which of the below usually contains great quantities of esters? ((1) point)
    A. Ale   B. Lager

22. Match the cheeses with their origin: (I) Spain; (II) Philippines; (III) Greece; (IV) France; (V) Wales; and (VI) Switzerland. ((½) point each) [max. 4 points]
    A. Kasseri   C. Kesong Puti   E. Roquefort
    B. Idiazábal   D. Hafod   F. Emmental

    For (1) bonus point: Cantal cheese's origin is from which of the above countries?

23. This is Argentina's most popular beverage.
    A. Classic coffee   C. Fernet-Branca with Coca Cola
    B. Yerba Maté   D. Malbec

24. Who is the first ever sushi chef to receive three Michelin stars? He invented the technique of massaging octopus for 40 minutes for the ideal texture. [max. 8 points]
    A. Eki Ichimura   C. Masayoshi "Masa" Takayama
    B. Jiro Ono   D. Nobu Matsuhisa

    1. For (2) bonus points: Name his famous restaurant.
    2. For (3) bonus points: This city has the most Michelin-starred establishments in the world.
    A. Kyoto   B. London   C. Paris   D. Tokyo

25. Match three tortes with their country of origin / person who invented it / person for whom it was made / its main ingredient(s) for (3) points; all six tortes for (8) points. No other derivatives.

Association to the Torte
I. German origin; key ingredients: kirschwasser liquor and maraschino cherries
II. Austrian origin; first made for Prince Metternich; key ingredients: apricot jam, chocolate glazing
III. Hungarian origin; invented by a delicatessen owner whose first name was József
IV. Finnish origin; named after a Finnish poet and is typically available from January to February 5 (the date of the poet's birthday)
V. Hungarian origin; key ingredients: buttercream and almond meringue; decorated with a fondant glaze
VI. Austrian origin; named after a city; has a lattice design on the top

    A. Sachertorte   D. Esterházy torte
    B. Black forest cherry torte E. Runeberg torte
    C. Linzer torte   F. Dobos torte (or Dobosh)

W. "MORE THAN INGREDIENTS"   177
(each question at least 3 points)

26. **Match three West African dishes below with their country of origin:**
    (I) Cape Verde; (II) The Gambia; (III) Ghana; (IV) Nigeria; and
    (V) Senegal. Match all six for (9) points. No other derivatives.
    A. Egusi soup with pounded yam   D. Cachupa stew
    B. Superkanja   E. Thieboudienne
    C. Waakye with Kelewele (spicy,   F. Nkatenkwan with Fufu
        fried plantains) and fish

27. **The super sweet, mild "Kula-grown" onion is produced only on which**
    Hawaiian island?
    A. Kauai   C. Maui
    B. Oahu   D. Molokai

28. **(I) This food was illegal to eat on Friday's, most Saturday's, and some**
    Wednesday's under the Tudor's Sumptuary Laws. ((2) points)
    A. Seal   B. Meat   C. Fish   D. Porpoise

    (II) If you're in Scotland or England and you're eating traditional
    shepherd's pie, what is the main ingredient? ((1) point)
    A. Lamb mince   B. Beef mince

29. **(I) The earliest known use of cocoa, as found on ancient pots, was in**
    what country? ((2) points)
    A. Mexico   C. Honduras
    B. Peru   D. Ecuador

    (II) To what European country was cocoa first brought from the
    Americas? ((1) point)
    A. England   C. Spain
    B. Portugal   D. Belgium

30. **This is the (unofficial) national dish of Colombia. (The other dishes are**
    also *muy deliciosos*.) [max. 4 points]
    A. Sancocho   D. Rondón
    B. Lechona   E. Puchero santafereño
    C. Bandeja paisa   F. Fritanga

    For (1) bonus point: From which region of Colombia is it originally?

31. **You are on a Zoom with three friends to plan your Trivia Lime, and**
    you're each in a different country: (I) Cameroon, (II) Ivory Coast, (III)
    Kuwait, and (IV) Oman. You each are eating a local dish while you
    chat. Match two dishes below with their origin for (1) point. Match all
    four dishes for (3) points. [max. 7 points]
    A. Mutabbaq samak   C. Shuwa
    B. Kedjenou with Attiéké (flaked cassava)   D. Ndolé

    If you earn the (3) points, for (2) bonus points each: One friend sips
    (A) *Habba Hamra*, while another is drinking (B) *Gnamakoudji*. Where
    above is each beverage commonly drunk?

W. "MORE THAN INGREDIENTS"
                    (each question at least 3 points)

32. **For the Tuareg, a Berber ethnic group who inhabits southern Sahara, their traditional foods include taguella flatbread. On special occasions and festivals, their drink of choice is which of the below? [max. 4 points]**
    A. Arajira (made from millet, milk, and water)
    B. Eshahid (strong sugary green tea)
    C. Akh (camel's milk)
    D. Eghajira (made from pounded millet, goat cheese, crushed dates)

    For (1) bonus point: The Tuareg are known for their men veiling their face with a dyed cloth, the color of which comes out as:
    A. Blue
    B. Burgundy
    C. Black
    D. Banana-yellow

33. **Match four of the national dishes below with their respective Caribbean country for the (3) points. Match seven for (8) points; and all ten correctly, receive (13) points. [max. 19 points]**

	Caribbean Country
A. Green turtle stew	I. Barbados
B. Oil down	II. Curaçao
C. Curry crab and dumpling	III. Cuba
D. Keshi yena	IV. Grenada
E. Callaloo soup	V. St. Martin
F. Ropa vieja	VI. Cayman Islands
G. Fish and fungi	VII. Tobago
H. Porc colombo	VIII. Guadeloupe
I. Goat water	IX. (British / U.S.) Virgin Islands
J. Flying fish and Cou-cou	X. Montserrat

    1. For (3) bonus points: *Arroz con gandules* **is the national dish of the Dominican Republic, while** *la bandera* **is the national dish of Puerto Rico.**
    A. True
    B. False

    2. For (3) bonus points: This is the unofficial number one local snack / street food in Trinidad & Tobago.
    A. Bake and Shark
    B. Pholourie
    C. Corn Soup
    D. Doubles
    E. Aloo Pie

Answers to questions in this Category can be found starting on page 275.

W. "MORE THAN INGREDIENTS"
(each question at least 3 points)

Category X: "COMPLICATED" WORDS (3-point category)

Part of an actual word (No Lie!)

methionylthreonylthreonylglutaminylalanylprolylthreonylphenylalanylthreonylglutaminylprolylleucylglutaminylserylvalylvalyl-
valylleucylglutamylglycylserylthreonylalanylthreonylphenylalanylglutamylalanylhistidylisoleucylserylglycylphenylalanylprolyl-
valylprolylglutamylvalylseryltryptophylphenylalanylarginylaspartylglycylglutaminylvalylisoleucylserylthreonylserylthreonyl-
leucylprolylglycylvalylglutaminylisoleucylserylphenylalanylserylaspartylglycylarginylalanyllysylleucylthreonylisoleucylprolyl-
alanylvalylthreonyllysylalanylasparaginylserylglycylarginyltyrosylserylleucyllysylalanylthreonylasparaginylglycylserylglycyl-
glutaminylalanylthreonylserylthreonylalanylglutamylleucylleucylvalyllysylalanylglutamylthreonylalanylprolylprolylasparaginyl-
phenylalanylvalylglutaminylarginylleucylglutaminylserylmethionylthreonylvalylarginylglutaminylglycylserylglutaminylvalyl-
arginylleucylglutaminylvalylarginylvalylthreonylglycylisoleucylprolylasparaginylprolylvalylvalyllysylphenylalanyltyrosylarginyl-
aspartylglycylalanylglutamylisoleucylglutaminylserylserylleucylaspartylphenylalanylglutaminylisoleucylserylglutaminyl-
glutamylglycylaspartylleucyltyrosylserylleucylleucylisoleucylalanylglutamylalanyltyrosylprolylglutamylaspartylserylglycyl-
threonyltyrosylserylvalylasparaginylalanylthreonylasparaginylserylvalylglycylarginylalanylthreonylserylthreonylalanylglutamyl-
leucylleucylvalylglutaminylglycylglutamylglutamylglutamylvalylprolylalanyllysyllysylthreonyllysylthreonylisoleucylvalylseryl-
threonylalanylglutaminylisoleucylserylglutamylserylarginylglutaminylthreonylarginylisoleucylglutamyllysyllysylisoleucyl-
glutamylalanylhistidylphenylalanylaspartylalanylarginylserylisoleucylalanylthreonylvalylglutamylmethionylvalylisoleucyl-
aspartylglycylalanylalanylglycylglutaminylglutaminylleucylprolylhistidyllysylthreonylprolylprolylarginylisoleucylprolylprolyl-
lysylprolyllysylserylarginylserylprolylthreonylprolylprolylserylisoleucylalanylalanyllysylalanylglutaminylleucylalanylarginyl-
glutaminylglutaminylserylprolylserylprolylisoleucylarginylhistidylserylprolylserylprolylvalylarginylhistidylvalylarginylalanyl-
prolylthreonylprolylserylprolylvalylarginylserylvalylserylprolylalanylalanylarginylisoleucylserylthreonylserylprolylisoleucyl-
arginylserylvalylarginylserylprolylleucylleucylmethionylarginyllysylthreonylglutaminylalanylserylthreonylvalylalanylthreonyl-
glycylprolylglutamylvalylprolylprolylprolyltryptophyllysylglutaminylglutamylglycyltyrosylvalylalanylserylserylserylglutamyl-
alanylglutamylmethionylarginylglutamylthreonylthreonylleucylthreonylthreonylserylthreonylglutaminylisoleucylarginyl-
threonylglutamylglutamylarginyltryptophylglutamylglycylarginyltyrosylglycylvalylglutaminylglutamylglutaminylvalylthreonyl-
isoleucylserylglycylalanylalanylglycylalanylalanylalanylserylvalylserylalanylserylalanylseryltyrosylalanylalanylglutamylalanyl-
valylalanylthreonylglycylalanyllysylglutamylvalyllysylglutaminylaspartylalanylaspartyllysylserylalanylalanylvalylalanylthreonyl-
valylvalylalanylalanylvalylaspartylmethionylalanylarginylvalylarginylglutamylprolylvalylisoleucylserylalanylvalylglutamyl-
glutaminylthreonylalanylglutaminylarginylthreonylthreonylthreonylthreonylalanylvalylhistidylisoleucylglutaminylprolylalanyl-
glutaminylglutamylglutaminylvalylarginyllysylglutamylalanylglutamyllysylthreonylalanylvalylthreonyllysylvalylvalylvalylalanyl-
alanylaspartyllysylalanyllysylglutamylglutaminylglutamylleucyllysylserylarginylthreonyllysylglutamylisoleucylisoleucylthreonyl-
threonyllysylglutaminylglutamylglutaminylmethionylhistidylvalylthreonylhistidylglutamylglutaminylisoleucylarginyllysyl-
glutamylthreonylglutamyllysylthreonylphenylalanylvalylprolyllysylvalylvalylisoleucylserylalanylalanyllysylalanyllysylglutamyl-
glutaminylglutamylthreonylarginylisoleucylserylglutamylglutamylisoleucylthreonyllysyllysylglutaminyllysylglutaminylvalyl-
threonylglutaminylglutamylalanylisoleucylmethionyllysylglutamylthreonylarginyllysylthreonylvalylvalylprolyllysylvalyl-
isoleucylvalylalanylthreonylprolyllysylvalyllysylglutamylglutaminylaspartylleucylvalylserylarginylglycylarginylglutamylglycyl-
isoleucylthreonylthreonyllysylarginylglutamylglutaminylvalylglutaminylisoleucylthreonylglutaminylglutamyllysylmethionyl-
arginyllysylglutamylalanylglutamyllysylthreonylalanylleucylserylthreonylisoleucylalanylvalylalanylthreonylalanyllysylalanyl-
lysylglutamylglutaminylglutamylthreonylisoleucylleucylarginylthreonylarginylglutamylthreonylmethionylalanylthreonyl-
arginylglutaminylglutamylglutaminylisoleucylglutaminylvalylthreonylhistidylglycyllysylvalylaspartylvalylglycyllysyllysylalanyl-
glutamylalanylvalylalanylthreonylvalylvalylalanylalanylvalylaspartylglutaminylalanylarginylvalylarginylglutamylprolylarginyl-
glutamylprolylglycylhistidylleucylglutamylglutamylseryltyrosylalanylglutaminylglutaminylthreonylthreonylleucylglutamyl-
tyrosylglycyltyrosyllysylglutamylarginylisoleucylserylalanylalanyllysylvalylalanylglutamylprolylprolylglutaminylarginylprolyl-
alanylserylglutamylprolylhistidylvalylvalylprolyllysylalanylvalyllysylprolylarginylvalylisoleucylglutaminylalanylprolylseryl-
glutamylthreonylhistidylisoleucyllysylthreonylthreonylaspartylglutaminyllysylglycylmethionylhistidylisoleucylserylseryl-
glutaminylisoleucyllysyllysylthreonylthreonylaspartylleucylthreonylthreonylglutamylarginylleucylvalylhistidylvalylaspartyllysyl-
arginylprolylarginylthreonylalanylserylprolylhistidylphenylalanylthreonylvalylseryllysylisoleucylserylvalylprolyllysylthreonyl-
glutamylhistidylglycyltyrosylglutamylalanylserylisoleucylalanylglycylserylalanylisoleucylalanylthreonylleucylglutaminyllysyl-
glutamylleucylserylalanylthreonylserylserylalanylglutaminyllysylisoleucylthreonyllysylserylvalyllysylalanylprolylthreonylvalyl-
lysylprolylserylglutamylthreonylarginylvalylarginylalanylglutamylprolylthreonylprolylleucylprolylglutaminylphenylalanyl-
prolylphenylalanylalanylaspartylthreonylprolylaspartylthreonyltyrosyllysylserylglutamylalanylglycylvalylglutamylvalyllysyllysyl-
glutamylvalylglycylvalylserylisoleucylthreonylglycylthreonylthreonylvalylarginylglutamylglutamylarginylphenylalanylglutamyl-
valylleucylhistidylglycylarginylglutamylalanyllysylvalylthreonylglutamylthreonylalanylarginylvalylprolylalanylprolylvalyl-
glutamylisoleucylprolylvalylthreonylprolylprolylthreonylleucylvalylserylglycylleucyllysylasparaginylvalylthreonylvalylisoleucyl-
glutamylglycylglutamylserylvalylthreonylleucylglutamylcysteinylhistidylisoleucylserylglycyltyrosylprolylserylprolylthreonyl-
valylthreonyltryptophyltyrosylarginylglutamylaspartyltyrosylglutaminylisoleucylglutamylserylserylisoleucylaspartyl-
phenylalanylglutaminylisoleucylthreonylphenylalanylglutaminylserylglycylisoleucylalanylarginylleucylmethionylisoleucyl-
arginylglutamylalanylphenylalanylalanylglutamylaspartylserylglycylarginylphenylalanylthreonylcysteinylserylalanylvalyl-
asparaginylglutamylalanylglycylthreonylvalylserylthreonylserylcysteinyltyrosylleucylalanylvalylglutaminylvalylserylglutamyl-

1. **For (1 ½) points each. (I) This German word means "a certificate from a doctor to a school that a student is too ill to take an exam."**
    A. Arbeitsunfähigkeitsbescheinigung
    B. Siebentausendzweihundertvierundfünfzig
    C. Schwangerschaftsverhütungsmittel
    D. Eichhörnchen

    (II) The word "Epäjärjestelmällistyttämättömyydellänsäkäänköhän" has the most umlauts of any word in its country. Which?
    A. Estonia   C. Germany
    B. Finland   D. Norway

2. **[SUPER-BONUS QUESTION—at least 007 points!!!!!] Let's (pretend to) be SPIES, INVESTIGATORS, or ASSETS, but no lock bags required. What do the acronyms / terminologies in the table mean? Decipher eight correctly for (7) points; and all 14 correctly for (15) points (7 + "_ _ _.." (or *huit*)). 2 EXTRA MINUTES.**

Spy Acronym / Terminology
I. BIRDWATCHER
II. BND
III. COBBLER
IV. CSIS
V. GHOUL
VI. KATSA
VII. LEGEND
VIII. CHATTERBELL
IX. ROLLED-UP
X. SHOE
XI. RADINT
XII. GRU
XIII. MUST
XIV. FIVE EYES

   A. German Foreign Intelligence Service
   B. A case officer in Mossad
   C. Swedish Military Intelligence and Security Service
   D. A spy who creates false passports, visas, diplomas, etc.
   E. British Intelligence slang for spy
   F. A false passport or visa
   G. Intelligence gathered from radar
   H. Canada's Foreign Intelligence Service
   I. When an operation goes badly, and an agent is arrested
   J. Someone who searches obituaries and graveyards for names of the deceased to be used by agents
   K. Russian military intelligence agency
   L. A fake life story created for a covert agent
   M. An intelligence sharing alliance of certain countries
   N. An open-source intelligence-based service

    If at least eight are answered correctly, for (3) points each:
    (I) Which "complicated" word do the clues in the table above spell?

    (II) SIGINT (signals intelligence) equals which of the below?
    A. COMINT + ELINT   C. PHOTINT + IMINT
    B. IMINT + ELINT   D. RADINT + COMINT

    (III) If "_ _ _ .." is Morse code for 8, which number is: "_ _ _ _ ."?
    A. 6   C. 7   E. 5
    B. 9   D. 0   F. 1

    (IV) In Tatsuya Endo's manga series *Spy x Family*, Yor Briar is a:
    A. Master spy   C. Professional assassin
    B. Precognitive dog   D. Telepath

X. "COMPLICATED" WORDS
(each question at least 3 points)

3. **For (1 ½) points each. (I) This Russian word means "somebody who drank more than they should have, but less than they could have."**
   A. Toska
   B. Pochemuchka
   C. Nedoperepil
   D. Perepodvypodvert

   (II) This Belarusian word means "tolerance and togetherness."
   A. Teşekkür ederim
   B. Zahaplennie
   C. Pamiarkounasc
   D. Znichka

4. **The following is a 1,000-foot / 305-metre-tall hill in Hawke's Bay, New Zealand. Its Māori name is:**
   "Taumatawhakatangihangakoauauotamateaturipukaka-pikimaungahoronukupokaiwhenuakitanatahu"
   (*Taumata.whakatangihanga.koauau.o.tamatea.turi.pukaka. piki.maunga.horo.nuku.pokai.whenua.ki.tana.tahu*)
   How many letters make up this word?
   A. 68   B. 72   C. 85   D. 94

5. **According to the Oxford English Dictionary, one of the below is the most complicated word in English because there are over 600 verbal usages for it (645 to be exact).**
   A. cut   B. fly   C. pat   D. run

6. **Unscramble any three words below. ((1) point each for (3) points) If you unscramble all five words correctly, then get (3) bonus points. [max. 6 points]**
   A. DRAEEAMARIC
   B. YQAMIUETIN
   C. KANSAMRA
   D. MGEASDANRI
   E. HTAZKEAD

   > Related Hints (not in any particular order because that'd be too easy): a color – charity – friendship – calmness – greeting

7. **ALL-Teams play question. Which team can say the following tongue twister the best in one go: no pause, no hesitation, no mistakes?**
   "Xavier, Xena, and Xochitl each has cymotrichous, xanthous hair, and each loves eating xylocarp under a xerophyte."

   Note: "Xavier" pronounced *zay-vee-eer*, "Xena" pronounced *zee-nuh*; "Xochitl" pronounced *soh-cheel*; "Cymotrichous" pronounced *cy-mot-ri-chous*; "Xanthous" pronounced *zan-thuhs*; "Xylocarp" pronounced *zahy-loh-kahrp*; "Xerophyte" pronounced *zeer-uh-fahyt*
   A. Team Cusco   D. Team Praslin   G. Team Zermatt
   B. Team Hamilton   E. Team Rotorua
   C. Team Krabi   F. Team Vava'u

   > Teams select the winner of this question (by majority vote only). The judge shall not intervene. If there's no consensus, then move on to another question in this category.

X. "COMPLICATED" WORDS
(each question at least 3 points)

8. One of the below is a **Welsh** word that means "a hug in a loving and protective way." [max. 6 points]
   A. Eunoia
   B. Cwtch
   C. Cawl
   D. Llanfairpwllgwyngyllgogerychwyrndrobwllllantysiliogogogoch
   E. Chwit-chwat

   For (3) bonus points: One of the above is the name of a village in Wales.

9. **"Archaeopteryx"** means:
   A. The first primitive dinosaur-like bird
   B. An extinct marine mollusk with a flat coiled spiral shell
   C. The study of archeological sites
   D. A library of archives of special arcane subjects

10. Match each word in the table with its meaning. ((1) point each)
    A. Habitual
    B. Lying
    C. Showing sorrow

"Complicated" word
I. Mendacious
II. Inveterate
III. Dolorous

11. I don't know how complicated is the following language, but it is a UNESCO classified "critically endangered language." In what country is the dialect **Griko** spoken in certain villages? [max. 5 points]
    A. France   C. Italy
    B. Spain   D. North Macedonia

    For (2) bonus points: What other dialect is spoken in the same region of that country?
    A. Aranese   B. Faetar   C. Aromanian   D. Corsican

12. **"Ittoqqortoormiit"** (pronounced I think '*it-oh-kwa-kwaor-tow-meet*') is one of the most remote settlements on Earth with a cool, complicated name to us non-locals. In which country / territory is it?
    A. Mongolia   B. Finland   C. Greenland   D. Iceland

13. Three words are spelled incorrectly. ((1) point each) [max. 6 points]
    A. Logorhia   D. Specific
    B. Ithmus   E. Ignominous
    C. Anathema   F. Vacuum

    For (3) bonus points (all or nothing): What is the correct British or U.S. English spelling of each word?

14. A **"situationship"** relationship may or may not be complicated. With which generation is the word mostly associated? [max. 6 points]
    A. Gen X   C. Millennials (Gen Y)
    B. Gen Z   D. Gen Alpha

    For (3) bonus points: The non-complicated word "skibidi" is associated with which generation above?

X. "COMPLICATED" WORDS
(each question at least 3 points)

15. This word means "a word having many syllables; an expression characterized by long-winded words."
    A. Supercalifragilisticexpialidocious   C. Synecdoche
    B. Onomatopoeia   D. Sesquipedalian

16. All of these words are considered difficult to pronounce, even for native English speakers, except for which one?
    A. Anemone   D. Sixth
    B. Phlegm   E. Rural
    C. Boondoggle

17. One of these complicated words means "beautiful, handsome."
    A. Pulchritudinous   C. Trichotillomania
    B. Polyphiloprogenitive   D. Consanguineous

18. Which is the correct spelling of these three word-pairs? ((1) point each)
    A. Dilate   C. Acommodate   E. Fuschia
    B. Dialate   D. Accommodate   F. Fuchsia

19. Say "otorhinolaryngological" (*oh-toh-rahy-noh-luh-ring-guh-loj-i-kuhl*) three times perfectly in one attempt. ((1) point each perfect pronunciation) It is Belmont's decision. No Steals. [max. 5 points]

    For (2) bonus points: What does the word mean?

20. Which of these three words is/are <u>not</u> in any English dictionary:
    (I) Floccinaucinihilipilification
    (II) Hippopotomonstrosesquippedaliophobia
    (III) Pneumonoultramicroscopicsilicovolcanoconiosis? [max. 6 points]
    A. (I)   D. (I) and (III)   G. (II) and (III)
    B. (II)   E. (I) and (II)   H. None is in the dictionary
    C. (III)   F. All are in the dictionary

    For (3) bonus points: The word "honorificabilitudinitatibus," meaning "with honorableness," was first used in which play?
    A. Yasmina Reza's *God of Carnage*
    B. William Shakespeare's *Love's Labour's Lost*
    C. Arthur Miller's *The Crucible*
    D. Oscar Wilde's *The Importance of Being Earnest*

21. Which is the correct spelling of these three word-pairs? ((1) point each)
    A. Acquiesce   C. Consciencious   E. Paraphenelia
    B. Aquiesce   D. Conscientious   F. Paraphernalia

22. This non-English word means "to take enjoyment or pleasure from someone else's misfortune(s)."
    A. Charcuterie   C. Schadenfreude
    B. Carte blanche   D. Ipso facto

X. "COMPLICATED" WORDS

(each question at least 3 points)

23. **Match each word in the table with its meaning. ((1) point each)**

    A. Traitor
    B. Having a fierce nature; belligerent
    C. Excessively complex and intricate

"Complicated" word
I. Byzantine
II. Quisling
III. Truculent

24. **One of these "complicated" German words to pronounce means "five-hundred fifty-five (555)." [max. 6 points]**

    A. Quietscheentchen
    B. Fünfhundertfünfundfünfzig
    C. Streichholzschachtel
    D. Siebentausendzweihundertvierundfünfzig

    For (3) bonus points: Which one of the above words means "7,254"?

25. **One of these "complicated" French words to pronounce means "rubber." [max. 6 points]**

    A. Serrurier
    B. Chirurgien
    C. Écureuil
    D. Caoutchouc

    Which word above means "locksmith"? ((3) bonus points)

26. **Three words are spelled incorrectly. ((1) point each) [max. 6 points]**

    A. Liaison
    B. Burbon
    C. Narcisisstic
    D. Epitome
    E. Embarass
    F. Occasion

    For (3) bonus points (all or nothing): What are their correct spellings?

27. **This non-English word means a "quality typically used in reference to art or decorations that is tacky or in bad taste."**

    A. Hoi polloi
    B. Zeitgeist
    C. Poshlust
    D. Kitschy

28. **Match two words in the table with their meaning for (3) points. Match all four words for (6) points.**

    A. Displaying immaturity; behaving in a silly, trivial way
    B. A person devoted to luxury or pleasure
    C. So focused on one's own needs, experiences, and wants, and does not consider anyone else's as important or relevant
    D. To treat with excessive indulgence; to (overly) pamper or spoil

"Complicated" word
I. Sybarite
II. Cosset
III. Puerile
IV. Solipsistic

29. **One of these words means "something that soothes or relieves pain."**

    A. Anodyne
    B. Laughter
    C. Diatribe
    D. Curmudgeon

X. "COMPLICATED" WORDS
(each question at least 3 points)

30. Unscramble four of these statements for (3) points. Unscramble all nine correctly for (18) points. No other points offered, but you have up to 4 minutes.
    A. RCSIHEH RMHETO RETUNA (3 words)
    B. WOHS YPHAMET (2 words)
    C. OPTS BLGAOL EITMCLA HEGCNA (4 words)
    D. EGVI A MDNA (3 words)
    E. HESIETGI CSMIU SI ITL (4 words)
    F. LYUGBLNI SI AESNKSWE (3 words)
    G. EB NLAEXI (2 words)
    H. VREESER CNOAE YTDXNEONGAOEI (3 words)
    I. YMOICT (1 word)

31. **One of these words is the longest word in the Spanish vocabulary. [max. 7 points]**
    A. Subductisupercilicarptor
    B. Anticonstitucionalissimamente
    C. Precipitevolissimevolmente
    D. Esternocleidooccipitomastoideos
    E. Sternocleidomastoid

    Bonus: From what language is each of the other four words? Options: English, Italian, Latin, Portuguese. ((1) point each)

32. **Match three words in the table with their meaning. ((1) point each) Match all five words correctly for (7) points.**

"Complicated" word
I. Puissant
II. Splenetic
III. Fatuous
IV. Tergiversation
V. Cognomen

    A. Evasion of a clear-cut statement; desertion of a cause/faith/position
    B. A (descriptive) nickname
    C. Powerful
    D. Often very irritable or bad-tempered
    E. Lack of intelligence or thought; disregarding reality

33. **Love can be simple. Love can be complicated. For the (3) points, match three versions of "love" below with their origin: (I) Proto-Indo-European; (II) Proto-Germanic; (III) Middle English; (IV) Sanskrit; (V) Old English; and (VI) Latin. Match all for (12) points. [max. 14 points]**
    A. Lubet   D. Lufu
    B. Lubhyati   E. Luve
    C. Leubh   F. Lubō

    If you earn at least (3) points, for (2) bonus points: Which band told us that "You Give Love A Bad Name"?
    A. Journey   C. Bon Jovi
    B. Survivor   D. Guns N' Roses

    Answers to questions in this Category can be found starting on page 276.

X. "COMPLICATED" WORDS
    (each question at least 3 points)

Category Y:
THE ARTS THROUGH
THE CENTURIES
(3-point category)

1. **[SUPER-BONUS QUESTION—at least 7 points!!!!!] (I) Breaking was created by African American youths from The Bronx, New York in the 1970s, and they further co-developed it with Puerto Rican youths into the 1980s ("B-boys" and "B-girls"). Pioneers were Mighty Zulu Kingz (who included Pow Wow and Sundance), Rock Steady Crew (who included Ken Swift and Richard "Crazy Legs" Colón), Dynamic Rockers (and its spun-off crew Dynamic Breakers), and New York City Breakers (who included Chino "Action" Lopez and Matthew "Glide Master" Caban). Which below is not a breaking move? ((7) points)**

    A. Windmill   C. Air flare   E. Applejack
    B. Dizzy run   D. Suicide   F. Nope, they all are moves

    (II) What is the first breakdancing-themed film? ((7) points)
    A. *Breakin'*   B. *Beat Street*   C. *Wild Style*   D. *Style Wars*
    For (3) bonus points to (II): State the year of its release in theaters.

    (III) A Pike pose is an example of which Breaking element? ((4) points)
    A. Toprock   C. Power move
    B. Downrock   D. Freeze

2. **One of these structures is not an example of Baroque architecture. (The images deliberately are not labeled.)**
    A. St. Paul's Cathedral (London)
    B. Palace of Versailles (Versailles)
    C. Karlskirche (Vienna)
    D. Chartres Cathedral (Chartres)

3. **What is the national musical instrument of Japan? [max. 9 points]**
    A. Yueqin   B. Koto   C. Mbalax   D. Steelpan

    (1) For (1) bonus point each: Where did the other instruments originate?
    (2) For (3) bonus points: Which is the main musical instrument played by world-renowned orchestras bp Renegades and Massy All Stars?

4. **Which one of these operas lists the incorrect composer? [max. 6 points]**
    A. Puccini's *Turandot*   C. Verdi's *Rigoletto*
    B. Wagner's *Der Freischütz*   D. Rossini's *Barber of Seville*

    For (3) bonus points: Which is the most popular form of opera in Hong Kong?
    A. Beijing (or Peking) Opera   C. Henan Opera
    B. Cantonese (or Yue Ju) Opera   D. Sichuan Opera

5. **(I) Renaissance refers to which era of the arts in European history? ((2) points)**
    A. From 12th to 13th centuries   C. In the 15th century only
    B. From 14th to 16th centuries   D. In the 14th century only

    (II) Who is not considered a Renaissance master? ((1) point)
    A. William Shakespeare   C. Sofonisba Anguissola
    B. Diego Velázquez   D. Giovanni Boccaccio

188   **Y. THE ARTS THROUGH THE CENTURIES**
(each question at least 3 points)

6. In a prestigious art exhibition of independent artists in Paris in April 1874, French art critic Louis Leroy saw the works of these artists and scathingly exclaimed: *"They painted nothing but impressions."* However, one of the artists below was not part of this group that led to the art movement known as Impressionism. Which one?

    A.   Renoir
    B.   Cassatt
    C.   Monet
    D.   Vermeer

7. (I) What was the name of the third *Game of Thrones* book written by George R. R. Martin? ((2) points)

    A.   *A Clash of Kings*
    B.   *A Storm of Swords*
    C.   *A Dance with Dragons*
    D.   *A Game of Thrones*

    (II) In what year was it published? ((1) point)
    A.   1995   B.   1998   C.   2000   D.   2005

8. Jane Austen wrote all of the following except:

    A.   *Emma*
    B.   *Persuasion*
    C.   *Sanditon*
    D.   *Wuthering Heights*
    E.   She wrote all. You can't fool us.

9. Which famous Japanese ukiyo-e artist created the shunga erotica masterpiece, *The Dream of the Fisherman's Wife*, in 1814? (*"Too risqué to show!"*) This particular work influenced later artists such as Pablo Picasso who painted his own version in 1903.

    A.   Moronobu
    B.   Sharaku
    C.   Utamaro
    D.   Hokusai
    E.   Hiroshige

10. These classic B-boy and B-girl national anthems were ideal songs for breakdancing battles. Match two classics with their artist(s) correctly, receive (3) points. Match all correctly for (12) points.

    A.   Afrika Bambaataa & Soulsonic Force
    B.   Newcleus
    C.   Planet Patrol
    D.   Twilight 22
    E.   M.A.R.R.S.
    F.   Man Parrish
    G.   Freeez

Classic Breaking Anthem
I. "I.O.U."
II. "Planet Rock"
III. "Play at Your Own Risk"
IV. "Hip Hop Be Bop (Don't Stop)"
V. "Pump Up the Volume (Extended Pump Up Mix)"
VI. "Electric Kingdom"
VII. "Jam On It"

11.

Matsue Castle   Osaka Castle   Phoenix Hall

Match the architectural image with the period in which the building was constructed in Japan. ((1) point each)

    A.   Azuchi-Momoyama Period
    B.   Edo Period
    C.   Meiji Period
    D.   Heian Period

Y. THE ARTS THROUGH THE CENTURIES

(each question at least 3 points)

12.

Which one of these structures is not an example of Gothic architecture? (The images deliberately are not labeled.)
A.   Florence Cathedral (Florence)
B.   Cologne Cathedral (Cologne)
C.   Pisa Cathedral (Pisa, Tuscany)
D.   Canterbury Cathedral (Canterbury, Kent)

13.   **For (1 ½) points each. (I) In what year was J. K. Rowling's *Harry Potter and the Half-Blood Prince* published? [max. 5 points]**
A.   2003   D.   2006
B.   2004   E.   "We can tell you instead what year the movie
C.   2005   was released."

(II) In what year was her *Harry Potter and the Goblet of Fire* published?
A.   1999   D.   2002
B.   2000   E.   "Uh, is that the book with the *Twilight* dude?"
C.   2001

For (2) bonus points: Harry Potter's wand coil was made of what?
A.   Dragon heartstring   C.   Unicorn tail hair
B.   Phoenix feather   D.   Horned serpent

14.   **Which list below shows these epic mangas in their correct order of publication, i.e., 1. oldest to 4. youngest? (2) bonus points for knowing your manga! [max. 8 points]**
A.   1. *Akira*; *Berserk*; *One Piece*; 4. *Full Metal Alchemist*
B.   1. *Attack on Titan*; *Dragon Ball*; *Bleach*; 4. *Hunter x Hunter*
C.   1. *JoJo's Bizarre Adventure*; *Naruto*; *My Hero Academia*; 4. *Death Note*
D.   1. *Berserk*; *Demon Slayer: Kimetsu no Yaiba*; *Vagabond*; 4. *Tokyo Ghoul*

For (3) bonus points: Which manga above did Kentaro Miura create?

15.   **For (1 ½) points each. (I) In what year was Mary Shelley's *Frankenstein* originally published? [max. 7 points]**
A.   1816   B.   1818   C.   1821   D.   1831

(II) In what year was Bram Stoker's *Dracula* originally published?
A.   1850   B.   1876   C.   1897   D.   1902

(I) For (1) bonus point: In September 2021, Christie's sold a first edition three-volume set of Shelley's *Frankenstein* at auction for:
A.   US$205,000   C.   US$1.17 million
B.   US$557,000   D.   US$1.28 million

(II) Who wrote the ghostly short story *Gibbet Hill*? ((3) bonus points)
A.   Mary Shelley   B.   Bram Stoker   C.   Washington Irving

190   **Y. THE ARTS THROUGH THE CENTURIES**
(each question at least 3 points)

16. **(I) As of early 2024, what was the most expensive comic book ever sold at auction or private sale (publicly known)? ((2) points)**
    A. *Action Comics #1* (featuring Superman) CGC 8.5 (1938)
    B. *Superman #1* CGC 8.0 (1939)
    C. *Amazing Fantasy #15* (featuring Spider-Man) CGC 9.6 (1962)
    D. *Action Comics #1* (featuring Superman) CGC 9.0 (1938)

    (II) What was the sale price? ((1) point)
    A. US$3.25 million
    B. US$5.3 million
    C. US$3.55 million
    D. US$6 million

17. **In 2014, this artist created an art installation waterfall of 10,000 recycled toilets, urinals, and sinks for the Foshan Pottery and Porcelain Festival at Shiwan Park in China's Foshan province.**
    A. Qui Zhijie
    B. Ai Weiwei
    C. Shu Yong
    D. Huang Yong Ping

18. **This author is renowned for his novels such as *The Old Man and the Sea*, *A Farewell to Arms*, which was inspired by his short tenure as an ambulance driver in World War I, and *For Whom the Bell Tolls*. He won the Nobel Prize for Literature in 1954.**
    A. Ernest Hemingway
    B. James Joyce
    C. Ian Fleming
    D. F. Scott Fitzgerald

19. **This German Baroque composer is known for his operas and oratorios. One of his most famous compositions is *Messiah*. He also grew blind as a result of several bad cataract surgeries performed by Dr. John Taylor. [max. 6 points]**
    A. Ludwig van Beethoven
    B. George Frideric Handel
    C. Johann Sebastian Bach
    D. Johannes Brahms

    For (3) bonus points: Name another composer who also went blind as a result of botched surgeries by Taylor. Hint: *St. Matthew Passion*.

20. **(I) All or nothing. Match the composer with her and his opera: (1) Georges Bizet; (2) Francesca Caccini; and (3) Vincenzo Bellini. ((2) points)**
    A. *La Liberazione di Ruggiero*   B. *Norma*   C. *Carmen*

    (II) Who composed *Tristan und Isolde*? ((1) point)
    A. Wolfgang Amadeus Mozart
    B. Richard Wagner
    C. Francesca Caccini

21. **Match two of the Latin genre music or dances below with their country of origin: (I) Cuba; (II) Mexico; (III) Dominican Republic; (IV) Puerto Rico; and (V) Panama. Match all for (7) points). [max. 11 points]**
    A. Bachata
    B. Ranchera
    C. Mambo
    D. Reggae en Español
    E. Reggaetón

    For (2) bonus points each: In which of the above countries, did (1) Rumba originate, and (2) Salsa originate?

Y. THE ARTS THROUGH THE CENTURIES

(each question at least 3 points)

22. **For (1 ½) points each. (I) Who is considered the first rap DJ?**
    A. Grandmaster Flash
    B. DJ Cool Herc
    C. DJ Red Alert
    D. DJ Marley Marl

    (II) What is the first rap song to be recorded and released (albeit on the B side of the album track) in 1979? [max. 6 points]
    A. "King Tim III (Personality Jack)"
    B. "Rapper's Delight"
    C. "Double Dutch Bus"

    For (3) bonus points: Who rapped and released the first hit rap song that brought rap music to the mainstream in 1979, with the lyrics *"Throw your hands up in the air and party hardy like you just don't care."*?
    A. The Fatback Band
    B. The Sugar Hill Gang
    C. Frankie Smith

23. **In celebration of the Queens of Hip-Hop, take (1) free point for Roxanne Shanté's "Roxanne's Revenge," then match two songs with the hip-hop artist(s) for (2) points; all the songs for (10) points. [max. 13 points]**

Hip-Hop Queen(s)
I. Missy Elliott
II. Lil Kim
III. Salt-N-Pepa and DJ Spinderella
IV. Queen Latifah and Monie Love
V. Cardi B
VI. Lauryn Hill
VII. MC Lyte
VIII. Nicki Minaj
IX. MC Sha-Rock
X. Foxy Brown
XI. Roxanne Shanté

    A. "Doo-Wop (That Thing)"
    B. "Shoop"
    C. "Ladies First"
    D. "Super Bass"
    E. "Ruffneck"
    F. "No Time"
    G. "Get Ur Freak On"
    H. "Bodak Yellow"
    I. "I'll Be"

    For (3) bonus points if you have at least (3) points: Who in the table is considered the first female rapper?

24. **Which of the below composers applied the technique** *Durchkomponiert* **(a composition that is not based on repeated verses; there is a different melody for each verse or stanza)? [max. 6 points]**
    A. Joseph Haydn
    B. Franz Schubert
    C. Robert Schumann
    D. (II) and (III) only
    E. (I) and (II) only
    F. (I) and (III) only
    G. All

    For (3) bonus points: Name a 1970s hit song that used this technique? Hint: The song is by a British "royal" band.

25. **Match these all-time famous ballets with their composer and original choreographer. Two correct (1) point; four correct (3) points. [max. 7 points]**

Composer, Original Choreographer
I. Pyotr Ilyich Tchaikovsky, Julius Reisinger
II. Ludwig Minkus, Marius Petipa
III. Léo Delibes, Arthur Saint-Léon
IV. Sergei Prokofiev, Rostislav Zakharov

    A. *Cinderella* (premiered 1945)
    B. *Swan Lake* (premiered 1877)
    C. *La Bayadère* (premiered 1877)
    D. *Coppélia* (premiered 1870)

    (1) bonus point each: Name the young woman, her prince, the sorcerer, and his daughter in *Swan Lake.*

Y. THE ARTS THROUGH THE CENTURIES
(each question at least 3 points)

26. **(I)** Who below was the creator of *Peter Pan*? ((1) point)
    (II) The Globe Theatre was accidentally burned down during one of this playwright's plays. This playwright below wrote *Richard III, Hamlet, The Taming of the Shrew, The Tempest,* and *All's Well That Ends Well,* among others. ((2) points) [max. 6 points]

A. Molière	C. Christopher Marlowe
B. William Shakespeare	D. James Matthew Barrie

    For (3) bonus points: During the performance of which play did the theatre burn down? Hint: "*A horse! A horse! My kingdom for a horse!*"

27. She is the youngest playwright at the age of 29 and the first African American to receive the prestigious New York Drama Critics' Circle Award. She is also the first Black woman to have her work produced on Broadway. [max. 6 points]

A. Lorraine Hansberry	C. Alice Childress
B. Ntozake Shange	D. Marita Bonner

    For (3) bonus points: What play is her magnum opus? Hint: When it debuted, Sidney Poitier played the role of Walter Lee.

28. All of these Japanese (or of Japanese descent) men were awarded the Nobel Prize: three in Literature and one for Peace. Who was the first to be awarded the Nobel Prize in Literature? [max. 5 points]

A. Kazuo Ishiguro	C. Yasunari Kawabata
B. Eisaku Satō	D. Kenazburō Ōe

    For (2) bonus points: Who above won the Nobel Prize for Peace?

29. Selecting from the list of composers below, answer two questions correctly for (3) points, all four questions for (5) points. [max. 10 points]
    (I) Who is considered the first classical composer in history of African origin? Born in Guadeloupe, he was also a virtuoso violinist. ((1) point)
    (II) Beethoven formerly dedicated his *Kreutzer* Violin Sonata No. 9 to this virtuoso violinist, but later he withdrew his dedication after they had a falling out. ((1) point)
    (III) Mozart is believed to have stolen the ideas of which composer's *Sinfonia Concertante* in his own *Sinfonia Concertante*? ((1) point)
    (IV) Who is the first known music theorist and published composer of choral music, born in Portugal and also of African descent, whose name and masterpieces were erased from history? ((1) point)

A. Florence Price	C. Vicente Lusitano
B. Joseph Boulogne, a.k.a. Chevalier de Saint-Georges	D. George Bridgetower
	E. Samuel Coleridge-Taylor

    For (1) bonus point each: Match the above composer with his/her orchestra or composition below.
    (1) *Symphony No. 1 in E minor*
    (2) Le Concert des Amateurs
    (3) *Hiawatha's Wedding Feast*
    (4) the composition manual *Introduttione Facilissima* (see image right of one page from the manual)
    (5) *Diatonica Armonica*

    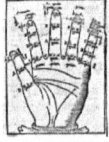
    Credit: IMSLP / Public Domain

Y. THE ARTS THROUGH THE CENTURIES
(each question at least 3 points)

NO OTHER TRIVIA LIKE THIS MASTERCLASS: VOLUME 1

30. (I) The earliest known and largest animal preserved rock art dates as far back as 6500 B.C.E. They are the Dabous Giraffes petroglyphs. In which country are these carvings? ((2) points) [max. 6 points]
    A. The Gambia   B. Niger   C. Namibia   D. Libya

    (II) What are the oldest known African art works south of the Equator? ((1) point)
    A. The ones found at the Apollo 11 caves in Namibia
    B. The zoomorphic head found in central Angola
    C. The Diepkloof Rock Shelter in South Africa
    D. The Blombos Cave Engravings in South Africa

    For (3) bonus points: In which seminal artwork did Pablo Picasso incorporate the ceremonial masks of the Dogon tribe of Niger?
    A. *Les Demoiselles d'Avignon*   B. *Head of a Woman*

31. This playwright, one of the founders of Modernism in theatre, is often referred to as the Father of Realism. Three of his plays are *An Enemy of the People*, *The Master Builder*, and *A Doll's House*.
    A. Henrik Ibsen   C. August Strindberg
    B. Arthur Miller   D. Anton Chekhov

32. For (1) point each. (I) What was the first single released in *Janet* by Janet Jackson? [max. 6 points]
    A. "Again"   C. "That's the Way Love Goes"
    B. "Any Time, Any Place" D. "You Want This"

    (II) Which Janet Jackson's music video won in the same year MTV's Award for Best Dance Video, MTV's Award for Best Choreography in a Video, MTV's Award for Best Female Video, and the Soul Train Music Award for Best Video of the Year?
    A. "You Want This"   C. "That's the Way Love Goes"
    B. "If"   D. "Rhythm Nation"

    (III) The iconic music video for "Rhythm Nation" was ahead of its time—with its conscientious lyrics, outfits, choreography, and filming (shot in black and white to portray its theme of racial harmony). With whom did Janet Jackson choreograph it?
    A. Paula Abdul   C. Barry Lather
    B. Tina Landon   D. Anthony Thomas

    For (3) bonus points: What is the name of Janet Jackson's fifth album?

33. Which of these novelists won the Pulitzer Prize for Fiction more than once? For (2) bonus points each: Match each author with his novel. [max. 11 points]

		Pulitzer Winning Novel
A. William Faulkner	D. John Updike	I. *Alice Adams*
B. Booth Tarkington	E. All	II. *The Underground Railroad*
C. Colson Whitehead	F. A and D	III. *A Fable*
		IV. *Rabbit at Rest*

Answers to questions in this Category can be found starting on page 276.

Y. THE ARTS THROUGH THE CENTURIES
         (each question at least 3 points)

Category Z:
BLIMEY! WHY NUMBERS?
WHY MATH? WHY PHYSICS?
(6-point category)

1. This was a 5th grade math problem from China for gifted students. What is the area of the "?" triangle?

   A.   4   C.   9
   B.   6   D.   12

2. **(I) A famous math problem: What does: $6 \div 2(1 + 2)$ equal? ((3) points)**
   A.   1   B.   12   C.   9   D.   18

   (II) Another famous math problem: What does: $9 - 3 \div \frac{1}{3} + 1$ equal? ((2) points)
   A.   1   B.   9   C.   7   D.   13

   (III) Solve for x: $\frac{4x-5}{2} + \frac{x+2}{3} = \frac{1}{2}$. ((1) point)

   A.   x = 2   B.   x = 3   C.   x = 1   D.   x = ½

3. Raul walks 7 km North in 2 hours and then 2.5 km South in 1 hour.
   (I) What is Raul's average <u>speed</u> for the whole journey? ((3) points)
   A.   1.5 km/h   D.   "Couldn't give a
   B.   2.2 km/h   rat's arse, with
   C.   3.2 km/h   all due respect."

   (II) What is Raul's average <u>velocity</u> for the whole journey? ((3) points)
   A.   1.5 km/h
   B.   "Still not give a rat's arse and starting to lose respect."
   C.   2.2 km/h   D.   3.2 km/h

4. **(I) This digit is considered the most significant number across religions, cultures, psychology. ((1) point)**
   A.   3   B.   4   C.   7   D.   1   E.   8

   (II) This physicist said: "If you only knew the magnificence of the 3, the 6, and the 9, then you would have the key to the universe." ((2 ½) points)
   A.   Albert Einstein   C.   Max Planck
   B.   Isaac Newton   D.   Nikola Tesla

   (III) "If you want to find the secrets of the universe, think in terms of energy, frequency and vibration." This quote is attributed to which physicist above? ((2 ½) points)

5. For (3) points each. **(I) In 2023, Google's next-gen Sycamore quantum processor could make a particular computation that would take Frontier, the world's fastest supercomputer, about 47.2 years to do. How many operational qubits below does Sycamore contain?**

   (II) In 2024, Google announced its new quantum computer Willow that performed in under 5 minutes a standard computation that would take Frontier 10^{25} years to do. How many qubits does Willow contain?
   A.   53   B.   105   C.   433   D.   70   E.   127

Z. BLIMEY! WHY NUMBERS? MATH? PHYSICS?
(each question at least 6 points)

6. **How many triangles are there in the image?**

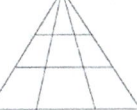

   A. 4
   B. 12   E. "Just 1! And Belmont, you
   C. 15   are annoying in a frigging
   D. 18   isosceles triangle way!"

7. **Root mean square** $= \sqrt{\dfrac{x_1^2 + x_2^2 + x_3^2 + \ldots + x_n^2}{n}}$

   Problem: Root mean square of
   $1^2 + 2^2 + 3^2 + 4^2 + 5^2 + 6^2 + 7^2$

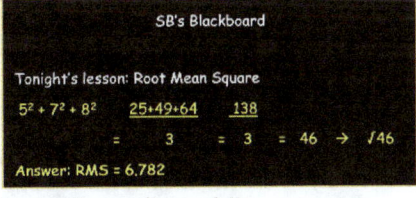

   A. 3.47
   B. 4.47
   C. 5.47
   D. "You're kidding, right?
   Without a calculator?! Our
   team will pass on the 6 points; we prefer to talk smack."

8. **What is the oldest known mathematical artifact? [max. 8 points]**
   A. Ishango bone (found in Democratic Republic of Congo)
   B. Lebombo bone (found in Eswatini)
   C. Quipu strings (found in Peru)
   D. Plimpton 322 tablet (found in Iraq)

   For (2) bonus points: Plimpton 322 resides at an Ivy League university in the USA. Venture a guess as to which one? If you guess wrong, you lose (2) of your original (6) points.

9. **Linear equation: A bookstore made $11,000, selling 3,000 math books and 1,000 physics books in a month. SB bought 1 math book and 1 physics book, and she paid $7. What was the price of each book?**
   A. Math book: $2   Physics book: $5
   B. Math book: $4   Physics book: $3
   C. Math book: $5   Physics book: $2
   D. Math book: $3   Physics book: $4

10. **(I) Logarithm: This number is equivalent to $4^9 + 4^3$. ((3) points)**
    A. 256   B. 1,024   C. 4,096   D. 8,192

    (II) Binary code: What is 7 in binary? ((3) points) [max. 10 points]
    A. 1000   B. 111   C. 110   D. 11

    For (4) bonus points: Quantum computing can store information in 0 or 1, and 0 and 1 simultaneously. A. True   B. False   C. Partially True

11. **Each question is (3) points.**
    (I) A quattuordecillion has [*] zeros in the short scale system.
    A. 24   B. 84   C. 45   D. 30

    (II) How many zeros are in the long scale system?
    A. 96   B. 84   C. 45   D. 30

Z. BLIMEY! WHY NUMBERS? MATH? PHYSICS?   197
(each question at least 6 points)

12. Each question is (3) points.
    (I) What are the possible number of handshakes among six people?
    A. 6   B. 12   C. 15   D. 20

    (II) What are the possible number of handshakes among seven people?
    A. 14   B. 21   C. 28   D. 7

13. **[SUPER-BONUS QUESTION—at least 7 points!!!!!] (I) The Large Hadron Collider at CERN in Switzerland generally uses 1.3 terawatt hours of electricity annually. That is equivalent to what? ((4) points)**
    A. The amount needed to power about 300,000 homes for a year in the United Kingdom
    B. About what a small city of about 230,000 inhabitants would use in a year
    C. Both   D. None of the above

    (II) As of 2024, in addition to Higgs Boson, the Large Hadron Collider has detected direct evidence of the following, except: ((7) points)
    A. Supersymmetry   C. Tetraquarks
    B. Neutrinos   D. Hypernucleus

    (III) CERN'S Search for Hidden Particles experiment will: ((6) points)
    A. Collide particles together in accelerators to search for "ghost" particles
    B. Crash particles into a large, fixed target to search for "ghost" particles

    (IV) The law of physics tells us that energy is: ((6) points)
    A. Concerned   C. Cray-cray   E. Constant
    B. Conserved   D. Contained   F. Collective

    (V) Which of the following is not a form of energy? ((6) points)
    A. Light   B. Heat   C. Sound   D. Friction

14.

SBH's Blackboard
Today's lesson: 6174

Example: 8757
1) $8775 - 5778 = 2997$
2) $9972 - 2779 = 7193$
3) $9731 - 1379 = 8352$
4) $8532 - 2358 = \underline{6174!!}$

Example: 1062
1) $6210 - 0126 = 6084$
2) $8640 - 0468 = 8172$
3) $8721 - 1278 = 7443$
4) $7443 - 3447 = 3996$
5) $9963 - 3699 = 6264$
6) $6642 - 2466 = 4176$
7) $7641 - 1467 = \underline{6174!!}$

"The answer is always 6174, and never beyond seven iterations." Start with any four-digit number (with at least two different digits) and then:
1) Arrange the digits of the four-digit number in descending and ascending order to make the largest and smallest numbers possible.
2) Subtract the smaller number from the larger number.
3) Take the answer and repeat steps 1 and 2.
4) <u>Within 7 steps, you will arrive at 6174</u>.
What is this mathematical concept called?
A. Baker Constant   D. Kaprekar Constant
B. Foias Constant   E. "Nonsense that SBH made up."
C. Planck Constant

15. **(I) Direct current (DC) flows in one constant direction. ((3) points)**
    A. True   B. False

    (II) DC was first produced by which physicist? ((3) points)
    A. André-Marie Ampère   C. Hippolyte Pixii
    B. Thomas Edison   D. Alessandro Volta

16. **(I) Pi (3.14159) (or to 39 decimal places,
    3.141592653589793238462643383279502884197) is a(n) _____
    number. ((3) points)**
    A. Rational   B. Irrational

    **(II) The circumference divided by the diameter of a circle is always
    equal to π. ((3) points)**
    A. True   B. False

17. **(I) (-7)(-6)(-2) = [?] ((2) points)**
    A. -15   B. -1   C. -84   D. -11   E. 84

    (II) -1^{50} = [?] ((2) points)
    A. 1   B. -1

    (III) -81 ÷ 3 ÷ -9 = [?] ((2) points)
    A. -9   B. 3   C. 9   D. -3

18. **(I) This mathematician invented the first mechanical calculator in 1642
    that did basic calculations. ((5) points)**
    A. Pierre de Fermat   C. Blaise Pascal
    B. John Wallis   D. Galileo Galilei

    (II) Where was he born? ((1) point)
    A. Italy   B. France   C. England   D. Germany

19. **(I) In what year did Swedish astronomer Anders Celsius invent his
    namesake temperature scale? ((3) points) [max. 8 points]**
    A. 1724   B. 1714   C. 1732   D. 1742

    **1. Bonus to (I): Celsius invented this scale while living in this city. The
    oldest Nordic university is located in this city. King Eric IX of Sweden
    is buried in a Gothic cathedral in this city. ((1) point)**
    A. Gothenburg   C. Malmö
    B. Uppsala   D. Stockholm

    **(II) In what years did physicist Daniel Gabriel Fahrenheit invent the
    alcohol thermometer then the mercury thermometer? ((3) points)**
    A. 1709, 1714   C. 1724, 1742
    B. 1714, 1724   D. 1709, 1724

    2. Bonus to (II): Where was Fahrenheit born? ((1) point)
    A. The Netherlands   C. Sweden
    B. Germany   D. Poland

Z. BLIMEY! WHY NUMBERS? MATH? PHYSICS?

(each question at least 6 points)

20. **(I) What does: 9 – 9 ÷ 9 + 9 – 9 ÷ 9 equal? ((3) points)**
   A.   0   B.   16   C.   7   D.   1
   (II) What does: 7 + 7 x 7 + 7 equal? ((3) points)
   A.   63   B.   196   C.   147   D.   105

21. 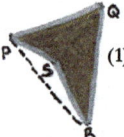 (1)   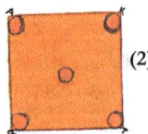 (2)

   (I) Which is a concave quadrilateral? ((3) points)
   (II) Which is a convex quadrilateral? ((3) points)
   A.   (1)   B.   (2)

22. **(I) This integer is the sum of its own proper divisors, other than the number itself. ((3) points)**
   A.   A prime number   C.   A composite number
   B.   A perfect number   D.   A complex number

   (II) One of the below is an example of this type of number. ((3) points)
   A.   7   B.   28   C.   2   D.   24

23. **(I) What is: "1 + 2 + 1 +1 + 3 + 3"? ((2) points) [max. 10 points]**
   A.   An equation   B.   An expression

   (II) What does: 4 x 3 ÷ 6 x 2 + 5 equal? ((2) points)
   A.   6   B.   54   C.   24   D.   9

   (III) Factor this polynomial: $3x^2 + 12x – 96$. ((2) points)

   For (4) bonus points: Which mathematician said, "*An equation means nothing to me unless it expresses a thought of God.*"?
   A.   G. H. Hardy   C.   John Edensor Littlewood
   B.   Gottfried Leibniz   D.   Srinivasa Ramanujan

24. **What is the cosine rule (or law of cosines)?**
   A. $c^2 = a^2 + b^2 – 2(ab) \cos(C)$
   B. $c^2 = a^2 + b^2 + c + 2(ab)$
   C. $c^2 = a^2 + b^2 + 2c – 2(ab) \cos(C)$
   D. $c^2 = a^2 + b^2 + 2(ab) \cos(C)$

25. **(I) $x = \dfrac{-b \pm \sqrt{b^2 - 4ac}}{2a}$ What is this formula? ((3) points)**
   A.   Quadratic formula   C.   Standard deviation
   B.   General relativity   D.   Distance formula

   (II) In 2019, which mathematician devised a new and easier version of this formula? ((3) points)
   A.   Prof. Po-Shen Loh   C.   Prof. John Stillwell
   B.   Prof. Caroline Klivans   D.   Prof. Terence Tao

26. The following sequence: "7, 22, 11, 34, 17, 52, 26, 13, 40, 20, 10, 5, 16, 8, 4, 2, 1" is an example of what?
    A. The Fibonacci Sequence   B. The Collatz Conjecture

27. <u>Plane geometry</u>. Match each of the below. ((1) point each)
    (I) (base) * (height)   (IV) ½ (base) * (height)
    (II) $\pi * r^2$ (V) $a^2+b^2=c^2$
    (III) $2\pi * r$ (VI) (length) * (width)
    A. Area of circle   D. Area of triangle
    B. Circumference of circle   E. Area of rectangle
    C. Area of parallelogram   F. Pythagorean theorem

28. (I) and (II) for (2) points each. A vigintillion has [*] zeros in: (I) the (American) short scale system; and (II) the (British) long scale system?
    A. 75   B. 84   C. 120   D. 63

    (III) The kilogram is defined currently by the weight of the IPK / Le Grand K stored in a vault in France. ((2) points)
    A. True   B. False

29. For (3) points each. (I) Jiuzhang 3.0, which Chinese physicist Pan Jianwei and his team developed, has calculated the most complex Gaussian boson sampling problem in one microsecond. The Frontier supercomputer would need more than 20 billion years to complete the same calculation. What type of quantum computing is Jiuzhang 3.0?
    A. Photon based / light based
    B. Electron based (superconducting)
    C. Atom based (cold atom or trapped ion)

    (II) Both or nothing. Which IBM quantum processor has (1) 433 functioning qubits, and (2) which has 1,121 functional qubits?
    A. Heron   B. Flamingo   C. Condor   D. Osprey

30. (I) To what number does this <u>magic square</u> add up? ((3) points)
    A. 42   B. 126   C. 336   D. 252

17	10	15
12	14	16
13	18	11

    (II) To what number does this <u>magic square</u> add up? ((3) points)
    A. 108   B. 144   C. 18   D. 54

9	2	7
4	6	8
5	10	3

31. (I) <u>Diophantine equation, $x^3 + y^3 + z^3 = k$</u>. Example, $1^3 + 1^3 + 1^3 = 3$. What does: $4^3 + 4^3 - 5^3 = k$? ((3) points)
    A. 9   B. 3   C. 11   D. 17

    (II) Which mathematician in April 2019 solved the "summing of three cubes = 33" equation that had stumped mathematicians for decades?
    $(8,866,128,975,287,528)^3 + (-8,778,405,442,862,239)^3 + (-2,736,111,468,807,040)^3 = 33$? ((3) points)
    A. Prof. Andrew Sutherland   C. Prof. Andrew Booker
    B. Dr. Karen Uhlenbeck   D. Prof. Terence Tao

Z. BLIMEY! WHY NUMBERS? MATH? PHYSICS?
(each question at least 6 points)

32. It's all about <u>number theories</u>. [max. 9 points]
   (I) 2 x 3 x 5 = 30   (V) 24
   (II) 2 x 3 x 7 = 42   (VI) 165
   (III) 66   (VII) 3 x 7 x 11 = 231
   (IV) 3 x 5 x 7 = 105   (VIII) 945

   1. Which of the above result(s) in or is/are a <u>pronic</u> number? Hint: It's the product of two consecutive integers. ((3) points)
   A.   All   D.   (II), (III)
   B.   (I), (V)   E.   (I), (II)
   C.   (II)   F.   (III), (V)

   2. Which of the above result(s) in or is/are an <u>abundant</u> or <u>excessive</u> number? Hint: It's where the sum of a number's proper divisors is greater than the number itself. ((3) points)
   A.   All   D.   (III), (IV), (V)
   B.   (I), (II), (III), (V)   E.   (IV), (VI), (VII), (VIII)
   C.   (I), (IV)   F.   (I), (II), (III), (V), (VIII)

   Bonus question if both above are correct: Which of the above result(s) in or is/are a <u>sphenic</u> number? Sorry, no hint. ((3) points)
   A.   (IV), (VI)   D.   (I), (II), (III), (IV), (VI), (VII)
   B.   (IV), (VI), (VII)   E.   (VI), (VII)
   C.   (I), (II), (III), (VII)   F.   "No hint, no answer. Sorry."

33. **(I)** In the early 1900s, quantum physicists suggested that atoms were a far better mechanism to keep time versus time based on Earth's rotation. ((3) points) [max. 18 points]
   A.   True   B.   False

   (II) Which clock time is the most accurate? ((3) points)
   A.   Mechanical clock   C.   Optical lattice atomic clock
   B.   Atomic clock   D.   Digital clock

   If you get both above correct, for (6) bonus points each:
   (1) From the list below, name the inventor of that clock.
   A.   Michio Kaku   D.   Isidor Rabi
   B.   Alain Aspect   E.   John Clauser
   C.   Hidetoshi Katori   F.   Anton Zeilinger

   (2) Which physicist above wrote *The God Equation: The Quest for a Theory of Everything* and *Quantum Supremacy: How the Quantum Computer Will Change Everything*?

Answers to questions in this Category can be found starting on page 277.

OY! We actually like NUMBERS, MATH, & PHYSICS. But really?! This was brutal!

Z. BLIMEY! WHY NUMBERS? MATH? PHYSICS?
(each question at least 6 points)

Category AA:
IN THE CONTINENTS
(3-point category)

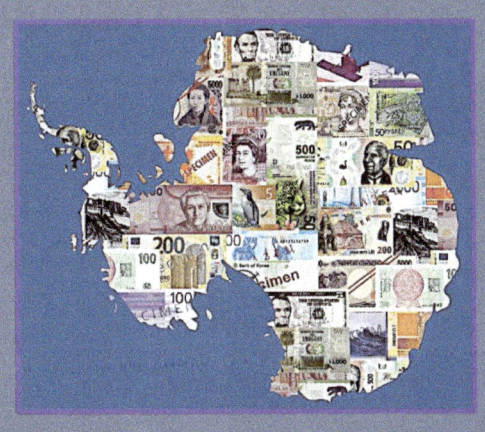

1. (I) These islands below have no permanent human residents but are homes to fur seals, elephant seals, and king penguins. At least one of the islands is actively volcanic and uninhabited. The Salvesen and Allardyce mountains are the highest peaks on one of the islands. Antarctica explorer Sir Ernest Shackleton is buried at Grytviken, a settlement on one of the islands. ((2) points) [max. 6 points]
    A. Scattered Islands
    B. Auckland Islands
    C. Galapagos Islands
    D. South Georgia and the South Sandwich Islands

    (II) The islands are territories of which country? ((1) point)
    A. Ecuador   C. New Zealand
    B. France   D. United Kingdom

    For (3) bonus points: In which ocean are the islands located?

2. [SUPER-BONUS QUESTION—at least 7 points!!!!!] The "S's":
    (1) Name 4 countries / territories in North and South America that begin with the letter S. ((2) points each)

    (2) Name 6 in Europe. ((2) points each)

    (3) All or nothing. Name 4 in geographic Asia. ((5) points)

    (4) Both or nothing. Name 2 in Oceania. ((3) points)

3. Name nine countries / territories that begin with the letter L. (1) point if you get 2 – 4 correct; (2) points if you get 5 – 6 correct; (3) points, only if answer 7 – 9 correctly.

4. This Central American country's crown jewel is the jade head of Kinich Ahau, the Mayan sun god. The ancient Mayan ruins of Xunantunich are located in its Cayo District. The Great Blue Hole, a giant marine sinkhole, is one of this country's natural wonders. What is its name?
    A. Costa Rica   C. Belize
    B. Honduras   D. Panama

5. One of these glaciers in Antarctica is also known as the Doomsday Glacier. Unfortunately, this nickname is appropriate. [max. 5 points]
    A. Denman Glacier
    B. Thwaites Glacier
    C. Pine Island Glacier (P.I.G.)
    D. Totten Glacier

    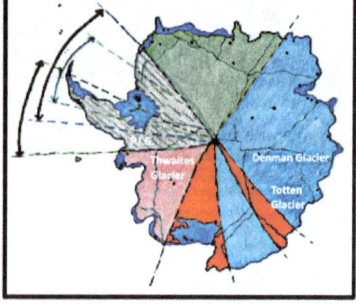

    For (2) bonus points: If this glacier collapsed entirely, global sea levels would increase by:
    A. 25 cm (9.8 in)   C. 65 cm (25.6 in)
    B. 45 cm (17.7 in)   D. 75 cm (29.5 in)

AA. IN THE CONTINENTS
(each question at least 3 points)

6. Which European country is 14; which country is 29; and which country is 31 on the map on the right? ((1) point each)

   A. Estonia
   B. Norway
   C. Latvia
   D. Lithuania
   E. Finland
   F. Sweden

7. If you're at any of the following research stations, at what country's outpost in Antarctica are you: (I) Casey Station; (II) Neumayer Station III; and (III) Palmer Station? ((1) point each)

   A. Germany   C. Australia
   B. UK   D. USA

8. This large island's climate is the mildest in Canada—ideal for its numerous vineyards. There is a substantial salmon habitat in its Englishman River. British Columbia's capital of Victoria is also on the island. What island is it?

   A. Cape Bretton Island   C. Vancouver Island
   B. Baffin Island   D. Newfoundland

9. (I) Only two countries in Africa were not colonized by European countries. For (2) points, what are they? Both or nothing. [max. 5 points]

   A. Ethiopia   D. Seychelles
   B. Sierra Leone   E. Liberia
   C. Madagascar

   (II) Name the capital of either of these two countries. ((1) point) If you name both capitals correctly, (2) extra points for you!

10. (I) Which country below was the first formally to claim territory in Antarctica? ((2) points) [max. 5 points]

   A. Argentina   D. Norway
   B. Australia   E. France
   C. United Kingdom   F. Chile

   (II) In which year? ((1) point)

   A. 1908   D. 1929
   B. 1923   E. 1933
   C. 1924   F. 1940

   For (2) bonus points, (1) point each: Which of the above countries has claimed (I) Peter I Island; and (II) Queen Maud Land?

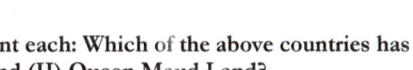

AA. IN THE CONTINENTS
(each question at least 3 points)

11. **(I) What is Oceania's most populous city? ((1 ½) points)**
     A.   Melbourne   C.   Port Moresby
     B.   Sydney   D.   Auckland

     (II) This is the national sport in most countries and territories in Oceania. ((1 ½) points)
     A.   Cricket   C.   Rugby
     B.   Football (Soccer)   D.   Australian Rules Football

12. **If you're at any of the research stations in the table, at what country's outpost in Antarctica are you? Answer any four correctly for (3) points; answer all correctly for (12) points. [max. 14 points]**

Research Station
I. Esperanza Base
II. Amundsen-Scott South Pole Station
III. Halley Research Station
IV. Maitri Station
V. Captain Arturo Prat Base
VI. SANAE IV
VII. Dumont d'Urville
VIII. Scott Base
IX. Syowa Station
X. Davis Station

A.   Argentina
B.   UK
C.   New Zealand
D.   USA
E.   Chile
F.   France
G.   South Africa
H.   Japan
I.   Australia
J.   India
K.   China

If you earn at least (3) points, for (2) bonus points: Which country will have a new research base in Antarctica on Inexpressible Island in Terra Nova Bay, Ross Sea? Hint: Some news outlets reported about it in 2023 but most others instead covered the Chinese spy balloon saga.

13. **(I) What is the largest country in South America <u>by area</u>? ((1 ½) points)**
     A.   Peru   B.   Colombia   C.   Brazil   D.   Argentina

     (II) What is the smallest sovereign country in mainland South America? ((1 ½) points)
     A.   Suriname   B.   Guyana   C.   Paraguay   D.   Uruguay

14. **Two ancient archeological settlements called Cocota and Landivar recently were found beneath dense vegetation, using a remote sensing technology called Lidar. These settlements of the Casarabe culture (between 500 and 1400 C.E.) had pyramids, elevated roads, causeways, and terraces. In what country were they found?**
     A.   Bolivia   C.   Mexico
     B.   Peru   D.   Egypt

15. **Nearly half of this country is below sea level. The country New Zealand was named after this country's southwestern province, Zeeland. Its official language is closely related to English. The Hague and Utrecht are the third and fourth largest cities in this European country.**
     A.   Belgium   C.   The Netherlands
     B.   Luxembourg   D.   Sweden

AA. IN THE CONTINENTS
     (each question at least 3 points)

16. This island is home to the cities of Tokyo, Kobe, and Osaka. It is Japan's largest island. Its highest point is Mount Fuji, while its lowest point is Hachirōgata. What is this island? [max. 6 points]

   A. Hokkaido   C. Kyushu   E. Okinawa
   B. Honshū   D. Shikoku

For (3) bonus points: What is Japan's smallest main island? Hint: Iva Valley and Ishiteji Temple with its Matra Cave are located there.

17. This is the largest island in South Korea. It is a popular island for honeymooners and those who desire to visit the adult theme park, Loveland. The dormant shield volcano Hallasan is located on this island. Local *Haenyo* (female divers), with an average age 65 years old, harvest shellfish by diving 10-20 metres (33-66 feet) below the water's surface without a breathing apparatus. What is the name of this island?

   A. Wolmido Island   C. Hongdo Island
   B. Jeju Island   D. Seonyudo Island

18. Around 7:14 a.m. (local time) on 30 June 1908, there was a massive explosion in this place. Tremors were felt across the world as far as England. In what is called the Tunguska event, there was no impact crater found. But about 2,072 square kilometres (800 square miles) of forest were ripped apart. Where did this 12-megaton explosion occur?

   A. Chinggis City   C. Bulunkul
   B. Atbasar   D. Siberia

19. This kingdom once controlled Iceland, St. John, and St. Thomas.

   A. Denmark   C. Sweden
   B. The Netherlands   D. United Kingdom

20.

Which African country is (12); which is (29); and which is (37) on the map? ((1) point each) [max. 6 points]

   A. Namibia   D. São Tomé and Principe
   B. Madagascar   E. Cabo Verde
   C. Seychelles   F. Democratic Republic of the Congo

For (3) bonus points, (1) point each: Which African country is (43); which is (45); and which is (8) on the map above? You do not need to get all of Q.20 correct to earn the bonus points.

AA. IN THE CONTINENTS
(each question at least 3 points)

21. Which central/east/south Asian country / territory is (32); which is (13); and which is (8)? ((1) point each) [max. 6 points]

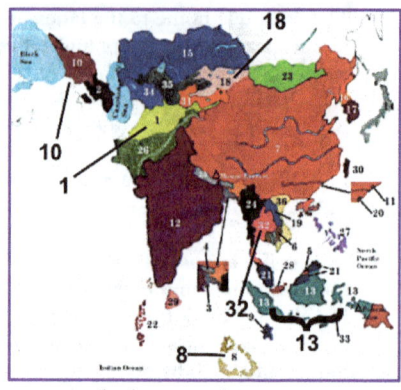

    A.   Georgia
    B.   Indonesia
    C.   Thailand
    D.   Cocos (Keeling) Islands
    E.   Afghanistan
    F.   Kyrgyzstan

For (3) bonus points, (1) point each: Which is (18); which is (10); and which is (1)? You do not need to get all of Q.21 correct to earn the bonus points.

22. In which African country is Spanish an official language?
    A.   The Gambia   C.   Gabon
    B.   Equatorial Guinea   D.   São Tomé and Principe

23. For (3) points, match three of the below with their city in the table; all for (8) points. [max. 12 points]

Indian City
I. Hyderabad
II. Jodhpur
III. Bangalore
IV. Shillong
V. Jaipur
VI. Mangalore
VII. Amritsar

    A.   This is the Blue City of India.
    B.   This is the Garden City of India.
    C.   This city is known as the City of Pearls.
    D.   This city is known as the Pink City.
    E.   This city is called the Rome of the East in India.
    F.   This is the Scotland of the East in India.

For (2) bonus points each: (1) Which one of the cities is known as the Golden City of India? (2) Which of the cities is known also as the Silicon Valley of India?

24. Which African country / territory / department is (42); which is (25); and which is (35) on the map? ((1) point each) [max. 6 points]

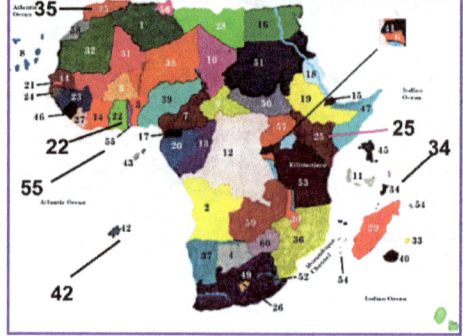

    A.   Kenya
    B.   Morocco
    C.   Ghana
    D.   Saint Helena
    E.   Togo
    F.   Mayotte

For (3) bonus points, (1) point each: Which is (55); which is (22); and which is (34)? You do not need to get all of Q.24 correct to earn the bonus points.

AA. IN THE CONTINENTS
(each question at least 3 points)

25. Snæfell and Castle Rushen are located on this island in the Irish Sea. This island's flag depicts a triskelion. The High Court of Tynwald, the oldest continuous parliament in the world, is of Norse origin, and is the parliament of this island. What is this island, whose capital is Douglas?

    A. Guernsey
    B. Jersey
    C. Isle of Man
    D. Shetland Islands

26. Tulip Mania took over this country in the 1630s. At its height, the average price of tulip bulbs could cost more than some houses. The rarest bulbs traded for as much as six times the average person's annual salary. Abel Tasman, an explorer from this country, was the first European to land on Australia and New Zealand.

    A. Denmark
    B. The Netherlands
    C. Sweden
    D. England

27. One of these countries is not one of the least densely populated places in the world. [max. 7 points]

    A. Namibia
    B. Singapore
    C. Greenland
    D. Mongolia

    For (4) bonus points: All or nothing. Which three Asian nations below were not colonized by European powers?

    A. Thailand
    B. Cambodia
    C. South Korea
    D. Singapore
    E. Laos
    F. Japan

28. What country did Francis Drake attack in the "Singeing of the King's Beard"?

    A. Spain
    B. France
    C. Portugal
    D. Scotland

29. Which Middle Eastern country / state in geographic Asia is (17); which is (1); and which is (14) on the map? ((1) point each) [max. 6 points]

    A. Jordan
    B. Yemen
    C. Syria
    D. Bahrain
    E. Oman
    F. Iran

    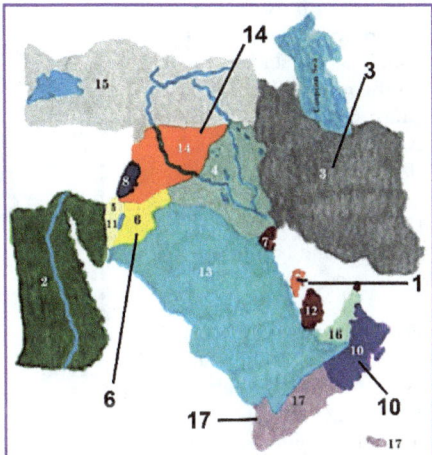

    For (3) bonus points, (1) point each: Which is (6); which is (10); and which is (3)? You do not need to get all of Q.29 correct to earn the bonus points.

AA. IN THE CONTINENTS
(each question at least 3 points)

30.

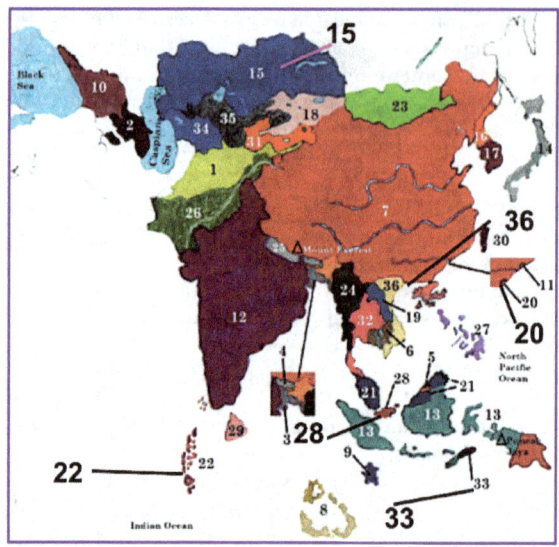

Which central/east/south Asian country / territory is (15); which is
(20); and which is (36) on the map? ((1) point each) [max. 6 points]

A. Singapore   D. Timor-Leste
B. Kazakhstan   E. Macau
C. Maldives   F. Vietnam

For (3) bonus points, (1) point each: Which is (22); which
is (33); and which is (28)? You do not need to get all of Q.30 correct to
earn the bonus points.

31. Which South American country
/ territory / department is (8);
which is (13); and which is (10)
on the map? ((1) point each)
[max. 6 points]

A. Colombia
B. Paraguay
C. Bolivia
D. Suriname
E. Falkland Islands
F. French Guiana

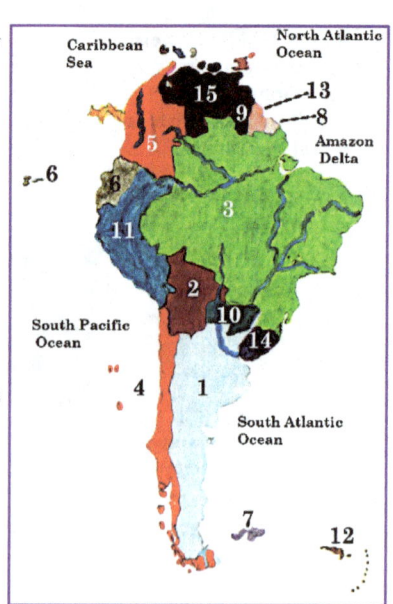

For (3) bonus points, (1) point
each: Which is (2); which is (5);
and which is (7)? You do not
need to get all of Q.31 correct
to earn the bonus points.

AA. IN THE CONTINENTS
(each question at least 3 points)

32. In 1592, Japanese samurai and military leader Toyotomi Hideyoshi invaded this then-region, but his attempt failed. The region's independence subsequently was recognized; and Taiwan, the Pescadores, and the Liaodong Peninsula in Manchuria were ceded to Japan in the Treaty of Shimonoseki signed by Japan and China in 1859. What was the region?
   A. Hong Kong
   B. Korea
   C. Myanmar
   D. Singapore

33. Africa has the richest concentration of natural resources amongst the continents. Although each country below may also contain the same mineral deposits as one another, match the mineral deposit with the country that it is found in some of the highest concentrations globally. [max. 6 points]

   A. Democratic Republic of the Congo
   B. Namibia
   C. Côte d'Ivoire
   D. Madagascar

Mineral Deposit
I. Nickel
II. Cobalt
III. Uranium

   For (3) bonus points: Which country above is one of the largest producers of cocoa in the world?

Answers to questions in this Category can be found starting on page 277.

AA. IN THE CONTINENTS

(each question at least 3 points)

Category BB:
CAPITALS
(4-point category)

1. Match the capital below with its country: (I) Tobago; (II) Bolivia; (III) Latvia; (IV) Malta; (V) Seychelles; (VI) Uzbekistan; and (VII) Fiji. Answer four capitals correctly, receive (4) points. Answer all eight correctly, receive (11) points. No other derivatives.
   A. Tashkent   D. Riga   G. Victoria
   B. Scarborough   E. Suva   H. La Paz
   C. Sucre   F. Valletta

2. Funafuti is the capital city of which country / territory? [max. 5 points]
   A. Mauritania   C. Norfolk Island
   B. Burkina Faso   D. Tuvalu

   For (1) bonus point: Not a capital, but where is the village A located?
   A. Finland   B. France   C. Norway   D. Liechtenstein

3. This is the capital of Bhutan. [max. 8 points]
   A. Phnom Penh
   B. Thimphu
   C. Kathmandu
   D. Bandar Seri Begawan

   (I) For (1) bonus point: What is the name of this 17th-century castle-monastery on the banknote, where legend has it that a demoness was banished into the rock of the hill where the monastery is located today?

   (II) For (3) bonus points ((1) point each): The other three cities listed above are the capitals of which countries?

4. What is the capital below of each country represented by its national flag to the right: (I) Flag 1; (II) Flag 2; (III) Flag 3; and (IV) Flag 4? ((1) point each)
   A. Prague
   B. Zagreb
   C. Ljubljana
   D. Praia
   E. Apia

   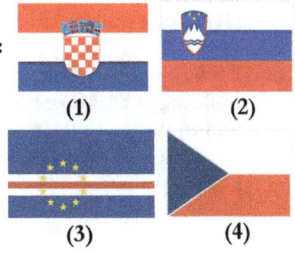

   (1) (2) (3) (4)

5. Name five country capitals in Europe that begin with the letter B.

6. Match the capital below with its country: (I) Bosnia and Herzegovina; (II) Zambia; (III) Sweden; (IV) Maldives; (V) Nauru; (VI) Grenada; and (VII) Oman. Answer four correctly, receive (4) points. Answer all seven correctly, receive (10) points. No other derivatives.
   A. Muscat   D. Sarajevo   G. Stockholm
   B. Malé   E. Lusaka
   C. Yaren   F. Saint George's

7. Benin has two capitals: (I) the official capital; and (II) the other is its largest city, port city, and de facto administrative capital. Which is which, for (2) points each?
   A. Cotonou   B. Porto-Novo   C. Abomey-Calavi

BB. CAPITALS
(each question at least 4 points)

8. On which date was D.C., the District of Columbia, the capital of the USA, founded? [max. 5 points]
   A. April 29, 1782
   C. July 16, 1790
   B. August 8, 1776
   D. July 12, 1792

   For (1) bonus point and for fun: In what year was DC, Detective Comics Inc., founded?
   A. 1934   B. 1937   C. 1949   D. 1955

9. Match the country with its capital below: (I) Kiribati; (II) Uruguay; (III) Bermuda; (IV) Monaco; (V) Jordan; (VI) Rwanda; and (VII) Barbados. Answer four correctly, receive (4) points. Answer all seven correctly, receive (10) points. No other derivatives.
   A. Kigali
   E. Bridgetown
   B. Tarawa
   F. Monte Carlo
   C. Montevideo
   G. Amman
   D. Hamilton
   H. Saint George

10. Match the capital with its Central American country: (I) Honduras; (II) Belize; (III) Nicaragua; and (IV) Costa Rica. ((1) point each correct answer) [max. 5 points]
    A. Managua
    C. Tegucigalpa
    B. San José
    D. Belmopan

    For an easy (1) bonus point: What is the capital of El Salvador?

11. Country capitals that begin with the letter R:
    (I) Name three in Europe. ((3) points)
    (II) Name one in Africa. ((1) point)

12. This capital is its country's second largest city. The capital's oldest building is St. Margaret's Chapel. The Palace of Holyroodhouse is within this capital. Its center is on the southern shore of the Firth of Forth. It was the first city in the world to have its own fire service. Lastly, you will find haggis on menus all across this capital.
    A. Cardiff
    C. London
    B. Belfast
    D. Edinburgh

13. The Itamaraty Palace (or Palace of the Arches) is a landmark in this country's capital city, which was once known as Plano Piloto. What is the city?
    A. Lisbon
    C. Buenos Aires
    B. Madrid
    D. Brasilia

14. What are the two capitals of Côte d'Ivoire? ((2) points each)
    A. Grand Bassam
    C. Abidjan
    B. Yamoussoukro
    D. Bouake

15. This capital city fell to the Soviet Union in 1945.
    A. London
    C. Prague
    B. Berlin
    D. Paris

BB. CAPITALS
(each question at least 4 points)

16. What is the capital of the country / territory in South America with the largest forest area as a percentage of its total land area?
    A. Caracas   C. Georgetown
    B. Cayenne   D. Paramaribo

17. Inhabitants of this capital have included the Paleo-Eskimo people, the Dorset people, Inuits, and Vikings. It holds the world's only Arctic nine-hole grass golf course. The iconic mountain Sermitsiaq can be seen from almost everywhere in this capital.
    A. Novosibirsk   C. Nuuk
    B. Oslo   D. Helsinki

18. This capital city was a center for science and mathematics during the rule of the Abbasid Caliphate. Its House of Wisdom was a renowned center of learning that was destroyed in 1258 during a siege. An attack of the city by the Mongols resulted in the death of the 37th caliph Al-Musta'sim.
    A. Baghdad   C. Ashgabat
    B. Beirut   D. Tehran

19. The oldest continuously operating university in the Americas is in this capital city. [max. 5 points]
    A. Santo Domingo   C. Santiago
    B. Lima   D. Mexico City

    For (1) bonus point: What is the university's name?

20. Match the capital with the statement associated with it. ((1) point each)
    (I) This is the coldest country capital in the world.
    (II) The Pan African Heritage World Museum is located here.
    (III) The most southerly Anglican church in the world, with its whalebone arch monument, is located here.
    (IV) This capital has a population of about 140 people.
    A. West Island   D. (Port) Stanley
    B. Abuja   E. Accra
    C. Ulaanbaatar   F. Moscow

21. The Thirty Tyrants ruled this capital city after its defeat in the Peloponnesian War. The Acropolis in this city was constructed during the rule by Pericles.
    A. Sparta   B. Nafplio   C. Corinth   D. Athens

22. Country capitals that begin with the letter D.
    (I) Name one in Europe. ((1) point)
    (II) Name one in Africa. ((1) point)
    (III) Name one in the Middle East region of Asia. ((1) point)
    (IV) Name one in geographic Asia (not located in the Middle East). ((1) point) [max. 7 points]

    (I) For (1) bonus point: Name another "D" country capital in Africa.
    (II) Name two other country capitals in geographic Asia that begin with the letter D. ((1) bonus point each)

BB. CAPITALS
(each question at least 4 points)

23. Match the capital with its Caribbean island: (I) Saint Barthélemy; (II) Curaçao; (III) Martinique; and (IV) Aruba. ((1) point each)
    A. Willemstad   C. Oranjestad
    B. Fort-de-France   D. Gustavia

24. This capital city is a major hub in Asia, and it is situated on the Tan-shui River. From 2004 to 2010, its financial center building was the world's tallest building.
    A. Singapore   C. Victoria City
    B. Kuala Lumpur   D. Taipei

25. The Hafsid Dynasty ruled this city during the medieval period. The grand Avenue Habib Bourguiba is the main street in this capital city. Carthage is a suburb of this city. The city's Bardo National Museum was originally a palatial complex of the Hafsid, and it contains one of the richest Roman mosaic collections in the world.
    A. Algiers   B. Tunis   C. Kigali   D. Tripoli

26. This capital was rocked by the Gordon Riots of 1780 that were motivated by anti-Catholic sentiment. A devastating four-day fire in early September 1666 in this capital left thousands of people temporarily homeless and it incinerated St. Paul's Cathedral.
    A. London   C. Cardiff
    B. Paris   D. Amsterdam

27. Which country has a new capital named Nusantara? [max. 18 points]
    A. Indonesia   C. Timor-Leste
    B. The Philippines   D. Malaysia

    There currently are 12 country and territory capitals that begin with N, including Nusantara. Name six of the other 11 capitals for (8) bonus points; name all 11 for (14) bonus points. No other derivatives. No bonus points will be earned if the main question is answered incorrectly.

28. SUPER-BONUS QUESTION—at least 7 points!!!!!] (1) Match the Caribbean island with its capital below: (I) Guadeloupe; (II) Saint Thomas, U.S. Virgin Islands; (III) Sint Maarten; (IV) Saint Kitts & Nevis; (V) Haiti; (VI) Turks & Caicos; (VII) Bonaire; (VIII) Saba; (IX) Tortola, British Virgin Islands; and (X) Saint Lucia. ((2) points each)
    A. Philipsburg   F. Port-au-Prince
    B. Cockburn Town   G. Charlotte Amalie
    C. Basse-Terre   H. Castries
    D. Kralendijk   I. The Bottom
    E. Basseterre   J. Road Town

    (2) Two countries above each shares their island geographically with another country (not listed). For (1) point each: What is the capital of each of those other countries?

    (3) What is the capital of the largest Caribbean island by area size? ((2) points)

216   BB. CAPITALS
               (each question at least 4 points)

29. Lapland is the northernmost region of Finland. Since 1927, it has been associated with the legendary residence of Santa Claus in the North Pole. What is the name of its capital, which lies about 2.6 kilometres (1.6 miles) south of the North Pole? *Leipäjuusto* (translated as "bread cheese" but also called the "squeaky cheese") with cloudberry jam is a must-try food when in this capital.

A. Kemi   B. Rovaniemi   C. Ranua   D. Tornio

30. This capital and largest city of Moldova lies along the Bâc River. It is called "The White Stone Town" because of its abundance of limestone buildings. It also is one of the greenest cities in Europe as it boasts 23 lakes and several parks, including the Stephen the Great Central Park, the oldest park in Moldova.

A. Chişinău (in the center)   C. Bălţi (in the north)
B. Tiraspol (in the east)   D. Bender (in the southeast)

31. This capital was the former capital of the Inca Empire in Peru from the 13th century until Spain's conquest in the 16th century. It is situated south of the sacred Urubamba Valley. [max. 6 points]

A. Isla del Sol   D. Ollantaytambo
B. Cusco   E. Inca Pisac
C. Machu Picchu

For (2) bonus points: One of the above was the royal estate town of Emperor Pachacuti. It also served as a stronghold for the Inca resistance against Spanish conquest.

32. What historical capital of Moravia is home to Czechia's Supreme Court and is the center of its judicial system? The city is famous for its gastronomy and modernist architecture, including the Villa Tugendhat that German architects Ludwig Mies van der Rohe and Lilly Reich designed.

A. Brno   B. Prague   C. Plzeň   D. Ostrava

33. What is the southernmost national capital city in the world of an independent nation? [max. 6 points]

A. Montevideo   C. Adamstown
B. Auckland   D. Wellington

For (2) bonus points: On which island or country is it located?
A. Te Ika-a-Māui (or North Island)
B. Pitcairn Island
C. Uruguay
D. Te Waipounamu (or South Island)

Answers to questions in this Category can be found starting on page 278.

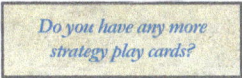

Do you have any more
strategy play cards?

BB. CAPITALS

(each question at least 4 points)

Category CC:
BODIES OF WATER
(3-point category)

1. What is the longest river in southern Africa? It starts in the Drakensberg Mountains in Lesotho. No crocodiles live in this river because the water is too cold. It was named after a Dutch ruling family. In one southern African nation, it is known as the Senqu River.

    A. Baakens River
    B. Molopo River
    C. Orange River
    D. Vaal River

2. This is the largest sea in the Philippines. [max 5 points]

    A. Bohol Sea
    B. Philippine Sea
    C. Sulu Sea
    D. Visayan Sea

    For (2) bonus points: This southeast Asian sea is located between Vietnam, the Philippines, and China. The sea is home to the heavily disputed Spratly and Paracel Islands. In China, it is called Nán Hǎi; in Vietnam, it is known as Biển Đông; in Indonesia, as Dagat Timog Tsina; and as Luzon Sea in the Philippines. What is the predominant name in English?

3. (I) This is the tallest waterfall (on land) in the world at 979 metres (3,212 feet). ((2) points) [max. 6 points]

    A. Victoria Falls
    B. Angel Falls
    C. Niagara Falls
    D. Tugela Falls

    (II) In which country/countries is it located? ((1) point)

    A. Canada and USA
    B. South Africa
    C. Venezuela
    D. Zimbabwe and Zambia

    For (3) bonus points: What is the name of the tallest and largest underwater waterfall in the world, plunging about 3,505 metres (11,500 feet)? Yes, there's such a thing.

4. This saline lake is the remains of the prehistoric Lake Bonneville. It is fed by the Bear, Jordan, and Weber Rivers in the USA. Robert Smithson's earthwork sculpture *Spiral Jetty* is on its northeastern shore.

    A. Lake Michigan
    B. Lake Tahoe
    C. Great Salt Lake
    D. Lake Ontario

5. This river forms the border between France and Germany, though it flows through six countries. It flows through Lake Constance, where it forms an inland delta. It originates in Switzerland and drains into the North Sea via The Netherlands. [max. 9 points]

    A. Volga River
    B. Rhine River
    C. Elbe River
    D. Danube River

    (I) For (3) bonus points: Which river above is the longest in Europe?

    (II) For (3) bonus points: Which river above passes through 10 European countries?

CC. BODIES OF WATER
(each question at least 3 points)

6. This muddy estuary is formed by the confluence of the Paraná River and the Uruguayan River. It forms part of the border between Uruguay and Argentina. Montevideo and Buenos Aires are on either side of it.
    A. Río Salado
    B. Río Bermejo
    C. Río Iguazú
    D. Río de la Plata

7. This river in Asia flows through six countries. It is home to some of the richest biodiversity of plant and fish species in the world, where in May 2022 a monstrous, endangered 661-pound (300-kilogram) stingray was caught. [max. 7 points]
    A. Mekong River
    B. Red River
    C. Kapuas River
    D. Salween River

    For (4) bonus points (all or nothing): Name all six countries.

8. This extremely cold sea (along with a strait bearing its name) separates Siberia from Alaska. It is separated from the Chukchi Sea of the Arctic Ocean by that same strait. It is near the chain of Aleutian Islands. Its waves are ferociously rough and can reach over 20 metres (66 feet) during storms! The International Date Line passes through its strait. What is this sea named after a Danish sea captain? [max. 6 points]
    A. Bering Sea
    B. Barents Sea
    C. North Sea
    D. Beaufort Sea

    For (3) bonus points: What is the name of the large, deep, submarine canyon situated in the center of the sea?
    A. Navarin Canyon   B. Pribilof Canyon   C. Zhemchug Canyon

9. This extremely salty body of water is located at the lowest point on Earth.
    A. Marmara Sea
    B. Dead Sea
    C. Lake Eyre
    D. Lake Assal

10. What is the largest natural lake in Japan? [max. 6 points]
    A. Lake Kawaguchi (think Mt. Fuji)
    B. Lake Biwa (think biwa musical instrument)
    C. Lake Kasumigaura (think freshwater pearls)
    D. Lake Chuzenji (think mountains above Nikko)

    For (3) bonus points: Which of the above is the oldest lake in Japan dating at least 4 million years old?

11. This sea flows into the Indian Ocean and it contains one of the world's northernmost shallow coral reefs, which is in the port of Eilat.
    A. Arabian Sea
    B. Aral Sea
    C. Mediterranean Sea
    D. Red Sea

12. This sea separates North Korea and South Korea from China. The Huang He, Yangtze, and Amnok (Yalu) rivers discharge sediments into this body of water.
    A. Black Sea
    B. Bohai Sea
    C. Sea of Japan
    D. Yellow Sea

CC. BODIES OF WATER
                    (each question at least 3 points)

13. **(I) One of these two seas is the cleanest sea on Earth. ((1 ½) points)**
    A. Weddell Sea   B. Norwegian Sea

    (II) One of these is the least polluted ocean on Earth. ((1 ½) points)
    A. (North) Atlantic Ocean   D. Southern Ocean
    B. (North) Pacific Ocean   E. (South) Pacific Ocean
    C. (South) Atlantic Ocean   F. Arctic Ocean

14. **Canadian forces raided the Port of Dieppe in this body of water in 1942. A tunnel running through this body of water connects at least two European countries. Its strait is the busiest shipping lane in the world.**
    A. North Sea   C. Celtic Sea
    B. English Channel (La Manche)   D. Bay of Biscay

15. **This is the largest freshwater lake in southeast Asia. UNESCO declared it as a biosphere reserve in 1997. About 170 villages float on the lake. [max. 4 points]**
    A Tonlé Sap   C. Macon Lake
    B. Lake Matano   D. West lake

    Bonus: In what country is it? ((1) point)
    A. Indonesia   C. Cambodia
    B. Philippines   D. Vietnam

16. **(I) All of the following lakes are located in Western Europe except: ((1 ½) points)**
    A. Lake IJssel   C. Lake Vänern
    B. Lake Annecy   D. Lake Maggiore

    (II) What is the largest lake in Central Europe? ((1 ½) points)
    A. Lake Onega   C. Lake Neusiedl
    B. Lake Balaton   D. Hallstätter See

17. **(I) For (2) points, the inland Caspian Sea is bordered by all of the following countries except:**
    A. Azerbaijan   D. Russia
    B. Iran   E. Turkmenistan
    C. Georgia   F. Kazakhstan

    (II) For (1) point, the Caspian Sea's water is:
    A. Freshwater   C. Completely saline
    B. Brackish

18. **This river flows through seven U.S. states and two nations, and it is especially known for its beautiful canyons and whitewater rapids. The two largest artificial reservoirs in the USA—Lake Powell and Lake Mead—are located along this river. However, both of these reservoirs are at severe risk of drying up.**
    A. Colorado River   C. Missouri River
    B. Kootenay River   D. Columbia River

CC. BODIES OF WATER

(each question at least 3 points)

19. Neva River and Nara River flow into this body of water, which is part of the Baltic Sea. Its main ports include Helsinki, Kotka, Tallinn, and Vyborg. It freezes over for three to five months during winter.
    A. Gulf of Bothnia   C. Bay of Gdańsk
    B. Gulf of Riga   D. Gulf of Finland

20. Match the coral reef with the ocean in which it is located. [max. 6 points]

Coral Reef
I. New Caledonia Barrier Reef
II. Great Barrier Reef
III. Mesoamerican Barrier Reef

    A. Atlantic Ocean   C. Indian Ocean
    B. Pacific Ocean   D. Southern Ocean

    For (3) bonus points: The Saya de Malha Bank is the largest submerged ocean single bank in the world. It also has one of the largest seagrass meadows in the world, which stores significant amounts of carbon— contributing its part for the climate. In what ocean listed above is it located?

21. What is the second-deepest lake in the USA with a depth of 1,645 feet (501 metres)? The Washoe Tribe's territory is centered near the lake. [max. 5 points]
    A. Lake Superior   C. Lake Tahoe
    B. Crater Lake   D. Lake Chelan

    For (2) bonus points: What is the deepest lake in the USA?

22. The islands of Wednesday, Saddle, Trinity, and Somerville are located in this ocean. This ocean covers about one-sixteenth of Earth's total ocean area, and it contains about 5.4% of the world's ocean water. The colossal squid (*Mesonychoteuthis hamiltoni*), the largest invertebrate on Earth, dwells here. [max. 6 points]
    A. Southern Ocean   D. Indian Ocean
    B. Arctic Ocean   E. Pacific Ocean
    C. Atlantic Ocean

    For (3) bonus points: What is the smallest ocean on Earth?

23. The Nile is the longest river in Africa. What is the second-longest river?
    A. Zambezi River   C. Niger River
    B. Congo River   D. Oued Rhumel

24. This body of water, once feared by sailors, has no land boundaries and coastlines. It is a spawning site for threatened and endangered eel, dolphinfish (or mahi-mahi), porbeagle shark, and white marlin. Humpback whales migrate to this sea annually. It is famous for its free-floating species of algae that reproduce vegetatively on the high seas.
    A. Florida Keys   C. Bering Sea
    B. Labrador Sea   D. Sargasso Sea

CC. BODIES OF WATER
                              (each question at least 3 points)

25. (I) All or nothing. Which ocean(s) does Egypt border? ((1) point)
(II) All or nothing. Which ocean(s) does Thailand border? ((1) point)
(III) All or nothing. Which ocean(s) does Svalbard border? ((1) point)
[max. 4 points]
A. Atlantic Ocean (or via one of its seas)
B. Pacific Ocean (or via one of its seas)
C. Arctic Ocean (or via one of its seas)
D. Indian Ocean (or via one of its seas)
E. Southern Ocean (or via one of its seas)

For (1) bonus point: All or nothing. Which ocean(s) does Belize border?

26. Which strait connects:
(I) South China Sea and the Andaman Sea, as well as the peninsula of Malaysia and the island of Sumatra in Indonesia? ((1) point)
(II) Tasman Sea and South Pacific Ocean? ((1) point)
(III) Gulf of Aden and the Red Sea? ((1) point) [max. 8 points]
A. Bab-el-Mandeb Strait   C. Cook Strait
B. Strait of Malacca   D. Bosporus (Bosphorus) Strait

(I) For (2) bonus points: What is the narrowest strait in the world? Hint: It is listed above.

(II) For (3) bonus points: What is the longest strait in the world? Hint: It too is listed above.

27. (I) Which ocean was referred to as the Aethiopian Sea / Ethiopian Ocean on some maps from the southern hemisphere as late as the mid-19th century? ((1) point)

(II) Which ocean used to be called the Eastern Ocean before 1515? ((1) point)

(III) Which explorer gave the Pacific Ocean its name of Mar Pacifico for "peaceful sea"? ((½) point)
A. Vasco Núñez de Balboa   D. Marco Polo
B. Christopher Columbus   E. James Cook
C. Ferdinand Magellan

(IV) Long before the name of Pacific Ocean, (1) the Māori, and (2) the original inhabitants of Hawaii, each called it by a different name. Match each name below with the peoples above. ((½) point)
A. Moananuiākea
B. Te Moana-Nui-a-Kiwa

28. What is the largest and longest fjord on Earth? [max. 5 points]
A. Scoresby Sund (Greenland)   D. Geirangerfjord (Norway)
B. Hardangerfjord (Norway)   E. Lynn Canal (USA)
C. Sognefjord (Norway)

For (2) bonus points: Which of the above is the deepest fjord in Norway?

CC. BODIES OF WATER
(each question at least 3 points)

29. This trans-Himalayan river's main tributaries include the Jhelum, Chenab, Beas, Ravi, and Sutlej. The Nar Canal flows away from this river. Rehman Dheri is an ancient urban city that was located along this river's west bank. This river, one of the longest in the world, flows southward through Pakistan and empties into the Arabian Sea.
   A. Swat River
   B. Kabul River
   C. Zanskar River
   D. Indus River

30. (I) All or nothing. Which ocean(s) does Canada border? ((1) point)
   (II) All or nothing. Which ocean(s) does Honduras border? ((1) point)
   (III) All or nothing. Which ocean(s) does Timor-Leste border? ((1) point) [max. 4 points]
   A. Atlantic Ocean (or via one of its seas)
   B. Pacific Ocean (or via one of its seas)
   C. Arctic Ocean (or via one of its seas)
   D. Indian Ocean (or via one of its seas)
   E. Southern Ocean (or via one of its seas)

   For (1) bonus point: All or nothing. Which ocean(s) does Israel border?

31. This lake is widely considered the oldest lake in the world. However, there is another old lake below, which if instead you select it, you'll receive the (3) points because there's controversy around it versus the former. No Steals. [max. 6 points]
   A. Lake Tanganyika
   B. Lake Zaysan
   C. Lake Baikal
   D. Caspian Sea

   (I) For (1) bonus point: Where is the lake located?

   (II) For (2) bonus points: Approximately how old is the lake?
   A. 9 million years old
   B. 65 million years old
   C. 25 million years old
   D. 5.5 million years old

32. This brackish inland sea spans from Denmark to Finland. It includes the Gulf of Bothnia, the Gulf of Finland, and the Gulf of Gdańsk. In the early Middle Ages, the Vikings of Scandinavia dominated its waters. Sadly, it is one of the most polluted seas in the world.
   A. Barents Sea
   B. Baltic Sea
   C. North Sea
   D. White Sea

CC. BODIES OF WATER
(each question at least 3 points)

33. **[SUPER-BONUS QUESTION—at least 7 wavy points!!!!!]** How well do you know Mother Earth's oceans?

A.   Arctic Ocean   D.   Pacific Ocean
B.   Atlantic Ocean   E.   Southern Ocean
C.   Indian Ocean

Each subquiz is (1) point, but if you answer all 15 subquizzes correctly, you'll earn (27) points, even before answering the bonus question correctly. You also have up to 5 minutes to complete the question. Good luck!

1)   Which ocean is the saltiest?
2)   Which ocean is the least salty?
3)   Which ocean experiences the full brunt of the Screaming Sixties?
4)   Which is the youngest ocean of (A) through (D) above?
5)   Which ocean's oil deposits make up about 40% of the world's oil production?
6)   Which ocean is home to most of the world's volcanoes?
7)   Which is the warmest ocean?
8)   In the last 200-plus years, the acidity of our oceans has increased by:
     A.   15%   B.   25%   C.   30%   D.   40%   E.   45%
     And it's not a good thing.
9)   Which ocean has the world's largest living structure that can be seen from the Moon?
10)   Which ocean has the strongest average winds of all the oceans?
11)   A mouthful of water from the ocean contains:
     A.   Millions of bacteria and billions of viruses
     B.   Billions of bacteria and millions of viruses
12)   Which ocean is the shallowest?
13)   Which is the oldest ocean?
14)   The IM1, a purported interstellar object or meteorite, crashed into which ocean on 9 January 2014?
15)   Our oceans globally are warmest during the month of March. However, on 1 August 2023, the average daily global sea surface temperature of our oceans broke record and reached:
     A.   20.96°C (69.73°F)   C.   20.95°C (69.71°F)
     B.   38.44°C (101.19°F)   D.   20.97°C (69.75°F)

If you earn at least (7) points above, you'll receive (3) bonus points if the following question is answered correctly:

To safeguard and recuperate marine nature, the High Seas Treaty (or BBNJ Agreement), formally adopted on 19 June 2023, aims to place what percentage of Mother Earth's seas into protected areas by 2030?

A.   10%   B.   20%   C.   30%   D.   40%

Answers to questions in this Category can be found starting on page 278.

CC. BODIES OF WATER
(each question at least 3 points)

Category DD:
MOUNTAINS, FORESTS, DESERTS
(3-point category)

1. The Monteverde Cloud Forest Biological Reserve is considered the most well-known cloud forest in the world. It's a few hours away from the Arenal Volcano National Park. Where is it located?
    A. Belize   B. Costa Rica   C. Colombia   D. Mexico

2. 16 January 2021 became the first time that climbers reached this mountain's summit in the winter. What is its name? [max. 5 points]
    A. Gangkhar Puensum   C. Mount Everest
    B. K2   D. Mount Baker

    For (2) bonus points: From which country are the climbers?

3. This dormant, snow-capped volcano is on the Armenian coat of arms and the Armenian ₹50000 banknote. It is the highest mountain in Türkiye. It is believed to be the location of the resting place of the biblical Noah's Ark after the flood described in the Bible's Genesis 6:9.
    A. Mount Ararat   C. Mount Nemrut
    B. Mount Erciyes   D. Mount Süphan

4. This is the tallest mountain in Tanzania. It has three volcanic cones—Kibo (dormant), Mawenzi (extinct), and Shia (extinct). What is this mountain, the tallest in Africa, known as *Uhuru* in Swahili?
    A. Mount Kenya   C. Mount Stanley
    B. Mount Karisimbi   D. Mount Kilimanjaro

5. (I) This inactive stratovolcano was once believed to be Earth's tallest mountain peak. It is the farthest point from the center of Earth due to Earth's equatorial bulge. Thus, it is the closest point on Earth to the stars. ((2) points)
    A. Mount Cotopaxi   C. Mount Antisana
    B. Mount Chimborazo   D. Mount Cayambe

    (II) In what South American country is it located? ((1) point)

6. In June 2023, it was reported that how many Amazon trees were felled in six years to feed the world's demand for Brazilian beef?
    A. More than 300 million   C. More than 800 million
    B. More than 500 million   D. More than 1 billion

7. (I) What is the world's largest bamboo forest? ((2) points)
    A. Anji Bamboo Sea (China)
    B. Arashiyama Bamboo Grove (Japan)
    C. Shunan Bamboo Forest (China)
    D. El Paraíso Del Bambú y la Guadua (Colombia)

    (II) Which bamboo forest above (pictured right) is located at the base of the "Storm Mountains"? ((1) point)

8. If you are visiting the national parks of Bannau Brycheiniog, Eryri, and Pembrokeshire Coast, where are you?
    A. England   C. Scotland   E. Isle of Man
    B. Northern Ireland   D. Wales

DD. MOUNTAINS, FORESTS, DESERTS
(each question at least 3 points)

9. This 4,478-metre-tall pyramid-shaped mountain is on the border of
    Switzerland and Italy. In its first ascent on 14 July 1865, four of the
    seven climbers perished. Edward Whymper, Peter Taugwalder and
    Peter Taugwalder Jr. survived. Iglu-Dorf, the world's largest snow igloo
    resort, is at the base of the mountain (in Zermatt). [max. 6 points]
    A. Monte Rosa   C. Matterhorn
    B. Dent Blanche   D. Weisshorn

    For (3) bonus points: What is the highest mountain located entirely on
    Swiss soil?
    A. Lyskamm   C. Weisshorn
    B. Dufourspitze   D. Dom

10. This mountain range includes the Accursed Mountains, Gjeravica
    Mountain, (Mali) Kozjak Mountain, Velika Mountain, Mosor
    Mountain, and Maglić Mountain. It separates the continental Balkan
    Peninsula from the Adriatic Sea.
    A. Julian Alps   C. Dinaric Alps
    B. Balkan Mountains   D. Albanian Alps

11. This valley, including its rainforest, in Australia is protected from
    logging because it was added to the Tasmanian Wilderness World
    Heritage Area in 2013. Prior to that, Forestry Tasmania (now
    Sustainable Timber Tasmania) managed it, and for some years pro-
    conservationists protested frequently against the company's
    controversial deforestation efforts. The valley is particularly recognized
    for its old growth forests, which are important carbon sequesters.
    A. Styx Valley   C. Walls of Jerusalem National Park
    B. Upper Florentine Valley D. Central Plateau Conservation Area

12. (I) This desert covers part of the United States and part of Mexico. It is
    the hottest desert in both countries. Many native peoples live in this
    desert, including the Yaqui, Seri, Tohono O'odham, and Cucapá. It also
    has two seasons of rainfall. ((2) points)
    A. Great Basin Desert   C. Chihuahuan Desert
    B. Sonoran Desert   D. Mojave Desert

    (II) Which of the above is the largest desert wholly situated in the USA?
    ((1) point)

13. What is the largest desert on Earth?
    A. Chihuahuan Desert   D. Arctic Polar Desert
    B. Sahara Desert   E. Arabian Desert
    C. Antarctic Polar Desert

14. What is the world's largest national park?
    A. Grand Canyon National Park (USA)
    B. Manú National Park (Peru)
    C. Northeast Greenland National Park (Greenland)
    D. Hamis National Park (India)

DD. MOUNTAINS, FORESTS, DESERTS
                (each question at least 3 points)

15. This is the tallest mountain in the UK and the British Isles.
   A. Aonach Mòr (Scotland)   D. Ben Nevis (Scotland)
   B. Scafell Pike (England)   E. Slieve Donard (Northern Ireland)
   C. Yr Wyddfa / Snowdon (Wales)

16. This mountain range was formed between 250 and 300 million years
   ago. Vast mineral resources are contained within it. Former Nomadic
   peoples such as the Khanty, Komi, Mansi, and Nenets live in the
   highest parts of this range, preserving their traditional ways of life. The
   range is in Western Russia and starts from the coast of the Arctic Ocean
   and stretches to the steppes of western Kazakhstan. It is this mountain
   range that separates the Eurasian landmass into two continents.
   A. Ural Mountains   C. Carpathian Mountains
   B. Kunlun Mountains   D. Altay Mountains

17. This mountain is the legendary home of the Greek gods and the site of
   Zeus's throne on its highest peak Mythikas. It is located near
   Thessaloniki, in the northeast region of Greece. It also is Greece's
   highest mountain. [max. 5 points]
   A. Mount Voras   C. Mount Pindus
   B. Mount Olympus   D. Mount Pelion

   For (2) bonus points: One of the mountains above was the kingdom of
   the half-human, half-horse centaur in Greek mythology.

18. What is the world's highest mountain that can be climbed without
   technical mountaineering equipment and special skills, if you follow the
   so-called "Normal Route"?
   A. Mont Blanc   C. Cerro Aconcagua
   B. Mount Kilimanjaro   D. K2

19. People incorrectly believe that there are no deserts in Europe. Of the
   five below, which is the largest desert in the continent? Two answers
   below, if either is selected, would be considered correct. No Steals.
   [max. 5 points]
   A. Oleshky Sands (Ukraine)   D. Deliblato Sands (Serbia)
   B. Tabernas Desert (Spain)   E. Oltenian Sahara Desert (Romania)
   C. Accona Desert (Italy)

   For (2) bonus points: Which of the above deserts often is used as a
   filming location, especially for Western genre films, because it
   resembles North American deserts?

20. What is the tallest sand dune in the world?
   A. Dune 7 (Namibia)   D. Duna Federico Kirbus (Argentina)
   B. Cerro Blanco (Peru)   E. Rig-e Yalan Dune (Iran)
   C. The Big Dipper (Wales)

21. This desert in Saudi Arabia contains the world's largest oil field,
   Ghawar.
   A. Al Araqana Desert   C. Rub' al Khali
   B. Al Nufud Al Kabir   D. Jubbah Desert

DD. MOUNTAINS, FORESTS, DESERTS   229
(each question at least 3 points)

22. This national park in the Canadian Rockies contains the southern portion of the Icefields Parkway as well as part of the Kicking Horse Pass. The Bow River flows through its main town. Its Castle Mountain served as an internment camp to hold immigrants from the Ukraine, Austria, Germany, and Hungary during World War I. It is Canada's first national park, and was once home to many indigenous peoples, including the Stoney Nakoda First Nation.

    A. Banff National Park   C. Kootenay National Park
    B. Yoho National Park   D. Jasper National Park

23. This mountain is the highest in Malaysia and Borneo and it is located on the Malaysian side. Species such as orangutans and the gigantic, carnivorous Rafflesia flower can be found on its slopes.

    A. Mount Jerai   C. Mount Kinabalu
    B. Mount Tahan   D. Mount Trusmadi

24. This stratovolcano is on Sumbawa Island, Indonesia. It was formerly the world's second-highest island peak at 14,100 feet (4,300 metres), before its height was reduced to 9,350 feet (2,850 metres) following one of the worst catastrophic eruptions in modern times in April 1815. Its slopes contain the ruins of a settlement that is referred to as "the Pompeii of the East."

    A. Mount Agung   C. Mount Sinabung
    B. Krakatoa   D. Mount Tambora

25. This mountain range's highest peak is Mount Nebo. It also hosts the Sundance Film Festival annually.

    A. Cascade Range   C. Teton Range
    B. Wasatch Range   D. Sawtooth Range

26. This is the largest remaining primeval forest in Europe. Hint: Europe's biggest mammal—the European bison—lives there.

    A. Cloosh Valley (Ireland)
    B. Kampinos Forest (Poland)
    C. Black Forest (Germany)
    D. Białowieża Forest (on the border between Belarus and Poland)

27. This mountain range is inhabited largely by Kurdish people. Kermanshah, Sulaymaniyah and Shiraz are cities located at the foot of this mountain range. Ancient Sumerians believed that the range contained the entrance to the Mesopotamian underworld of Kur.

    A. Zagros Mountains   C. Mount Cudi / Judi
    B. Shir Kuh   D. Mount Soffeh

28. All of the following volcanoes are in the horseshoe-shaped Ring of Fire except: [max. 6 points]

    A. Mount Saint Helens   C. Mount Nyiragongo
    B. Krakatoa   D. Mount Merapi

For (3) bonus points: What percentage of Earth's volcanoes are in the Ring of Fire?

    A. 30%   B. 50%   C. 65%   D. 75%

230   **DD. MOUNTAINS, FORESTS, DESERTS**
(each question at least 3 points)

29. Name the deepest cave in the world, as measured thus far.
    A. Sarma Chevé   C. Lamprechtsofen
    B. Veryovkina Cave   D. Krubera-Voronya Cave

30. **[SUPER-BONUS QUESTION—at least 7 points!!!!!] (I)** Hawaii's Mauna Loa, Venus's Maat Mons, Iceland's Skjaldbreiður, and Mars's Olympus Mons are examples of this type of volcano. ((4) points)
    A. Caldera volcano
    B. Composite volcano (or stratovolcano)
    C. Shield volcano   D. Cinder volcano

    (II) This stratovolcano in Europe has the largest base conference. ((3) points)
    A. Beerenberg (Norway)   C. Mount Hekla (Iceland)
    B. Mount Etna (Italy)   D. La Palma (Spain)

    (III) This is a large submarine volcano in Europe. ((3) points)
    A. Mount Pico (Portugal)   C. Marsili (Italy)
    B. Öræfajökull (Iceland)   D. Mount Teide (Spain)

    (IV-1) There are no active volcanoes in Greenland.   A. True   B. False
    (IV-2) There are two known, mapped, and dormant volcanoes under the Greenland ice sheet. (Each (IV) is (3) points.)   A. True   B. False

31. Where is the largest verified impact crater (i.e., the place created when meteorites hit the Earth's surface) on Earth?
    A. Chicxulub crater (Mexico)   C. Sudbury Basin (Canada)
    B. Vredefort crater (South Africa) D. Popigai crater (Russia)

32. For (1 ½) points each. **(I)** Mount Siple (at 10,203 feet / 3,110 metres) is a potentially active volcano. It is believed to be the most remote mountain never climbed. Where is it located?
    A. Alaska   B. Nunavut   C. Siberia   D. Antarctica

    (II) Because mountaineering is prohibited in this country, Gangkhar Puensum, which reaches 24,836 feet / 7,570 metres, is believed to be the highest unclimbed mountain in the world. Where is it located?
    A. Mongolia   B. Malaysia   C. Bhutan   D. Laos

33. Submarine volcanoes are located beneath the ocean's surface, commonly near mid-ocean ridges where tectonic plates move towards or away from each other. They erupt as the seafloor rips itself apart to allow magma through into the water. The magma cools very quickly and often turns into volcanic glass. (*Fascinating!*) All of the below are submarine volcanoes except: [max. 6 points]
    A. West Mata (Tonga)   D. Kick 'em Jenny (Grenada)
    B. Mount Babuyan (Philippines)   E. Kavachi (Solomon Islands)
    C. Tamu Massif (east of Japan)

    For (3) bonus points: What type of volcano is it?

    Answers to questions in this Category can be found starting on page 279.

DD. MOUNTAINS, FORESTS, DESERTS

(each question at least 3 points)

231

Category EE:
GODS, GODDESSES,
AND MANY MYTHS
(2-point category)

1. This mythological black dog haunted the Peel Castle in the Isle of Man.
    A. Fang
    B. Cerberus
    C. Moddey Dhoo
    D. Sirius

2. What Aegean island is the mythological birthplace of Apollo and Artemis?
    A. Mykonos
    B. Naxos
    C. Athens
    D. Delos

3. All of these are mythological creatures except:
    A. Sleipnir
    B. Chang'e
    C. Aqrabuamelu
    D. Lernaean Hydra

4. St. Patrick banished snakes from this country.
    A. Scotland
    B. Jersey
    C. Ireland
    D. Wales

5. This god was the father of Artemis, Apollo, Dionysus, Caerus, and Athena, among others. [max. 5 points]
    A. Zeus
    B. Prometheus
    C. Poseidon
    D. Hades

    (I) For (1) bonus point: Who commonly is considered his eldest child?
    (II) For (1) bonus point: Who is his youngest child?
    (III) For (1) bonus point: Who is believed to be his favourite child?

6. Only one of the following is completely correct. Which one? [max. 3 points]
    A. Norse mythical figures/creatures: Frigg, Dagda, Thor, Rhiannon
    B. Egyptian mythical figures/creatures: Khnum, Ra, Bastet, Ebisu
    C. Indian mythical figures/creatures: Naga, Garuda, Nezha, Durga
    D. Japanese mythical figures/creatures: Sang-Je, Pangu, Izanagi, Paritegi
    E. Americas mythical figures/creatures: Coyote, Lusca, Atabey, Tezcatlipoca

    For (1) bonus point: What is this fine-looking specimen called? Hint: It's Japanese.

7. Known as the dog-bird, this enormous, winged creature possessed great wisdom. She could exist for up to 1,700 years before she would dive into a fire that she created to die, and then give birth to herself again. She was a prominent figure in the story of the hero Zal. What is her name in Persian mythology?
    A. Huma
    B. Kamak
    C. Chamrosh
    D. Simurgh

8. After Ariadne gave this legendary hero a ball of thread to find his way out of Daedalus's labyrinth, he slew the fearsome minotaur of the Cretan king Minos. Who was he?
    A. Pirithous
    B. Theseus
    C. Perseus
    D. Lycomedes

EE. GODS, GODDESSES, AND MANY MYTHS

(each question at least 2 points)

9. This Japanese moon god killed Ukemochi, the food goddess, with his sword after he witnessed her pulling rice and millet from her ears and nose. (He was disgusted at the sight.) After the killing, this god and Amaterasu were never seen together.
    A. Tsukuyomi   C. Susanoo
    B. Raijin   D. Fujin

10. Which mythical Mayan bird demon replaced his jeweled teeth with maize after they were knocked out by one of the "Hero Twins," Hunahpu and Xbalanque?
    A. Zipacna   C. Camazotz
    B. Vucub Caquix (Seven Macaw)   D. Cabrakan

11. In ancient mythology, the manticore was a fearsome beast with the head of a man, the body of a lion, and the tail of a scorpion. It feared dragons, but would eat anything except:
    A. Bulls   C. Elephants
    B. Human beings   D. Lions

12. These mythological Greek creatures had the torso of a human and the lower body of a horse. There are different versions of their creation. In one myth, they were born of Ixion and the cloud-goddess Nephele. In another, they were children of Centaurus and Magnesian mares. Perhaps the most famous and intelligent of these creatures is Chiron.
    A. Centaur   C. Chimera
    B. Minotaur   D. Griffin

13. This Egyptian deity is a god of agriculture, vegetation, and fertility, as well as god of the underworld. He was murdered and dismembered by his jealous brother.
    A. Osiris   C. Anubis
    B. Set   D. Horus

14. This fierce Æsir god, son of Odin and Jörð, is destined to kill and to be killed by Jörmungandr, the Midgard Serpent. He wields the powerful Mjöllnir hammer. He is an unrelenting defender of the Aesir and their fortress, Asgard. [max. 4 points]
    A. Viðarr   B. Thor   C. Váli   D. Baldr

    (I) For (1) bonus point: What was the name of his first wife?
    (II) For (1) bonus point: What was the name of his second wife?
    A. Sif   B. Sigyn   C. Järnsaxa   D. Freyja

15. This Titan god of fire is associated with the creation of mortals. He stole Zeus's lightning bolt and gave fire to humanity. Zeus punished him by chaining him to a rock in the Kaukasos (Caucasus) Mountains and had an eagle eat his liver daily. [max 4 points]
    A. Epimetheus   C. Oceanus
    B. Prometheus   D. Cronus

    For (2) bonus points: What was the name of the eagle?

234   EE. GODS, GODDESSES, AND MANY MYTHS
(each question at least 2 points)

16. According to legend, whom did St. Peter meet along Via Appia while he was fleeing Emperor Nero's persecutions in Rome?
   A. Archangel Gabriel   C. Archangel Michael
   B. Jesus   D. St. Paul

17. This Greek god, a sibling of Zeus, resided in a place (of the same name) with his wife and niece Persephone. In Greek mythological canon, he was one of the most peaceful and impartial gods. His weapon was a bident, a two-pronged tool resembling a pitchfork.
   A. Cronus   B. Eris   C. Chiron   D. Hades

18. This Akan folklore character is a god of all knowledge of stories, who completed three difficult tasks to give all the stories of the world from the Sky God to the children of Earth.
   A. Rafiki   C. Adze
   B. Eshu   D. Anansi

19. Viracocha, Inti, Pachamama, and Mama Quilla were gods and goddesses of which Mesoamerican people?
   A. Aztec   C. Maya   E. Chimú
   B. Zapotec   D. Inca

20. [SUPER-BONUS QUESTION—at least 7 points!!!!!]
   (1) (I) Sunna or Sól; (II) Amaterasu; (III) Apollo; (IV) Lugh; (V) Utu or Shamash; (VI) Liza; and (VII) Surya are considered what kind of god or goddess? ((3) points)
   A. Sun god or goddess   C. Fertility god or goddess
   B. Moon god or goddess   D. Thunder god or goddess

   (2) What is the nationality, religion, or mythology of each of the above gods and goddesses? ((2) points each)

21. In Norse mythology, Fenrir, Geri, Freki, and Hati are:
   A. Dogs   D. Horses
   B. Wolves   E. Snakes/serpents
   C. Gods and Goddesses

22. This god's wife was Amphitrite, and their children included Triton and Rhodos. This god also fathered two sons with Medusa. He competed against Athena for the love of the people—she created a useful olive tree; he created a saltwater spring or horses, depending on the myth.
   A. Zeus   C. Poseidon
   B. Oceanus   D. Hades

23. This Greek figure blinded Polyphemus, the cyclops son of Poseidon and Thoosa, in order to escape his cave. He lost 11 of his 12 ships to cannibalistic giants. He spent almost nine years on an island of the nymph Calypso. Athena was his protectress. When he returned home to Ithaca to reunite with his family, only his faithful old dog and his nurse first recognized him.
   A. Odysseus   C. Agamemnon
   B. Achilles   D. Telemachus

EE. GODS, GODDESSES, AND MANY MYTHS   235
(each question at least 2 points)

24. In various ancient mythologies, this sacred bird flew eternally over the earth, never landing. The bird symbolized elevation and enlightenment, as well as compassion and fortune. Any attempt to injure it would bring one great misfortune, while seeing it flying overhead would bring one great blessing. What is this bird?
   A. Saena   C. Huma
   B. Chamrosh   D. Peri

25. This ancient Greek town was the location of the Oracle of Apollo. It also was home to the revered priestess Pythia as well as the feared dragon Python that Apollo killed.
   A. Athens   C. Crete
   B. Corinth   D. Delphi

26. One of the below is a Japanese god who is the protector of children, the weak, and travelers.
   A. Kannon   C. Ame-no-Uzume
   B. Jizō   D. Inari

27. In Egyptian mythology, who is the god of the Earth? [max. 4 points]
   A. Ra   C. Geb
   B. Shu   D. Ptah

   His sister is the sky goddess. What is her name? ((2) bonus points)
   A. Bastet   C. Sekhmet
   B. Nut   D. Maat

28. This Earth Mother of the Aztec Empire gave birth not just to animals and vegetation, but also to the Sun, the Moon, and the stars.
   A. Cōātlīcue   C. Chalchiuhtlicue
   B. Toci   D. Mictēcacihuātl

29. In certain African mythology, this goddess, who sometimes appears as a mermaid and with a snake, symbolizes good fortune, health, and wealth.
   A. Shun   C. Mami Wata
   B. Mawu   D. Ahia Njoku

30. This god accidentally killed his lover Semele while she was pregnant. He saved their unborn child from the womb and kept him sewn into his thigh until the baby was ready to be born. [max. 4 points]
   (I) Who is the god? ((1) point)
   A. Zeus   C. Poseidon
   B. Hades   D. Chiron

   (II) Who is the son? ((1) point)
   A. Heracles   D. Carystus
   B. Dionysus   E. Zagreus
   C. Pegasus

   For (2) bonus points: One of the gods above in (I) or (II) is represented as the constellation Sagittarius. Which one by name?

236   EE. GODS, GODDESSES, AND MANY MYTHS
              (each question at least 2 points)

31. **Who is the Māori Mother Earth goddess? [max. 4 points]**
    A. Papatūānuku   C. Ranginui
    B. Tangaroa   D. Rehua

    Who is the Māori Sky Father god? He is listed above. ((2) bonus points)

32. **This highly skillful god is one of the most important in Celtic mythology. Among other key attributes, he was a god associated with thunderstorms and he was a warrior king who led the Tuatha Dé Danann to victory against the Fomorians.**
    A. Cernunnos   C. Aengus
    B. Lugh   D. Ogmios

33. **This Buddhist deity embodies compassion. She is the goddess of mercy.**
    A. [K][Q]uan Yin   C. Mazu
    B. Green Tara   D. Palden Lhamo

Answers to questions in this Category can be found starting on page 279.

Don't worry, even the gods and goddesses would be struggling to get to 50 points! LOL!

EE. GODS, GODDESSES, AND MANY MYTHS   237
(each question at least 2 points)

Category FF:
HISTORY, HERSTORY, THEIRSTORY, [Y]OURSTORY
(3-point category)

1. Siblings Patria Mercedes, María Argentina Minerva, and Antonia María Teresa are national heroines of the Dominican Republic. They were brave and fearless activists against Rafael Trujillo's rule. On November 25, 1960, all three sisters were assassinated on their way to their homes. Decades later, the United Nations designated November 25 as the International Day for the Elimination of Violence Against Women. By which nickname are the sisters often referred to affectionately and admiringly?

    A. Las Flores
    B. Las Leonas
    C. Las Mariposas
    D. Las Hermanas Valientes

2. He is a national hero. He was the founder and strong ruler of the first centralized state of the Tajiks—the Samanid Dynasty. He lived from 849 until 907. One central Asian country's currency is named in his honor. The banknote below depicts a representation of him and his tomb located in Uzbekistan.

    A. Ibn Sīnā
    B. Ismoil Somoni
    C. Rūdhakī
    D. Ulūgh Beg

3. Dame Zaha Hadid, legendary Iraqi-British architect, was the first female to win the prestigious Pritzker Architecture Prize in 2004. She died in 2016, at age 65. Her works appear also on certain country banknotes. Her major works include the following, except for one: [max. 4 points]

    A. Heydar Aliyev Centre (Azerbaijan)
    B. Sheikh Zayed Bridge (UAE)
    C. Guangzhou Opera House (China)
    D. National Museum of Qatar (Qatar)
    E. MAXXI Museum (Italy)

    For (1) bonus point: Hadid designed just one private residence (a $140 million project)—a futuristic house half-submerged into the ground in a forest. Where is this house?

    A. USA   C. France   E. Switzerland
    B. Bahrain   D. Russia   F. UK

4. This pirate was active in the South China Sea in the early 19th century. She is perhaps the most successful pirate in history. After the death of her husband-pirate Zheng Yi, she subsequently commanded more than 1,000 vessels, the largest of which was the Red Flag Fleet, and over 70,000 pirates. She defeated the Qing Dynasty navy, the British, and the Portuguese empires in conflicts. In 1810, she was even able to negotiate with the Qing government a pardon for her and her crew along with a pension for her crew in exchange for her retirement from piracy. She also retained her immense wealth and went on to become a gambling house owner.

    A. Lin Siniang   C. Hua Mulan
    B. Ching Shih

5. This former gladiator, once a Thracian soldier, led a revolt of enslaved gladiators and the poor in the Third Servile War against the Roman Republic. Marcus Licinius Crassus defeated him at Senerchia in southern Italy in 71 B.C.E.

   A. Spiculus
   B. Crixus
   C. Spartacus
   D. Flamma

6. Until the age of 9, this woman spoke only Dutch. Born into slavery, she gained her freedom in 1826. She was an abolitionist, a women's right activist, and an author. One of her most famous speeches is "Ain't I a Woman?". She is the first Black woman to sue a White male in a U.S. court and prevail. She also is the first Black woman to be recognized with a statue in the U.S. Capitol building. Who is she?

   A. Harriet Tubman
   B. Sojourner Truth
   C. Sarah Forten
   D. Elizabeth Freeman

7. This Dominican friar, known for his prophesies and for standing up to corruption, burned so-called sinful literature, art, and jewels in the bonfire of the vanities in Florence. He introduced a democratic government in Florence after a brief departure of Medici rule.

   A. Alexander VI
   B. Domenico da Pescia
   C. Lorenzo the Magnificent
   D. Girolamo Savonarola

8. All of the following were allies of Germany at some point (known as the "Axis powers") during World War II except:

   A. Italy
   B. Japan
   C. Hungary
   D. China

9. This queen was married to King Louis VII of France at the age of 15. She later married King Henry II of England after her divorce from Louis VII on the grounds of consanguinity. Years later, King Henry II imprisoned her. Her full freedom was restored once her son Richard the Lionhearted took over the throne.

   A. Isabelle of France
   B. Eleanor of Aquitaine
   C. Emma of Normandy
   D. Queen Anne

10. This ancient Greek philosopher soundly believed that human wisdom begins with recognizing one's own ignorance. [*True that….Recognized!*] After being tried on charges of impiety and corrupting the youth, he accepted his guilty charge and declared that "*the life which is unexamined is not worth living*," before drinking hemlock poison.

    A. Plato
    B. Aristotle
    C. Socrates
    D. Thales of Miletus
    E. Protagoras

11. This person was the daughter of Emperor Gaozu of Tang. She assisted her father in overthrowing the Sui Dynasty with her own women's army that she herself commanded. Who is this powerful woman?

    A. Han E (Han Guanbao)
    B. Liang Hongyu
    C. Zhao of Pingyang
    D. Empress Taimu

FF. HISTORY, HERSTORY, THEIRSTORY, [Y]OURSTORY
(each question at least 3 points)

12. This political and spiritual leader, originally from the state of Gujarat, entered into a pact with Lord Irwin after he led the Salt March from 12 March to 6 April 1930. The Salt March was a nonviolent protest of civil disobedience against British rule in India. He also introduced the ideology of *Satyagraha*—which emphasized the power of truth, firmly holding to that truth, and the demand to search for truth.
    A. Mohandas "Mahatma" Gandhi
    B. Jawaharlal Nehru
    C. Chakravarti Rajagopalachari "Rajaji"
    D. Subhash Chandra

13. This visionary mystic and military leader, who believed she was acting under divine guidance, led the French army to victory at the besieged city of Orléans against the English in 1429, during the Hundred Years' War. She was later captured in 1430 outside of Compiegne and subsequently charged by an English tribunal with heresy and for wearing men's clothing. She was burned at the stake in 1431 at the age of 19. Years later, her sentence was revoked and annulled. Pope Benedict XV canonized her in 1920.
    A. Catherine of Alexandria
    C. Jeanne Hachette
    B. Joan of Arc
    D. Joanna of Flanders

14. Constantinople was invaded at least 34 times throughout its history by various empires, e.g., (I) the siege of Constantinople in 1203; (II) the siege of Constantinople in 1260; and (III) the siege of Constantinople in 1394.
    Who were the invaders in each of the above sieges? ((1) point each) [max. 6 points]
    A. Mongol Empire
    C. Ottoman Empire
    B. Crusaders
    D. Nicaea Empire

    If at least two answers are correct, for (3) bonus points: Who above won the fall of Constantinople in May 1453?

15. This tyrannical emperor was the fifth and final Roman emperor of the Julio-Claudian dynasty. He and his mother Agrippina allegedly poisoned his younger stepbrother Britannicus; he later had Agrippina killed, and his wife Octavia executed. He built the Domus Aurea, a lavish palatial complex, soon after the Great Fire of Rome in 64 C.E. He loved the coastal area of Baiae where a lot of his debauchery occurred.
    A. Tiberius
    C. Commodus
    B. Nero
    D. Caligula

16. A published front-page story of Sarah Page's false assault accusation against Dick Rowland, a Black male, triggered this riot in a U.S. state that led to the destruction of city blocks and the murders of more than 300 Black residents of its Greenwood District (the "Black Wall Street").
    A. Pequot Massacre
    C. Tulsa Race Massacre
    B. Rosewood Massacre
    D. Rock Springs Massacre

17. **[SUPER-BONUS QUESTION—at least 7 Amazonian points!!!!!]**
(1) Match each female warrior in the table with the statement associated with her below. Up to 4 minutes. ((3) points each)

Legendary Female Warrior
I. Queen Gudit (or Yodit)
II. Micaela Bastidas Puyucahua
III. Rani Velu Nachiyar
IV. Tomoe Gozen
V. Queen Ana Nzinga
VI. Granny Nanny
VII. Fu Hao

A. She led many military campaigns, including the defeats of the Tu-Fang and the Bafang, rivals of the Shang dynasty.

B. She led the Windward Maroons of Jamaica against the British during the First Maroon War from 1720 to 1739.

C. She was a Peruvian rebel who fought against Spanish colonialism. She was a leader of the Inca revolt of 1780.

D. She was a 10th-century leader of Abyssinia (now Ethiopia) who ruled for four decades.

E. She was queen of Ndongo and Matamba who fought back against Portuguese control of Angola, including by allying with the Dutch. She fought alongside her troops until she reached her sixties.

F. She was the first Indian queen from Tamil Nadu to wage war with East India Company to fight against British colonial power.

G. She was a 12th-century samurai, an Onna-Bugeisha, who was a leading commander in the Genpei War. Her name first appeared in the Japanese military epic *The Tale of the Heike*.

(2) The Dahomey female warriors were an elite, fearless, fighting force. From which country were they? ((1) point)
A. Benin   B. Senegal   C. Nigeria   D. Sierra Leone

18. **For (1 ½) points each. (I) Which countries were involved in the first Opium War (1839-42)? [max. 4 points]**
A. China against Great Britain
B. China against France
C. Japan against China
D. Japan against Vietnam

(II) Which countries were involved in the second Opium War (1856-60)?
A. France and Vietnam against Japan
B. Great Britain against China and Japan
C. France against Japan
D. Great Britain and France against China

For (1) bonus point: Into which country was opium imported illegally?

19. **This member of the Lemhi Shoshone Tribe was instrumental in the Lewis and Clark Expedition of land west of the Mississippi River in the USA. Her knowledge of plants was extraordinary. [max. 6 points]**
A. Lozen
B. Dahteste
C. Sacagawea
D. Pocahontas

For (3) bonus points: What is the name of her son who was born during the expedition on February 11, 1805? A representation of him is on a US-dollar coin along with her.

FF. HISTORY, HERSTORY, THEIRSTORY, [Y]OURSTORY
(each question at least 3 points)

20. Both or nothing. (I) Which country below was not involved in the 19th-century War of the Pacific, also known as the Saltpeter War?

    A. Peru   B. Chile   C. Ecuador   D. Bolivia

    (II) Over which valuable mineral deposit in the Atacama Desert was the dispute?

    A. Nitrate   B. Salt   C. Gold   D. Nickel

21. This 9th-century Frankish leader established the Carolingian Empire that stretched from northern Europe to Italy and Spain. He ruled from 768 until his death in 814. He was the first Holy Roman Emperor. He instituted economic reforms. He also abandoned the gold standard and put Europe on the same silver currency, making trade easier. He was devoted to his children but went so far as not to allow any of his daughters to marry while he was alive. He loved roasted meat and detested the advice of his doctors to restrict himself to boiled meat during the last four years of his life.

    A. Charlemagne   C. Charles the Bald
    B. Louis the Pious   D. Charles the Younger

22. Match the great and highly influential Persian poets of the Middle Ages with their descriptions below: (I) Rumi; (II) Saadi; and (III) Rūdakī. Answer one correctly for the (3) points; all three correctly, (8) points. No Steals. [max. 8 points]

    A. This 13th-century poet is best known for his poetic work: the *Bustan* (*The Orchard*). This work explored the importance and practice of virtue in one's life. He also wrote the celebrated *Gulistan*. A line in it states: "*Whoever does no good in the time of ability will see distress in the time of inability.*" (Chapter VIII, Admonition 15)

    B. This court poet of the Samanids and accomplished musician and singer was born in the town of Rudak (in Tajikistan). He is considered the Father of Persian Literature. The concepts of diwan (a collection of selected works of a poet), the ghazal (short lyrical form with rhyming couplets), qasida (long form satiric poem), and rubai (quatrain) have been attributed to him. Only about 52 of his works have survived.

    C. This 13th-century mystical poet, scholar, and Sufi theologian wrote in Farsi, Turkish, Arabic, and Greek. One of his greatest works is the *Masnavi*, a six-volume masterpiece that begins with:
        "*Listen to the reed and the tale it tells,*
        How it sings of separation…"

23. This musical artist broke her/his own all-time record for biggest streaming year for any artist in Spotify history, with over 10.3 billion streams within the first two months of the artist's album release in 2022. [max. 10 points]

    A. The Weeknd   B. Bad Bunny   C. Drake   D. Taylor Swift

    (1) For (3) bonus points: What is the name of the album?
    (2) For (4) bonus points: The concert tour of which artist above brought in a staggering US$1.04 billion in gross sales across the first 60 shows?

24. **Match each description below with the famous pirate: (I) Blackbeard; (II) Black Bart; (III) Calico Jack; and (IV) Henry Every. ((1) point each below) [max. 5 points]**

   A. This Wales-born pirate plundered and burned ships along the coasts of West Africa, Brazil, the Caribbean, and even as far north as Newfoundland Canada. He wore bright red silk finery in battle. His self-designed flag portrayed himself standing with a sword in hand, astride two skulls labeled A.B.H. ("A Barbadian's Head") and A.M.H. ("A Martinican's Head") flown over his *Royal Fortune* ship. He was one of the most successful pirates (known also for his fashion sense) during the Golden Age of Piracy.

   B. This England-born pirate had two female pirates in his crew, Anne Bonny (his lover) and Mary Read. He operated in The Bahamas and Cuba and his flagship was *Kingston*. He and his crew were captured in Jamaica where they were tried, convicted, and executed in November 1720. His body was gibbeted on display at an entrance to Port Royal to deter other pirates.

   C. This England-born pirate operated out of New Providence in The Bahamas, after leaving Jamaica. His main ship was *Queen Anne's Revenge*, and he had a crew of over 300 men. In May 1718, he blockaded the port of Charleston Harbor in South Carolina, USA. He was killed in battle some months later by Lieutenant Robert Maynard and his crew.

   For (2) bonus points: Which of the above pirates captured the *Ganj-i-Sawai*, a treasure ship of Aurangzeb (the Mughal Emperor of India), in September 1695? He and his crew made off with cargo estimated to be worth between £325,000 and £600,000 at the time.

25.

   These two folio vellum leaves above (Leaf I and Leaf III, respectively) are from which 1375 historical atlas? The 14th-century atlas focuses primarily on the territories around the Mediterranean Sea, but also covers part of the west coast of Africa, Scandinavia, and Asia—all as known at the time. The full map is meant to lay flat, and it is oriented with the North at the bottom. Owned by King Charles V, it is preserved in the Bibliothèque national de France. Hint: Abraham Cresques was the cartographer.

   A. Catalan Atlas
   B. Medici-Laurentian Atlas
   C. Theatrum Orbis Terrarum (Epitome of the Theatre of the World)
   D. Tabula Peutingeriana (Peutinger Table)

FF. HISTORY, HERSTORY, THEIRSTORY, [Y]OURSTORY
(each question at least 3 points)

26. **This person became monarch at the age of 18 in 1837. [max. 9 points]**

    A. Queen Emma
    B. Queen Elizabeth I
    C. Empress Go-Sakuramachi
    D. Queen Victoria
    E. Queen Isabella II

    For (3) bonus points each:
    (I) Which woman above succeeded to the throne when she was just three years old?

    (II) Which woman above abdicated the throne in favour of her nephew?

27. **This Native American woman was America's first major prima ballerina. She was the first prima ballerina of the New York City Ballet. She was the first American to dance with the Paris Opera Ballet. She was one of the "Five Moons," and the character of the Firebird was her signature role. [max. 6 points]**

    A. Myra Yvonne Chouteau
    B. Moscelyne Larkin
    C. Maria Tallchief
    D. Marjorie Tallchief
    E. Rosella Hightower

    For (3) bonus points: Which Native American tribe is her heritage?

    A. Shawnee Tribe
    B. Osage Nation
    C. Choctaw Nation
    D. Peoria Tribe
    E. Eastern Shawnee Tribe

28. **Match the Roman Catholic pope with the description of his (alleged) death below. ((½) point each correct answer) [max. 5 points]**

Roman Catholic Pope
I. Stephen VI
II. John XIV
III. Leo V
IV. John VIII
V. John X
VI. Benedict VI
VII. John XII

    A. This pope allegedly was first poisoned and then clubbed to death by his own clerics.
    B. This pope was strangled to death by a priest on order of Crescentius I.
    C. This pope was imprisoned by Antipope Boniface VII, where he died either from starvation or was poisoned.
    D. Within a few months after instigating the Cadaver Synod, this pope was imprisoned and strangled by other prelates.
    E. This pope was deposed then imprisoned by Christopher, a cardinal priest, under the orders of Sergius III, where he later died.
    F. This pope was deposed, imprisoned, and allegedly smothered with a pillow.

    (I) For (1) bonus point: This pope (from the table above) was beaten badly by the husband of a woman with whom he was caught in bed. He succumbed to his injuries three days later.

    (II) For (1) bonus point: Which commandment in the Roman Catholic tradition is *"Thou shalt not covet thy neighbour's wife"*?

    A. Seventh
    B. Eighth
    C. Ninth
    D. Tenth

FF. HISTORY, HERSTORY, THEIRSTORY, [Y]OURSTORY
(each question at least 3 points)

29. Match two statements below with the female warrior in the table. Match all three for (7) points. [max. 8 points]

Legendary Female Warrior
I. Petra "Pedro" Herrera
II. Boudicca
III. Khutulun
IV. Mai Bhago

A. This 13th-century warrior was the great-great-granddaughter of Chinggis Khaan. She dominated the wrestling ring and was a feared and fearless warrior on the battlefields in her defense of Mongolia and Kazakhstan against Kublai Khaan.

B. This Sikh warrior led a group of 40 Sikh soldiers (who had been deserters) against 10,000 soldiers of the Mughal Empire in the Battle of Muktsar in 1705.

C. This Celtic queen warrior of Iceni led her people against Roman rule and occupation.

For (1) bonus point: From which country is Petra Herrera?
A. Bolivia   B. Chile   C. Colombia   D. Mexico

30. This indigenous author and chronicler wrote *El primer nueva corónica y buen gobierno* (or *Nueva Corónica*), a 1,189-page document, written mainly in Spanish, and also in Quechua and Latin. It included 398 of his drawings of the Inca Empire. His document was addressed to King Philip III of Spain, who it is believed never to have received it. *Nueva Corónica* was the strongest critique of Spain's colonial rule in the Americas and the injustices of the rule, including of forced labour in mercury and silver mines. The chronicler argued that the Spanish were foreign settlers of his country, and he wrote that: "*It is our country because God has given it to us.*" He also highlighted the history and sophistication of Andean civilization. Today, *Nueva Corónica* is housed in the Royal Library of Denmark. Who is the author? [max. 6 points]
A. Paul Rivet   C. Blas Valera
B. Felipe Guamán Poma   D. Fray Martín de Murúa

For (3) bonus points: About which country in the Americas was he writing?
A. Peru   B. Colombia   C. Chile   D. Bolivia

31. During this golden age period of Japanese history: Chinese influences declined. The aristocratic Fujiwara family was quite powerful. Two esoteric Buddhist sects, the Tendai and the Shingon, gained prominence during the period. The Byōdō-in temple near Kyōto was built. Katakana and Hiragana Japanese scripts were developed. Royal court was depicted in *The Tale of Genji*. The famous Japanese poem "Iroha" and the *Pillow Book* essays were written. [max. 12 points]
A. Nara   C. Kamakura Shogunate
B. Edo   D. Heian

(I) For (3) bonus points: Which period immediately preceded it?

(II) For (6) bonus points: Which below shows certain of Japan's historical periods in their correct order from earliest to latest?
A. Muromachi→ Heian→ Azuchi-Momoyama→ Nara→ Edo→ Kamakura
B. Nara→ Heian→ Kamakura→ Muromachi→ Azuchi-Momoyama→ Edo

FF. HISTORY, HERSTORY, THEIRSTORY, [Y]OURSTORY
(each question at least 3 points)

32. **Which is the first recorded peace treaty in history? [max. 6 points]**
    A. Peace of Philocrates (Athens and Macedon)
    B. Peace of Antalcidas (Persia and Greece)
    C. Treaty of Kadesh (Hittites and Egypt)
    D. Treaty of the Thirty Years Peace (Athens and Sparta)

    For (3) bonus points: Which of the above treaties brought an end to the First Peloponnesian War?

33. **Rome did not fall in one day. Western Rome's battles with the so-called "Barbarian" tribes were major contributing factors to the collapse of its empire. Match each conflict below with the tribe who attacked Rome in the 5th century. ((1) point each)**

    A. This tribe successfully sacked Rome over a three-day period, starting on the night of 24 August 410 C.E.
    B. This tribe raided Rome, plundering it for 14 days, from 2 June through 16 June 455 C.E.
    C. This tribe staged a successful revolt against Orestes, a Roman general, on 23 August 476 C.E., and later deposed and exiled Orestes's son Emperor Romulus Augustulus on 4 September. The leader became the first Barbarian to rule in Rome.

"Barbarian" Tribe
I. King Gaiseric and the Vandals
II. Odoacer and the Sciri
III. King Alaric and the Visigoths

Answers to questions in this Category can be found starting on page 280.

Category GG:
THE SCIENCES ROCK!
(4-point category)

1. **Who first took an X-ray image of the DNA structure in 1952 (the "Photo 51")?**
   A.   James Watson
   B.   Rosaland Franklin
   C.   Maurice Wilkins
   D.   Francis Crick

2. **One of these statements is not a true attribute of iodine. Which one?**
   A.   Iodine is found in seaweed.
   B.   Iodine is used in photography.
   C.   Iodine's atomic number is 23.
   D.   Iodine's atomic mass is 126.9044.

3. **This is not a trick question. Koalas are related to:**
   A.   Bears   B.   Sloths   C.   Monkeys   D.   Wombats

4. **All of the following are true facts of Krypton (Kr) except:**
   A.   Krypton is green.
   B.   Krypton is odorless.
   C.   Krypton's mass is 83.80
   D.   Krypton's autonomic number is 36.

5. **(I) What is the primary function of the Tympanum? ((1) point)**
   (II) What is the primary function of the Incus? ((1) point)
   A.   To store wax
   B.   To vibrate in response to sound waves and transmit them to the middle ear
   C.   To transmit vibration from the malleus to the stapes
   D.   To clear mucus and other secretions from the middle ear

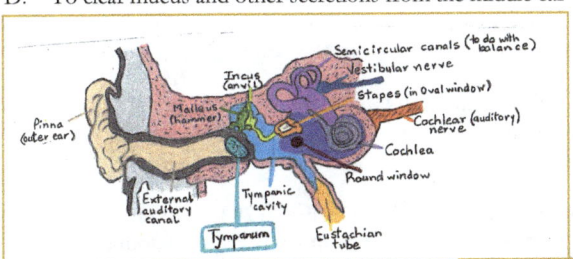

   (III) All or nothing. Name the three main parts of the inner ear. They also are shown in the above image. ((2) points) [max. 6 points]

   If you have at least (2) points, for (2) bonus points: What reflexology point (shown right) corresponds to the ear?
   A.   12   B.   7   C.   15   D.   9

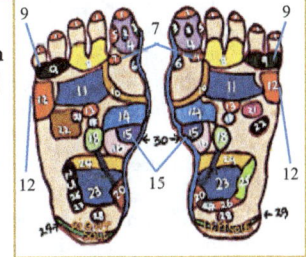

6. **How many X chromosomes are in the female cells of humans and many other mammals? How many X chromosomes are in male cells?**
   A.   1 in females, 1 in males
   B.   2 in females, 1 in males
   C.   1 in females, 2 in males
   D.   2 in females, 0 in males

GG. THE SCIENCES ROCK!
(each question at least 4 points)

7. **For (2) points each. (I) When did the Holocene period begin?**
   A. About 2 million years ago   C. About 15,000 years ago
   B. About 11,700 years ago   D. About 5 million years ago

   (II) Each of these is a stage of the Pleistocene epoch/era except:
   A. Gelasian   D. Mesozoic
   B. Ionian   E. Calabrian
   C. Tarantian

8. **(I) At what point on the Celsius and Fahrenheit scales is the temperature in degrees the same? ((2) points) [max. 8 points]**
   A. -40°   B. -32°   C. -25°   D. -10°

   (II) The [X] scale, used mainly in engineering, starts at absolute zero but uses Fahrenheit units. ((1) point)
   A. Kelvin   B. Rankine

   (III) The [Y] scale, widely used in scientific equations and calculations, starts at absolute zero but uses Celsius units. ((1) point)
   A. Kelvin   B. Rankine

   For (4) bonus points: From May 2019, one of the above scales was redefined in terms of the Boltzmann constant (and no longer in terms of the triple boiling point of water).

9. **How many Y chromosomes are in the female cells of humans and many other mammals? How many Y chromosomes are in male cells?**
   A. 1 in females, 1 in males   C. 0 in females, 2 in males
   B. 0 in females, 1 in males   D. 1 in females, 2 in males

10. **What is this unit of time, 10^{-21}, called?**
    A. Nanosecond   C. Zeptosecond
    B. Attosecond   D. Picosecond

11. **This proposal was rejected in 2024, but in 2022, a team of research scientists proposed that the Anthropocene epoch began in:**
    A. The year 2000   C. Between 1984 and 1990
    B. The year 1945   D. Between 1950 and 1954

12. **(1) Mature human red blood cells do not contain nuclei or mitochondria, and so, they do not have DNA. ((1) point)**
    A. True that, as shocking as it is!
    B. False, did you not study biology?!

    (2) Which is (I) in the diagram to the right? Which is (II)? Which is (III)? ((1) point each)
    A. Nucleoplasm
    B. Nucleolus
    C. Nuclear Pore
    D. Chromatin

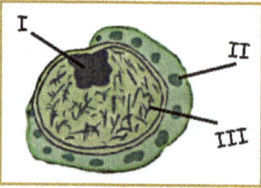

GG. THE SCIENCES ROCK!
(each question at least 4 points)

13. DNA and RNA are nucleic acids found in living cells. Which else is/are
true? [max. 10 points]
(I) DNA is a single strand of nucleotides folded onto itself, while RNA
has a paired double strand.
(II) RNA is a single stranded sugar phosphate ribose.
(III) RNA can be formed spontaneously in basaltic glass.
(IV) RNA is a carrier of genetic codes in some viruses.
(V) A DNA strand is about 6 feet (2 metres) long if stretched out.

A. (I) only   E. (II), (IV), and (V)
B. (II) only   F. (I), (IV), and (V)
C. (I) and (III)   G. (II), (III), (IV), and (V)
D. (II) and (III)   H. (I), (III), and (IV)

For (3) bonus points each:
1. Which structure is RNA?
A. (1)   B. (2)

2. Thymine is found in [ ],
while Uracil is found in [ ].
A. DNA   B. RNA

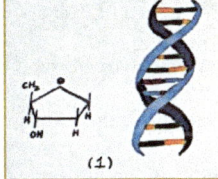 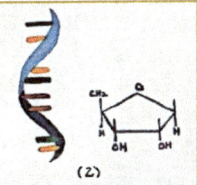

(1)   (2)

14. What is the latest supersonic aircraft, hoping to take the boom burst out
of supersonic travel? Hints: Its engines are above the wing rather than
below as those on the Concorde. It made its debut in January 2024.
A. X-59   C. X-51A   E. X-43A
B. X-66   D. X-15

15. Who discovered that when a beam of colored light enters a liquid, a
fraction of the light scattered by the liquid is of a different color?
A. Venki Ramakrishnan   C. Chandrasekhara Venkata Raman
B. Subrahmanyan Chandrasekhar   D. Homi Jehangir Bhabha

16. At -196°C, nitrogen exists in what state?
A. Gas   B. Liquid   C. Solid   D. ½ Liquid, ½ Gas

17. Match the galaxy with its constellation below: (I) Eyes Galaxies (NGC
4435, NGC 4438); (II) Black Eye Galaxy (M64); (III) Southern Pinwheel
Galaxy (M83); and (IV) NGC 474 Galaxy. ((1) point each) [max. 8
points]
A. Pisces   D. Hydra
B. Coma Berenices   E. Boötes (the Herdsman)
C. Virgo   F. Hercules

For (4) bonus points: The mega-large structures, the Big Ring and its
companion Giant Arc, are pushing us to rethink our understanding of
the universe. Both are nearest to which constellation above?

18. Which of the following elements are in the Nonmetal Group on the
periodic table: (I) Hydrogen; (II) Lithium; (III) Carbon; (IV) Oxygen;
(V) Mercury; and (VI) Phosphorus.
A. All   C. (I), (III), (IV), (VI)
B. (I), (II), (VI)   D. (II), (III), (IV), (V)

GG. THE SCIENCES ROCK!
(each question at least 4 points)

19. **Ancient inventions from this country include the compass, an earthquake detector, umbrella, and porcelain.**
    A. China   B. South Korea   C. India   D. Japan

20. **(I) Name the Post-Transition Metal element with chemical symbol Pb and atomic number 82. ((2) points)**
    A. Lead   B. Thallium   C. Bismuth   D. Tin

    (II) Name the Transition Metal element with chemical symbol Fe and atomic number 26. ((2) points)
    A. Scandium   C. Manganese
    B. Titanium   D. Iron

21. **Which of the following is not true about Xenon (Xe) gas?**
    A. It is colorless.
    B. It does not react with oxygen and other elements.
    C. It is odorless.
    D. It is used to make the lamps of belisha beacons.

22. **These organisms live in the Mariana Trench. Match the organism with its scientific name: (I) Black seadevil anglerfish; (II) Dumbo octopus; (III) Fangtooth; and (IV) Goblin shark? ((1) point each)**
    A. Grimpoteuthis   C. Melanocetus
    B. Mitsukurina owstoni   D. Anoplogaster cornuta

23. **What temperature is absolute zero (or zero Kelvins)? It is the temperature at which a thermodynamic system reaches its lowest possible energy, and where there is no motion and no heat.**
    A. -273.15°C / -459.67°F   C. -227.78°C / -378°F
    B. -270.56 °C / -455°F   D. -262.22°C / -440°F

24. **What unit(s) of measurement do astronomers use to determine the distances to nearby stars? [max. 8 points]**
    A. Light-years   D. (A) and (B)
    B. Parallax (or parsec)   E. (A), (B), and (C)
    C. Astronomical unit

    For (2) bonus points each: Which of the below can be used to measure: (I) Distances in our Galaxy, and to nearby galaxies; and (II) Distances to objects far, far away?
    A. Redshift and Hubble's Law   B. Cepheid variables

25. **When this element is combined with tin, it forms bronze. When it is combined with zinc, it forms brass. Which element is it?**
    A. Gold   B. Silver   C. Copper   D. Nickel

26. **Which of the following occurred first?**
    A. Otto Lilienthal built the monoplane hang glider.
    B. The Wright Brothers successfully flew an aircraft.
    C. Guglielmo Marconi broadcasted the first transatlantic radio signals.
    D. Albert Einstein propounded the general theory of relativity.
    E. Max Planck introduced the quantum theory.

GG. THE SCIENCES ROCK!
(each question at least 4 points)

27. **(I) How many different types of amino acids are there in a string in the human body? ((2) points) [max. 12 points]**

    A.   15   B.   10   C.   30   D.   20

    (II) About how many known protein-coding genes are expressed in the human body? ((2) points)

    A.   7,500   B.   10,000   C.   15,400   D.   Over 20,000

    For (4) bonus points each: (1) What software platform using AI can accurately predict 3D models of protein structures? Hint: In November 2020, it was recognized as a solution to the 50-year-old "protein-folding problem."

    A.   Baker   C.   FEIG-R2
    B.   AlphaFold2   D.   Zhang

    (2) Who and/or which lab is/was associated with the above platform?

    A.   Yang Zhang Lab   C.   Demis Hassabis, Mustafa Suleyman
    B.   David Baker   D.   Michael Feig (Feig Lab)

28. Maintained since 1947, the Doomsday Clock represents how close we are to destroying the world with dangerous technologies of our own making. It informs us of how many metaphorical "minutes to midnight" humanity has remaining. [max. 6 points]
    (I) At what time was the device set in January 1947? ((2) points)

    A.   11:50 p.m.   C.   11:53 p.m.
    B.   11:52 p.m.   D.   11:55 p.m.

    (II) At what time was it set in January 2022? ((2) points)

    A.   11:58 p.m.   C.   100 seconds to midnight
    B.   90 seconds to midnight   D.   75 seconds to midnight

    For (2) bonus points: Using the answers above in (II), what time was the Doomsday Clock set at on 23 January 2024?

29. French physicist Léon Foucault introduced this device in 1851 to demonstrate the rotation of Earth.

    A.   Pendulum   C.   Sundial
    B.   Oscillator   D.   Water clock

30. **For (2) points each. (I) Which one of the following sharks can walk on land, possibly up to 30 metres (almost 90 feet) using its paddle-shaped fins, and for up to two hours? [max. 5 points]**

    A.   Hammerhead   C.   Tiger
    B.   Epaulette   D.   Bull

    (II) How many known species of this "walking" shark are there?

    A.   1   B.   6   C.   3   D.   9

    For (1) bonus point: As of 2024, these walking sharks have been found in all of the below places, except:

    A.   Australia   C.   Thailand
    B.   Indonesia   D.   Papua New Guinea

GG. THE SCIENCES ROCK!

(each question at least 4 points)

31. **[SUPER-BONUS QUESTION—at least 7 points!!!!!]**
    (1) All matter except dark matter is made of molecules. ((4) points)
    A. True   B. False

    (2) Based on current understanding of cosmology, dark energy is not distributed evenly throughout the universe. ((2) points)
    A. True   B. False

    (3) What are the four fundamental forces at work in the universe? ((3) points each)
    A. Gravitational force   D. Negative force
    B. Weak force   E. Electromagnetic force
    C. Neutral force   F. Strong force

    (4) Which fundamental force is the weakest strength? ((1) point)

    (5) Which two fundamental forces have infinite range? ((2) points each)

    (6) The below are examples of which subatomic particles: (I) Fermions (matter), and (II) Bosons (forces)? ((4) points)
    A. Gluons, Gravitons, Photons, W particles, Z particles
    B. Electrons, Neutrinos, Neutrons, Protons, Quarks

    (7) In which value does: (I) a Fermion have a spin, and (II) a Boson have a spin? ((3) points)
    A. Odd half-integer value (e.g., ½, 1 ½ , 2 ½)
    B. Integer value (e.g., 0, 1, 2)

32. This famous fossil skeleton was discovered by Kamoya Kimeu and Richard Leakey in 1984 in an area in Kenya. It is of a *Homo erectus* from about 1.6 million years ago. The skeleton is 40% complete (only about 108 bones were found). There are plausible theories regarding the cause of death of this *Homo erectus*. [max. 8 points]
    A. Turkana Boy   B. Lucy   C. Ardi   D. Selam

    For (4) bonus points, (2) points each: (I) Which of the above is the skeleton of a two-and-a-half or three-year-old female *Australopithecus afarensis* who lived about 3.3 million years ago?
    (II) In which country was the fossil found?
    A. Egypt   B. Kenya   C. Ethiopia   D. Senegal

33. In 2022, which device did scientists in Japan modify to enable it to read and record dreams, along with another machine? ((2) points each below) The "dream machine" measures brain activity while one sleeps. An algorithm reconstructs the dreams, and the result is a playback of those dreams.
    A. A modified endoscope   D. A modified otoscope
    B. A modified cardiogram   E. A modified polygraph
    C. A modified MRI scanner   F. An electroencephalogram (EEG)

Answers to questions in this Category can be found starting on page 280.

GG. THE SCIENCES ROCK!
               (each question at least 4 points)

NO OTHER TRIVIA
LIKE THIS MASTERCLASS
BE STRATEGIC....BE YOU

BE STRATEGIC.   BE SWEET.   BE MEAN.   BE GUILELESS.
BE A GOOD SPORT.   BE CONNIVING.   BE EMPATHETIC.
BE CALCULATED.   BE WICKED.   BE BOLD.   BE KIND.
BE ASTUTE.   BE CUT-THROAT.   BE SMART.   BE CHILL.

I.   Choose one play <Smile>

1.   **BE A GOOD SPORT**. Get 5 free points and give 5 points to another team of your choice.

2.   **BE CALCULATED.** Get 5 free points and take away 5 points from another team of your choice.

3.   **BE KIND**. Get 5 free points and give 3 points each to at least three other teams.

BE YOU

BE STRATEGIC. BE SWEET. BE MEAN. BE GUILELESS.
BE A GOOD SPORT. BE CONNIVING. BE EMPATHETIC.
BE CALCULATED. BE WICKED. BE BOLD. BE KIND.
BE ASTUTE. BE CUT-THROAT. BE SMART. BE CHILL.

II.   **Choose one play <Smile>**

1. **BE CUT-THROAT.** Take away 4 points each from <u>two</u> other teams, 5 points each from <u>three</u> different teams, and 6 points from <u>one</u> other team.* As a reward, receive 6 points.

> *If there aren't seven teams, you must at least take away 4 points from one team, and 6 points from another team.

2. **BE STRATEGIC.** Receive 7 points just for selecting this strategy play card.

BE YOU

BE STRATEGIC.   BE SWEET.   BE MEAN.   BE GUILELESS.
BE A GOOD SPORT.   BE CONNIVING.   BE EMPATHETIC.
BE CALCULATED.   BE WICKED.   BE BOLD.   BE KIND.
BE ASTUTE.   BE CUT-THROAT.   BE SMART.   BE CHILL.

III.   **Choose one play \<Smile\>**

1.   **BE SMART**. With this card, you get 3 points now for selecting this
strategy play card, AND
one extra turn immediately after your next regular turn, AND
you may choose the same Category consecutively.

2.   **BE CONNIVING**. With this card, you get one extra turn
immediately after your next regular turn, PLUS
you can ask one other team to collaborate with you on that extra
turn*, PLUS
you can choose your favorite Category (even if it was played in the
round immediately before), PLUS
you must take 3 points away from *any* team, after you've played that
turn.

> *The other team can refuse. If they
> don't, they share the points for that
> full question equally with you.

BE YOU

BE STRATEGIC.   BE SWEET.   BE MEAN.   BE GUILELESS.
BE A GOOD SPORT.   BE CONNIVING.   BE EMPATHETIC.
BE CALCULATED.   BE WICKED.   BE BOLD.   BE KIND.
BE ASTUTE.   BE CUT-THROAT.   BE SMART.   BE CHILL.

IV.   **Choose one play <Smile>**

1.   **BE CHILL**. Don't task your brain. Get the points of the next question on your turn for free, while you and your teammates shoot the breeze, and perhaps distract everyone else who chooses to attempt the question. You must tell the judge your Category and question number now.
If you happen to select the Super-Bonus question, you must choose a different question in the Category on your turn.

2.   **BE WICKED**. Pick any team to skip their next regular turn and deny their ability to steal from the team who replaces them.

BE YOU

BE STRATEGIC.   BE SWEET.   BE MEAN.   BE GUILELESS.
BE A GOOD SPORT.   BE CONNIVING.   BE EMPATHETIC.
BE CALCULATED.   BE WICKED.   BE BOLD.   BE KIND.
BE ASTUTE.   BE CUT-THROAT.   BE SMART.   BE CHILL.

V.   **Choose one play <Smile>**

1.   **BE ASTUTE.** Get 5 free points, AND
     choose the next Category for the team two numbers away from you
     (*e.g.*, if you're team 1, you'll select for team 3; if you're team 4, you'll
     select for team 6; if you're team 7, you'll select for team 2, etc.).
     They choose the question. (For avoidance of doubt, it cannot be a
     question already played.)

2.   **BE MEAN.** Get 6 free points, AND
     choose any two teams to miss their next respective turn (though
     they can still steal), AND
     take away 3 points from each of the remaining teams.

BE YOU

BE STRATEGIC.   BE SWEET.   BE MEAN.   BE GUILELESS.
BE A GOOD SPORT.   BE CONNIVING.   BE EMPATHETIC.
BE CALCULATED.   BE WICKED.   BE BOLD.   BE KIND.
BE ASTUTE.   BE CUT-THROAT.   BE SMART.   BE CHILL.

VI.   Choose one play <Smile>

1.   **BE EMPATHETIC.** Give away this card to the team with the lowest score presently, and that team receives 5 points. In return, you get 3 free points, and hopefully they'll say "thank you" genuinely. If that team is you, give the card to the second lowest scoring team for the same points.

2.   **BE SWEET.** Give away this card to the team with the second lowest score presently, and that team receives 4 points, while you get 3 points. If that team is you, give away instead to the third highest scoring team for the same points.

3.   **BE GUILELESS.** Get 1 point now, AND
if you answer your question(s) correctly on your next regular turn, you receive double the points of the main question(s), including if that question happens to be the Super-Bonus question, but regular points for the Bonus question(s).

BE YOU

BE STRATEGIC.   BE SWEET.   BE MEAN.   BE GUILELESS.
BE A GOOD SPORT.   BE CONNIVING.   BE EMPATHETIC.
BE CALCULATED.   BE WICKED.   BE BOLD.   BE KIND.
BE ASTUTE.   BE CUT-THROAT.   BE SMART.   BE CHILL.

VII.   **Choose one play <Smile>**

1.   **ALL-TEAMS-PLAY.** All teams answer the next question. The **judge** selects the Category and the question*. The first team to answer the entire question (including Bonus questions, if any) correctly, wins 8 additional points.

2.   **ALL-TEAMS-PLAY**. All teams answer the next question. **Your team** selects the Category and the question*. The first team to answer the entire question (including Bonus questions, if any) correctly, wins 5 additional points.

> *For the avoidance of doubt, it cannot be a question already answered.

BE YOU

BE STRATEGIC. BE SWEET. BE MEAN. BE GUILELESS.
BE A GOOD SPORT. BE CONNIVING. BE EMPATHETIC.
BE CALCULATED. BE WICKED. BE BOLD. BE KIND.
BE ASTUTE. BE CUT-THROAT. BE SMART. BE CHILL.

VIII.   **Choose one play <Smile>**

1.   **BE CHILL.** Receive 3 points just for selecting this strategy play card, and smile to the other teams.

2.   **BE BOLD**. Bet half of your team's current score by selecting a question from a Category not played so far or the least played. On your next regular turn, if you answer the <u>full</u> main questions(s) correctly, you receive 3 times your wager, in addition to the points shown for the main question(s). Answering the Bonus question(s) is what it is…a bonus.

    But if you answer (any of) the full main question(s) incorrectly, you lose your wagered score plus 3 points must be taken off your then present unwagered score. And yes, you can end up with zero points or in the negative.

    There will be no Steals allowed on that play. All attention is on your team. If you happen to select the Super-Bonus question, you must choose a different question in the Category.

3.   **BE STRATEGIC**. Auction this strategy play card for the highest bid points. The "winning" bidding team must deduct the points from their current score before they play 2 above. If no bidder or accepted bid, this strategy play card becomes null and void.

.

BE YOU

NO OTHER TRIVIA
LIKE THIS MASTERCLASS
THE ANSWERS

Category A. Country Leaders	Category B. Wait… What Happened?	Category C. "Independence"
1. (I) A; (II) C.	**1.** C. Bonus: *Salvator Mundi* ~1500.	**1.** B. Bonuses: (I) Mary Katharine Goddard. (II) C.
2. (I) B; (II) C.	**2.** B.	**2.** D.
3. (I) D; (II) C.	**3.** D.	**3.** A. Bonus: C.
4. (I) C; (II) B.	**4.** D.	**4.** C.
5. (I) A, C, D. (II) B. (III) B.	**5.** A. Bonus: A, D.	**5.** C.
6. B.	**6.** C.	**6.** D. (20 May 2002)
7. (I) C; (II) C.	**7.** D.	**7.** B.
8. (I) A; (II) C. Bonus: Eroni Kumana, Biuku Gasa.	**8.** A.	**8.** B.
9. (I) C; (II) B.	**9.** B (at Lituya Bay).	**9.** C.
10. D.	**10.** B. The other site was Támchen.	**10.** A. Bonus: B.
11. A.	**11.** C.	**11.** C.
12. B. Bonuses: (I) D. (II) India; Sri Lanka; United Kingdom; Israel.	**12.** Date 1: B. Date 2: D.	**12.** B.
13. A.	**13.** B.	**13.** D.
14. D.	**14.** A.	**14.** A.
15. D.	**15.** C.	**15.** C.
16. C.	**16.** C. Bonuses: (I) A. (II) D. (III) A.	**16.** D.
17. D. Bonus: It allowed a daughter of the king to rule in his stead should he not produce a male heir.	**17.** B.	**17.** (1) (I) C. (II) E. (III) F. (IV) A. (V) D. (VI) B. (VIII) G. (IX) C. (2) (VII).
18. C.	**18.** B.	**18.** D. Bonus: A.
19. B.	**19.** A.	**19.** C.
20. A. Bonus: B.	**20.** B. Bonus: C.	**20.** B.
21. C. Bonus: C.	**21.** D.	**21.** D.
22. A (III), (I). B (II), (IV). C (VII), (VI). D (I), (III). E (IV), (V). F (VI), (VII). G (V), (II).	**22.** B.	**22.** A.
23. D. Bonus: Philip II.	**23.** C. Bonus: B.	**23.** D.
24. B. Bonuses: (I) Naha Stone. (II) D.	**24.** C. Bonus: B.	**24.** C.
25. B. Bonus: D.	**25.** A. Bonus: The "Glomar response" or the "Glomar denial."	**25.** B.
26. D. Bonus: A.	**26.** D.	**26.** C.
27. A.	**27.** A. Bonus: B.	**27.** D.
28. C.	**28.** C.	**28.** B.
29. (I) A. (II) D.	**29.** B.	**29.** A.
30. (I) C. (II) B. Bonuses: (I) D; (II) *The Anglo-Saxon Chronicle*.	**30.** (I) H. (II) D. (III) G. (IV) F. (V) A. (VI) E. (VII) C. (VIII) J. (IX) B. (X) I.	**30.** C.
31. (I) D; (II) E. Bonus: B.	**31.** A. Bonus: D.	**31.** C.
32. C; G; H; J.	**32.** G.	**32.** B.
33. A. Bonuses: (I) C. (II) E.	**33.** C.	**33.** A.

Category D. Sports Champion	Category D. Sports Champion continued	Category E. "JAMS" (continued)
1. (I) B. Bonus: B. (II) D.	**18.** D. (*All are Canadian.*) Bonuses: (I) B. (II) C.	**3.** A: (VI), (V). B: (V), (III). C: (IV), (I). D: (VII), (II). E: (II), (VII). F: (I), (IV). G: (III), (VI). Bonus: D, E.
2. B. Bonuses: (I) C. (II) C.		
3. (I) B (Men's); C (Women's). (II) D. (III) A.	**19.** B. Bonuses: (I) B. (II) C.	
4. B. Bonus: A.	**20.** (I) C. (II) D. (III) B. Bonuses: (1) E. (2) Germany, Spain.	
5. C, with 88. Bonuses: (I) D. (II) B.		**4.** (I) G; (II) F; (III) B; (IV) D; (V) C; (VI) E; (VII) J; (VIII) K; (IX) A; (X) I; (XI) H. Bonuses: (I) 3 (E, F, K). (II) D, J. (III) G.
6. A. Bonuses: (I) Larry Bird, Kevin McHale, Robert Parish, Dennis Johnson. (II) 1. D. 2. Magic Johnson, Kareem Abdul-Jabbar, James Worthy, Michael Cooper, A.C. Green.	**21.** C.	
	22. A. Bonus: C.	
	23. (I) D. (II) A. (III) B. Bonus: C.	
	24. (I) B; C, with 82. *If only answer one, (1) point.* (II) A with 18.	**5.** F. Bonus: B.
7. (I) E; (II) B; (III) C; (IV) D; (V) H; (VI) A. (VII) F. Bonuses: (I) A (6x). (II) C.		**6.** (I) E; (II) H; (III) G; (IV) C; (V) B; (VI) A; (VII) F; (VIII) D. Bonus: B.
	25. C with 5. Bonuses: (I) Uruguay. (II) Croatia.	
8. D. Bonuses: (I) B (a Black Canadian player at Halifax Eureka, in 1906). (II) A (Canadian, from 1958).	**26.** (I) C. (II) A. (III) C. (IV) B. (V) D. (VI) B. (VII) C.	**7.** (I) B; 1. (II) A. Bonuses: (I-1) D; (I-2) A; (I-3) B. (II) B. (III-1) D; (III-2) C.
	27. (I) A. Bonus: 1995, 2007, 2019, 2023. (II) A.	**8.** (I) B. (II) C. (III) D, A, C, B. (IV) B. (V) A.
9. (I) A. Bonus: Kenya. (II) C. Bonuses: F. Time: 2:00:35.		**9.** (I) G; (II) B; (III) H; (IV) E; (V) M; (VI) A; (VII) J; (VIII) C; (IX) K; (X) F; (XI) L; (XII) I; (XIII) D.
	28. D. Bonuses: (I) B. (II) A (6 GM, 2 BM).	
10. (I) A. (II) A. (III) B. Bonuses: (1) E; (2) USA.	**29.** (I) B; (II) A; (III) B.	
11. C. Bonus: C.	**30.** D. Bonuses: (I) C. (II) Chris Evert. (III) C. (IV) 2022.	**10.** (I) B; (II) B. Bonus: C.
12. A: III, VII. B: III, VII. C: III, VII. D: III, VII. E: III, VII. F: III, VII. G: III, VII. Bonus: These are the years Serena and Roger won the same Grand Slams, a total of 7. *Thank you, GOATS!*		**11.** B. Bonuses: (I) C. (II) Bon Jovi. (III) A.
	31. (I) B. (II) C. Bonuses: World: C. Olympics: B.	**12.** A (III); B (IV); C (II); D (XI); E (VIII); F (X); G (III); H (VII); I (VI); J (I); K (XII); L (XIII); M (IX); N (V).
	32. C. *Gracias, GOAT!* Bonuses: (I) A. (II) 2022. (III) B.	
13. (I) A; (II) Zaire. Bonuses: (I) B. (II) Ali; (III) At the end of the 14th round.		**13.** (I) B; (II) A; (III) B.
	33. B. Bonuses: (I) C. (II) Bob Baffert. (III) D. (IV) A.	**14.** A. Bonuses: (1) D; A; F; C. (2) C. (3) B. (4) B.
14. A.		
15. (I) B; (II) C. Bonuses: (1) D. (2) A.	**Category E. "JAMS"**	**15.** A (IX); B (VIII); C (VII); D (III); E (II); F (V); G (VI); H (I); I (XI); J (IV); K (X). Bonus: B.
16. (I) A; (II) B; (III) C. Bonuses: (1) 1991; (2) USA.	**1.** D. Bonuses: (I) "The Boomin' System." (II) B.	
17. B.	**2.** (I) B; (II) B; (III) B. Bonus: A.	**16.** A. Bonuses: (I) *Heart Break.* (II) E.

Category E. "JAMS" (continued)	Category E. "JAMS" (continued)	Category F. Geography 235 (continued)
17. C, D. Bonuses: (I) *Madonna*. (II) A. *Desperately Seeking Susan*. 1985. **18.** (I) J; (II) I; (III) A; (IV) B; (V) K; (VI) D; (VII) G; (VIII) E; (IX) H; (X) C; (XI) F; (XII) L. Bonus: Barbados (Rihanna). Dominican Republic (El Alfa El Jefe). Jamaica (Beenie Man, Bob Marley, Buju Banton). Puerto Rico (Bad Bunny, Ozuna). Saint Vincent (Kevin Lyttle, Skinny Fabulous). Trinidad (Bunji Garlin, Destra, Kes, Machel Montano, Nailah Blackman). **19.** C. Bonus: A. **20.** (I) C; (II) C. **21.** (I) B. Bonus: "Miss You Much (Extended Version)"; (II) A; (III) B. **22.** A (IV); B (II); C (V). Bonuses: D (III); E (VI); F (XI); G (I); H (X); I (VIII); J (IX); K (VII); L (XII). **23.** (I) C; F. (II) A; G. (III) B; J. (IV) H. (V) D. (VI) E; I. **24.** (I) B; (II) F; (III) G; (IV) J; (V) A; (VI) H; (VII) C; (VIII) E; (IX) I; (X) D. **25.** A (IV). B (VIII). C (V). D (I). E (XI). F (IX). G (II). H (VII). I (X). J (VI). K (III). L (VIII). **26.** A (III). B (I). C (II). Bonuses: (I) C; (II) B. **27.** A (I). B (IV). C (II). Bonuses: (I) *Do The Right Thing*. Public Enemy. (II) C. (III) D. **28.** (I) C; (II) B. Bonuses: (1) E. (2) D.	**29.** B; E. Bonus: *Once Upon a Time in Shaolin*. **30.** C; G. Bonus: H. **31.** C. Bonus: B. **32.** (I) D; (II) E; (III) B; (IV) F; (V) C; (VI) A. Bonuses: (I) B; (II) D. **33.** (I) I; (II) G; (III) A; (IV) D; (V) B; (VI) L; (VII) F; (VIII) C; (IX) K; (X) J; (XI) H; (XII) M; (XIII) E. **Category F. Geography 235** **1.** (I) Canada, Costa Rica, Chile, Curaçao, Cayman Islands, Cuba, Colombia. (II) Czechia (Czech Republic), Croatia. (III) Cameroon, Côte d'Ivoire (official name), Comoros, Cabo (Cape) Verde, Central African Republic, Chad. (IV) Cambodia, China, Christmas Island, Cocos Island, Cyprus. Bonus: Cook Islands. **2.** D. Bonuses: (1) C. (2) Krung Thep or Bangkok. **3.** C. **4.** A. Bonus: Sri Lanka. **5.** D. **6.** Egypt, England, Ecuador, Estonia, Equatorial Guinea, El Salvador, Eswatini (formerly Swaziland), Eritrea, Ethiopia, Easter Island, East Timor (officially, it is Timor-Leste).	**7.** (I) Puerto Rico, Panama, Peru, Paraguay. (II) Pakistan, Philippines, Palestine (State of). (III) Palau, Papua New Guinea, Pitcairn Islands. Bonus: Poland, Portugal. **8.** D. Bonuses: (I) Cordoba. (II) Honduras. **9.** B. Bonuses: (I) E; (II) D. **10.** (I) D; (II) B. **11.** D. **12.** A. **13.** (I) Montserrat, Mexico, Martinique. (II) Moldova, Malta, Monaco, Montenegro. (III) Malaysia, Maldives, Myanmar, Mongolia, Macau. (IV) Marshall Islands, Micronesia. Bonus: Mayotte, Malawi, Morocco, Mauritius, Mozambique, Mali, Mauritania, Madagascar. **14.** C. **15.** D. Bonuses: (I) United Kingdom; (II) Portugal. **16.** C. **17.** C. **18.** (I) A; (II) C. **19.** Ireland, Italy, Isle of Man, Iceland, India, Indonesia, Israel, Iran, Iraq, Ivory Coast. Bonus: Islamabad. **20.** A. **21.** B. **22.** C. Bonus: B. **23.** (I) D. (II) B.

Category F. Geography 235 (continued)	Category G. Big Screen, Small Screen (continued)	Category G. Big Screen, Small Screen (continued)
24. (11) D; (14) C; (15) B. Bonus: A.	12. (I) E. (II) G. (IV) C. (V) B. Bonus:	33. (I) H. (II) B. (III) G. (IV) A. (V) J. (VI)
25. C.	2004 = (III).	E. (VII) D. (VIII) I.
26. B.	13. (I) D; (II) B; (III)	(IX) C. (X) F.
27. B.	C; (IV) Shaguar.	
28. C. Bonus: B.	14. C.	**Category H. Country**
29. C.	15. C.	**Flags**
30. Nicaragua, Norway, The Netherlands, North Macedonia, Namibia, Niger, Nigeria, North Korea, Niue, Nepal, New Zealand, Norfolk Island, New Caledonia, Northern Mariana Islands, Nauru.	16. B.	
	17. E. Bonus: D.	1. B.
	18. A.	2. A.
	19. F. Bonuses: 2002 - 2008.	3. (I) A=3; B=4; C=2; D=5; E=1; F=6. (II) The Five Pillars of Islam.
	20. A; D.	
	21. C.	
	22. E.	4. B. Bonus: Iceland.
31. (I) B; (II) B.	23. 1: (I) I. (II) C. (III)	5. D. Bonus: Mer-
32. (I) B; (II) C; (III) D.	D. (IV) F. (V) D. (VI)	Lion; national flag;
33. (I) D: Belgium, Spain, Andorra, Monaco, Italy, Luxembourg, Germany, Switzerland. (II) C: South Africa, Namibia, Zambia, Zimbabwe. (III) B: China, India.	G. (VII) E. (VIII) H. (IX) A. (X) D. (XI) G. (XII) J. (XIII) E. 2: A (VI). B (III). C (V). D (IV). 3: B.	coat of arms; national anthem "Maluja Singapura"; national flower: Singapore orchid.
	24. (I) C. (II) D. (III) A. (IV) B.	6. (1) B; (2) C; (3) A. A dog. Bonuses: (I) Christmas Island; (II) A.
	25. A (IV). B (V). C (I). D (III), (II). E (VII). F (II). G. (VI). H (IV), (I).	
Category G. Big Screen, Small Screen		7. (I) C; (II) D; (III) B; (IV) E; (V) A.
	26. C.	8. C.
1. E.	27. (I) D. Bonus:	9. A.
2. (I) B. (II) D.	Alejandro González	10. C. Bonus:
3. B (Best Foreign Language Film). Bonus: B.	Iñárritu. (II) B.	Paraguay.
4. B.	28. A (IX); B (VI); C (I); D (VII); E (IV); F (III); G (VIII); H (X); I (II); J (V).	11. A.
5. B. Bonus: John Hughes: *16 Candles, Breakfast Club, Ferris Bueller's Day Off, Uncle Buck, Pretty in Pink, Home Alone,* the first three *National Lampoon's Vacation,* and *Planes, Trains & Automobiles.*		12. (1) B. (2) A.
		13. C. Bonus: D.
	29. (I) D. (II) B. Bonuses:	14. (I) C. (II) C. Bonuses: (I) A triskelion; (II) Medusa.
	1. (I) D; (II) B.	
	2. December 1983.	15. A.
6. E.	30. C. Bonuses: (I) C, D. (II) 1. A. 2. E.	16. (Flag 1) B; (Flag 2) D. Bonus: (Flag 3) C.
7. B.	31. (I) D. (II) G. (III) B. (IV) H. (V) E. (VI) A. (VII) F. (VIII) C. Bonus: *Da 5 Bloods.*	17. (I) D; (II) A.
8. C, D.		18. (I) A. (II) D. (III) E. (IV) F.
9. F. Bonus: *227.*		
10. (I) B; (II) D. Bonuses: (I) B, C, D. (II) C.		19. A. Bonus: D.
	32. (I) B. (II) C. (III) D. (IV) A. Bonus: D.	20. (I) D; (II) A.
11. (I) B; (II) C. Bonuses: (I) March 21st. (II) B.		21. (Flag 1) D; (Flag 2) B. Bonus: C.

Category H. Country Flags (continued)	Category I. Earth's "Spheres"	Category I. Earth's "Spheres" continued
22. (I) C. Bonus: Kuwait City; (II) B. Bonus: Khartoum. 23. C. 24. (Flag 1) G. (Luanda); (Flag 2) A. (Port-of-Spain); (Flag 3) F. (Port Moresby); (Flag 4) B. (Abu Dhabi). 25. Flag 2. Bonus: Malta (St. George on his horse slaying a dragon). Note too that the Presidential Standard of Lithuania has a dragon. 26. (Flag 1) B. (Vientiane), (Flag 2) C. (Vaduz). Bonus: (I) E. (Skopje). 27. (Flag 1) D; (Flag 2) B. 28. (1) D; (2) B. Bonus: Dominica; El Salvador; Nicaragua. 29. (1) D. (Palikir); (2) B. (Gaborone); (3) A. (No one central capital, but will also accept: Alofi, Nukunonu, or Fakaofo); (4) C. (Djibouti). 30. (1) D; (2) B. 31. (Flag 1) C. (Bern); (Flag 2) A. (Copenhagen); (Flag 3) D. (Tbilisi); (Flag 4) B. (Nuku'alofa). 32. A (Flag 4); B (Flag 1). Bonuses: (I) C (Flag 3); D (Flag 2). (II) Flag 5 = South Korea; Flag 6 = North Korea. 33. (Flag 1) C; (Flag 2) A; (Flag 3) B; (Flag 4) D. Bonuses: A; Paris.	1. (I) D; (II) D; (III) D. Bonuses: (1) C. (2) A. 2. C. Bonuses: (a) Argentina; (b) USA; (c) Iran; (d) Russia. 3. C. Bonuses: (I) C. (II) D. 4. (I) D. (II) A. 5. (I) B. (II) D. (III) F. (IV) C. (V) E. Bonus: A. 6. (I) B (70.8%). (II) B. (III) A. 7. (I) A; (II) A. 8. (I) (i) C; (ii) Tanzania. (II) B in 2014. 9. (I) D; (II) B. 10. (I) D; (II) B. 11. (1) (I) H; (II) A; (III) D; (IV) K; (V) C; (VI) J; (VII) F; (VIII) G; (IX) B; (X) E; (XI) I. (2) B. 12. B: e.g., owls, most parrots, most woodpeckers. (*Other facts: A: e.g., Northern three-toed woodpecker; C: e.g., most common birds; D: e.g., swift.*) 13. (I) C; (II) C. 14. (I) C; (II) D. Bonus: D. 15. (I) B; (II) A. 16. (I) A; (II) C; (III) C; (IV) B. Bonuses: (1) B; (2) D (typically). 17. D. 18. (I) A; (II) D. 19. (I) A; (II) B; (III) B. 20. (I) A; (II) B. 21. D 22. C. 23. (I) C. (II) A. (III) D. (IV) B. 24. (I) B; (II) A. 25. D. 26. C.	27. 1. (I) E; (II) C; (III) A; (IV) B; (V) D. 2. B. 3. A. Bonuses: (I) D-double-prime or D". (II) Crust and Upper Mantle. 28. (I) B. (II) A. (III) C; E. (IV) D. 29. C. 30. (I) C; (II) A; (III) E; (IV) B; (V) D. 31. B. 32. 1) A. 2) B. Bonuses: (I) B. (II) A. 3) I) A; II) B. 33. (I) D. (II) C. **Category J: Land and Sea Forms** 1. C. 2. C. Bonus: Hong Kong UNESCO Global Geopark. 3. D. 4. A; Bonus: Dugong. 5. A. 6. D. 7. B. Bonus: C. 8. C. Bonus: Swiss engineer Jacques Piccard and U.S. navy lieutenant Don Walsh. 9. (I) D; (II) E; (III) C; (IV) B; (V) A. 10. A. 11. 1) B; 2) D. 12. (I) B; (II) C; (III) A-Portugal; B-Norway; C-UK; D-UK; F-Brazil. Other facts: *The other islands that are part are St. Helena (UK), Gough Island (UK), Ascension Island (UK), and Bouvet Island (Norway).* 13. (I) C; (II) A. 14. D. 15. (I) C; (II) D.

Category J: Land and Sea Forms (continued)	Category K. World Slangs / Sayings / Cool Words (continued)	Category L. "Show Me the $¥€£"
16. D. Bonuses: (1) A. (2) F. (3) E.	**8.** C.	**1.** B. Bonus: A.
17. B. D.	**9.** C.	**2.** A. (I); B. (II); C. (V); D. (III); E. (IV). Bonuses: €5 = (VII); €200 = (VI).
18. D.	**10.** A.	
19. C. Bonuses: (I) D; (II) B; (III) A.	**11.** B.	
20. C.	**12.** A (III); B (I); C (II).	**3.** B. Bonus: Bryn Mawr, Pennsylvania.
21. (I) C. (II) A. (III) B. (IV) E. (V) D. Bonus: Andros Coral Reef.	**13.** A.	**4.** D.
	14. (I) B; (II) D; (III) C; (IV) A.	**5.** (I) C. (II) B. *It actually was the $1000 banknote.*
22. (I) I. (II) F. (III) D. (IV) J. (V) A. (VI) E. (VII) G. (VIII) B. (IX) C. (X) H.	**15.** B.	**6.** (1) A (I); B (VII); C (II); D (VI); E (XI); F (XII); G (IV); H (IX); I (X); J (III). (2) (I) Lithuania. (II) Slovenia.
	16. B. Bonuses: (I) No childbirth. (II) No marriage. (III) No sex. (IV) No dating.	
23. (I) B. (II) A.		
24. (I) C; (II) C.	**17.** 1. (I) I; (II) D; (III) A; (IV) C; (V) F; (VI) H; (VII) E; (VIII) G; (IX) B. 2. B.	**7.** A. 10%. Bonuses: (I) A; (II) A.
25. B.		**8.** C.
26. A.	**18.** A. Bonus: They were similar to the Berserkers, but they wore wolf pelts, and had the "spirit of wolves" in them.	**9.** D.
27. (I) D; (II) B; (III) A; (IV) C. Bonus: D.		**10.** D.
28. (I) C. (II) A.		**11.** (I) B. (II) F.
29. B.		**12.** (I) C. (II) D.
30. B. Bonus: A.	**19.** (I) C; (II) D. Bonus: A.	**13.** (I) C. (II) C. Bonus: DeepMind (London) and Google Brain AI (Silicon Valley).
31. B.	**20.** D.	
32. D. Both hot springs are interconnected. Uniquely, when one lake's temperature and water level increase, the temperature and outflow of the other decrease. Bonus: B.	**21.** C.	
	22. B.	**14.** (I) B; (II) E; (III) F; (IV) D; (V) A; (VI) C.
	23. D. Bonus: C.	**15.** (I) C; (II) B; Bonus: E.
	24. (I) C; (II) F; (III) A; (IV) E; (V) D; (VI) B. Bonus: "Quiet hiring."	**16.** B.
33. (I) B; (II) E; (III) A; (IV) C; (V) D. Bonus: Lut Desert.		**17.** (I) D; (II) E; (III) B; (IV) A; (V) F; (VI) C. Bonus: Australian Dollar.
	25. A.	
	26. E.	
Category K. World Slangs / Sayings / Cool Words	**27.** A.	**18.** D. Bonus: C.
	28. D.	**19.** D.
	29. B.	**20.** (I) C; (II) B; (III) C.
	30. C.	
1. C.	**31.** B. Bonus: A.	**21.** (I) C; (II) A; (III) D.
2. A.	**32.** A.	**22.** A.
3. B.	**33.** D. Bonuses: (I) C. (II) F. (III) D. (IV) H.	**23.** B. Bonus: D.
4. C.		
5. (I) C. (II) A.		
6. (I) D; (II) C.		
7. (I) B. (II) C. Bonus: "Go on."		

NO OTHER TRIVIA LIKE THIS MASTERCLASS
(THE ANSWERS)

Category L. "Show Me the $¥€£" (continued)	Category L. "Show Me the $¥€£" (continued)	Category M. Scientists and Geniuses (continued)
24. (A) Morgan Stanley; (B) Nintendo Co. Ltd.; (C) Tencent Holdings Limited. Bonuses: (I) Berkshire Hathaway Inc. (II) NVIDIA Corp. (III) Taiwan Semiconductor Manufacturing Company Limited. (IV) Joby Aviation, Inc. (V) Rigetti Computing, Inc. (VI) Defiance Quantum ETF. **25.** (I) B; (II) D; (III) A; (IV) F; (V) E; (VI) C. Bonuses: ESB = Croatian; BČE = Maltese; ЕЦБ = Bulgarian. **26.** (I) C; (II) A; (III) D; (IV) B. Bonuses: (I) "There are plenty of alternatives" (Deutsche Bank). (II) "There are reasonable alternatives" (Goldman Sachs). (III) "There is a realistic alternative" to stocks (Insight Investment). **27.** (I) E; (II) H; (III) A; (IV) L; (V) D; (VI) G; (VII) J; (VIII) I; (IX) K; (X) F; (XI) C; (XII) B. **28.** (A) Costco Wholesale Corp.; (B) Alibaba Group Holding Limited; (C) Goldman Sachs Group, Inc. Bonuses: (A) LVMH Moët Hennessy – Louis Vuitton, Société Européenne; (B) Hermès International SA; (C) Kering SA; (D) Mastercard Inc. **29.** A, C, E, F, G, I. **30.** A (III); B (I); C (VI); D (II); E (IV); F (V).	**31.** B. Bonus: F. **32.** A, C, E. **33.** C. Bonus: D. **Category M. Scientists and Geniuses** **1.** (I) E; (II) B; (III) G; (IV) F; (V) C; (VI) D; (VII) A. **2.** (I) D. (II) D. Bonus: E. **3.** (I) C. (II) B. (III) A. (IV) E. (V) D. **4.** (I) D; (II) E, (III) A; (IV) B; (V) F; (VI) C. **5.** (I) B; (II) B. **6.** D. Bonus: *Hidden Figures*. **7.** 1. (I) B; (II) D; (III) C; (IV) A. 2. Country of birth: (I) Austria; (II) India; (III) Mexico; (IV) USA. **8.** C. **9.** C. **10.** B. **11.** C. **12.** D. **13.** E. or B. Some historians now believe that Merit-Ptah never existed. **14.** D. **15.** B. **16.** D. **17.** B. **18.** C. **19.** A. **20.** A. Bonuses: (1) D. (2) C. **21.** B. **22.** C. Bonus: C, Singularity by 2045. **23.** B. Bonus: A. **24.** D. **25.** D. Bonuses: C, G, D, F. **26.** A. Bonus: B.	**27.** D. **28.** B. Bonus: C. **29.** C. Bonus: A. **30.** A. Bonus: B. **31.** B. **32.** E. Bonuses: (I) C. (II) A. (III) B. **33.** A. Bonuses: (I) $1^3 + 12^3$; (II) $9^3 + 10^3$. (III) C. **Category N. Landmarks and Monuments** **1.** B. Bonus: Uzbekistan, Pakistan, Tajikistan. **2.** D. **3.** D. Bonus: A. **4.** (I) (1) E; (2) D; (3) B; (4) C; (5) A. (II) Doric. (III) 2-Roman. **5.** A. Bonuses: (I) A; (II) Lorgnette. **6.** C. Bonus: D. **7.** B. Bonus: A. **8.** A. **9.** D. Bonus: Peru. **10.** D. Bonus: Potala Palace, in Lhasa. **11.** A. Bonus: D. **12.** A. **13.** C. **14.** A. **15.** D. **16.** C. Bonus: B. **17.** A. Bonus: Djamaa el Djazaïr. **18.** C. **19.** B. **20.** A. **21.** C. **22.** A. Bonuses: 1. C. 2. A. **23.** A: (II); B: (I). Bonus: Romania. **24.** D. Bonus: C. **25.** D.

Category N. Landmarks and Monuments (continued)	Category O. "Enlightenment" (continued)	Category P. "Doctor"
26. B. Bonus: Madrid-Barajas Airport Terminal 4; London Heathrow Airport Terminal 5.	**20.** (11) B; (22) C; (33) A. Bonus: B.	**1.** C. Bonus: E.
27. C.	**21.** (I) D; (II) B. Bonuses: (I) D; (II) C.	**2.** D. Bonuses: 14: A; 23: D.
28. B.	**22.** A.	**3.** B. (John A. "Jack" Hopps. The surgeons: Wilfried Bigelow, John Callaghan.) Bonus: C.
29. B. Bonuses: (I) A; (II) D.	**23.** B.	
30. D.	**24.** A.	**4.** (I) B. (II) A. Bonuses: 1. (I) A. (II) E. 2. B.
31. C. Bonuses: 1. B; 2. A; 3. C.	**25.** B. Bonuses: (I) France; (II) Albigensian.	**5.** D.
32. B.	**26.** D. by St. Hilary of Poitier in the 4th century. Bonus: Church leaders banned the song as there was Church outcry because (1) the lyricist Placide Cappeau was an atheist; (2) the composer Adolphe Adam was Jewish; (3) some of the lyrics such as *"Chains shall He break for the slave is our brother"* and *"In His name, all oppression shall cease"* were frowned upon as being activist and lacking musical taste.	**6.** D. Bonus: E.
33. D.		**7.** (I) B; (II) D.
		8. A.
Category O. "Enlightenment"		**9.** 528 = B. 741 = D.
		10. A.
1. C.		**11.** A (II); B (V); C (III); D (I); E (IV); F (VI); G (VII).
2. (I) D; (II) B; (III) F. Bonus: Taoism.		**12.** B.
3. B.		**13.** A.
4. D. Bonus: A.		**14.** C.
5. C. Bonus: A.		**15.** (I) B; (II) A.
6. (I) F; (II) B.		**16.** C.
7. A (II); B (IV); C (I); D (V); E (III).	**27.** B.	**17.** B.
8. (I) A; (II) C; (III) B. Bonus: gold, myrrh, frankincense.	**28.** C.	**18.** D.
	29. A. Bonuses: (I) B. (II) A.	**19.** A.
9. D.	**30.** C. Bonuses: (I) A. 4th Sikh Guru. (II) B. 3rd Sikh Guru.	**20.** C.
10. B. Bonuses: (1) D. (2) 1 (V). 2 (III). 3 (II). 4 (I). 5 (IV).	**31.** E.	**21.** D. Bonus: D.
11. (I) (1) B; (2) E; (3) G; (4) D; (5) A; (6) H; (7) C; (8) F. (II-1) A. (II-2) D.	**32.** D.	**22.** A.
12. (I) C; (II) C.	**33.** (I) D. (II) B. Bonus: Author's answer is B, but there is no single correct answer. So, enjoy the freebie.	**23.** A, C. Bonus: D.
13. (I) D. (II) B.		**24.** K. Bonus: Henrietta Lacks.
14. C.		**25.** B. Bonus: Legume.
15. (I) D; (II) A; (III) B; (IV) C.		**26.** C.
16. B.		**27.** D.
17. D. Bonuses: Lakshmi, Sarasvati, Ganga.		**28.** A. Bonuses: (1) B. (2) C.
18. (I) D. (II) A (3); B (5); C (2); D (4); E (1).		**29.** C.
19. A.		**30.** A. Bonuses: (I) B. (II) D. (III) E. (IV) F. (V) I. (VI) A.
		31. (1) A (V); B (III); C (I); D (XI); E (II); F (X); G (I); H (VI); I (II); J (VIII); K (IX); L (VII); M (IV); N (III); O (I). (2) B.

Category P. "Doctor" (continued)	Category Q. Masterpieces (continued)	Category R. True or False (continued)
32. B.	28. D.	19. A.
33. C. Bonuses: (I) D.	29. C.	20. A.
(II) B.	30. C, E, G. Bonuses:	21. (I) A. (II) A
	(I) B. (II) E.	(*Bamburg*). Bonus: False
Category Q. Masterpieces	31. B.	(*2022 NYC Comic Con*).
	32. A. Bonus: B.	22. B (*It was #42*).
	33. A (I); B (VI); C	23. A.
1. B. Bonuses: (I) B (*in Germany*). (II) G (*Antwerp was part of the Southern Netherlands back then*).	(IV); D (V); E (II); F (III). Bonuses:	24. (I) C (*in the 9th century, not the 8th c.*); (II) A.
	1. (I) Colombia;	
	(II) Colombia;	25. B (*He authored no texts, as he believed writing to be inferior to dialogue*).
	(III) Argentina;	
	(IV) Mexico; (V)	
2. D. Bonus: A-France; B-Poland; C-England; D-USA.	Brazil; (VI) Mexico.	26. B (*English is a West Germanic language in the Indo-European language family*).
	2. Frida Kahlo.	
3. C.		
4. A.	**Category R. True or False**	27. A.
5. A. Bonus: A.		28. A (*under Aniconism*).
6. B. Bonus: C.		29. B.
7. B.	1. (I) A. (II) A.	30. (I) A. (II) A.
8. (I) C; (II) A; (III) D. Bonus: B.	2. B. Bonuses: Wadi Al-Hitan (Whale Valley)–Egypt; Western Ghats–India; Works of Gaudi–Spain.	31. (I) B. (II) B.
		32. (I) A. (II) B (*Spain won in 2010*). (III) B (*He was born in England*). (IV) A. (V) C (*Stan Wawrinka won in 2015*). (VI) A. (VII) A (*The word is the chemical name for titin, the largest protein*). (VIII) B. (IX) A. (X) A. (XI) A.
9. C.		
10. F.		
11. D.		
12. C.		
13. D.	3. A.	
14. (I) B; (II) C.	4. (I) A. (II) C (*Incas lived in S. America; Aztecs lived in N. America—Mexico*).	
15. E.		
16. C. Bonus: "*Index Librorum Prohibitorum*" ("List of Prohibited Books").		33. B (*It is Area 51*).
	5. A.	**Category S. "First" or "Only"**
	6. B (*1 metre*).	
17. D.	7. B. Bonus: C (*it passes through Bolivia*).	
18. C. Bonus: A.		1. B. Bonuses:
19. B.	8. (I) A (*Grevy's, mountain, plains*). (II) A.	(I) Trinidad & Tobago.
20. D. Bonus: C; C.		(II) Bat.
21. B.	9. B.	2. (I) D. (II) B.
22. A. Bonus: C.	10. B.	Bonuses: *The Tale of Genji;* Murasaki Shikibu.
23. C.	11. A.	
24. D.	12. B (*It is Freemasonry*).	
25. A. Bonus: C.	13. A.	3. B. *Wow, GOAT!* Bonus: Steffi Graf.
26. B.	14. A.	
27. (1) A (V); B (IV); C (III); D (II); E (I); F (II). (2) C. But it was nominated for 16 Tony's in 13 categories. (3) 3. (4) B. (5) Rick Riordan.	15. (I) B; (II) A.	
	16. (I) A. (II) A. Bonus: B (*Nijo Castle*).	4. A.
	17. B. Bonus: Dart.	5. B. Bonus: B.
	18. A.	

Category S. "First" or "Only" (continued)	Category T. Potpourri continued	Category U. "Who Said This?"
6. D. Bonuses: (I) Liechtenstein. (II) 1984.	6. (I) C; (II) E; (III) A; (IV) B; (V) D; (VI) F; (VII) J; (VIII) G.	1. (I) A; (II) C; (III) D.
7. E.	7. B.	2. A.
8. (I) D. (II) B.	8. C.	3. C.
9. B.	9. (I) C. (II) D.	4. C.
10. D. Bonus: A, D.	10. A.	5. (I) A; (II) C; (III) B; (IV) D.
11. C. Bonus: B (but ceramics were used).	11. A (II); B (III); C (IV); D (I). Bonuses: (II) (1) Jamaica. (2) Jamaica. (3) Trinidad & Tobago.	6. D.
12. C. Bonuses: (I) B. (II) A.		7. (I) C; (II) E; (III) B; (IV) D; (V) A.
13. A.		8. (I) B; (II) D; (III) E; (IV) A; (V) C.
14. D.	12. C. Bonuses: 2 ox; 3 tiger; 12 pig/boar.	9. (I) E; (II) B; (III) D; (IV) A; (V) C.
15. A.	13. B.	10. (I) A; (II) B; (III) D.
16. B.	14. (I) A; Bonus: Donna Summer. (II) C.	11. Sun Tzu. Bonus: *The Art of War.*
17. C.	15. (I) A. (II) C.	12. (I) B; (II) C; (III) A.
18. A.	16. D.	13. (I) = C; (II) = A; (III) = B.
19. (I) C. (II) A.	17. (I) D; (II) B; (III) C.	14. A.
20. C.	18. B. Bonus: A.	15. (I) B. (II) D.
21. D. Bonus: *La Bougie du Sapeur.*	19. B.	16. (I) A; (II) A.
22. D.	20. B.	17. D.
23. (I) E; (II) C.	21. C.	18. D.
24. (I) D. (II) B. Bonus: A.	22. D.	19. C.
25. (I) B (1570). (II) A (It's also called *The Babylonian Map of the World*).	23. D. Bonus: A.	20. B.
	24. A.	21. B.
	25. A.	22. D.
26. C. Bonus: B.	26. D. Bonus: E.	23. A.
27. (I) C. (II) A.	27. A. Bonus: When you're playing in costume ("mas") in a Carnival band, as you approach a judging point, these are the instructions given to remain in or go to your mas section within the band.	24. C.
28. B. Bonuses: (I) B. (II) D.		25. D.
29. 1: H. 2: (I) E. (II) F. (III) B. (IV) G. (V) A. (VI) D. (VII) C.		26. B.
30. (I) C; (II) B; (III) D.		27. C.
31. (I) D by Run DMC. (II) A by Blondie.		28. (I) C; (II) A.
32. B.		29. A
33. (I) D. (II) C. (III) C. Bonus: C.		30. D.
	28. A. Bonus: *Fidelio* (a.k.a. *Lenore*).	31. C.
	29. A.	32. B.
Category T. Potpourri	30. C.	33. (I) B. (II) C. (III) A. (IV) B. (V) D. (VI) B.
1. C.	31. D.	
2. B. Bonus: Ukraine.	32. C.	
3. A (IV); B (III); C (II); D (I).	33. B. Bonuses: (I) B; (II) C; (III) A.	
4. C.		
5. B.		

Category V. What's out There in the Universe? The Answer: A Lot!!!!!	Category V. What's out There in the Universe? The Answer: A Lot!!!!! (continued)	Category W. "More than Ingredients" (continued)
1. C. Bonus: A.	**24.** (I) B; (II) D; (III) C; (IV) A; (V) F.	**14.** (I) A; (II) B (*durum wheat semolina and water*).
2. (I) D; (II) C.	**25.** D.	**15.** A (III); B (I); C (II).
3. (I) B (It's ~69% dark energy, ~26% dark matter). (II) B.	**26.** A.	**16.** A.
4. A. Bonus: B.	**27.** (I) D; (II) A.	**17.** C.
5. (I) D; (II) C; (III) A. Bonus: A.	**28.** (I) C; (II) B.	**18.** D.
6. (I) D; (II) C. Bonus: D.	**29.** C.	**19.** B.
7. (I) C; (II) B.	**30.** D. Bonus: Prada.	**20.** B; G; H.
8. (I) B; (II) B.	**31.** B.	**21.** (I) B; (II) A; (III) A.
9. C.	**32.** A. Bonus: D.	**22.** A (III); B (I); C (II); D (V); E (IV); F (VI). Bonus: (IV).
10. C. Bonuses: (I) B, D. (II) Any of these answers accepted: A. as suggested by astrophysicist Avi Loeb; C. as suggested by chemist Jennifer Bergner and researcher Darryl Seligman.	**33.** 1: B (~238,855 miles / 384,400 km). 2: A. 3: (I) D; (II) A; (III) B; (IV) C; (V) E. 4: C. 5: A. 6: B.	**23.** B.
11. (I) C; (II) B.		**24.** B. Bonuses: 1. Sukiyabashi Jiro (Sushi Jiro). 2. D.
12. B.	Category W. "More than Ingredients"	**25.** A (II). B (I). C (VI). D (V). E (IV). F (III).
13. (I) C. (II) A.	**1.** D.	**26.** A (IV); B (II); C (III); D (I); E (V); F (III).
14. (I) A; (II) C.	**2.** C.	**27.** C.
15. A.	**3.** (I) B. (II) (i) C. (ii) A. (iii) B. (iv) D. Bonus: The two winners were: E--*Kagoshima for Best Breeding Bull*, and D--*Miyazaki prefecture for Best Beef Quality*.	**28.** (I) B; (II) A.
16. D.		**29.** (I) D (*from the Mayo-Chinchipe culture some 5300 years ago*); (II) C.
17. A.	**4.** D.	**30.** C. Bonus: Antioquia.
18. B.	**5.** D. *It's more like a savoury crepe than a pizza.* Bonus: C.	**31.** A (III); B (II); C (IV); D (I). Bonuses: A (IV); B (II).
19. (I) A; (II) D.		**32.** D. Bonus: A.
20. D.	**6.** (I) C; Bonus: D. (II) C.	**33.** A (VI); B (IV); C (VII); D (II); E (V); F (III); G (IX); H (VIII); I (X); J (I). Bonuses: 1. B (It's the reverse). 2. D.
21. (I) A; (II) B. Bonus: B.	**7.** B.	
22. D.	**8.** D.	
23. D. Olympus Mons is the largest planetary mountain, while Rheasilvia is on the asteroid Vesta, and is barely 100 metres (315 feet) taller than Olympus Mons! But if you said B, I'll give you the point because I can.	**9.** B.	
	10. A.	
	11. D.	
	12. 1. A (III); B (II); C (VII); D (VIII); E (I); F (IV); G (V); H (VI); I (IX). 2. C.	
	13. (I) C (618-907). (II) B.	

Category X. "Complicated" Words	Category X. "Complicated" Words (continued)	Category Y. The Arts through the Centuries (continued)
1. (I) A; (II) B.	27. D.	12. C.
2. (I) E; (II) A; (III) D; (IV) H; (V) J; (VI) B; (VII) L; (VIII) N; (IX) I; (X) F; (XI) G; (XII) K; (XIII) C. (XIV) M. Bonuses: (I) Clandestine. (II) A. (COMINT (communications intelligence), ELINT (electronic intelligence)). (III) B. (IV) C.	28. (I) B. (II) D. (III) A. (IV) C.	13. (I) C; (II) B. Bonus: B.
3. (I) C. (II) C.	29. A.	14. A. Bonus: *Berserk*.
4. C.	30. A: Cherish Mother Nature. B: Show Empathy. C: Stop Global Climate Change. D: Give A Damn. E: Eighties Music Is Lit. F: Bullying Is Weakness. G: Be Xenial. H: Reverse Ocean Deoxygenation. I: Comity.	15. (I) B. (II) C. Bonuses: (I) C. (II) B.
5. D.		16. (I) A; (II) D.
6. A. Camaraderie; B. Equanimity; C. Namaskar; D. Smaragdine; E. Tzedakah.		17. C.
7. ALL-Teams Play.		18. A.
8. B. Bonus: D.	31. D. Bonuses: A: Latin. B: Portuguese. C: Italian. E: English.	19. B. Bonus: C.
9. A.	32. (I) C. (II) D. (III) E. (IV) A. (V) B.	20. (I) (1) C; (2) A; (3) B. (II) B.
10. (I) B. (II) A. (III) C.	33. (I) C; (II) F; (III) E; (IV) B; (V) D; (VI) A. Bonus: C.	21. A (III); B (II); C (I); D (V); E (IV). Bonuses: 1 (I). 2 (I).
11. C. Bonus: B.		22. (I) B; (II) A. Bonus: B.
12. C.		23. A (VI); B (III); C (IV); D (VIII); E (VII); F (II); G (I); H (V); (I) X. Bonus: (IX).
13. A; B; E. Bonuses: Logorrhea. Isthmus. Ignominious.	**Category Y. The Arts through the Centuries**	24. G. Bonus: "The Bohemian Rhapsody" (Queen).
14. B. Bonus: D.	1. (I) F. (II) C. Bonus: 1983. (III) D.	25. A (IV); B (I); C (II); D (III). Bonuses: Princess Odette; Prince Siegfried; Baron Von Rothbart; Odile.
15. D.	2. D.	
16. C.	3. B. Bonuses: (1) A-China; C-Senegal, The Gambia; D-Trinidad & Tobago. (2) D.	26. (I) D. (II) B. Bonus: *Richard III*.
17. A.	4. B (correct is Carl Maria von Weber). Bonus: B.	27. A. Bonus: *A Raisin in the Sun*.
18. A; D; F.	5. (I) B. (II) B.	28. C. Bonus: B.
19. *Oh-toh-rahy-noh-luh-ring-guh-loj-i-kuhl*. Bonus: relating to the medical practice involving the ear, nose and throat.	6. D.	29. (I) B. (II) D. (III) B. (IV) C. Bonuses: (1) A. (2) B. (3) E. (4) C. (5) D.
	7. (I) B; (II) C.	30. (I) B; (II) D. Bonus: A.
20. F. Bonus: B.	8. D.	31. A.
21. A; D; F.	9. D.	32. (I) C; (II) B; (III) D. Bonus: *Janet* (1993).
22. C.	10. (I) G. (II) A. (III) C. (IV) F. (V) E. (VI) D. (VII) B.	33. E. Bonuses: A (III). B (I). C (II). D (IV).
23. (I) C. (II) A. (III) B.	11. Matsue Castle: B. Osaka Castle: A. Phoenix Hall: D.	
24. B. Bonus: D.		
25. D. Bonus: A.		
26. B; C; E. Bonuses: Bourbon. Narcissistic. Embarrass.		

Category Z. Blimey! Why Numbers? Why Math? Why Physics?	Category Z. Blimey! Why Numbers? Why Math? Why Physics? (continued)	Category AA. In the Continents (continued)
1. C.	32. (1) E. (2) F. Bonus: D (*it's a positive integer that is the product of three distinct prime numbers*).	13. (I) C; (II) A. *French Guiana is the smallest country by area, but it is an overseas department of France.*
2. (I) C (*applying PEMDAS/BODMAS*). (II) A; (III) C.		
3. (I) C. (II) A.	33. (I) A; (II) C (but for a very long time, it was B). Bonuses: (1) C. (2) A.	14. A.
4. (I) C. (II) D. (III) D.		15. C.
5. (I) D; (II) B.		16. B. Bonus: D.
6. D.		17. B.
7. B.		18. D.
8. B. Bonus: Columbia University.	**Category AA. In the Continents**	19. A.
9. A.		20. (12) F; (29) B; (37) A. Bonuses: (43) D; (45) C; (8) E.
10. (I) C. (II) B. Bonus: A.	1. (I) D. (II) D. Bonus: (South) Atlantic Ocean.	
11. (I) C; (II) B.	2. (1) Saba; St. Martin; St. Maarten; St. Kitts & Nevis; St. Lucia; St. Vincent & the Grenadines; Suriname. (2) San Marino; Scotland; Serbia; Slovakia; Slovenia; Spain; Sweden; Switzerland. (3) Saudi Arabia; Singapore; South Korea; Sri Lanka; Syria. (4) Samoa; Solomon Islands.	21. (32) C; (13) B; (8) D. Bonuses: (18) F; (10) A; (1) E.
12. (I) C (*based on formula: n*(n-1)/2*). (II) B.		22. B.
13. (I) C. (II) A. (III) B. (IV) B. (V) D.		23. A (II); B (III); C (I); D (V); E (VI); F (IV). Bonuses: 1. (VII). 2. (III).
14. D.		24. (42) D; (25) A; (35) B. Bonuses: (55) E; (22) C; (34) F.
15. (I) A; (II) D.		25. C.
16. (I) B; (II) A.		26. B.
17. (I) C; (II) A; (III) B.	3. Lithuania, Liechtenstein, Latvia, Lesotho, Lebanon, Luxembourg, Laos, Liberia, Libya.	27. B. Bonus: A, C, F.
18. (I) C; (II) B.		28. A.
19. (I) D; Bonus (1): B. (II) A; Bonus (2): D.	4. C.	29. (17) B; (1) D; (14) C. Bonuses: (6) A; (10) E; (3) F.
20. (I) B; (II) A.	5. B. Bonus: C.	
21. (I) A; (II) B.	6. (14) A; (29) C; (31) D.	30. (15) B; (20) E; (36) F. Bonuses: (22) C; (33) D; (28) A.
22. (I) B; (II) B.	7. (I) C; (II) A; (III) D.	
23. (I) B. (II) D. (III) 3(x − 4) (x + 8). Bonus: D.	8. C.	31. (8) F; (13) D; (10) B. Bonuses: (2) C; (5) A; (7) E.
24. A.	9. (A) and (E). Addis Ababa; Monrovia.	32. B.
25. (I) A; (II) A.	10. (I) C; (II) A. Bonuses: (I) D; (II) D.	33. (I) D; (II) A; (III) B. Bonus: C.
26. B.	11. (I) B; (II) C.	
27. (I) C; (II) A; (III) B; (IV) D; (V) F; (VI) E.	12. (I) A; (II) D; (III) B; (IV) J; (V) E; (VI) G; (VII) F; (VIII) C; (IX) H; (X) I. Bonus: K.	
28. (I) D. (II) C. (III) B (*now based on the Planck constant h*).		
29. (I) A (*with 255 detected photons*). (II-1) D. (II-2) C.		
30. (I) A; (II) C.		
31. (I) B; (II) C.		

Category BB. Capitals	Category BB. Capitals (continued)	Category CC. Bodies of Water
1. A (VI); B (I); C (II); D (III); E (VII); F (IV); G (V); H (II).	**22.** (I) Europe: Dublin (Ireland). (II) Africa: Dakar (Senegal), Djibouti (Djibouti), Dodoma (Tanzania). (III) Middle East Region: Doha (Qatar), Damascus (Syria). (IV) Asia: Dushanbe (Tajikistan), Dhaka (Bangladesh), Dili (East Timor).	**1.** C.
2. D. Bonus: C.		**2.** B. Bonus: South China Sea.
3. B. Bonuses: (I) Simtokha Dzong (*Sangak Zabdhon Phodrang / Palace of the Profound Meaning of Secret Mantra*s). (II) A–Cambodia; C–Nepal; D–Brunei.		**3.** (I) B; (II) C. Bonus: Denmark Strait cataract (between Iceland and Greenland).
		4. C.
		5. B. Bonuses: (I) A; (II) D.
		6. D.
4. (Flag 1) B; (Flag 2) C; (Flag 3) D; (Flag 4) A.	**23.** (I) D; (II) A; (III) B; (IV) C.	**7.** A. Bonus: Cambodia, China, Laos, Myanmar, Thailand, Vietnam.
5. Bern, Brussels, Belgrade, Budapest, Berlin, Belfast, Bucharest, Bratislava.	**24.** D.	**8.** A. Bonus: C *(it's larger than the Grand Canyon in the USA)*.
	25. B.	
	26. A.	
6. A (VII); B (IV); C (V); D (I); E (II); F (VI); G (III).	**27.** A. Bonus: Nassau (The Bahamas), New Delhi (India), Nuuk (Greenland), Nicosia (Cyprus), Niamey (Niger), N'djamena (Chad), Nairobi (Kenya), Nouakchott (Mauritania), Naypyidaw (Myanmar), Nouméa (New Caledonia), Nuku'alofa (Tonga).	**9.** B.
7. (I) B; (II) A.		**10.** B. Bonus: B.
8. C. Bonus: A.		**11.** D.
9. (I) B; (II) C; (III) D; (IV) F; (V) G; (VI) A; (VII) E.		**12.** D.
		13. (I) A; (II) D.
		14. B.
10. A (III); B (IV); C (I); D (II). Bonus: San Salvador.		**15.** A. Bonus: C.
		16. (I) C (in Sweden, Northern Europe). (II) B (in Hungary).
11. (I) Reykjavik, Riga, Rome; (II) Rabat (Morocco).	**28.** (1) (I) C; (II) G; (III) A; (IV) E; (V) F; (VI) B; (VII) D; (VIII) I; (IX) J; (X) H. (2-1) Saint Martin: Marigot. (2-2) Dominican Republic: Santo Domingo. (3) Havana (of Cuba).	**17.** (I) C; (II) B.
12. D.		**18.** A.
13. D.		**19.** D.
14. B; C.		**20.** (I) B. (II) B. (III) A. Bonus: C.
15. B.	**29.** B.	**21.** C. Bonus: B.
16. D.	**30.** A.	**22.** A. Bonus: B.
17. C.	**31.** B. Bonus: D.	**23.** B.
18. A.	**32.** A.	**24.** D.
19. B. Bonus: National University of San Marcos (May 1551).	**33.** D. Bonus: A.	**25.** (I) 2 oceans: A; D. (II) 2 oceans: B; D. (III) 2 oceans: A; C. Bonus: A only.
20. (I) C; (II) E; (III) D; (IV) A.		**26.** (I) B. (II) C. (III) A. Bonuses: (I) D. *It also connects the Black Sea to the Sea of Marmara.* (II) B.
21. D.		**27.** (I) Atlantic Ocean. (II) Indian Ocean. (III) C. (IV) (1) = B. (2) = A.
		28. A. Bonus: C.
		29. D.

Category CC. Bodies of Water (continued)	Category DD. Mountains, Forests, Deserts	Category EE. Gods, Goddesses, and Many Myths
30. (I) 3 oceans: A; B; C. (II) 2 oceans: A; B. (III) 2 oceans. B, D. Bonus: 2 oceans: A; D. **31.** C. Bonuses: (I) Siberia; (II) 25M (C). If chose Zaysan (B), then Bonuses: Kazakhstan; and 65M (B). **32.** B. **33.** (1) B. (2) A. (3) E. (4) B. (5) C. (6) D. (7) C. (8) C. (9) D. (10) E. (11) A. (12) A. (13) D. (14) D. (15) A (*C was the prior record reached on 29 March 2016, while the sea surface temperatures in the U.S. State of Florida hit B during the last week of July 2023*). Bonus: C.	**1.** B. **2.** B. Bonus: Nepal. **3.** A. **4.** D. **5.** (I) B. (II) Ecuador. **6.** C. **7.** (I) C; (II) B. **8.** D. **9.** C. Bonus: D. (*B is taller but it's partly in Italy.*) **10.** C. **11.** B. **12.** (I) B. (II) A. **13.** C. **14.** C. **15.** D. **16.** A. **17.** B. Bonus: D. **18.** C. **19.** D. (the largest sand desert) or E. (the largest desert that is not a natural land formation). Bonus: B. **20.** D. **21.** C. (also called the Empty Quarter Desert). **22.** A. **23.** C. **24.** D. **25.** B. **26.** D. **27.** A. **28.** C (in the Democratic Republic of the Congo). Bonus: D. **29.** B, at 7,257 feet / 2,212 metres. **30.** (I) C. (II) B. (III) C. (IV-1) A; (IV-2) B. (None). **31.** B. **32.** (I) D. (II) C. **33.** B. Bonus: Cinder cone volcano.	**1.** C. **2.** D. **3.** B. **4.** C. **5.** A. Bonuses: (I) Athena; (II) Caerus; (III) Athena. **6.** E. Bonus: Kylin. **7.** D. **8.** B. **9.** A. **10.** B. **11.** C. **12.** A. **13.** A. **14.** B. Bonuses: (I) C; (II) A. **15.** B. Bonus: Aetos Kaukasios / Caucasian Eagle / Aethon. **16.** B. **17.** D. **18.** D. **19.** C. **20.** 1. A. 2. (I) Norse. (II) Japanese. (III) Greek, Roman. (IV) Celtic. (V) Sumerian. (VI) West African. (VII) Hinduism. **21.** B. **22.** C. **23.** A. **24.** C. **25.** D. **26.** B. **27.** C. Bonus: B. **28.** A. **29.** C. **30.** (I) A. (II) B. Bonus: Chiron. **31.** A. Bonus: C. **32.** B. **33.** A.

Category FF. HIStory, HERstory, THEIRstory, [Y]OURstory	Category FF. HIStory, HERstory, THEIRstory, [Y]OURstory (continued)	Category GG. The Sciences Rock! (continued)
1. C.	**29.** A (III); B (IV); C (II). Bonus: D.	**18.** C.
2. B.	**30.** B. Bonus: A.	**19.** A.
3. D. Bonus: D.	**31.** D. Bonuses: (I) A. (II) B.	**20.** (I) A; (II) D.
4. B.	**32.** C. Bonus: D.	**21.** B.
5. C.	**33.** (I) B; (II) C; (III) A.	**22.** (I) C; (II) A; (III) D; (IV) B.
6. B.		**23.** A.
7. D.	**Category GG. The Sciences Rock!**	**24.** D. Bonuses: (I) B; (II) A.
8. D.		**25.** C.
9. B.	**1.** B.	**26.** A (from 1891 - 1894). (Note: B – *1903*; C – *1901*; D – *1905*; E – *1900*.)
10. C.	**2.** C (53).	
11. C.	**3.** D.	
12. A.	**4.** A.	**27.** (I) D. (II) D. Bonuses: (1) B. (2) C.
13. B.	**5.** (I) B. (II) C. (III) Cochlea, Semicircular canals, Vestibular nerve. Bonus: D.	**28.** (I) C. (II) C. Bonus: B.
14. (I) 1203 = B; (II) 1260 = D; (III) 1394 = C. Bonus: 1453 = C.		**29.** A.
15. B.	**6.** B.	**30.** (I) B. (II) D. Bonus: C.
16. C.	**7.** (I) B; (II) D.	**31.** (1) A. (2) B. (3) A; B; E; F. (4) A. (5) A; E. (6) A (II). B (I). (7) (I) A. (II) B.
17. (1) (I) D; (II) C; (III) F; (IV) G; (V) E; (VI) B; (VII) A. (2) A.	**8.** (I) A. (II) B. (III) A. Bonus: Kelvin.	
18. (I) A. (II) D. Bonus: China by the British.	**9.** B.	**32.** A. Bonuses: (I) D. (II) C (in Dikika).
19. C. Bonus: Jean Baptiste Charbonneau.	**10.** C. (Note: *(A=10⁻⁹); (B=10⁻¹⁸); (D=10⁻¹²)*.)	**33.** C; F.
20. (I) C. (II) A.	**11.** D.	
21. A.	**12.** 1. A. 2. (I) B; (II) C; (III) D.	
22. (I) C; (II) A; (III) B.	**13.** G. Bonuses: (1) B. (2) A; B.	
23. B. Bonuses: (1) *Un Verano Sin Ti*. (2) D.	**14.** A.	
24. (I) C; (II) A; (III) B. Bonus: (IV).	**15.** C.	
25. A.	**16.** B.	
26. D. Bonuses: (I) E. (II) C.	**17.** (I) C; (II) B; (III) D; (IV) A. Bonus: E.	
27. C. Bonus: B.		
28. A = IV. B = VI. C = II. D = I. E = III. F = V. Bonuses: (I) VII. (II) C.		

El Fin…La Fin…The End
until Volume 2

CATEGORIES: **A.** Country Leaders (4 pts). **B.** Wait…What Happened? (2 pts). **C.** "Independence" (1 pt). **D.** Sports Champion (3 pts). **E.** "JAMS" (3 pts). **F.** Geography 235 (3 pts). **G.** Big Screen, Small Screen (2 pts). **H.** Country Flags (2 pts). **I.** Earth's "Spheres" (5 pts). **J.** Land and Sea Forms (5 pts). **K.** World Slangs / Sayings / Cool Words (2 pts). **L.** "Show Me the $¥€£" (3 pts). **M.** Scientists and Geniuses (3 pts). **N.** Landmarks and Monuments (1 pt). **O.** "Enlightenment" (3 pts). **P.** "Doctor" (2 pts). **Q.** Masterpieces (3 pts). **R.** True or False (2 pts). **S.** "First" or "Only" (3 pts). **T.** Potpourri (2 pts). **U.** "Who Said This?"(5 pts). **V.** What's out There in the Universe? (4 pts). **W.** "More than Ingredients" (3 pts). **X.** "Complicated" Words (2 pts). **Y.** The Arts through the Centuries (3 pts). **Z.** BLIMEY! Why Numbers? Why Math? Why Physics? (6 pts). **AA.** In the Continents (3 pts). **BB.** Capitals (4 pts). **CC.** Bodies of Water (3 pts). **DD.** Mountains, Forests, Deserts (3 pts). **EE.** Gods, Goddesses, and Many Myths (2 pts). **FF.** HIStory, HERstory, THEIRstory, [Y]OURstory (3 pts). **GG.** The Sciences Rock! (4 pts).

#	Cusco	Hamilton	Krabi	Praslin	Rotorua	Vava'u	Zermatt

CATEGORIES: **A.** Country Leaders (4 pts). **B.** Wait…What Happened? (2 pts). **C.** "Independence" (1 pt). **D.** Sports Champion (3 pts). **E.** "JAMS" (3 pts). **F.** Geography 235 (3 pts). **G.** Big Screen, Small Screen (2 pts). **H.** Country Flags (2 pts). **I.** Earth's "Spheres" (5 pts). **J.** Land and Sea Forms(5 pts). **K.** World Slangs / Sayings / Cool Words (2 pts). **L.** "Show Me the $¥€£" (3 pts). **M.** Scientists and Geniuses (3 pts). **N.** Landmarks and Monuments (1 pt). **O.** "Enlightenment" (3 pts). **P.** "Doctor" (2 pts). **Q.** Masterpieces (3 pts). **R.** True or False (2 pts). **S.** "First" or "Only" (3 pts). **T.** Potpourri (2 pts). **U.** "Who Said This?"(5 pts). **V.** What's out There in the Universe? (4 pts). **W.** "More than Ingredients" (3 pts). **X.** "Complicated" Words (2 pts). **Y.** The Arts through the Centuries (3 pts). **Z.** BLIMEY! Why Numbers? Why Math? Why Physics? (6 pts). **AA.** In the Continents (3 pts). **BB.** Capitals (4 pts). **CC.** Bodies of Water (3 pts). **DD.** Mountains, Forests, Deserts (3 pts). **EE.** Gods, Goddesses, and Many Myths (2 pts). **FF.** HIStory, HERstory, THEIRstory, [Y]OURstory (3 pts). **GG.** The Sciences Rock! (4 pts).

#	Cusco	Hamilton	Krabi	Praslin	Rotorua	Vava'u	Zermatt

CATEGORIES: A. Country Leaders (4 pts). **B.** Wait…What Happened? (2 pts).
C. "Independence" (1 pt). **D.** Sports Champion (3 pts). **E.** "JAMS" (3 pts).
F. Geography 235 (3 pts). **G.** Big Screen, Small Screen (2 pts). **H.** Country Flags (2 pts).
I. Earth's "Spheres" (5 pts). **J.** Land and Sea Forms (5 pts). **K.** World Slangs / Sayings /
Cool Words (2 pts). **L.** "Show Me the \$¥€£" (3 pts). **M.** Scientists and Geniuses (3 pts).
N. Landmarks and Monuments (1 pt). **O.** "Enlightenment" (3 pts). **P.** "Doctor" (2 pts).
Q. Masterpieces (3 pts). **R.** True or False (2 pts). **S.** "First" or "Only" (3 pts).
T. Potpourri (2 pts). **U.** "Who Said This?"(5 pts). **V.** What's out There in the Universe?
(4 pts). **W.** "More than Ingredients" (3 pts). **X.** "Complicated" Words (2 pts). **Y.** The
Arts through the Centuries (3 pts). **Z.** BLIMEY! Why Numbers? Why Math? Why
Physics? (6 pts). **AA.** In the Continents (3 pts). **BB.** Capitals (4 pts). **CC.** Bodies of
Water (3 pts). **DD.** Mountains, Forests, Deserts (3 pts). **EE.** Gods, Goddesses, and
Many Myths (2 pts). **FF.** HIStory, HERstory, THEIRstory, [Y]OURstory (3 pts).
GG. The Sciences Rock! (4 pts).

#	Cusco	Hamilton	Krabi	Praslin	Rotorua	Vava'u	Zermatt

CATEGORIES: A. Country Leaders (4 pts). **B.** Wait…What Happened? (2 pts). **C.** "Independence" (1 pt). **D.** Sports Champion (3 pts). **E.** "JAMS" (3 pts). **F.** Geography 235 (3 pts). **G.** Big Screen, Small Screen (2 pts). **H.** Country Flags (2 pts). **I.** Earth's "Spheres" (5 pts). **J.** Land and Sea Forms(5 pts). **K.** World Slangs / Sayings / Cool Words (2 pts). **L.** "Show Me the $¥€£" (3 pts). **M.** Scientists and Geniuses (3 pts). **N.** Landmarks and Monuments (1 pt). **O.** "Enlightenment" (3 pts). **P.** "Doctor" (2 pts). **Q.** Masterpieces (3 pts). **R.** True or False (2 pts). **S.** "First" or "Only" (3 pts). **T.** Potpourri (2 pts). **U.** "Who Said This?"(5 pts). **V.** What's out There in the Universe? (4 pts). **W.** "More than Ingredients" (3 pts). **X.** "Complicated" Words (2 pts). **Y.** The Arts through the Centuries (3 pts). **Z.** BLIMEY! Why Numbers? Why Math? Why Physics? (6 pts). **AA.** In the Continents (3 pts). **BB.** Capitals (4 pts). **CC.** Bodies of Water (3 pts). **DD.** Mountains, Forests, Deserts (3 pts). **EE.** Gods, Goddesses, and Many Myths (2 pts). **FF.** HIStory, HERstory, THEIRstory, [Y]OURstory (3 pts). **GG.** The Sciences Rock! (4 pts).

#	Cusco	Hamilton	Krabi	Praslin	Rotorua	Vava'u	Zermatt

CATEGORIES: A. Country Leaders (4 pts). **B.** Wait…What Happened? (2 pts).
C. "Independence" (1 pt). **D.** Sports Champion (3 pts). **E.** "JAMS" (3 pts).
F. Geography 235 (3 pts). **G.** Big Screen, Small Screen (2 pts). **H.** Country Flags (2 pts).
I. Earth's "Spheres" (5 pts). **J.** Land and Sea Forms(5 pts). **K.** World Slangs / Sayings /
Cool Words (2 pts). **L.** "Show Me the $¥€£" (3 pts). **M.** Scientists and Geniuses (3 pts).
N. Landmarks and Monuments (1 pt). **O.** "Enlightenment" (3 pts). **P.** "Doctor" (2 pts).
Q. Masterpieces (3 pts). **R.** True or False (2 pts). **S.** "First" or "Only" (3 pts).
T. Potpourri (2 pts). **U.** "Who Said This?" (5 pts). **V.** What's out There in the Universe?
(4 pts). **W.** "More than Ingredients" (3 pts). **X.** "Complicated" Words (2 pts). **Y.** The
Arts through the Centuries (3 pts). **Z.** BLIMEY! Why Numbers? Why Math? Why
Physics? (6 pts). **AA.** In the Continents (3 pts). **BB.** Capitals (4 pts). **CC.** Bodies of
Water (3 pts). **DD.** Mountains, Forests, Deserts (3 pts). **EE.** Gods, Goddesses, and
Many Myths (2 pts). **FF.** HIStory, HERstory, THEIRstory, [Y]OURstory (3 pts).
GG. The Sciences Rock! (4 pts).

#	Cusco	Hamilton	Krabi	Praslin	Rotorua	Vava'u	Zermatt

CATEGORIES: **A.** Country Leaders (4 pts). **B.** Wait…What Happened? (2 pts).
C. "Independence" (1 pt). **D.** Sports Champion (3 pts). **E.** "JAMS" (3 pts).
F. Geography 235 (3 pts). **G.** Big Screen, Small Screen (2 pts). **H.** Country Flags (2 pts).
I. Earth's "Spheres" (5 pts). **J.** Land and Sea Forms(5 pts). **K.** World Slangs / Sayings /
Cool Words (2 pts). **L.** "Show Me the $¥€£" (3 pts). **M.** Scientists and Geniuses (3 pts).
N. Landmarks and Monuments (1 pt). **O.** "Enlightenment" (3 pts). **P.** "Doctor" (2 pts).
Q. Masterpieces (3 pts). **R.** True or False (2 pts). **S.** "First" or "Only" (3 pts).
T. Potpourri (2 pts). **U.** "Who Said This?"(5 pts). **V.** What's out There in the Universe?
(4 pts). **W.** "More than Ingredients" (3 pts). **X.** "Complicated" Words (2 pts). **Y.** The
Arts through the Centuries (3 pts). **Z.** BLIMEY! Why Numbers? Why Math? Why
Physics? (6 pts). **AA.** In the Continents (3 pts). **BB.** Capitals (4 pts). **CC.** Bodies of
Water (3 pts). **DD.** Mountains, Forests, Deserts (3 pts). **EE.** Gods, Goddesses, and
Many Myths (2 pts). **FF.** HIStory, HERstory, THEIRstory, [Y]OURstory (3 pts).
GG. The Sciences Rock! (4 pts).

#	Cusco	Hamilton	Krabi	Praslin	Rotorua	Vava'u	Zermatt

CATEGORIES: A. Country Leaders (4 pts). **B.** Wait…What Happened? (2 pts).
C. "Independence" (1 pt). **D.** Sports Champion (3 pts). **E.** "JAMS" (3 pts).
F. Geography 235 (3 pts). **G.** Big Screen, Small Screen (2 pts). **H.** Country Flags (2 pts).
I. Earth's "Spheres" (5 pts). **J.** Land and Sea Forms(5 pts). **K.** World Slangs / Sayings /
Cool Words (2 pts). **L.** "Show Me the $¥€£" (3 pts). **M.** Scientists and Geniuses (3 pts).
N. Landmarks and Monuments (1 pt). **O.** "Enlightenment" (3 pts). **P.** "Doctor" (2 pts).
Q. Masterpieces (3 pts). **R.** True or False (2 pts). **S.** "First" or "Only" (3 pts).
T. Potpourri (2 pts). **U.** "Who Said This?"(5 pts). **V.** What's out There in the Universe?
(4 pts). **W.** "More than Ingredients" (3 pts). **X.** "Complicated" Words (2 pts). **Y.** The
Arts through the Centuries (3 pts). **Z.** BLIMEY! Why Numbers? Why Math? Why
Physics? (6 pts). **AA.** In the Continents (3 pts). **BB.** Capitals (4 pts). **CC.** Bodies of
Water (3 pts). **DD.** Mountains, Forests, Deserts (3 pts). **EE.** Gods, Goddesses, and
Many Myths (2 pts). **FF.** HIStory, HERstory, THEIRstory, [Y]OURstory (3 pts).
GG. The Sciences Rock! (4 pts).

#	Cusco	Hamilton	Krabi	Praslin	Rotorua	Vava'u	Zermatt

CATEGORIES: **A.** Country Leaders (4 pts). **B.** Wait…What Happened? (2 pts). **C.** "Independence" (1 pt). **D.** Sports Champion (3 pts). **E.** "JAMS" (3 pts). **F.** Geography 235 (3 pts). **G.** Big Screen, Small Screen (2 pts). **H.** Country Flags (2 pts). **I.** Earth's "Spheres" (5 pts). **J.** Land and Sea Forms(5 pts). **K.** World Slangs / Sayings / Cool Words (2 pts). **L.** "Show Me the \$¥€£" (3 pts). **M.** Scientists and Geniuses (3 pts). **N.** Landmarks and Monuments (1 pt). **O.** "Enlightenment" (3 pts). **P.** "Doctor" (2 pts). **Q.** Masterpieces (3 pts). **R.** True or False (2 pts). **S.** "First" or "Only" (3 pts). **T.** Potpourri (2 pts). **U.** "Who Said This?"(5 pts). **V.** What's out There in the Universe? (4 pts). **W.** "More than Ingredients" (3 pts). **X.** "Complicated" Words (2 pts). **Y.** The Arts through the Centuries (3 pts). **Z.** BLIMEY! Why Numbers? Why Math? Why Physics? (6 pts). **AA.** In the Continents (3 pts). **BB.** Capitals (4 pts). **CC.** Bodies of Water (3 pts). **DD.** Mountains, Forests, Deserts (3 pts). **EE.** Gods, Goddesses, and Many Myths (2 pts). **FF.** HIStory, HERstory, THEIRstory, [Y]OURstory (3 pts). **GG.** The Sciences Rock! (4 pts).

#	Cusco	Hamilton	Krabi	Praslin	Rotorua	Vava'u	Zermatt

CATEGORIES: A. Country Leaders (4 pts). **B.** Wait…What Happened? (2 pts).
C. "Independence" (1 pt). **D.** Sports Champion (3 pts). **E.** "JAMS" (3 pts).
F. Geography 235 (3 pts). **G.** Big Screen, Small Screen (2 pts). **H.** Country Flags (2 pts).
I. Earth's "Spheres" (5 pts). **J.** Land and Sea Forms(5 pts). **K.** World Slangs / Sayings /
Cool Words (2 pts). **L.** "Show Me the $¥€£" (3 pts). **M.** Scientists and Geniuses (3 pts).
N. Landmarks and Monuments (1 pt). **O.** "Enlightenment" (3 pts). **P.** "Doctor" (2 pts).
Q. Masterpieces (3 pts). **R.** True or False (2 pts). **S.** "First" or "Only" (3 pts).
T. Potpourri (2 pts). **U.** "Who Said This?"(5 pts). **V.** What's out There in the Universe?
(4 pts). **W.** "More than Ingredients" (3 pts). **X.** "Complicated" Words (2 pts). **Y.** The
Arts through the Centuries (3 pts). **Z.** BLIMEY! Why Numbers? Why Math? Why
Physics? (6 pts). **AA.** In the Continents (3 pts). **BB.** Capitals (4 pts). **CC.** Bodies of
Water (3 pts). **DD.** Mountains, Forests, Deserts (3 pts). **EE.** Gods, Goddesses, and
Many Myths (2 pts). **FF.** HIStory, HERstory, THEIRstory, [Y]OURstory (3 pts).
GG. The Sciences Rock! (4 pts).

#	Cusco	Hamilton	Krabi	Praslin	Rotorua	Vava'u	Zermatt

CATEGORIES: A. Country Leaders (4 pts). **B.** Wait…What Happened? (2 pts).
C. "Independence" (1 pt). **D.** Sports Champion (3 pts). **E.** "JAMS" (3 pts).
F. Geography 235 (3 pts). **G.** Big Screen, Small Screen (2 pts). **H.** Country Flags (2 pts).
I. Earth's "Spheres" (5 pts). **J.** Land and Sea Forms(5 pts). **K.** World Slangs / Sayings /
Cool Words (2 pts). **L.** "Show Me the $¥€£" (3 pts). **M.** Scientists and Geniuses (3 pts).
N. Landmarks and Monuments (1 pt). **O.** "Enlightenment" (3 pts). **P.** "Doctor" (2 pts).
Q. Masterpieces (3 pts). **R.** True or False (2 pts). **S.** "First" or "Only" (3 pts).
T. Potpourri (2 pts). **U.** "Who Said This?"(5 pts). **V.** What's out There in the Universe?
(4 pts). **W.** "More than Ingredients" (3 pts). **X.** "Complicated" Words (2 pts). **Y.** The
Arts through the Centuries (3 pts). **Z.** BLIMEY! Why Numbers? Why Math? Why
Physics? (6 pts). **AA.** In the Continents (3 pts). **BB.** Capitals (4 pts). **CC.** Bodies of
Water (3 pts). **DD.** Mountains, Forests, Deserts (3 pts). **EE.** Gods, Goddesses, and
Many Myths (2 pts). **FF.** HIStory, HERstory, THEIRstory, [Y]OURstory (3 pts).
GG. The Sciences Rock! (4 pts).

ACKNOWLEDGMENTS

I want to thank Kendra Muntz, Jerry Bennett, Chad Layne, and P.J. Hoover for being on this trivia journey with me. I earnestly appreciate your advice and contributions. I'd like also to thank NKB for certain illustrations—you always come through for me; thank you to Angie Gruber, Arvi Mohan, and Nadine Muhlematter for photos that you shared with me to use in this volume. And a special shout-out to the Turkot family. Lastly, a humungous thank you to my children and husband for playing this trivia with me months on end, devising your personal strategies on how to win, and for your insights on what questions should be made "easier." We had a lot of laughs too.

****

ABOUT THE AUTHOR

SB Hilarion is the author and lead illustrator of the narrative nonfiction books in the *Raising Young Scholars Series*. She is passionate about traveling to experience and then showcase world cultures. She lives with her family and about 100 houseplants.

****

www.ingramcontent.com/pod-product-compliance
Lightning Source LLC
Chambersburg PA
CBHW061603120626

46550CB00004B/1598